Ian Sayer is a successful tra~~~~~~~~~~~~~~
a leading investigator in ~~~~~~~~~~~~~~~
German history and has assembled one of the largest private
archives of original World War II documents in Britain. He
is the co-author with Douglas Botting of *Nazi Gold: The Story
of the World's Greatest Robbery and its Aftermath*.

Douglas Botting is a writer and documentary film-maker
whose books and television programmes have reflected his
interest in travel, exploration and modern German and
Soviet history. His books include *Humboldt and the Cosmos*, *In
the Ruins of the Reich* and (with Ian Sayer) *Nazi Gold*.

AMERICA'S SECRET ARMY

The Untold Story of the Counter Intelligence Corps

IAN SAYER
and
DOUGLAS BOTTING

FONTANA/Collins

For the men and the women of the CIC
without whom there would have been no story,
and to the memory of the legendary
Major Ann Bray
whose dream has now been realized.

First published by Grafton Books 1989

First published in 1990 by Fontana Paperbacks
8 Grafton Street, London W1X 3LA

Copyright © Ian Sayer and Douglas Botting 1989

Printed and bound in Great Britain by
William Collins Sons & Co. Ltd, Glasgow

CONTENTS

ACKNOWLEDGEMENTS

Former CIC Agents who provided assistance above and beyond the call of duty:

Arthur S. Hurlburt, Medford, Maryland (Lt. Col. Retd), (President, National Counter Intelligence Corps Association and Member of the Military Intelligence Association of New England); James H. Ratliff, Cincinnati, Ohio; Duval A. Edwards, Seattle, WA, (Member NCICA Board of Governors); Col. Earl S. Browning Jr., USA, Retd, Fairfax, Virginia.

NCICA:

National Counter Intelligence Corps Association, National HQ, Columbus, Ohio; Special Agent, Major Ann Bray, 1905–1976.

Former CIC Agents with whom we have corresponded:

Colonel Aaron Bank, USA, Retd, San Clemente, California; Clark A. Barrett, San Mateo, California; Richard W. Beebe, Sioux City, Iowa; Francis T. Brown, Westchester, PA; Stephen W. Bumball, Rahway, New Jersey; John M. Curran, Santa Barbara, California; Nelson V. N. Dungan, Somerville, New Jersey; David W. Fuller, Bangor, Maine; Ted Girouard, Critz, Virginia; Hyman W. Goodwin, Providence, Rhode Island; Kenneth B. Hale, Indianapolis, Indiana; Ronald M. A. Hirst, Wiesbaden, West Germany; John P. Hogan, Riverside, Illinois; Edward T. Howard, Delray Beach, Florida; George J. Kimmel, Ashland, PA; Richard B. Kirkpatrick, Chevy Chase, Maryland (deceased); Edward R. Koudelka, Sun City, Arizona; William Larned, Greenwich, Connecticut; Anthony W. Lobb, Greenville, New York; William F. Loebl; Albert C. Losche, Indianapolis, Indiana; Paul McCarty, Newton, Maryland; James H. Marion, Columbus, Ohio; Robert R. Richards, Columbus, Ohio; Joseph Rosen; William R. Spilmann, Wellesley, Maryland; Michael J. Suszan, Birmingham, Michigan; Bradley W. Vaughan, Tempe, Arizona; Arnold H. Weiss; David Wright, Rockville, Maryland.

US ORGANIZATIONS:

Army Counter Intelligence Corps Veterans Inc.

Department of the Army:

US Army Intelligence and Security Command, Fort George G. Meade, Maryland: Thomas F. Conley, Chief, Freedom of Information/Privacy Office; Robert J. Walsh Jr., Chief, Freedom of Information/Privacy Office.

General Services Administration:

National Archives and Records Service, Washington DC: Frank G. Burke, Acting Assistant Archivist for the National Archives; Amy Schmidt, Military Field Branch, Military Archives Division; John E. Taylor, Military Reference Branch, Military Archives Division.

CIA Washington DC:

Lee S. Strickland, Information and Privacy Co-Ordinator.

Department of State, Washington DC:

Louis Schwartz Jr., Director Diplomatic Security Service; H. Eugene Bovis, Acting Director, Classification/Declassification Center, Bureau of Administration.

US Department of Justice:

Federal Bureau of Investigation, Washington DC: Emil P. Morchalto, Chief, Freedom of Information, Privacy Acts Section, Record Managements Division.

ORGANIZATIONS (EUROPE):

The Stars and Stripes, Darmstadt, West Germany: G. Smith.

Other individuals:

Tom Agoston, Hamburg; Willi Gerl, Garmisch; William C. Wilson, Douglasville, Georgia; Melanie Borland; Ann Lane; Julia Beavor; Carrie Beeks; Pret Houston.

GLOSSARY

The words 'counter intelligence' necessarily crop up rather frequently in this book. Of all the possible ways of spelling this term, we have chosen one of the American military variants. In US Army parlance, counterintelligence (all one word) is a generic term referring to all the various measures employed by all members of the military in order to deny vital information to the enemy; while counter intelligence (two words, which strictly speaking should be capitalized) is a specific term for a specialist aspect of counterintelligence which is carried out by a particular body of the military specially trained for this function – for many years, the Counter Intelligence Corps. For the sake of simplicity and consistency, it is the spelling of this latter, specific term – counter intelligence – that we have chosen to employ throughout this book.

Abwehr	Military and counter intelligence arm of the German armed forces
AEF	American Expeditionary Force (World War I)
AFHQ	Allied Forces Headquarters
ATIS	Allied Translation and Interpretation Section
BDJ	Büro Deutschen Jungen (League of Young Germans)
CBI	China-Burma-India
CID	Criminal Investigation Division
CIG	Counter Intelligence Group
CIT	Combat Interrogation Team
DAD	Department of the Army Detachment
DP	Displaced Person (refugee)
ECIC	European Command Intelligence Center
EEI	Essential Elements of Information
ETOUSA	European Theater of Operations – US Army
EUCOM	European Command
FBI	Federal Bureau of Investigation
FFI	Forces of the Interior (French)
FHO	Fremde Heere Ost (Foreign Armies East)
G-2	General Staff Officer (G-2 Section) dealing with Intelligence
GIS	German Intelligence Service
GPU	Soviet Secret Political Police (renamed OGPU in 1923)
GRU	Chief Intelligence Directorate of Soviet General Staff
KPD	German Communist Party

LVF	La Volonté Française
MGB	Soviet Ministry for State Security
MIS	Military Intelligence Section (also Military Intelligence Service)
MVD	Soviet Ministry for Internal Affairs
NCAC	Northern Combat Area Command
NCICA	National Counter Intelligence Corps Association
NKVD	The People's Committee of Internal Affairs
NSC	National Security Council
NSDAP	Nationalsozialistische Deutsche Arbeiterpartei (National Socialist Workers' Party – the Nazi Party)
NSFK	NS-Fliegerkorps (National Socialist Flying Corps)
NSKK	NS-Kraftfahrerkorps (National Socialist Motor Corps)
NSV	Nationalsozialistische Volkswohlfahrt (National Socialist Public Welfare Organization)
OMGUS	Office of Military Government United States
ONI	Office of Naval Intelligence
OPC	Office of Policy Co-ordination
OSI	Office of Special Investigations (US Air Force Justice Department)
OSO	Office of Strategic Operations
OSS	Office of Strategic Services
OUN	Organization of Ukrainian Nationalists
PWE	Prisoner of War Enclosure or Political Warfare Executive
RAD	Reichsarbeitsdienst (Reich Labour Service)
RIS	Russian Intelligence Services
RSHA	Reichssicherheitshauptamt (Reich Security Head Office)
S-2	Lower echelon military intelligence officer
SB	Special Branch
SCI	Special Counter Intelligence
SD	Sicherheitsdienst (Security Service of the SS)
SHAEF	Supreme Headquarters, Allied Expeditionary Force
SIM	Servizio Informazioni Militari (Italian Counter Espionage Service)
SOE	Special Operations Executive
SSU	Strategic Services Unit
SWPA	South West Pacific Area
Ultra	Highly secret information derived from messages intercepted and decoded by the British from the Germans' Enigma code machine
UNRRA	United Nations Relief and Rehabilitation Administration
USAF	United States Army Forces
USAFFE	United States Army Forces Far East
USFET	United States Forces European Theater
WDGS	War Department General Staff

'To remain in ignorance of the enemy's condition simply because one grudges the outlay of a hundred ounces of silver in honours or emoluments is the height of inhumanity.'

Sung T'ai Tsu
Chinese General and Emperor of China
AD 960–976

'The CIC has more adventure stories buried in its secret files than a month's output of blood and thunder comic books. Unfortunately for the reading public, these bona fide cloak and dagger stories are not for publication.'

William Attwood
New York Herald Tribune, Paris
7 March 1947

INTRODUCTION

One February evening in 1983 a retired American intelligence agent and college professor by the name of Erhard Dabringhaus was watching TV at his home in Sarasota, Florida, when his attention was riveted by an item of news that flashed up on the screen in front of him. An obscure Nazi war criminal and former SS Hauptsturmführer by the name of Klaus Barbie had just been extradited from Bolivia to France, where he was to stand trial charged with numerous crimes, including the torture and murder of members of the Resistance and the deportation of Jewish children to the extermination camps, committed during the time he was head of the Gestapo in Lyons during the war.

Dabringhaus peered intently at the haggard face of the 70-year-old ex-Nazi on the screen and his mind went back many years to Bavaria after the war and a tall, thin, ferret-faced German with thin lips and a scar on his right cheek who looked like a shoe salesman and spoke German with a clipped, military delivery. An arrogant, bragging sonofabitch, Dabringhaus remembered, but intelligent, efficient, reliable. For all the years that had passed since those wild, havoc days, there was no doubt that he was looking at the same man. Augsburg, 1949. Dabringhaus picked up the phone and dialled the local TV station.

'That guy, Barbie,' he said. 'Used to work for American intelligence, did you know that? I was the agent who ran him. He was a full-time salaried informant of the CIC. That's Counter Intelligence Corps. Never heard of it? Well, you have now.'

And so the cat and the scandal were out of the bag. For the first time the world at large learned of the existence of the CIC, America's secret army, though only as a shadowy, hush-hush organization that operated in the murky, *Third Man* world of spy and counter-spy in the ruins of occupied Germany after the war. In the public's perception the CIC was a double-dealing secret American intelligence outfit like the CIA, a bunch of spooks that in the best tradition of a

Len Deighton or John le Carré spy novel had deceitfully and shamefully betrayed the rules of honour and justice by expediently making use of the services of an ex-Gestapo officer and known war criminal to further their own ends in the secret intelligence war against the Communists during the direst, dourest days of the Cold War.

Though Ian Sayer and Douglas Botting had already come across the CIC some years previously during the course of research for their book, *Nazi Gold – The Story of the World's Greatest Robbery*, precious little else was generally known about this reclusive organization that had so suddenly surfaced from obscurity. The public did not know that in four great wars in this century – World War One, World War Two, the Korean war and the Vietnam war – the Counter Intelligence Corps had served with selfless distinction and probity in the Allied cause as the United States Army's first line of defence against enemy espionage, sabotage and subversion in more than 60 countries around the world; nor that in the early post-war years, as America's only overt, fully functioning intelligence agency, the CIC had been a guardian of western security, an unsung bastion of defence for the cause of free democracy against Communist totalitarianism.

It was a sad irony that of all the myriad cases CIC agents had been involved in, in war and peace, only the aberrant case of Klaus Barbie had ever impinged upon the public's awareness. Nothing was said or written about all those often intriguing and sometimes amazing investigations which spanned the whole spectrum of secret endeavour and human character – the case of the Rhine Maiden, the hunt for General Tojo, the resurrection of Konrad Adenauer, the confrontation with Otto Skorzeny, the master of sabotage and Germany's super-spy, to mention but a few – nor the massive security operations surrounding the D-Day invasion, the atom bomb project, the Pacific invasions and other historic endeavours in which CIC was intimately involved. Nor was the public aware of the roll-call of leading diplomats, judges, lawyers, university professors and newspapermen who had served in the CIC, including such famous names as Henry Kissinger, President Nixon's Secretary of State; the novelist J. D. Salinger, author of the best-selling *The Catcher in the Rye*; the successful composer Leroy Anderson; and Aaron Bank, father of the Vietnam special operations commandos, the Green Berets.

America's Secret Army, then, is the hitherto untold story of the exploits, adventures, triumphs and failures of this far-flung but little-known intelligence organization of the American military – spawned, like the British MI5 and MI6 and the Italian SIM, from

Military Intelligence. Its long and immensely varied history spans half a century of global conflict and upheaval, half a century of struggle against those agents of twentieth century darkness, the spies and saboteurs of the Fascist, Nazi, Imperial Japanese and Communist powers. The CIC, it should be said at the outset, is not to be confused with that other far-flung American organization, the CIA, or Central Intelligence Agency, which it preceded and then overlapped, and by which it was sometimes impersonated, and to which a number of its own agents defected in the course of their professional advancement. To put it at its simplest, in the field of intelligence the CIC's job was to catch spies; the CIA's job was, and is, to run them. The former was an organization of the US Army, the latter is an agency of the US Government.

Nobody actually ever called the CIC a secret army. That epithet is the authors'. But it seems an appropriate sobriquet. The CIC was not, strictly speaking, a secret organization, even though it did at times run covert operations, and its agents often wore plain clothes, and even in uniform carried no unit identification or even badges of rank. But the CIC was in some curious way a very private, very recondite affair. Extraordinarily little publicity, either popular or professional, ever came its way. Though it was part of the Army establishment, and had its agents attached to almost every army, corps and division, few members of the military had heard of it, or understood what its agents were supposed to be doing; and many who came across them viewed them with the gravest suspicion. One 1942 Army report complained loudly about the advanced degree of secrecy that existed within the CIC establishment in the USA. 'Telephones were not listed,' ran the report, 'the locations of offices were secret, and the identity of resident agents concealed. This is in direct contrast to the FBI.'

It was not altogether surprising that the CIC appeared to keep such a low, enigmatic profile. For one thing, it suffered a major setback at home when in the winter of 1943–4 President Roosevelt attempted to have the whole organization abolished, or at any rate banished from the continental United States, after blowing up in wrath at a CIC report alleging that the President's wife had been enjoying sexual congress with an air force sergeant she happened to know. This served to give the CIC a lower profile than they might otherwise have had, at any rate on the home front.

For another thing, the CIC could be an odd bunch when they chose, and present an unnerving image. They did not always conform to the military stereotype. Even the lowest ranking members of a CIC team frequently had IQs higher than the average army officer's. One team of 20 agents, for example, was found to have 27 university degrees among them, including several Doctors of Philosophy and a private who was a Master of Arts. The CIC as a whole spoke a babel of languages. They came from a daunting variety of high-status professions in their civilian careers. Their ranks included bankers, lawyers, professors, journalists and county sheriffs, and men who were to become famous in diverse walks of life. At times they enjoyed extraordinary power far beyond the normal expectations of their rank and status, and a freedom of movement and right of access which could be alarming to the conventional regimental mind. This unusual freedom from geographical boundaries – political or military – was authorized by none less than the US Chief of Staff, General George C. Marshall, who decreed that agents were free to operate 'with minimum restrictions upon movements or channels of communication', and should not be impeded 'by the observance of standard customs and prohibitions'.

Intermittent attempts to raise CIC's profile had little effect in blowing away the cloud of unknowing which surrounded this exclusive organization like a thick sea fog. The first – and last – that the mass of the army ever heard about it was a brief item in the army newspaper *Stars and Stripes* which described the CIC as 'one of the army's hush-hush departments'. The first the general public ever knew about it was a picture article in *Look* magazine about a CIC team in action in the 1943 Sicilian campaign. Two more years passed before there was any other reference in the American press. Then another article, entitled 'G-Men in Khaki', appeared in *The American* magazine, which drew a rather fuller picture:

Few people, even the Army itself, knows much about the Counter Intelligence Corps, for obviously it must operate behind a smoke screen of secrecy. CIC has two major functions. First, to catch enemy spies, saboteurs and subversive agents. Second, to prevent our military plans and secrets leaking out to the enemy.

The Corps is a puzzling mixture of G-men [FBI agents] and plain GI. Although its agents scoff at any cloak-and-dagger mystery about themselves, they have, in fact, done detective work that rivals any Oppenheim novel. They have caught literally hundreds of enemy agents. By recovering lost Allied secret papers and by discovering equally secret enemy ones, they have unquestionably saved thousands of American lives.

But they are also soldiers. They have ridden the very first waves of every African or European (and many a Far Eastern) invasion, by landing craft, glider and parachute. They have done front-line intelligence work that has won them many medals and more compliments.

Not the least of the CIC romance lies in its own agents, who remain as nearly anonymous as possible, never appear in print, and sometimes fool even their friends about their real jobs. Perhaps no other army unit has men of such consistently high caliber – men of astonishing talent, experience and education. In the London office alone there were 8 PhDs. The composite experiences of one group were typically startling. Among them, they had raced cars in Italy, newspapered in Paris, studied science in Germany, taken scientific photographs in Alaska, taught political science, prospected for gold.

Their teachers were America's best – former secret service agents, FBI aces, narcotics investigators, military intelligence experts. They learned all known detective arts, and also such things as jujitsu, enemy spy methods, the almost magical powers of interrogation. They became crack pistol shots. They also got rigorous, toughening field training.

This almost frightening thoroughness has turned out agents superbly efficient and versatile. They have to be both. Today a CIC agent may find himself posing as anything from a deserter to a diplomat, from a clerk to a colonel. One day he may lounge in a smart London bar; the following week he may be assaulting an enemy invasion beach. He may be interviewing a beggar or a general, a duchess or a prostitute; he may be wearing a dinner jacket or torn trousers.

Almost without exception, they would laugh at transferring to any other branch of the service. For now they are having adventures that a few years ago would have seemed the wildest dreams of some novelist. They are on the inside of great happenings.

On these great happenings, several agents broke into print once the war was over. Two wrote their memoirs and one turned to fiction. Another wrote a piece for the March 1948 issue of the magazine *Varsity* relating the sensational tale of how he broke into the world's biggest, most closely guarded secret – the Manhattan Project plant, which was then manufacturing the world's first atomic bomb – simply to test the security system. Another regaled readers of the *Saturday Evening Post* with an account of how he and his CIC colleagues caught no less than 500 enemy spies in the course of their long counter-espionage haul from the burning sands of the North African desert to the snowy foothills of the Italian Alps.

But still the CIC made no impact on the public of the nation whose security it had been pledged to preserve. The glory and the glamour went to other clandestine wartime organizations such as the rival American positive and political intelligence gathering outfit known as the OSS, or Office of Strategic Services (the forerunner of the CIA); and the British resistance and sabotage organization called SOE, or Special Operations Executive. Conversely, to the CIC's arch opponents – the German Gestapo and SD, the Japanese Kempei Tai, and SMERSH (the counter intelligence branch of Russian military intelligence, deadly rivals of MI6's fictional special agent, James Bond, and the exact Russian equivalent of CIC) – accrued the notoriety.

And so, in this quiescent state of near oblivion, things seemed destined to remain till the end of time – until Klaus Barbie's extradition and trial. More than 40 years after the CIC's involvement with this notorious Nazi, and more than 10 years after its own demise, the CIC had finally hit the headlines in a way it had never envisaged. The spy catchers, the scourge of the Nazis, the mortal foe of the Gestapo, had employed a notorious Gestapo thug and war criminal as an American spy. The outrage sent shockwaves. Not only had the CIC taken on Barbie knowing that he was wanted for war crimes by their allies, the French, but they had arranged for him to be spirited away to a safe sanctuary in South America when the outcry grew too hot. Since the Barbie affair the CIC's name has cropped up several times again in public – almost always in a controversial area. In 1988, for example, the Office of Special Investigations at the Department of Justice in Washington DC reported the results of its latest inquiries and confirmed that the post-war Austrian CIC Detachment had also employed notorious former Nazis and Gestapo agents as informants and spies – at least 13 of them, in fact, including several war criminals responsible for the deaths of a number of civilians in Nazi-occupied countries.

So instead of being covered in the glory which was its due, the CIC was daubed with calumny, its image tarnished by the actions of a few agents who, under the pressure of extreme and extraordinary circumstances, compromised their own rules. It was partly for this reason, perhaps, that the National Counter Intelligence Corps Association of America decided to give their assistance to the authors' projected history of the CIC, and to make available such written material, agent contacts and other assistance as could be rendered at this late date, so many years after the events concerned. This decision marked the culmination of years of official and unofficial efforts by CIC members to make available to the general public a popular but comprehensive and balanced account of the history of the Corps of which they were so proud. At the same time, support was also forthcoming from the Army Counter Intelligence Corps Veterans.

The first effort had been made shortly after the end of World War Two. In 1947 two freelance authors, Fletcher Pratt and Thomas M. Johnson, of New York, were authorized to write a history of the CIC and began collecting documentary material and recording agents' first-hand accounts of their CIC exploits with a view to writing a book of the 'full, true story of the Counter Intelligence Corps in war and peace . . . an informal history of an informal outfit . . . a service as unique as hitherto it has not been celebrated'. Pratt and Johnson were seasoned and reliable pros with a string of other books to their name. Johnson had been a war correspondent for the *New York Sun* in World War One and written one of the few accounts of American military intelligence in that conflict, *Our Secret War*. Pratt had served as a Navy correspondent in World War Two and written a history of the Pacific front, *The Marines' War*. The two of them were given every assistance in their new venture by the CIC and loaded with a mass of historically priceless documents. By late 1948 they had written a substantial chunk of the book and had it vetted by the Department of the Army. Publication was scheduled for 1949 and the CIC waited with bated breath. But nothing happened. No book appeared. Pratt and Johnson were never seen or heard of again and the priceless material they had made off with was never recovered.

The CIC picked up the pieces and began to write an in-house account of the Corps themselves. The project proved a massive and daunting one. The history spanned a period of more than a quarter of a century, involving some 25,000 CIC personnel serving in 300 CIC detachments in more than 60 countries. Examination of the records showed that many wartime field reports had been lost or destroyed and that former agents were scattered across the globe, many of them untraceable or already deceased. Records of some of the 200 or more CIC detachments that had served in World War Two were entirely absent, especially those that had fought under General MacArthur in the Pacific war, where there was not even a full roster of personnel and even the names of the detachment commanders were unknown. Many sensitive counter intelligence documents had been classified as Top Secret and had not yet been downgraded. The view from 'the other side of the hill', in the form of enemy or Soviet records of counter intelligence interest, were missing. But the research team under Lieutenant Colonel Franklin P. Jordan and Major Ann Bray persisted, and by 1955 they had produced a document 4250 pages long and divided up into 30 volumes. This dense and hefty work was promptly classified as confidential and locked away in the vaults of the US Army Intelligence Center at Fort Holabird, Maryland, where it was to gather dust for another quarter of a century.

Nothing daunted, Ann Bray still dreamed of bringing the achievements of the CIC before a greater public. With the active help and encouragement of former Special Agent Duval A. Edwards, a CIC veteran of the Pacific war and a member of the Board of Governors of the National CIC Association, Ann Bray set to work on a shorter historical work. But the project was faced with numerous difficulties, not least the author's tragic illness and death, and at a formal meeting in the Pentagon the NCICA Board decided to release all materials in their possession in order to assist the present authors to complete the work on which they had already embarked. This co-operation, all the more generous for having been extended to two foreign nationals, has made a major contribution to this, the first full story of the Counter Intelligence Corps ever brought before the public. Subsequently Sayer and Botting became the first and only honorary members of the NCICA.

It is a story whose beginnings go back more than 70 years, to America's first hesitant involvement in the mud and blood of the Western Front – the first of those global mass slaughters which have distinguished the twentieth century from all the centuries which preceded it. It is to that distant and terrible conflict, the Great War, that we turn now.

PROLOGUE:
AMERICA'S SECRET ARMY

The Counter Intelligence Corps of the United States Army had its distant origins in the Corps of Intelligence Police in World War One. Formed shortly after America joined the war on the Allied side in the summer of 1917, the CIP was intended to provide the counter intelligence support of a group of enlisted specialists to the security of the American Expeditionary Force in France. In the short period of the war that was left to run, the CIP proved itself worthy of being a permanent part of the Army, both at home and overseas. This was a remarkable achievement, considering that at the outbreak of World War One the US Army did not have any kind of intelligence service at all.

The new organization was saddled, however, with an unfortunate name. For the Corps of Intelligence Police was not in fact an official Corps; nor was it involved at that time in intelligence (that is, finding out what your enemies were planning and doing) but in counter intelligence (that is, preventing your enemies finding out what your own side was planning and doing); nor was it in any way a police force since it had no police powers and no interest in pure crime. What the CIP really was was a secret service, and this was the term which Colonel (later General) Van Deman, the founder of American military intelligence, had always wanted to call the American military organization responsible for counter espionage operations. But Secret Service was a name that had been claimed by the US Treasury, who refused to part with it. So for the pioneer band of 50 agents assigned for counter intelligence duties under the direction of the Commanding General of the American Expeditionary Forces in war-torn France, Corps of Intelligence Police it remained.

Those 50 pioneer counter-spies had not been easy to find. When Colonel Van Deman outlined to the heads of America's leading detective agencies the qualifications required in the sort of men he was looking for – outstanding personal character, military aptitude, fluent linguistic ability in French and German, social poise and diplomatic manner – a one-eyed old private eye was heard to remark: 'There ain't no such animal.' Adverts in the New York and New Orleans papers resulted in the recruitment of a miniature French Foreign Legion. One candidate had a police record. One was mentally unbalanced. One was a French deserter. One was pro-German. One was a Communist who had done time in Blackwell's Island Penitentiary for Red demonstrations against the property of John D. Rockefeller. Several were just morons. One officer described them as 'a delegation of "Cajuns" from Louisiana, a sprinkling of French Canadians, a coterie of Harvard men; their professional antecedents ran the gamut of occupations. If there were any "Secret Service" men among them . . . well, I didn't meet them.' A recruiting officer's notes provided thumb-nail sketches of some of these unlikely lads. One was described as a 'sharp Creole'; another as 'an Englishman, with all characteristics appended'; another as 'Hebrew, very shrewd'. One was found to need 'democratization', another 'pep'. Any kind of French language would do – Cajun, Canadian or French with any sort of foreign accent. What was remarkable was how well this motley crew was to perform once it got to the war.

The newly-formed CIP set sail for Europe on 12 October 1917 on board the SS *Powhattan*, formerly the SS *Hamburg* of the Hamburg –American Line. Thirteen days later they arrived at St Nazaire, and were arrested by US Marines 'on suspicion' the moment they set foot on French soil. Once this embarrassing mistake had been rectified the group shuffled off to Paris, where, passing rapidly from one extreme to another, they were billeted in the luxury Hotel Quai d'Orsay, causing a high-ranking French officer to inquire nervously whether it was the usual custom of the American Army to billet enlisted men in the best hotels. On 5 December the Corps left Paris for the American Expeditionary Force headquarters town of Chaumont, and late in the evening formed ranks beside the deserted station to march under a cold winter moon to yet another extreme change of address – an unfinished barracks, without flooring, shutters or heat.

This brand new bunch of tyros was officered by intelligence officers of the Military Intelligence Division – in effect, CIP officers in all but name – and given a crash course in counter intelligence techniques by British Intelligence instructors at Le Havre. The British had already had the benefit of three years' experience of this sort of work on the Western Front, as a history of American G-2 (military intelligence) in France was to acknowledge: 'It is impossible to overestimate the assistance the British Intelligence Service afforded G-2, not only through their records and the information they communicated, but also in lending the benefit of the experience they had gained previous to America's entry into the war and which was indispensable as a basis for the establishment of the American Service.'

A document outlining the principles of conduct of the Corps of Intelligence Police was soon produced and remained essentially the same through the period of peace and two wars that followed. The primary mission of the Corps was counter espionage work. In the execution of this mission CIP agents were expected to exercise the virtues of saints and the self-denial and austerity of monks. As CIP personnel enjoyed greater freedom of action than other soldiers, self-discipline was essential. Agents were never to lose their tempers. They were to avoid the use of slang and profanity and not partake of tobacco in the presence of women. They had to be careful whom they mixed with. Association with prostitutes or women of immoral character should be avoided except on duty. 'The work devolving upon Intelligence Police will leave no time to take part in social life,' the report concluded glumly. 'Therefore private associates should not be cultivated. Your entire time will be occupied with your duties. Do not frequent military messes or canteens. Attend strictly to business.'

Very soon the CIP began to perceive the magnitude of the task they had taken on. The execution by a French firing squad in September of the Dutch dancing girl and spy, Mata Hari, had dramatically brought to the world's attention the extent of German espionage and sabotage operations. Less spectacular but just as deadly was the German 'army' of low-level espionage agents infiltrated into every section of France. One German organization, which was ostensibly a mutual benefit association for hotel employees, operated some 1500 agents in France, and this was just one of a number of German 'front' organizations. German agents were recruiting Spanish labourers to work on the construction of dozens of American depots in France, and were regularly recruiting Belgian and Dutch citizens for intelligence work. 'It is no secret,' warned the American Chief of Staff in France, 'that in this war the United States is pitted against an enemy with a splendid spy system.'

So splendid, indeed, that within a month General Pershing was requesting authority to increase the CIP's strength from the original 50 men to 750, of whom 450 had been delivered by the end of hostilities. Of these, a third worked in the Front Zone, comprising the American segment of the 400-mile fighting front and some 400 miles of Swiss frontier, and the rest in the Rear, a counter intelligence coverage spread over some 80,000 square miles of north-western

France, including supply ports, military depots, rest areas and over 30 French cities, along with more than 400 miles of the borders with Spain and Italy. Other agents worked on special projects. One was assigned to General Pershing's private train. One specialized in Bolshevism, another in counter intelligence aspects of civilian labour. One became an expert in German–Spanish espionage, another in surveillance, another in undercover work.

The chief function of the CIP with the armies was 'control of the civil population and the detection and prevention of espionage'. At the front the CIP men were involved in combat counter intelligence among the combat divisions on the fighting lines. This was a dangerous and uncomfortable place to be and a number of CIP agents became casualties in the carnage, though none are known to have lost their lives. There were all sorts of strange problems. In the vicinity of Verdun, German agents in American uniforms were a peculiar headache. So were gypsies and 'other persons of this character' who tended to wander through No Man's Land at random at any odd hour. Laundresses required special scrutiny – they could pick up a lot of useful information from soldiers' uniforms and were known to signal to enemy aeroplanes by laying out washing on the grass in a coded pattern. When entering captured cities or towns with the advance troops, CIP agents had to round up suspected enemy collaborators on the 'Black' list and seek out friendly and reliable locals on the 'White' list. The biggest task was screening the mass of refugees and line-crossers that came pouring through the American positions to escape the fighting up front, especially before the final push when 30 American divisions massed for the all-out offensive that terminated in the Armistice on 11 November 1918. All the CIPs of the Front Zone, and all available agents from the Rear Zone, had to be massed across the American positions in order to screen out suspects from this surging tide of humanity.

Both at the front and the rear it was correctly assumed that the German intelligence service was primarily interested in Order of Battle data, and safeguarding this data took up much CIP time. Regiments had to be stopped from parading through ports and towns with regimental colours flying and regimental numbers clearly printed on everything from the big bass drum to the kitchen trailer. CIP agents were instructed in detail on the various means used by espionage agents for conveying information:

Information has been discovered written on the inside of en-velopes, underneath a photograph, underneath a postage stamp and on the gummed edges of envelopes. Instances have been known where messages have been written on the back of a woman in invisible ink. Hiding places for papers have included double collars or ties, hollow heels, hollow buttons and shoe laces. Information has been discovered in the hollow stem of an artificial flower placed in the middle of a bouquet of real flowers or in a woman's hat. Messages have been found rolled up very small and carried in a gelatine sheath in the mouth or other parts of the body, in newspapers by marking certain words with a pinhole, written on bandages, indicated by stitches in embroidery or in a hem, enclosed in coins which are sawed in half, hollowed out and soldered together again with the messages inside . . .

Agents were warned to watch out for signals such as flashing lights, puffs of smoke, windmills, church clock faces, devices in haystacks or corn stooks, strange movements of cattle, sheep, stray dogs and pigeons. They were instructed to observe closely all foreigners, repatriates, persons in French uniform in American areas, persons in American uniform in French areas, as well as 'those generally supposed to be half-witted'. Persons in certain specific occupations – horse-dealers, wine merchants, caravan traders, fruit pedlars, bargees, whores, gamblers, cocaine dealers, black-marketeers or bootleggers, and anyone who deliberately cultivated the friendship of officers or men – also had to be closely watched.

A report from Vichy listed suspects who fell into the criminal category. One was a refined, attractive and intelligent woman called Bertha, who had made the acquaintance of many American officers, but refused to accept any money from them, telling them that she was 'liberally supplied with cash by a young man in Marseilles'. Another was a young woman called Wanda, who signed herself in letters as Contesse. Wanda was well known in Germany and had been deported from Paris a few months previously. She ran an opium den in Vichy and was noted for establishing close relations, *recherché des amants*, with Allied officers. She was reported as being very expensive and as having charged '1500 francs for a single night'. Two men were also on the Vichy suspect list. One was a former professional boxer who was a 'pal' of a professional gambler. The other was an American of Alsatian birth with no visible means of support.

The war in France ended before the overseas counter-espionage service had come fully on stream or established adequate informant nets and a full rota of trained agents. Statistically the CIP had handled over 3700 cases, of whom three had been convicted of espionage, 107 interned, and 119 expelled from the war zone, making a total of 229 neutralized suspects. But statistics alone did not provide a proper measure of efficiency. As one officer noted: 'No one will ever know how many enemy agents were turned back, nor to what extent we succeeded in preventing the leakage of information, the dissemination of propaganda and similar enemy activities.'

France was not the only arena in which the CIP was involved in World War One and its aftermath. In July 1918, following the Bolshevik Revolution in Russia, the war was extended to two Russian fronts when President Wilson, against the advice of his Secretary of War and Army Chief of Staff, yielded to British and French pressure for a joint Allied Northern Russia military expedition in support of the anti-Bolshevik forces of the White Russian government under Admiral Kolchak. One American contingent – the AEF, Siberia, comprising about 9000 men – landed at Vladivostok in August. Another American contingent – the AEF, Northern Russia, which was about 5000 strong – landed in Archangel the following month. This war of intervention, the so-called 'Russian Adventure', continued long after the end of the war against Germany, and was not finally terminated until March 1920, when the AEF, Siberia, evacuated Vladivostok.

In Siberia few counter intelligence problems presented themselves. But in Northern Russia, where the British were actually fighting the Bolsheviks with American troops in support, there were exceptional difficulties. The extreme isolation and severe arctic weather, the friction generated by close association with strange nationalities like the Serbians, Karelians, Finns, Poles, Lithuanians and White Russians, the resentment felt by American troops at being under British command, the even greater resentment felt at not being allowed home like their comrades in France at the end of the war in Europe – all these stresses and grievances led to a considerable crisis in morale and some novel problems for American counter intelligence in the Soviet Union. Thirteen mutinous incidents occurred among British, French, Russian and American units. The most serious American incident involved a company of the 339th Infantry. On 30 March 1919 the entire company refused to pack sleds for a movement order. Investigation revealed that the mutiny had been instigated by a disaffected agitator working for the Soviets, who had successfully politicized the other men in the company with Communist propaganda deliberately fed to him by Soviet agents in the hope of further breaking down American morale.

The counter intelligence problem far away in the wilds of Russia was nothing like as serious as it was in the familiar domestic environment of the United States. Out of a total US population of just over 100 million in 1917, more than 28 million, or over a quarter, were either foreign born or children of parents who were foreign born. A large proportion of these still had family ties with what were now enemy nations, and thus presented a considerable potential source of subversion. A large body of people of German origin were openly hostile to the nation's war aims and sympathetic to the cause of their original homeland. These American-Germans constituted the biggest security risk in the USA, but not the only one. There were also the Austro-Hungarians, the Turks and Bulgarians, and last but not least the Irish, whose compatriots across the water were already locked in a violent war of liberation against the British. The problem was aggravated by the fact that there was ample evidence the Germans had built up an extensive agent network in America and were bent on causing havoc and mayhem on a grand scale.

It was hardly surprising, therefore, that when Colonel Van Deman began the organizing of Army Military Intelligence, he felt the principal emphasis should be laid on counter intelligence. Yet at no time were there ever more than about 250 agents of the CIP operational in America, together with those officers of the Military Intelligence Division who were responsible for directing their activities. Nonetheless, this relatively puny band was up against ruthless, ambitious and brilliant opponents.

The big cities were the front line of the security war inside America. In Washington DC, the capital, the need for undercover investigations of individuals and organizations was so great that the CIP brought in a complete team of plain clothes men, most of them selected from the Metropolitan Police Department of New York City, whose existence in the city was unknown except to the three officers who controlled their operations. 'This,' stated Colonel Van Deman, 'was probably the beginning of the organization later known as the Counter Intelligence Corps.'

While Chicago was always a problem because of the subversion cases arising out of the huge German-American population living there, New York remained by far the biggest centre in the United States for German sabotage and espionage operations. New York was the hub of America's effort to supply war materials to the Allies in Europe and these materials were the target of frequent German sabotage attempts both on land and sea. Perhaps the most accomplished New York saboteur was Dr Walter T. von Scheele, one of Germany's pre-war spies in America, who had successfully bribed dock hands in New York to place incendiary bombs on a total of 36 cargo ships sailing for Europe, thereby destroying goods worth more than $10 million. While trying to reconstruct one of his incendiary devices for the benefit of American intelligence after his capture, von Scheele accidentally blew himself up, and died of pneumonia a few months later before he could be put on trial.

More dangerous still were the master saboteurs, Kurt A. Jahnke and Lothar Witzke, described by British intelligence as 'the most deadly sabotage team in history'. Jahnke was a naturalized American citizen who had served some time in the United States Marines. Witzke was a German Navy lieutenant who had entered America illegally after escaping from Valparaiso, where he had been interned after the German cruiser *Dresden* was captured and sunk off Chile.

Operating under the direction of the German Consul General in San Francisco, Jahnke and Witzke between them had already blown up the Navy Yard at Mare Island, San Francisco, and destroyed two million pounds of ammunition on Black Tom Island in New York harbour in a series of huge explosions which could be heard as far away as Philadelphia. In addition, Jahnke had been suspected of blowing up the munitions plant at Kingsland, New Jersey, in a four-hour detonation of half a million three-inch high-explosive shells which completely wrecked the plant. An informant report from Mexico City early in 1918 warned:

> The present task of promoting a mutiny in the US Army has been entrusted by Berlin to one of their star agents, K. A. Jahnke of Mexico City. This event is scheduled for the autumn. Jahnke has also taken under his wing the general supervision of sabotage in the United States, the Panama Canal and American possessions generally, including especially sabotage of ships transporting war material. His program has been approved by the German Government with available credit of 100,000 marks per month and an additional large commission on results accomplished. He has already had some experience in control of German agitators, defeatists and International Workers of the World agitators in this country and is regarded as the ideal man for the job ... Intelligence Officers will probably never have the pleasure of meeting Mr Jahnke personally, but it is not unlikely that he will give them something to think about. Hence this note in advance.

It was Jahnke who sent Witzke on the trip to the United States which was to culminate in his arrest and mark him down in the annals of American counter espionage as the only German agent to be condemned to death in the United States in World War One. The handling of the case by the CIP Special Agent Byron S. Butcher represented exceptionally skilful counter intelligence work by any standards. When German agents in the United States fled across the border into Mexico after war had been declared, Butcher managed to recruit an informant, code name A-1, to report on German espionage activities in that country. A-1 (an anti-German Pole by the name of Dr Paul Altendorf, then serving as a Colonel in the Mexican Army) soon ingratiated himself into Witzke's confidence and accompanied the saboteur on his last fateful trip.

Witzke, it seemed, had a fondness for wine and women. In his cups he made a number of hair-raising statements to A-1 which were later to be used in evidence against him. 'There is something terrible going to happen on the other side of the border when I get there,' he told A-1 after they set off for the States. 'I will have saved Germany. You will see it in the papers. I do not know whether I will come back alive from this trip or not, as I may be killed.' Witzke told A-1 that it was he who had been responsible for the deaths of 16 people, including six children, in the Mare Island explosion, and added: 'I have many lives on my conscience and I have killed many people and will now kill more.'

While Witzke was otherwise engaged during an overnight stop at a bawdy house at Mazatlan, Mexico, A-1 seized the opportunity to get in touch with the American Consul and report details of the itinerary Witzke would follow when he crossed into the USA. On 1 February 1918 Witzke stepped over the border into the United States and into the muzzles of the revolvers of Special Agent Butcher and Captain Linscomb of Military Intelligence. He was handcuffed, bundled into a car and taken to a camp and searched. American currency and Mexican gold was found on him, together with one Russian and one Mexican passport, the names of several girls he had met in towns along the way, and an amorous letter to one of his conquests in Berkeley, California. Later that day, Captain Linscomb and Special Agent Butcher crossed into Mexico to search Witzke's baggage, in which they found a secret letter code and cipher table for sending encoded telegrams, together with an encoded letter from the German Embassy in Mexico City which when deciphered read as follows:

15.1.18. To the Imperial Consular Authorities in the Republic of Mexico. Strictly Secret. The bearer of this is a subject of the Empire who travels as a Russian under the name of Pablo Waberski. He is a German secret agent. Please furnish him protection and assistance on request, and also advance him on demand up to one thousand pesos in Mexican gold, and send his code telegrams to this Embassy as official consular despatches.

Witzke was imprisoned in Houston, Texas, but refused to make any statements. Later it transpired that Germany had been planning a mass uprising in America, to be handled through German secret agents and organizations in the United States. Witzke was to have met delegates of the International Workers of the World from New Mexico, Arizona and California and plan a campaign whereby, in his words, 'Hell would break loose in the United States,' with the blowing up of mines, factories, railroads, bridges and telegraph and telephone systems. Witzke was tried, found guilty and sentenced to be hanged. Three times he attempted to escape and on the third attempt succeeded, though he was soon recaptured. In May 1920 his sentence was commuted to life by President Wilson, and in 1923, following pressure from the German Ambassador, he was returned to Germany, where he was decorated with the Iron Cross, First and Second Class. His only regret, he said, was that when he had once had informant A-1 at the point of a pistol he had not pulled the trigger.

As World War One ended with the armistice so many thought was peace, the Corps of Intelligence Police could be justly proud of its record. But ahead lay the difficult inter-war years of military retrenchment and austerity; years which saw the rise of Hitler, Mussolini and Imperial Japan, and the spread of high-level Communist espionage and subversion nets throughout the Americas; years of the Great Crash and the Depression in which disarmament and appeasement were the order of the day among the Western powers, and American army intelligence virtually ceased to exist, and army counter intelligence shrank to six men and a dog.

Only two days after the end of the war, Colonel Van Deman had warned: 'We might be entering on a period of even greater danger to the civilization of the world than the one through which we have just passed.' Events rapidly seemed to prove him right. Almost immediately reports of Communist disturbances came pouring in from all over Europe, followed shortly afterwards by the discovery that Bolsheviks were attempting to incite American and British troops on the Rhine to open mutiny. At the same time, the first of many Soviet espionage agents arrived in the United States at the beginning of an intensive undercover campaign which was to infiltrate the highest circles of American government.

The new danger to the security of the United States had little effect in saving the CIP from near extinction. Within three months of the Armistice its numbers had been halved. By January 1920 it was down to 18 men. By the time the Communists had made a bid for popular power in the USA and the National Guard and Federal troops had to be called out to suppress the Boston police strike and restore order during the coal strikes in West Virginia, the CIP had almost ceased to exist. CIP agents were well aware that subversion of the Armed Forces was the primary mission of Communists in the United States, for instructions from the Moscow-based Comintern to the Communist Party of America clearly stated: 'One of the most important aims at present is the organization of Communist nuclei among soldiers and sailors.' But public aversion to investigations of Americans continued to grow and the Secretary of War was to record: 'It is very obvious that the American people are very sensitive with regard to any military interference in their affairs.' In February the Secretary of War issued a directive that provided for the complete elimination of the Corps of Intelligence Police. The following month the Director of Military Intelligence in Washington explained:

> The counterespionage service will be discontinued as it is believed that there is no longer any necessity for such an organization in the Military service. The activities of the German Secret Service are no longer a source of danger to the Army. The only menace we will have to combat is the radical propaganda that the Reds may try to disseminate in the Army, and the activities of Red agitators. This can be successfully met by requiring each organization commander to keep his own ranks free from radical influence ... The fact that radical organizations, such as the Union of Russian Workers, the International Workers of the World, the Communist Party of America and the Communist Labor Party are openly advocating the overthrow of the Government by force should be carefully explained to the noncommissioned officers in each organization.

By August 1920 the Corps reached a low of six men and a dog, all of whom were eligible for discharge. Though it was saved from total extinction a few months later, when a permanent peacetime CIP force was finally authorized, years of neglect ensued. CIP was so starved of funds and agents that for the best part of the next 20 years the principal counter intelligence activities of the Army were carried on in American territories overseas, in Hawaii, Panama and the Philippines, and along the Mexican border. Proposals to reinforce CIP presence in the army corps areas of mainland America were greeted with at least one strongly dissentient voice. In view of the circumstances surrounding the final demise of the Counter Intelligence Corps nearly half a century later, the opinions of the commander of Seventh Corps were both important and prescient, and are still relevant today:

> In my opinion in time of peace in America, radicalism, communism, and efforts to overturn the existing form of government are political questions with which the Army should in no wise concern itself, any more than it should concern itself in questions of religion or party politics. I do not believe that the Army has the right, the knowledge or the facilities for determining what individuals or organizations in America stand for good government and what stand for bad government. The President of the United States is the Commander in Chief for the Army. And if enough laborites, radicals, anarchists or what not get together to elect him and other public officials in accordance with the laws and constitution of the United States, it is the duty of the Army to support them. The Army cannot condemn individual citizens or groups of citizens because of their political views so long as they come within the provisions of the laws which the Army itself is required to enforce . : . The contrary confirms the sentiment 'Standing armies are a menace to free peoples!'

The 1930s were dramatic days in the history of the world. In Europe, they saw the rise of the dictators Hitler, Mussolini and Franco; in the Far East, the Japanese invasion of Manchuria and Shanghai. Abroad, there was a strong whiff of war and malevolence in the air. At home, the Nazis, Japanese and Soviets extended their espionage nets; in America's possessions in the Philippines, Japanese agents continued their secret operations and actively encouraged Filipino subversion. In mainland America espionage cases leapt from an average of 35 a year in the early 1930s to 250 in 1938 and to more than 1600 in 1939. Yet throughout this decade of mounting crisis at home and abroad, the fortunes of military counter intelligence continued to decline. CIP could get no more men and no more money. The rest of the army was little better off. By mid 1939, as the Japanese battled their way into China and the Nazis massed their armies on their eastern frontiers, the United States Army totalled less than 200,000 men and could barely afford to train them. The mighty United States possessed the peacetime army of a third-rate military power – and an intelligence organization that was commensurate.

Of this dismal period of unpreparedness and retrenchment General Eisenhower was to comment later: 'Within the War Department a shocking deficiency that impeded all constructive planning existed in the field of intelligence. The fault was partly within and partly without the Army. The American public has always viewed with repugnance everything that smacks of the spy; during the years between the two World Wars no funds were provided with which to establish the basic requirement of an intelligence system – a far-flung organization of fact-finders.'

This picture did not change when Hitler marched into Poland on 3 September 1939 and began the Second World War. It did not change when the German army overran France and the Low Countries and German air force began to bomb the cities of Britain. It did not change as the Japanese in central China broke through to the Yangtse gorges and launched a violent air assault on the key city of Chungking. Not until Christmas 1940, more than a year after the start of the war, was authorization given for an increase of strength in the CIP.

War Department intelligence began belatedly to stir. In 1941 it increased its strength ten times over. By the summer the CIP suddenly found itself with a chief, a training school, ample funds and provision for more than 500 agents. Soon it was to get a new badge and a new name deemed more appropriate to its present and future role – the Counter Intelligence Corps. It was also to get a clear directive as to its mission:

> The mission of the Counter Intelligence Corps is to contribute to the operations of the Army Establishment through the detection of treason, sedition, subversive activity, and disaffection, and the detection, prevention, or neutralization of espionage and sabotage within or directed against the Army Establishment and the areas of its jurisdiction.

But the Corps had barely six months to sort out its heaven-sent treasure of men and riches. On the fateful morning of 7 December 1941, as the first step in the Japanese plan for the conquest of the Pacific, an air armada of 360 Japanese warplanes swooped down without warning on the United States Pacific fleet at anchor in Pearl Harbor, Hawaii, in a pre-emptive strike which accounted for five American battleships and nearly 2500 lives. Though the raid was a limited tactical success, it brought an immediate response from a vengeful United States.

America was at war again.

1

WAR GAMES USA

The war caught the American counter intelligence community as flat-footed as everyone else in the States. On New Year's Day 1942, when the old Corps of Intelligence Police was rechristened the Counter Intelligence Corps, this little-known organization had but a handful of personnel, most of them still novices at the counter intelligence game. More importantly, global war had thrust upon the Corps a gamut of new and unprecedented problems requiring urgent solution if effective progress was to be made.

The tremendous responsibility of recruiting, training and equipping new agents in an expanding organization capable of operating globally in untested situations fell on the minuscule headquarters of the Chief, Counter Intelligence Corps, which was housed at that time in a single small room in the Munitions Building, Washington DC, under the command of Major (later Colonel) H. Gordon Sheen, the CIC's first CO. As the United States armed forces rushed into full mobilization on a total war footing, Major Sheen estimated that his work load increased by 250 per cent in a few months, and to meet his rapidly growing commitments he moved the CIC headquarters into a second room, then into larger premises, and finally out of Washington altogether into a girls' hostel in a college in Charles Street, Baltimore. From here, for the first two years of the war, headquarters exercised a centralized control of CIC activities and grappled with the myriad headaches presented not only by their country's acknowledged enemies but by the machinations of the military hierarchy on their own side as well.

One of the most perplexing problems confronting the nascent CIC was the continual misunderstanding of the CIC's mission by commanders and G-2s in the field. Since the CIC was virtually unknown to the Army at large when the war began, some misunderstanding was inevitable. But cases of the blatant misuse of the Corps' highly specialized agents by the divisional intelligence officers who controlled their operations on active service were legion. At best CIC agents might be assigned to combat intelligence duties or even sent to the front in an infantry role; at worst enlisted CIC personnel would be put on routine duties or even fatigues – humdrum army tasks which were far beneath the very special qualifications and abilities of the agents involved. As early as March 1942 the Adjutant General advised all commanding generals: 'The primary mission of these agents is undercover operations for the detection and investigation of espionage, sabotage, disaffection, disloyalty and general subversion. They should not be used to perform other duties which can be equally well accomplished by other personnel having fewer specialist qualifications.'

Early the following year a tentative field manual known as Technical Manual 30–215 strenuously emphasized the CIC role. It was the mission of the CIC to 'provide effective counter-espionage, counter-sabotage, and counter-subversive security for the unit to which it is assigned.' It was not the CIC's job to 'assume the responsibility for tactical security, combat counter intelligence or counter-subversive installations for all field force units.' CIC personnel were to be encouraged to 'exercise initiative to the fullest extent'. Agents could be expected at all times to 'resort to any means, methods or strategems necessary to accomplish the mission assigned.' In vain the manual cried out in the wilderness. A CIC lieutenant complained: 'I am familiar with the CIC Manual, which is apparently our bible, but to try to put some of that doctrine into practice here would be the worst possible mistake. Both the Divisional G-2 and the camp intelligence officer would see red.' As late as May 1943 – nearly a year and a half after America's entry into the war – the CIC's new Chief, Colonel H. R. Kibler, was still unclear what the CIC's role in combat was supposed to be, and agents in the field and top-level G-2s and field commanders all had their own opinions on the subject. It was not until D-Day in Normandy that the matter was officially resolved, and in practice agents in combat zones even then often had to take matters into their own hands and go their own way.

If *what* the CIC was supposed to do was one major point of debate, *who* was supposed to do it was another, even more pressing one. Four months after Pearl Harbor the CIC still numbered barely more than a thousand non-commissioned officers. Not until July 1942 did the Adjutant General authorize the number at which the strength of the CIC was to be set: 12 colonels, 28 lieutenant colonels, 55 majors, 136 captains, 156 first lieutenants, 156 second lieutenants, 80 master sergeants, 300 technical sergeants, 750 staff sergeants, 1049 sergeants, 1900 corporals and 352 privates first class – a little under

5000 men in all. But the CIC never, in fact, achieved this total during the war. In February 1943 the Chief of Staff of the Army was asked to double the proposed number to nearly 10,000 on the grounds that the Corps was now involved in an ever-increasing multiplicity of tasks all round the world. 'The presence of American forces in hostile and semi-hostile countries has given rise to counter-espionage, counter-sabotage and general counter-subversive problems of extraordinary volume and importance,' ran the letter of request from General Strong, G-2 to the Chief of Staff. 'The continued operation of American forces in such areas and the eventual invasion of other hostile countries will increase these problems which are complicated by differences in language, race and custom, and create additional demands for Counter Intelligence Corps personnel qualified to combat enemy agents under such circumstances.' This and subsequent requests for an increase in strength met with a consistently evasive or uncompliant response from the Chief of Staff. By September 1943 there were still less than 5000 officers and agents serving in the CIC, of whom 1729 were serving overseas. The total never seems to have risen substantially above this figure at any later point in the war, though the US Army as a whole was to soar to a strength of some 12,000,000.

In spite of the urgent pressures of war and the need to expand and deploy in great haste, the CIC did not lower its extremely high standards for officers and agents. After Pearl Harbor many men of military age flocked to the CIC office in Washington to volunteer their services, some of them intrigued by the glamorous prospects of undercover assignments, others hoping to avoid combat duties in front-line units. Most of them were disappointed. Major Sheen warned prospective candidates:

> The Counter Intelligence Corps does not solicit applicants. Nine out of ten applicants are rejected. To be a Special Agent the applicant must possess certain linguistic, investigative, legal, technical, or other ability qualifications peculiar to the mission of the Corps. The officers and men of the Corps are aggressive, daring, determined, shrewd, resourceful and self-reliant. Their loyalty to their country and the Army is unquestionable. The most important word in the vocabulary of the Corps is DUTY. Their discipline is largely self-imposed and severe.

A successful candidate for the job of CIC agent had to be between 25 and 45 years of age and to have completed eight weeks' basic military training. In some cases CIC agents were posted to tactical detachments without having done their basic training, but in general the rule was the agents must first qualify as soldiers. They also had to pass an exhaustive background investigation and prove to be absolutely loyal, honest, reliable and courageous. They had to be in first-class physical condition. They had to have had prior experience in investigative work as an attorney, investigator, accountant, journalist or similar profession; alternatively (or for that matter additionally) they needed to demonstrate a fluency in a foreign language – most urgently Brazilian Portuguese, Spanish, French, Dutch, German, Italian, Russian, Polish, Hungarian, Latvian, Lithuanian, Arabic, Chinese, Japanese and Korean. The CIC was the first racially integrated unit in the US Army. It was completely integrated, out of functional necessity, with blacks and orientals, back in 1942. The rest of the Army was not integrated until Eisenhower became President. The FBI, by contrast, had no blacks and just did not hire them. When they had need of a black agent they would borrow one from a CIC office. Black agents were required for assignments with black troops in the United States, Africa and Australia, and Polynesian agents were required on rare occasions for special operations in the South Pacific. Irrespective of the applicant's colour, mother tongue or specialist abilities, every prospective CIC agent of enlisted rank had to have a high IQ (120 or more) and a high-school education, and every prospective CIC officer (except, eventually, those who were awarded a battlefield commission) had to be a college graduate.

Given such astronomically high qualifications for the job, it was clear that a majority of the CIC's personnel were going to be men of a calibre and ability far above their actual grade and rank. Almost all personnel within the Corps were officer material, yet few were destined to become officers and most were condemned to stick in absurdly low ranks for years on end, even though they numbered in their ranks lawyers, bankers, university professors, even an author or two. Men of the calibre demanded by the CIC were easily able to gain promotion and commissions in other branches of the Army, but those who chose to stay in the Corps could wait two years for promotion. This was the CIC's Achilles heel, for it came near to destroying morale and proved a grave handicap to operations in the field.

Among enlisted ranks the main distinction was between Agent and Special Agent. The title of Special Agent was a highly coveted one, for it denoted a man who had proved himself worthy of the most exacting duties and responsibilities. Only the War Department was empowered to create Special Agents, a title available only to sergeants or men of higher rank. The real problem was with officer rank. In May 1943 the CIC posited an ideal roster of one officer to one enlisted man – an extraordinarily high proportion of commissioned ranks by normal military standards. Though such a ratio was turned down by the Army, the CIC repeatedly attempted to have a greater number of its agents commissioned. 'The personnel of this Corps is of officer calibre,' General Strong reminded the Chief of Staff. 'The character of work being done by these men is work which should be done by commissioned officers. Its counterpart is done in the Navy by commissioned officers and in civilian life by carefully trained and well-paid special agents of the Federal Bureau of Investigation.' This was absolutely correct; but the Chief of Staff remained unmoved. Special Agents were forbidden to accept direct commissions, except for battlefield ones, mainly because it was feared that the head-hunting of such men for the US Army's officer corps would leave the CIC denuded of most of its finest personnel.

At times the impact of these strictures on agents' morale was catastrophic. In the first seven months of 1943, nearly 12 per cent of CIC personnel left the Corps to seek greater opportunities of advancement elsewhere. In October of the same year all CIC promotions were frozen. Perhaps it was at this point that the ordinary agents of the CIC renamed their organization the Corps of Indignant Corporals. The situation was paradoxical, not to say odd. In practice, irrespective of a CIC man's nominal rank, on active service in the field he often wielded an authority and influence, and enjoyed an independence of judgement and action, matching that of a senior tactical commander. This, needless to say, did not always suit the senior tactical commander, who as often as not resented being advised what to do in the counter intelligence field by a soldier from a peculiar outfit who was not of commensurate rank. Since the question of rank put agents at such an extreme disadvantage, one solution was for the agents to conceal their rank. In the United States most CIC agents wore civilian clothing, and in the field their uniforms usually bore no badges of rank – in fact, were often civilian uniforms (rather like war correspondents' uniforms) with only a brass 'US' on each collar. It was further recommended that military passes and similar documents in an agent's possession should not reveal the agent's rank or his connection with the CIC.

In course of time, when some senior commanders and G-2s became better indoctrinated about the CIC's mission and the special expertise and value of its agents, the dilemma of rank was often overlooked. And certain legendary agents, endowed with a larger-than-life presence and style – they were known in the business as BTOs, or Big Time Operators – managed to conduct themselves amongst foreign military and political figures (such as the French Resistance) in such a seigneurial way that they were treated at the very least as if of colonel rank – as in any other branch of the Army they might well have been. But by and large little credit accrued to the Army high command for their handling of an acute dilemma, never properly solved, that revealed a fundamental incomprehension of the circumstances in which CIC operations were conducted. The problem obsessed CIC agents throughout the war and for long afterwards. As one agent (Duval Edwards) reminded the authors:

I sometimes fear that you might lose sight of a major, daily CONFLICT that confronted CIC agents: doing a job in spite of army officers who were ignorant of the CIC mission, and in spite of their own lack of officer rank in most instances. In fact, to my way of thinking and that of the great majority of us who served during World War Two, the central theme of our history in our minds was pursuing our mission in spite of official interference, official misuse, even official non-use of CIC talent. In February 1944 a communication from Allied Force HQ to all American forces regarding CIC's mission and operations helped to bring an end to much of the misuse of CIC personnel in the European Theatre. Unfortunately this communication never saw the light of day in General MacArthur's headquarters in the Pacific, so the CONFLICT between army officers and enlisted CIC agents never lessened there as it apparently did in Europe. But I would warrant that there continued to be incidents in Europe where agents had to work around officers in order to accomplish their mission.

Another agent was more forthright:

Aside from a few beach landings under enemy fire, most CIC agents' battles were against officers in their own Army – the kind who forced them to be on time for mess and stand in chow lines when everything from surveillances to distant investigations kept them constantly on the go, seven days a week. Martinets and fools were a constant handicap, but in our own case we got off to a good start in France by charming the combat officers into believing how important our mission was – so we went straight from beginners to missionaries to fully-fledged pros in record time.

In spite of these built-in difficulties, the CIC remained an élite corps of high-calibre men whose exceptional talents enabled them to sidestep many of the obstacles needlessly set in their path. As Special Agent Nelson V. N. Dungan recalled: 'Essentially, in our operations and personal living conditions in the European Theatre much more consideration was usually given to us than even high-ranking officers. We had great latitude in our work and we rarely lacked adequate, if not luxurious, living conditions.' It was the rule that CIC agents lived in the best style that circumstances permitted, no matter what trials and dangers confronted them. As General Patch, the Commanding General of the US Seventh Army in the European campaign, once remarked: 'I always have the second-best house in town because the CIC reserves it for me.' The implication being that the CIC always had the first-best house.

More important than concealment of rank, which was largely a mechanism for beating the people on their own side, was conceal-ment of identity, which was rightly considered vital in operations against the people on the enemy side, or other counter intelligence targets. Agents were required to sign an oath that they would conceal their membership of the CIC at all times, and even from their own families, except in the conduct of official business. The degree of secrecy surrounding the CIC was extreme – infinitely greater than that of the FBI, for example. Former Special Agent Duval A. Edwards recalled his wartime training days in the States:

> Our instructors said over and over that not even our relatives, best friends, Sunday school teacher or creditors must know of our work or of the existence of CIC. Some of the agents from the Washington DC office told a most remarkable tale of how well the secrecy of the CIC was being kept there. According to our informers, an army general, preparing for the first general staff meeting after Pearl Harbor, asked J. Edgar Hoover to furnish FBI men to protect the meeting. Hoover suggested: 'Why don't you use your own plainclothes organization?' To which the general reportedly replied: 'My God, do we have one?'

Later Duval Edwards's respect for the advisability of secrecy got its stiffest jolt when a munitions factory in his district reported a 'hot' sabotage case and asked if he could come out and take charge of the investigation straightaway.

> I did. That is, I got as far as the gate of the plant, where an army MP stopped me cold. There had been some sabotage in the plant and he wasn't admitting anyone; orders, he told me. But look here, fellow, here are my credentials. Yeah, says he, anyone can fake those. So then I pulled out the flashy gold badge with 'War Department Military Intelligence' on it, which we were supposed to show only people who couldn't read. I read the four words for

him but he still shook his head. Finally, after two hours and twenty
arguments and a call to the commanding general, I got in. But you
can see what I mean about this secrecy stuff.

It was in the South West Pacific Theatre that Edwards's secrecy
psychosis began to disappear. The new army headquarters gave
the order for army and civilians to be acquainted with the CIC's
existence and function. He wrote at the end of the war:

We were glad to comply but it seemed a little late in the game. For
instance, during the battle for Manila, while the struggle for the
old walled section raged fiercely, there was I – twenty safe blocks
away from a 'Veectoree' party, conscientiously acquainting a
Filipino girl with the existence and mission of the CIC, telling her
how the loyal Filipinos could help us get evidence on collaborators
and Japanese spies. A young American soldier stood nearby with
his mouth hanging open at this revelation of CIC 'secrets'. After a
few minutes of intense listening, he strode over to me, pushed me
firmly and not too gently into a seat, and whispered: 'Listen, bud,
if you are in intelligence, you'd better stop spreading the news
around, or I'll have to report you for loose talking, see?' And he
strolled away before I could ask how things were in the States
when he left.

In the European Theatre, in the rear areas of the war front, where
enemy saboteurs and spies could be expected to be operating, every
effort was made to conceal the identities of CIC agents. In combat
zones, however, when working closely with tactical troops, agents
were sometimes required to wear bright red and black 'CIC'
armbands which identified them as CIC agents when entering a town
or operational area for the first time – an act of self-advertisement
which many agents branded as folly to be avoided whenever possible.
Indeed, the matter of the armbands and all they stood for was
sometimes a burning issue in some detachments. One Special Agent
recalled just such a moment while approaching the Normandy
invasion beach of Omaha on D+28. When first the ship's commander and then the CIC detachment commander, Lieutenant
Hardin, ordered all 'soldiers' to police the decks, the Special Agent
and his colleagues refused to budge so long as they were obliged to
wear the hated armbands.

I sat on one of those toadstool-like bollards, stubbornly unmoving,
while everyone watched me.
'You have an order,' said Hardin, with steel in his voice.
'*We're* not going to disgrace CIC by doing it in these armbands,'

I replied stubbornly, hinting mutiny by using the plural. 'We'll take them off and do it incognito.'

'You won't take them off and you'll do as you're told,' was Hardin's scorching response.

'You can transfer me to the infantry any time you like, Lieutenant,' I replied defiantly, 'but the reason will be for supporting our proper mission, not for disobeying orders.'

It was a deadly impasse for me, because everyone was watching, secretly rooting for me. Hardin glowered as only he could glower and walked away. We did not pick up a thing but stood our ground. He never told me, but Hardin – a really gutsy guy – must have taken it up with top intelligence after we were in Normandy. Nothing was ever said again, but the armbands disappeared and Hardin suddenly dropped his Lieutenant's bars and appeared with a simple brass 'US' on each collar, like the rest of the detachment. We won.

In general, the CIC shunned publicity, and for most of the duration of the war remained an organization almost unknown to the American public at large and a puzzle to many units in the US Army as well. In November 1943 an Inspector General's report indicated an advanced degree of secrecy within the CIC establishment in the Zone of the Interior (as the continental United States was then called in Army parlance). By contrast the existence and purposes of the FBI were widely publicized, their offices known, telephones listed, and public support and co-operation encouraged. Only one irritant stung the Corps into a brief spasm of press publicity during World War Two, and that was the OSS, the rival organization set up in June 1942 to collect positive intelligence. As perceived by the CIC, the OSS were 'befuddled amateurs with an inexhaustible supply of funds and a veil of mysticism' who muddled up CIC's own intelligence operations and claimed the credit for CIC's intelligence achievements. But as things began so they continued. To the OSS fell the glamour; to the CIC fell the grind. The CIC were to end the war as secreted from the public as they began it.

Such a specialist organization as the CIC clearly required highly specialist training. There were a number of training establishments for CIC personnel – the Preliminary Training Schools run by the various Service Commands (these Commands were based in nine different areas and carried out all the military responsibilities of the continental United States apart from the Military District of Washington); the CIC Advanced Training School in Chicago, which imparted the specialist techniques of counter intelligence work; the CIC Staging Area in Baltimore, which provided a conditioning course and a crash programme of combat training for CIC agents about to be posted to overseas divisions; and the Military Intelligence Training Center at Camp Ritchie, which for a while took CIC agents for aspects of intelligence and special operations training.

When army counter intelligence training for World War Two began in February 1941, some months before the United States' entry into the war, there were still only 42 trained investigators in an army of some 1,640,000 men, and within a very short period nearly 150 more had to be trained in investigative skills in a four-week crash course held in a room in the Army War College in Washington DC. It was intended purely for personnel serving in the Zone of the Interior and dealt almost exclusively with criminal matters, using the FBI as a model. As the number of trainees expanded it became increasingly difficult to squeeze them into the cramped accommodation available in the capital, so in November 1941, a few weeks before Pearl Harbor, the training school was moved to the ampler premises of an athletic club in Chicago. This proved no more than a temporary solution. America's declaration of war following the Japanese attack on Pearl Harbor in December led to an immediate increase in CIC strength to more than 1000 and severe overcrowding in the new premises. The CIC was forced to move premises again, this time to 66 East 11th Street on Chicago's South Side, which in November 1942 was opened up as the CIC Advanced Training School, at which CIC personnel who had passed through a Preliminary Training School and completed a qualifying period as apprentice agents in a field office could receive further training.

In preliminary training the bulk of the course consisted of investigation work and the programme was exhaustive. Students were taught the finer points of observation and description, interrogation, surveillance, undercover work, search and arrest, lock picking, fingerprinting, bugging, phone-tapping, plaster casts, secret writing and techniques for reading it using ultra-violet lamps and chemical reagents, investigative photography using the Speed Graphic, Bantam, Minox and 16mm movie cameras, codes and ciphers, bombs and infernal machines, lie detectors and truth serum and much, much else besides. At the Advanced Training School, however, there was a gradual shift in the training curriculum away from criminal investigative work at home towards the CIC's major task in World War Two, counter espionage and counter sabotage duties with tactical commands in Theatres of Operations overseas. Though the school still produced investigators, many of them were to be 'gumshoes' in combat, and with combat experience came a new sense of realism which was reflected in the greater relevance of the CIC training curriculum. Courses in subjects like enemy and allied political intelligence and police systems, interrogation techniques, frontier control, and a résumé of CIC operations in overseas Theatres were added. Students were obliged to regard themselves as soldiers first and agents second, attend classes in uniform and learn unarmed combat as well as small-arms weapon firing.

The need for combat training became all the more necessary as an increasingly large proportion of CIC agents were posted to fighting units at war fronts all round the world. An agent had to learn how to continue functioning in the hurly-burly of a front-line command, and how to survive under fire, even though the CIC mission did not strictly require that agents should carry out their tasks so near the sharp end of war. Neither the eight weeks' basic training which most CIC agents had to go through when they joined the army, nor the tinkering with weapons and combat techniques which they received in the desk and blackboard environment of the Advanced Training School in Chicago were considered adequate. So from July 1943 agents were given intensive combat training at a CIC Staging Area at Fort Holabird, Baltimore, with additional specialized training at other military centres. For men used to desk jobs the training was tough. In the first week they practised marksmanship with the .45 automatic pistol, .38 revolver, sub-machine gun and M1 rifle, and learned map-reading, tent-pitching and other requisites of the military life. At the end of the week they were transferred to Fort Hunt in Washington for specialist courses of a classified nature involving courses in prisoner-of-war handling such as escape and evasion, and resistance to interrogation.

After four days at Fort Hunt, the trainees were moved on to the Military Intelligence Training Center at Camp Ritchie, where they were instructed in the arts of knife fighting, house fighting, street fighting, unarmed combat, scouting, patrolling and identification of the enemy. Then they moved on again, this time to Fort Belvoir for more battle training in mines, booby traps, search and disposal of explosives, and camouflage. This was followed by a motor vehicle course and a week of intensive physical conditioning. Eventually the Staging Area training programme was extended from four to six weeks, with additional training in and around Baltimore in such specialist CIC matters as port and harbour security, ship search and industrial security. The programme was brief but it was vital. In those few weeks CIC agents were transformed from civilians to soldiers, mentally and physically conditioned to confront the stress and rigours of combat. As a CIC agent in New Guinea wrote to his former training CO:

> The first battle that every man in this section fights is the one to keep himself physically fit. A soldier must be in perfect shape when he comes here, and he must know how to keep himself in shape. That is his first duty.
>
> The US Army is mainly a civilian army, but do not let them act like civilians when they get into an operations zone. Give them hell now, and they will thank you for it later.

A major disruption of CIC training occurred at the beginning of 1944 when, for exceptional reasons that will be explained later, the CIC's own training establishments were closed down and all agents destined for overseas service were put through an eight-week course at the Military Intelligence Training Center at Camp Ritchie which was mainly geared to needs other than counter intelligence.

That, then, was the system. Most of the men of the CIC in World War Two were passed through that production-line from induction to battlefield. For many it was experience unforgettable not only for its own inherent interest and excitement but for the many ironies and absurdities which seem inseparable from army life – especially army life a side-step away from the routine norm. Arthur S. Hurlburt, later a Lieutenant Colonel in the professional Army, was to recall those strange times with great good humour and affection in an extended letter to his granddaughter, Julie, written 45 years after the event. In August 1942, the young Arthur Hurlburt, then an artilleryman in a Coast Artillery Corps regiment stationed on Rhode Island, received Confidential orders to report to an obscure army-requisitioned office in Boston, along with a number of his fellow artillerymen. So his CIC adventures began:

> Surprising to me, no one knew we were coming. They got us all together and told those of us who lived in the area to go home. Those who did not live nearby were told to get a room somewhere and send home for civilian clothes. We were all instructed to pack our uniforms in the back of a closet somewhere and leave them there. We were to turn up the following Monday morning in civvies. This was *not* like the army.
>
> I recall vividly the first morning – the first hour. There was a lieutenant by the name of Cameron who showed movies and slides of terrorist activities, bombings and knifings, with all the gory details. When the films were over he came out on the stage and

told us we were starting in a career of just what we had been looking at. If any of us had weak stomachs, now was the time to find out. The bus was waiting and would take anyone back where they came from, with no questions asked. Sure enough, a handful of people got up and left. I decided I wasn't going to be flushed out by such tactics from something that might turn out interesting.

So Arthur Hurlburt stayed and found himself in the CIC. 'No lover of gore was I,' he wrote, 'especially my own. But I never regretted my decision. We had mixed emotions at finding ourselves in an élite group with a minimum IQ of 120, though, when Officers' Candidate School required 110. And we were all Corporals!'

The preliminary course of basic CIC training at the Boston CIC School lasted only two weeks and then the student agents were turned loose under the eye of an experienced man – 'experienced' in the sense that he had two or three months more service than the students had. 'It says quite a bit about the people charged with the responsibility of building up a Counter Intelligence Corps post haste,' noted Hurlburt, 'especially when you recognize that the British had been in this business in MI5 for centuries, the French with their Sûreté for at least 150 years, and the Russians with the Czar's old organizations, which went back centuries.' One of their principal functions after preliminary training was to conduct investigations on people who were being considered for assignment to sensitive positions in the Army. They were also to investigate incidents of espionage, disaffection and sabotage. Some of them would go undercover for long periods. Some did this in the Boston area. Others went undercover as far away as Thule, Greenland.

One of our first investigative jobs was to do background investigations on each other. This made us the first, and as far as I know, the only outfit in the Army where each and every member had the right of refusal over other members – sort of like a fraternal lodge with its black ball.

There were a few pieces of equipment we were issued and required to carry. One was a set of credentials. They looked similar to FBI credentials, on stiff material, folded in the middle, of a size to fit in a shirt pocket. They contained a picture of the bearer, with a seal in one corner, and the printed declaration that you were an Agent of the Counter Intelligence Corps, authorized to conduct investigations. The credentials ordered every person under Army jurisdiction to assist you in any way required, and requested all other citizens to do the same. In 1942, with the nation gearing itself up to a maximum war effort, these credentials opened every door, from the local sheriff's office to the State's Bureau of Vital Statistics or the Dean of Harvard Law School. They enabled us, as Corporals, to speak in confidence with senior officers as easily as with privates.

In some ways we operated like salesmen. We had a mileage allowance – I think it was 6 cents a mile for the car – plus an unquestioned expense account. But we had no territories. It was stated from above that you cannot turn a man loose to catch a spy and expect him to remain behind artificial barriers when the spy recognizes no such barriers. Those two things, the ability to move about anywhere, anytime, plus the fact that no doors were closed to us, when added to the feeling that we were finally in a position to do something that really could count, even as Corporals.

Another piece of equipment we carried was a reason why we were in civilian clothes. Remember, this was during a time when practically all healthy young men were in uniform, and regulations were that one would wear the uniform at all times. My alibi was a 4F draft card. 4F was the classification given to people physically or mentally unfit for induction into the armed forces.

The only other piece of equipment we were required to carry at all times was a weapon. Later on our personal weapon was a 4-inch barrel .38 revolver. But in the early days they had none of these. We were issued .45 revolvers from the Spanish–American War. Revolvers, of course, take rimmed ammunition, to keep the shells from dropping out of the cylinders. The Army had run out of rimmed .45 ammo at some time since 1898, and all that was available was the rimless kind. You could drop this rimless ammunition into the chamber of your .45 revolver and it would drop right out onto your feet. There was no way to keep it in the gun. We never could figure out why we had to carry it anyway. It weighed about 4 lbs loaded and was about 11 inches long. There was no possible way to conceal one on the human body, so we carried them in our briefcases. One morning, in getting on the street car, someone's briefcase came open and the revolver dropped on the floor of the street car. The man who dropped it very casually reached down and picked it up, while all the passengers glanced the other way, as though this happened every morning.

At Preliminary Training School the CIC students had been given a Threat Analysis from the Military Intelligence point of view. According to this, there were four principal threats to the security of the United States. Curiously, though the Japanese Empire was the nearest and most imminent danger, it was not regarded as one of the main threats to America's security. 'The Japanese Empire was not seen as an ideology,' Arthur Hurlburt recalled. 'It was not perceived as a movement which could gain converts within the US, even if it wanted to, which did not seem to be the case. The four principal threats out there in the world were: National Socialism in the form of Hitler's Germany; Fascism as in Mussolini's Italy; the Falange as in Franco's Spain; and Communism in Stalin's Russia. The first three were seen as short-term threats. They could be destroyed or contained in the foreseeable future. Communism was the long-term threat, the most insidious of the lot, and it was seen as taking years, maybe a generation, to contain.'

Perhaps not surprisingly, therefore, one of Hurlburt's first tasks after leaving basic school was to check out the Communist backgrounds of persons under CIC investigation. Some were members of Communist organizations with the most patriotic sounding names – like the Samuel Adams School in Boston, 'an out and out center of Marxist propaganda', and the Abraham Lincoln Brigade, a group of fervent young American Marxists based in New England who had fought on the revolutionary side in the Spanish Civil War. Strictly speaking, CIC investigations of this nature within the continental United States were properly confined to persons of interest to the military. Civilian cases were handled by the FBI.

In the course of 1943 Arthur Hurlburt and his fellow agents turned to other extraordinary duties involving the control and surveillance of American industry and installations:

Once war was declared, the Army was given the security responsibility of the war effort, nationally. The CIC was the eyes and ears of the Commanding General of each Corps Area in carrying out this responsibility. Every little plant was turned to the war effort. Factories that made tea bags were turned into manufacturers of hand grenades. Manufacturers of electrical consumer goods changed to making aerial searchlights, generators, airplane parts. Almost our whole society was tuned to war production. Transportation was a vital war effort and could not be interrupted. Port facilities were war production and could not be closed. Today there is a common perception that there was great unanimity of purpose and direction about the war effort, in all segments of society. On the contrary, there was a constant pressure from persons who wanted to either subvert the war effort or change its direction. Here and there they succeeded in closing down a war production plant. There was one attempt to close a port. But the

Commanding General had wide authority. He could surround a facility with troops and order the people inside to keep on working. He could, and did, seize a number of war plants when there was one or another threat, and operate them as he saw fit. He could seize a port, induct all the personnel into the Army, put them under Army orders and send in Army officers to execute the orders. In a way, that was almost like Clint Eastwood saying, 'Make my day.'

In the First Corps Area the CIC effort was headed by Special Agent Isadore Zack. Iz, as he was known, laid on the Commanding General's desk every Friday morning a complete report on the state of health of the New England and Northern New York area, as it related to this effort. He and his team of Agents kept their collective finger on the pulse of the area. At no time during the war was the General caught unawares. Numbers of seizures were made and at no time did the situation get out of hand. This CIC effort was considered vital enough to keep a crew continually on the job right through the war, until the cessation of hostilities.

Eventually Hurlburt was sent to the finishing school for senior agents, the Advanced Training School at Chicago. The instructors were mostly field grade officers in their 50s and 60s – 'retreads from World War One'. Some were successful lawyers, one was a former State Trooper 'who had been in more gun-fights than he could count', another was an old-time member of the Chicago Bomb Squad. Others were former FBI agents, Treasury and Secret Service agents. Such men had some unusual skills and knowledge to impart. Hurlburt learned how to derail a train with the least amount of explosive, how to bug a room, conduct a raid and make an arrest:

We were taught to search a room with two men, one to do nothing but watch and see every single item that was picked up was put back in precisely the same position it was in before. If it was a surreptitious search and you moved something from here to there, the subject would know you had been there and the benefit of the search, either positive or negative, would be lost. At the opposite extreme, we were also taught to habitually leave something placed just so as you left a room, so you could tell if anyone had searched it while you were gone. A dime could be placed between two handkerchiefs in a drawer in such a way that even lifting just one corner would disturb the dime without it being even noticed. Putting a hair on a light switch or a phone or the top of a closed drawer would give away anyone's presence.

Hurlburt and his fellow agents were also taught lockpicking and safecracking in the Chicago School. At first this had caused some problems, since there was no qualified instructor for this shadowy subject. A certain Lieutenant Teeple, a former English teacher who had returned from the South Pacific Theatre, was delegated to teach this course by the Commandant. 'I'm an English teacher,' the Lieutenant protested. 'I don't know the first thing about criminal activities like that. Where will I find out about it?' The Colonel pointed to his office door and said: 'Outside that door is the whole of the USA. Out there is the answer. Go find it.' And find out he did, first from the Chicago Police, and then a safecracking expert in New York, and finally the Yale Safe and Lock Company in Connecticut, which provided him with more theory and some sample cut-away locks and lock-picking kits. 'These kits became standard issue,' Arthur Hurlburt recalled. 'Everyone had one, along with his .38, handcuffs, sap [blackjack] and badge. We learned how to drill a tiny hole in the thin back of a padlock, just big enough for a hairpin, in just the right place so a hairpin could trip the locking mechanism, then cover the hole with grease and dirt so no one would be aware you had been there.'

It was not just skills that the Chicago School was trying to impart, but attitudes as well – especially self-confidence, inquisitiveness, adaptability to new and differing circumstances, and timing.

We *had* to be good [Hurlburt wrote to his granddaughter]. We were going to face the experts. The opposition was the best the world had to offer. The Japanese Kempei Tai had had ten years of hot war experience behind them in China and South East Asia. The Gestapo and the Military Intelligence Services of Germany had had four years of hot war plus another six years of controlling and subjugating their own population. The NKVD [a forerunner of the KGB] had at least two hundred years of experience under the Tsars before Lenin. The British were aces and had given our top people advice and assistance, but they would not be with us. And the game was not tiddley winks. It was for real. If we weren't good enough, the world your mother would grow up in would be entirely different.

Before being posted overseas, personnel who had finished their course at the Advanced School were sent for further specialized and operational training in the CIC Staging Area which, at such centres as Fort Meade, Fort Holabird and Fort Hunt, transformed hundreds of CIC agents from civilians to soldiers in record time. Specialized subjects include marksmanship, tent-pitching and other military routines, camouflage, mines, booby traps and disposal of explosives, riding motor-bikes and driving tanks, port security and ship search. In the winter of 1943–4 intensive operational training took place at Camp Ritchie, the Military Intelligence Training Center in the Blue Ridge Mountains of Maryland, not far from Roosevelt's country retreat of Shangri-La (later re-developed into the Presidential complex known as Camp David) and the present-day underground emergency installations of the alternative Pentagon in the event of a nuclear war.

Camp Ritchie was essentially a training centre for all specialized US tactical intelligence personnel – photo interpreters, POW interrogators, interpreters and order of battle specialists. Because the Army automatically sent to Ritchie anyone who spoke foreign languages or had good working knowledge of foreign countries, there was a dense concentration of the most educated recent immigrants, including a number from show business. Seventy-five of Arthur Hurlburt's CIC colleagues joined him on the intensive course at Camp Ritchie, along with a number of other military intelligence types – and the future Secretary of State in the Nixon Administration, Henry Kissinger.

Camp Ritchie stuck in the memories of all who had passed through it. It was an unusual place in a variety of ways. For a start the normal week lasted eight days there – seven days of work, and the eighth day off. And there was an awful lot of enemy activity at Ritchie. A large army unit was employed solely in enacting enemy military activity. 'On a typical day,' recalled one former Ritchie graduate, Thomas O. Schlesinger, 'one could see a complete battery of German horse-drawn artillery clatter across the parade ground. Walking by a classroom building one might see a class form into ranks and practise German short-order drill. On night field exercises in the Blue Ridge Mountains, men staggering into an exercise station half dead with fatigue had to get an "abandoned" Japanese radio functioning to learn the compass azimuth to the next station.'

Life at Ritchie was hard but morale-boosting. Arthur Hurlburt recalled:

Ritchie was a finishing school for outdoor, rough and tumble, last minute cramming before going overseas – a midwinter adventure, in the mountain snow. Much of it was done in the middle of the night, and most of it alone, or with at most one other man. At Ritchie we fired a familiarization course with just about every weapon known to man, mostly enemy types. We worked with hand grenades, concussion grenades, explosives, crawled under live gun fire, examined all sorts of captured enemy uniforms and insignia. But the map reading was king. We would study in a hot classroom during the day, then at night go out into the mountains to practise what we had learned. The first lesson was how to follow a compass course. We were dropped off a truck, two by two, and given a course to walk, up over the top of the mountain, through thick woods and briar patches, in the pitch black night. The next day we would go on to learn something new, like the different kinds of North: Grid North, Magnetic North and True North, azimuth and back azimuth. That night we would go out in the trucks again and be dropped off in twos or threes with a compass, flashlight and map. The next day we would study contours, elevations, signs and symbols. The next night a whole corner of the map would be blanked out, not a mark or a word on a circle 8 inches in diameter. We were to meet the truck at 11 at the center of the circle. Next it would be foreign maps. The French and Germans have entirely different signs and symbols from ours. Our maps were real maps of the actual countryside in Maryland, but in French or maybe German.

The whole course at Ritchie gave us all a good deal of self-confidence, since we knew we would be travelling in a strange place in small groups or alone – not like Infantry soldiers, where the Captain tells people where to go. And it worked out exactly like that, too. Most of the time I was away from even my own people, from ten to over a hundred miles, sometimes without any Americans at all around. When I got hurt in the Philippines, at Damuguete, Negros Oriental, I was 108 miles away from Detachment HQ. Most infantrymen would shudder to be that far away from the rest of their men. Ritchie was a good training ground for what we faced. It was physically toughening as well as mentally sharpening, so that overseas weather, distance, aloneness and strange terrain were never insurmountable. We were very fortunate to be heading overseas with superb training for the job ahead of us. Many men, drafted later, received only six weeks of basic training and found themselves a few weeks later overseas and under fire.

As the war progressed, the rapid expansion in the number of agents in the CIC was matched only by the special equipment required for operations by CIC detachments in the field. By the end of 1943 the inventory numbered more than a hundred items, from equipment for observation, identification, examination and preservation of evidence to sound detection and recording devices, weapons and defensive equipment. The CIC supply catalogue included such arcane devices of the trade as ultra-violet ray lamps, moulage supplies (for mould making), lockpicking and latent fingerprinting sets, iodine fumers, Recordographs and Speak-O-Phone disc recorders, blackjacks, handcuffs and Colt .45s. It was an imbalanced list. In the western desert during the North African campaign, for example, CIC detachments found themselves bowed under the weight of a generous supply of moulage weighing 40 lbs but with totally inadequate transport by which to transport it – or for that matter themselves and the rest of their kit.

Transport was a headache almost to the end. In the States agents were expected to provide their own cars and claim mileage. In Iceland requests for trucks for use by the CIC were repeatedly turned down. In Bermuda for the entire duration of the war the CIC were forced to borrow a pick-up truck from the post engineer. In North Africa agents in combat conditions had to resort to liberating motor vehicles from the French colonials or from their own Army in order to move about at all. In the summer of 1943 the CIC won the entitlement to one jeep for every two agents, and a subsequent Table of Organization and Equipment finally clarified the right of CIC tactical detachments to transport of their own. But canny agents with long experience of the monolithic waywardness of the Army learned to by-pass the military system and jealously guard whatever came their way, especially in the matter of vehicles, billets and rations.

Towards the end of 1943, when World War Two was at its height, the efforts of the burgeoning CIC to achieve proper recognition and status suffered a sudden and catastrophic set-back. Though the real cause for this sensational turn of events was not known to most members of the CIC at the time, and even at the present day is a matter of some controversy, the effect was only too clear: in the space of a few months the CIC in the Zone of the Interior was largely dismantled, its headquarters shut down, its agents posted elsewhere, its files destroyed. Though the CIC continued to operate overseas, within the United States it had virtually ceased to exist; and when an urgent request for agents for the Normandy invasion was received from General Eisenhower's headquarters, the CIC had great difficulty fulfilling it.

So what happened? As far as can be pieced together, the sequence of events went like this. During the course of 1942 and early 1943, as part of the CIC's Countersubversive System in the US, CIC agents placed under surveillance a 33-year-old Army Air Force sergeant by the name of Joseph P. Lash, a personal friend of both Eleanor and Franklin Roosevelt who was under suspicion because of his association with leftist groups. According to a memo dated 31 December 1943 and submitted to the FBI by CIC agent G. C. Burton, the CIC had uncovered a liaison between Lash and the wife of the US President and had actually bugged a sexual encounter between them in a hotel room. This information had been given to Burton by two CIC colonels who had been privy to the investigation.

In his memo Burton reported that when President Roosevelt heard of the bugging he summoned two top Army intelligence officers – in all probability Colonel H. R. Kibler, the CIC Chief, and Brigadier General W. A. Holbrook, an officer on the G-2 Staff – to a meeting at the White House at 10 o'clock one night. At this meeting the two officers played a recording which 'indicated quite clearly that Mrs Roosevelt and Lash engaged in sexual intercourse during their stay in the hotel room.' Burton's memo continued:

> After this record was played, Mrs Roosevelt was called into the conference and was confronted with the information, and this resulted in a terrific fight between the President and Mrs Roosevelt. At approximately 5:00 am the next morning the President called General Arnold, Chief of the Army Air Corps, and upon his arrival at the conference ordered him to have Lash outside the United States and on his way to a combat post within 10 hours.
>
> After the conference was over it was learned that the President had ordered that anybody who knew anything about this case should be immediately relieved of his duties and sent to the South Pacific for action against the Japs until they were killed.

Lash and ten other airmen were at once banished from the weather forecasting school in Grand Rapids, Michigan, where they were attending a course, and summarily despatched to the Japanese war front in the South Pacific. According to a later statement by Colonel Kibler, the Inspector General's investigation of the CIC was ordered by General George Marshall, the Army Chief of Staff, after repeated insistence by his deputy, General Joseph T. McNarney, that he should stifle a CIC report that was 'personally embarrassing' to persons high in the government. Colonel Kibler refused to elaborate on the nature of the 'embarrassing' report, but did say that though communism was involved, the business concerned a personal matter unrelated to communism.

Retribution came thick and fast. The CIC noted in a post-war report:

> The first indication that something amiss had attracted the attention of officials high in the Roosevelt Administration came in

April, when the Deputy Chief of Staff requested a list of all agents operating in Washington by name. At a period when the Allies were rushing preparations for the invasion of France, this request from a general officer high in the War Department must be construed as more than a passing interest in CIC affairs. There was little time in those hectic days for consideration of trivia at top echelons.

Even as the Inspector General probed into the scope and function of the CIC, Brigadier General Holbrook reported that 'in July information was given orally to Counter Intelligence section that it would be reduced radically in the scope of its functions.' The CIC annals noted: 'The forces opposed to the CIC did not wait for the Inspector General's report to wreak their vengeance. On 5 November – the day before the report was published – CIC was ordered to withdraw its agents from the District of Columbia in a move that strengthens the theory that the investigators were about to uncover embarrassing information about certain high officials.'

The report that followed was damning to the CIC and criticized it at every opportunity – the lack of adequate military training, the inclusion of hearsay, rumour and gossip in CIC report-writing, the centralization of CIC control at War Department, the duplication of investigative activities between the CIC and the Provost Marshal General within the Zone of Interior, and much else besides. The proper place of the CIC was with tactical units in theatres of operations, the Inspector General declared. CIC agents should be recruited and trained exclusively for combat activities.

The acceptance of the Inspector General's report at the end of the month led to immediate and drastic steps to curtail CIC's jurisdiction within the USA and to ship CIC agents out to the overseas theatres. CIC agents who remained in America were to merge their functions with those of criminal investigators of the Provost Marshal General in a single investigative body known as the Security Intelligence Corps, which succeeded the CIC in the United States with effect from 1 January 1944. The Countersubversive System was ended and all manuals, reports and personnel records were burnt. At the end of January the Advanced Training School in Chicago was closed down, followed a few days later by the CIC Staging Area at Fort Holabird (though it continued to be used as a transit camp for agents destined for the Normandy landings and North West European campaign). On 10 February Colonel Kibler stepped down as CIC Chief and five days later the CIC Headquarters in Baltimore were officially dissolved. The Counter Intelligence Corps within the continental

United States had nominally ceased to exist. Nine hundred and
sixty-three CIC agents were merged with 900 Provost Marshal CID
agents into the new SIC, 718 CIC agents remained with the Air
Force, 516 with the ground forces, and 162 with the Manhattan
Project (the manufacture of the atomic bomb). By that time nearly
two-thirds of the CIC's total strength were already with their
overseas commands. It was not until May 1946, nearly a year after the
end of the war, that the political climate in Washington changed and
the CIC was fully reinstated as an integral part of the Army at home
as well as abroad.

Commenting on this cataclysm, possibly unprecedented in American military history, CIC annals observe: 'The speed with which
top-echelon approval was stamped on the Inspector General's report
left little doubt that someone—possibly Communists who still held
key positions in government – was determined to halt CIC investigative activities in the United States.' This was written at a time when
anti-Communist fervour was rampant in post-war USA, and when
the CIC was still in the dark about the true instigator of their demise
in the US, little guessing that it was their own wartime President who
had been to blame.

How justified was President Roosevelt in the draconian revenge he
took on the CIC? Former agent Burton has said he knows no more
than the two CIC colonels told him, and did not hear the recording
that was at the centre of the scandal. Joseph Lash, who contrary to
plan survived the war, vehemently denies ever having laid a finger on
the President's wife, who was 26 years older than him at the time.
The President's son, Franklin Roosevelt Jr, has commented on the
White House meeting described by Burton: 'The whole episode is
unbelievable. It would have been out of character for my father and
mother to have acted the way they are reported to have acted.' A
much respected former CIC officer, Lieutenant Colonel Anthony
W. Lobb, also doubts the validity of the story. Before joining the
CIC, Lobb was a US Secret Service Agent in the White House Detail
between 1941 and March 1942, and knew both Lash and Mrs
Roosevelt, having seen them often at the White House or at Eleanor
Roosevelt's cottage, Vall-Kill, near Hyde Park. He has written to say:

In my opinion Mrs Roosevelt would *never* have done the things
that were reported, ostensibly, by some CIC people. I don't doubt
that some eager-beaver CIC agents might have been interested.

Mrs Roosevelt was always a friendly, polite, educated woman. I
talked to her many times. When on Secret Service duty in the
White House we had a night post on the 2nd floor by FDR's

bedroom. There were four agents on night duty (plus a detail of uniformed White House police). One agent was in the door post at a time, 2 hours on, etc. From 11 pm to 7 am the shift rotated. I recall many nights (the night tour was 30 days) I talked to Mrs R. She had a room several doors down from FDR. I recall she would walk by without shoes or slippers, always smiling and friendly. She once told me: 'Don't mind me, I wander around all night long.' She would always go to FDR's door and in her high voice would call in 'Good night, Franklin!' He usually just mumbled 'G'night!'

For 40 years FBI documents that might have revealed the truth of the matter were kept from the light of day – for most of the time in the cabinets ('three cabinets of cancer', as one official described them) containing highly sensitive confidential files held personally by the Bureau's chief, J. Edgar Hoover. Now that these files have been released it is possible to construe that CIC agent Burton or his sources may have muddled reports on two separate incidents involving Lash, as a later FBI memo quite certainly does. The CIC report concerning the first incident covers a meeting between Lash and Mrs Roosevelt at the Urbana-Lincoln Hotel in Urbana, Illinois, on 5 March 1943. On this occasion Lash had the room next to Mrs Roosevelt and her aide, Malvina Thompson. The report does not disclose that there was any bugging of the rooms or any sexual misconduct between the parties. The investigator in charge of the surveillance remained in the hotel lobby until 10.15 pm and was then ordered to discontinue surveillance.

A week later Lash again checked in at the same hotel, this time with a young woman by the name of Trude Pratt, whom he was later to marry. This time the room was bugged and surveillance continued into the night. The officer who wrote the CIC report on this second incident reported that on this occasion Lash and his girlfriend 'appeared to be greatly endeared to each other and engaged in sexual intercourse a number of times.'

If the names in the two reports were indeed mixed up then it would seem that it was the recordings of the sighs and endearments of Trude Pratt, and not Eleanor Roosevelt, that filled the Oval Room and the President's outraged ears during that fretful all-night meeting in the White House in March 1943. If that is indeed the case it follows that the CIC's own demise in the United States was a consequence of the CIC's own bungling and that a night of romance in Urbana had a public consequence out of all proportion to its private significance.

There is one final twist to this odd episode. One of the by-products of the White House backlash was the termination of the Counter-subversive System. Or so it seemed. However, according to Arthur Hurlburt, the order was never properly carried out. When the command was given to cease any investigations of known or suspected Communists and destroy all files on such persons immediately, eight of the nine Corps Area Commanders took the remarkable step of disobeying this order. Taking their careers (and more) in their hands, they merely moved the files into warehouses and other hiding places until the inspection teams from Washington had been and gone, and then brought the files back into their offices again. Arthur Hurlburt commented:

It is very difficult for the civilian mind to grasp the enormity of what they had done. Here were people at the top of their careers, who had spent their entire working lives under military discipline, always obeying and enforcing orders no matter how distasteful they might be. Asking them to disregard a lawful order would be on the magnitude of asking a Priest to profane the Host in public, maybe even worse. I cannot conceive of them doing such a thing without at least conferring with each other and possibly even with higher authority, which would have been General Marshall. The result was the exclusion of Communists from positions of influence in the Army, for the time being, even as they were worming their way into the Departments of State, Agriculture and other parts of the civilian bureaucracy. Maybe they even went as far as to deem the order unlawful, which is really the only excuse for disobeying. Fortunately for them, they were never called to account for it, and we, you and I, know it or not, and like it or not, were and are the beneficiaries.

2

THE THIN BLUE LINE

When the war became a global war the CIC became a global organization – a thin blue line of counter intelligence and security outposts that encircled the world. Wherever an American soldier shouldered a gun, wherever an American plane took off on a mission, wherever an American Navy ship tied up or merchant ship set sail with troops and supplies, there the clever young men of the Corps, with their low pay and high IQ, waited and watched, ferreted and sleuthed, totally committed to their task of protecting the American war effort against those ingenious and dedicated sons and daughters of darkness and Cain – the enemy intelligence agents and saboteurs, the informers, suborners, traitors, stirrers up of insurrection and strife – whose cells and nets were everywhere.

CIC detachments were formed in every Theatre of Operations – in Europe, the Mediterranean, the Pacific, North Africa and the Middle East, India, Burma and China. Agent teams were established at every stepping stone along the attenuated air transportation routes – in the Caribbean, British Guiana and Brazil, remote Atlantic islands like Ascension, bases in black Africa like Liberia, Gold Coast and Sudan, North African cities like Cairo and Marrakech (in Morocco). Altogether 7,500,000 men and 127,000,000 tons of supplies went through army posts served by CIC units. Inevitably service in many of these far-flung and exotic posts in time of war entailed a life-style both fraught and strange.

Iceland was one of the extremer, more isolated postings. Situated roughly half-way between New York and Moscow on the great-circle air route from America to Europe, this bleak, treeless, glaciated island hugged the rim of the Arctic Circle, enjoying the worst of the weather that the North Pole and the North Atlantic could throw at it. For CIC agents freshly posted out of Chicago or Baltimore, arriving at this outpost of World War Two was not so much like going to war as embarking on an old-time expedition of exploration. There were ice-covered wastes to cross, bubbling mud volcanoes, 3,700 miles of rugged coastline indented by countless fjords, remote lakes and mountains, six months of polar blizzards and winter dark when agents were expected to go about their clandestine business on skis and snow-shoes. For long stretches of the year many parts of the island were cut off from the outside world and from each other. For many agents, keeping their lonely vigil over harbours and aero-dromes and the miles of uninhabited coast where it was feared German agents would most likely dare to tread, the 'real' war of Anzio, Guam and Omaha Beach must have seemed a world away.

Yet Iceland had a vital part to play in the global war, for it straddled the strategically important northern Atlantic convoy route which helped keep open Britain's supply line of war matériel from the United States, as well as the Arctic route for convoys bound for Murmansk in support of the Russian front. For a long period during the Battle of the Atlantic a lethal gap in protective air cover for the convoys existed in the mid-Atlantic. This gap – 'torpedo junction' they called it in Iceland – was beyond the range of both US-based and UK-based aircraft, and it was here that the U-Boat wolf packs wrought their greatest havoc among Allied ships. By basing long-range planes in Iceland it was possible to cover a substantial area of this gap. Moreover, there was a large British and American naval base in Iceland and it was from here that Royal Navy and American Navy warships patrolled the shipping lanes and escorted the Murmansk convoys. Icelandic ports offered a half-way staging post for trans-Atlantic naval and merchant ships, a refuelling air base for bombers and other aircraft being sent to join squadrons in England, and a refuge for waifs and strays from the Atlantic battle, especially the survivors (of various nationalities) from torpedoed merchant ships.

Given Iceland's strategic location it was almost inevitable that British troops would occupy the island once German armies had invaded Denmark, whose king was Iceland's titular sovereign. Though Britain's intentions were principally to deny Iceland to the Germans, the Icelanders gave the British a cool welcome, for the island had been neutral for centuries and had no army, navy or defences, and no intention of getting sucked into anybody else's fight. Though the Prime Minister pleaded for courtesy to be shown to the British troops, the islanders were suspicious – were they about to be annexed into the British Empire? In May 1941, the anniversary of the British occupation, many of the inhabitants wore black arm bands in protest.

When the Americans arrived to assist (and subsequently relieve) the British in their occupation duties later that summer, their welcome was no less frigid. Four thousand four hundred Marines were followed by 5000 ground troops (an advance detachment of the 5th Division) and a Pursuit Squadron of the Air Corps. Eventually there were 40,000 Americans stationed in Iceland, or one to every three Icelanders, most of them in the south-west corner of the island in the vicinity of Reykjavic and the US air base at Keflavic and big navy base at Hvalfjordur. The first CIC personnel, Special Agents Weldon M. Jacobs and Donald S. Connell, arrived from the States in November and were put under the command of a G-2 officer from the Iceland Base Command by the name of Major (later Colonel) Richard D. Stevens. The new detachment found itself operating among the Icelanders in a difficult atmosphere of mutual antipathy. As Edward Koudelka, who joined CIC in Iceland later that summer, recalled:

> For reasons I just could not initially fathom, there seemed to be a mutual dislike between Americans and Icelanders. To most GIs, the Icelanders were 'fish-eaters' and '*mojacks*'. The latter term had no specific meaning. It just *sounded* derogatory. There were often altercations in town between Icelanders and Americans. Usually this took place at some café where a very weak beer (about one per cent alcohol content) was available. The Icelanders responded to the belligerent Americans in kind. What better way to hurt these young men more than doing everything possible to prevent them from meeting and enjoying the company of those lovely blonde, or red-haired, nicely proportioned Icelandic girls? Icelandic men did not take kindly to the possibility of Americans enticing away their girlfriends, sisters or wives. They had a term for women who acted friendly with Americans. Such a woman was placed in a category socially called *Astand*. The young lady would be shunned by her countrymen and ostracized until shamed back into the fold. The *Astand* discipline worked very effectively. The possibility of amatory adventure was almost nil for the young Americans.

Many Americans found it difficult to comprehend what made Icelanders tick. In its history and ethnic make-up Iceland was almost the exact opposite of the United States, a melting pot of many nationalities. The Icelanders were staunchly proud of their ancient culture, their old Norse language and their snow-white pure pedigree, and desperately anxious that these should not be despoiled by the Americans. Already they were complaining that instead of the high-class troops that President Roosevelt had promised, they had been sent uncouth hillbillies from Kentucky and Tennessee. Then one day the local morning paper erupted in outrage. *SVARTUR*

ISLENDINGUR! screamed the headline. Black Icelander! A local reporter had seen a black American navy man – most probably a ship's cook from one of the warships at the navy base – walking around the streets in Reykjavic and leapt to an alarming vision of racial apocalypse on the island. 'Does this mean,' the reporter asked his readers, 'that one of our Icelandic girls, *Astand* notwithstanding, will bring forth a black Icelander, despoiling our traditions?' The answer was no, but the navy was doubtless alerted to the general concern, and no black service personnel were seen enjoying shore leave on Icelandic soil again.

Such an incident, so abhorrent by the standards of today, must be viewed within the context of racial opinions held at the time, rather than as an expression of Nazi racial ideology extolling Nordic supremacy absorbed by a section of the Icelandic population. Before the war the Nazis had made considerable efforts to cultivate support among Icelanders and form a potential Fifth Column along the lines of the Quislings in Norway. Even during the war a small element of the population held pro-Nazi views, while a rather larger element continued to be pro-German. Since Iceland was under American occupation, part of the CIC's job was to keep a check on all persons considered security risks among the Icelandic population, using the so-called Z List of top suspects provided by the British, who had seized it in the German Legation in Reykjavic within minutes of first landing on the island in 1940. In the event of a German invasion of Iceland, Z List suspects were to be rounded up and shipped out to internment on the Isle of Wight in England; in the meantime, they were to remain under regular CIC surveillance. In fact most Icelanders were more pro-Icelandic than anything, and gradually warmed to the Allied cause as the war progressed.

The embryonic CIC detachment confronted a number of unusual problems. For a start, none of them spoke Icelandic, at least in the early days. Icelandic is a difficult language to learn, and though the CIC employed native interpreters the language barrier adversely affected the efficiency of the detachment. Later the CIC managed to secure the services of several intelligence officers who spoke Icelandic or something akin to it and eventually the Iceland detachment had its own roster of linguists. Notable among these was Special Agent Leroy Anderson, a Harvard graduate and former arranger with the Boston Pops Orchestra under Arthur Fiedler, who could read Icelandic and translated the Icelandic daily papers as part of CIC's daily intelligence input. Leroy Anderson later gained world-wide fame as the composer of popular light music pieces like 'Sleigh Ride' and 'Blue Tango'. Some ten other officers and enlisted agents were of Icelandic background, and another 20 of Scandinavian background with varying degrees of skill in communicating with Icelanders.

The CIC also had assistance from two intelligence officers who, though not strictly CIC, worked with the CIC throughout the war. One was a US Navy intelligence officer with an Icelandic background, Lieutenant Valdimar Bjornson. The other was a British intelligence officer with a Danish background by the name of Captain F. R. Stevenson, who ran specialist courses for agents newly recruited into the CIC from American ground forces based in Iceland. One of his most memorable courses was on interrogation techniques, which he adapted from his knowledge of Gestapo methods. This, according to one of his students, Edward Koudelka, is how Stevenson put the lesson across:

The Gestapo method of interrogation, the Captain said, had been very effectively used by the Nazis in their occupied territories, and we could learn a good lesson here. Example: A bridge had been blown up by some resistance group, and there were several suspects rounded up and brought in for interrogation. At first they would be sequestered so that they would not have an opportunity to compare or otherwise prepare their stories. Each would then be brought in separately for questioning. After allowing the suspect to sit for a while and 'stew' (particularly stressful if, in fact, he was culpable), a smiling Nazi interrogator would sit down, relaxed-like, and start out with small talk – anything from the weather, the suspect's family, children, occupation, etc. Then occasionally he would intersperse a comment or question, not specifically about the incident under investigation, but about explosions or fires in general. Still basically small talk, but getting closer to the subject. The suspect would be carefully observed for any eye movement, nervous actions or body language when this talk came close to the subject. After building up the tension slowly, the smiling stopped, the interrogator's face became stern, and with accusatory questions the suspect would be directly confronted with the act. The climax would be an out-and-out accusation of guilt, and a conclusion on the part of the interrogator of the culpability of the accused.

The psychological effect of these tactics worked well, according to our instructor. The suspect would find himself in an untenable position and would often be ready to make a deal, to implicate others to obtain leniency. This was particularly effective with suspects who had not had experience of being interrogated. In other words, a real 'cool' or hardened suspect who could think on his feet might wriggle out with some mental gymnastics, but the novice was no match for these experts.

Of course, for the 'cool' type, the Nazis were not averse to using threats or actual torture. We were advised not to use such coercive tactics, and I never heard of such methods by CIC agents before or during my period of service.

Language remained a problem for a while and in turn provoked additional problems, for not only did it hamper counter intelligence operations amongst an initially aloof and incomprehensible local populace, but it led to serious clashes of personality and even frequent bitter arguments and loss of temper between the agents and their superiors. The early agents had arrived in Iceland in civilian clothes, which is how they had dressed on assignment in the States and how they wished to dress on undercover work in Iceland. But Major Stevens, doubting how they could work under cover at all when they could not speak a word of the language, ordered them into uniform – an order they quarrelled over and grumbled about and in the end only half complied with, so that some days agents were to be seen in uniform and other days in civilian clothes, and the local Icelanders, observing this, dubbed their outfit 'the chameleon – the lizard that changes colours'.

Personal differences were rife in the pioneering days of the CIC watch over Iceland, but they faded away as the war escalated and their own duties began to absorb more of their energies, especially after July 1942, when the Americans took over responsibility for the occupation from the British and Iceland became part of the European Theatre of Operations. Though relations with the Icelanders improved greatly as time went by, especially when it became apparent to the local populace that the Allies were beginning to win the war against the Germans, morale amongst the agents sometimes wavered. Partly this was due to the long tours of service of up to two years on the island, rarely with any prospect of promotion. Partly it was due to conditions of life in this dour and wintry part of the world.

Physically Iceland was a hard nut to crack. As one CIC agent put it, Iceland was 'a land of dreary, cloudy, long summer days of supposed midnight sun, and raw, damp, chilling winters when night begins at three o'clock in the afternoon, and there is no spring or fall.' The centre of the southern part of the island was covered by the largest glacier in Europe, *Vatnajökul*. The one rough dirt road across the island was only usable for two months of the year and it was virtually impossible to cross from the south-west to the east coast except on foot or on the back of a tough little Icelandic pony. The long, wild coastline was a counter intelligence nightmare, for its innumerable fjords were ideal places for clandestine landings by enemy agents coming ashore from German U-Boats. There were no railways and the roads connecting the coastal fishing villages were in a dreadful state at the best of times and closed by snow drifts for six months of the year. To make matters worse, the Iceland detachment suffered more than usually from the Army's entrenched assumption that the CIC could function without any means of transportation of their own. In a vain effort to acquire more agents and more jeeps and trucks to cover the wild open spaces of this rugged island, the commanding general, General Bonesteel, shot off a memo to Army in Washington in which he explained: 'Iceland must be considered as three separate and distinct sectors which are isolated from each other except for telephone or radio communication, and movements by ship, a considerable portion of the year. This means that each of these sectors must be self-sustaining tactically and for counter intelligence measures.'

By May 1943 there were nine officers and 98 enlisted agents operating with the CIC in Iceland, many of them taken into the organization from other units on the island with little formal training. Reykjavic, the capital and main port, remained the CIC's headquarters and the scene of greatest activity for much of the war, for among the CIC's many duties was the unusual one of conducting the entire customs and immigration inspection of all non-military people and ships entering and leaving Iceland. But a number of the agents were distributed in single 'cells' in the outlying areas of the island, where some of them were completely cut off from the world for six months or more. For these men it was a lonesome job and they had to dig deep into their personal resources to carry it through. But once an agent was accepted as the *Amerikinskur Njosnari* (the American spy) by the village population life became a little more relaxed and integrated. There would be the frequent custom of taking coffee and cake, invitations to dinner – boiled fish, roast mutton, ptarmigan and sheep's head complete with eyes – and Saturday night dances in the school hall, a far cry from the dreaded *Astand* of Reykjavic and the bigger settlements. There were fishing trips to the mountain falls for Icelandic salmon, climbs among the fog-girt hills, the occasional midsummer dip in the freezing Arctic sea. When the lone agents began to go native – or, as Colonel Stevens put it, 'when the mountains start to close in on you' – they were posted to a bigger village in another part of the island, often having to tramp there cross-country on foot.

But in spite of the monotony and isolation it was an important job. Much of the work entailed watching the sky for enemy aircraft, watching the shore for German submarines, checking the fishing villages for strangers, and monitoring fishing activity and travel in coastal rear areas. The Germans maintained a ceaseless intelligence interest in activities in and around Iceland. This was not just to report convoy movements to U-Boat headquarters. The Allies had made a special effort to convince the Germans that the build-up of American troops in Iceland was the preamble to an invasion of Norway, then in German hands. To find out more about this the Germans sent long-range reconnaissance aircraft over Iceland, but this proved unsatisfactory because the weather was often bad and when it was good the Americans shot the planes down and captured the crews. The Germans then decided to recruit Icelandic students in Denmark, train them at one or other of their Abwehr spy schools and land them from U-Boats on the east coast of Iceland equipped with radios. This also proved unsatisfactory. One of the first Icelandic agents landed by the Germans turned out to be a cousin of the CIC's star agent in Iceland, Leon Zeuthen, who had a number of aunts and uncles living on the island. Inevitably, the moment the cousin set foot on the rocky shore of his homeland the whole family knew about it, including Zeuthen. Detachment Commander Major (later Colonel) Earl S. Browning recalled: 'The agent was successfully "doubled" and sent back only the information we wanted the Germans to have. This was done so skilfully that the Germans asked for advice as to when and where more agents should be sent. The result was that the CIC met them and apprehended them when they arrived.'

In one such incident in the spring of 1944, Agent Anthony Fricano, acting on a tip from a civilian informant, caught two enemy agents while they were asleep in a farm house on the east coast. Both were native Icelanders who had been trained in Germany and then returned to Iceland on an espionage mission. In another incident a few weeks later Agents Dwight P. Miller Jr and Kenneth F. Haan were warned by another civilian informant in Seydisfjordur that three suspicious strangers had been spotted in the area. The place where the strangers were hiding out was in remote and difficult country, and the two agents had to make a dangerous boat journey up a raging river, followed by a long and exhausting mountain climb through deep snow to reach it. Their endeavour was rewarded and they captured three enemy agents – a German soldier and two Icelanders – who under interrogation revealed that they had landed from a U-Boat only three days previously. All three were trained enemy espionage agents who had been sent to Iceland in order to radio back information on convoys and shipping movements and military and naval activities on the island. According to Edward Koudelka, a total of seven enemy agents were apprehended while on espionage missions to Iceland.

If conditions were rugged in Iceland, they were verging on intolerable in Alaska. In this huge wilderness appendage of the continental United States, the extreme winters and almost non-existent communications adversely affected the operational capacity of CIC units. Inks and carbon paper froze in the low temperatures and cameras had to be heated before they would function, as did the vacuum tubes of sound equipment, which otherwise would burst in the cold. Only two phone lines connected Anchorage and Fairbanks, the main towns of this vast region, and it was often quicker to send a letter than make a call because of the inordinately long wait for a phone reservation. Roads were bad and ripped tyres to shreds, so to get anywhere in a hurry it was best to take a bush pilot's float plane and land on the nearest lake or stream to your chosen destination. But if Alaska was tough it was at least, in a sense, home ground. Not so another bleakly northern centre of CIC activity, the Atlantic-battered island of Newfoundland, then still a British possession.

Separated from Canada only by St Lawrence Bay, and lying directly across the Atlantic from the mass of war-torn Europe, Newfoundland occupied a key strategic position in the eastern defences of Canada and the USA alike. Though the primary responsibility for the defence of the island rested with Canada, the US established four big military and naval installations there, as well as a chain of coastal artillery emplacements round the rugged 6000-mile coastline. The US Army was also responsible for the defence of the Avalon peninsula, which is where most of the Newfoundland population lived and included the capital city and main port of St John's.

Like Alaska and Iceland, the terrain of Newfoundland was rugged and in many parts impenetrable. Communications were poor and the weather depressing – cold and wet, with violent gales and torrential rain sweeping across the island almost continuously. An extra dimension of difficulty was added by the Newfoundland people, whose lethargy did much to impede the Allies' preparations for war. The Newfoundlanders were indifferent to the war effort, and slow to comply with even the most rudimentary defence measures, such as blackout. They resented the presence of American and Canadian troops on the island, and isolationist, anti-British, anti-American, pro-German and pro-Nazi sentiments were rife amongst the civilian labour force – particularly in their cups on dreary winter nights when morale was even lower than usual.

Two CIC Special Agents in Newfoundland, Joseph Gilbert and Jack Blue, who had been working undercover among the civilian contract labour on the island, one as a truck driver, the other as a shipping expert in the docks, reported the frustration their cheerless and unfruitful duties brought them. 'Jack and I haven't been able to accomplish a thing here,' wrote Gilbert, 'and I don't believe that the whole set-up here is accomplishing much. I don't intend any criticism of anyone in these statements. But there don't seem to be any leads on anything and I'll be darned if I can dig any up. Jack and I both feel like we are wasting our time. The job is finishing up here and all the Americans will soon be gone.'

Very different were the tropical postings towards the south of the American continent. In many ways life was easier here, physically at least. But the devious web of Latin American loyalties and Nazi perfidies caused many a headache to hard-pressed CIC agents operating in an alien ambience. This was especially the case in Panama.

Even before America's involvement in the war, the Panama Canal – America's strategic military and economic life-line connecting the Atlantic and Pacific Oceans – had been a major counter intelligence preoccupation. One of the biggest problems in Panama were the so-called Blue Moon Girls – the local name for the night club hostesses and cabaret dancers who plied their charms, or more, in the down-town clubs and dives of Panama City and Colón. Because there were so many of them, and they came from such dubious backgrounds, the Blue Moon Girls posed grave intelligence difficulties for the CIC. Ostensibly their job was to mingle with the male clientele in the clubs and charm and cajole them into buying more drinks at very high prices, a major source of profit to the establishment for which they worked, and for the girls themselves. Obviously these girls were a prime intelligence target for enemy secret agents seeking information on military and shipping matters, and the situation was highly fluid. There were at least ten cabarets in Panama City and another ten in Colón. Fresh armies of opportunistic young women were constantly arriving from all parts of Central and South America to find employment as dancers, singers, hostesses and good time girls, taking the place of other girls who were on the move to other hang-outs in other locales.

Three such girls were the objects of special scrutiny by the CIC over a period of time. One was Adriana Barahona, a Chilean girl who worked at the Rialto Cabaret in Panama City. Adriana was the former mistress of the Head of the Abwehr (the Intelligence Service of the German High Command) for eastern South America, General Friedrich Wolf, whose cover was that of German Military Attaché first to Chile and then to Argentina. Adriana's closest friend at the Rialto was another hostess by the name of Ernestyna del Carmen Arias Olave, a companion of the former pro-Nazi, anti-American President of Panama, Dr Arnulfo Arias.

Another girl with dubious connections working at the Rialto was a French dancer from Argentina by the name of Genevieve Batel. Genevieve was the ex-mistress of Dr Karl Wilhelm Koerner, known to the American Embassy in Buenos Aires as a code operator in the German Embassy and a Nazi agent and spy. While living with Koerner in Argentina the French girl also prostituted herself to other men, raising the possibility that Koerner was using her as a tool to gain intelligence information. Reviewing the CIC report on the first two girls, the Commanding General, Caribbean Defense Command, declared: 'It is more than possible that Barahona and Arias are serving as sources of information to someone in Argentina, and their employment in a place habitually frequented by members of the military service is undesirable...' He therefore requested their deportation, along with that of their fellow danseuse and night companion of known Nazis, Genevieve Batel.

Eventually, at about the time of Pearl Harbor, CIC investigations revealed that one cabaret in particular, the Florida, in Colón, was being used as an espionage centre where the hostesses were constantly endeavouring to wheedle information from military personnel and merchant seamen. It seemed that the owner of the Florida, a certain Manuel Cunquero, had bought the club from a known Nazi agent and was sending regular sums of money to an Argentine bank strongly suspected of handling Axis interests in South America. The CIC put the club under mail surveillance and in January 1942 determined that Cunquero was in direct contact with a number of persons throughout Latin America, including the employees of a certain Captain George Gough, known as the 'King of Belize', who was a member of a wealthy family in British Honduras that controlled extensive shipping interests in the Caribbean. Gough was a known smuggler who had engaged in rum-running during the prohibition days in the US and ran a number of brothels in both Belize (British Honduras) and Colón. His connection with the Florida case stemmed from the fact that some of his ships were being used to transport native labourers (who had been using the club as a mail drop) from the Republic of Panama to British Honduras, where the war had created an acute labour shortage.

Further investigations revealed much more startling evidence about Gough's activities. Not only was he passing on espionage information gathered by the busy girls of the Florida club, but he was using his fleet of ten auxiliary schooners to refuel German U-Boats, with which he was allegedly communicating by short-wave radio. In May 1942 agents of the Panama Canal CIC Detachment boarded Gough's vessels and conducted a thorough search. As it happened, there was insufficient fuel on board for a submarine refuelling operation, but among the papers confiscated by the CIC agents were classified blueprints of naval air stations at Coca Solo and San Juan. This discovery led to the seizure of the vessel on which they were found and the arrest of the crew and 30 passengers who were subsequently charged by the American authorities. 19 of Gough's aides, from longshoremen to cabaret dancers, were also taken into custody. George Gough himself made off in one of his own boats but was intercepted by a US Navy float plane while on his way to Argentina and taken back to Panama under arrest. In America the press jubilantly hailed the breaking of what they called the 'Caribbean Spy Ring'.

But the most sensational investigation ever conducted by the Panama CIC Detachment ended in anti-climax. Though the US Army Intelligence Chief in the Panama Canal Department confidently claimed that submarine sinkings had perceptibly diminished since the case was publicized, Gough and his associates were never brought to trial. This was in all probability due to inexperience in this aspect of their counter intelligence duties on the part of the agents involved, a lack of knowledge of the law of evidence and failure to co-ordinate with the US Attorney who could have helped in the preparation of evidence. The King of Belize went free. The girls of the Florida club continued to ply their trade. The U-Boats continued to lurk among the Caribbean reefs and isles until the Allies despatched them to their watery Valhalla.

The Middle East was an even more complex and devious hotbed of intelligence and intrigue. With its internecine rivalries, its closet politics and arras treacheries, its cross-currents of religious and nationalistic fanaticism, the Arab world presented to the fresh young soldier from the New World as complex a picture of ancient deviousness as old Europe was to do, but raised to the hundredth degree. Added to this was the grand strategic design which enmeshed the whole region as powerful foreign powers – Nazi Germany and the Soviet Union, Great Britain and France – jostled and elbowed one another for influence and supremacy, one eye on the region's rich oil resources, and the other on its crucial strategic position astride the Mediterranean and the route to the East.

Though the Middle East was predominantly a British sphere of influence, and intelligence matters largely in British hands, the need for American counter intelligence in the region became paramount the moment the US began to establish a military presence in support of the Allied war effort in the region. The American build-up escalated considerably during the dark days of 1942 as the Germans advanced simultaneously on Egypt and Stalingrad and the Caucasus in what was seen by Allied strategists as a gigantic Nazi pincer movement threatening the whole of the Middle East. As the situation reached crisis point, and Axis armies bombarded the British last line of defence at El Alamein, the first contingent of CIC agents was ordered to Cairo. On 20 September 1942 four officers and 27 agents set sail from New York for Suez and by 12 November they had set up the first Middle Eastern CIC headquarters in Heliopolis, near Cairo.

From this small nucleus CIC penetration of the region spread rapidly. By December field offices in Eritrea and the Levant had been established. By February 1943 another field office had been set up in Teheran for coverage of Iran and Iraq, and as the months followed more offices were added in a network which spread throughout the Middle East and much of Africa: in Beirut and Tripoli in Lebanon, and Aleppo and Damascus in Syria; in Tel Aviv and Haifa in Jerusalem and Jaffa in what was then Palestine; in Ahwaz and Isfahan in Iran, and Baghdad and Mosul in Iraq; in Alexandria, Port Said and Suez in Egypt; in Turkey, Libya, North Africa, the Gold Coast and Sudan.

When they first arrived the CIC's mission was to subdue or eliminate the espionage and sabotage activities of Axis agents working in the area. But by the time they had settled in the whole military situation had changed. With the British advance in Libya and the Allied landings in Morocco and Algeria, the Germans were at last being driven out of Africa; and with the Russian victory at Stalingrad the German threat to the Middle East by way of the Caucasus had been removed. From now on the CIC's main task was increasingly directed towards positive intelligence in the form of collection of political information.

The German retreat in North Africa led to a reduction but not a cessation of Axis intelligence activities. With their withdrawal they left behind organized intelligence groups and innumerable collaborators. By means of sophisticated propaganda campaigns they had also had some success in influencing the minds of non-belligerent populations, exploiting anti-colonial feelings against Allied nations and convincing many of an ultimate Axis victory. Even after they had been driven out of Africa, the Germans and Italians continued to launch intelligence ingressions against Allied positions throughout the region. Although proven espionage and sabotage by Axis agents was limited, professional spy and saboteur networks did exist, and were continually reinforced by agents coming in by parachute or submarine.

These incursions occurred on all fronts. In October 1944, for example, the CIC in Palestine intercepted a German parachute group of five agents, two of them members of the Gestapo, equipped with radio sets, sabotage material, arsenic for use as a poison, forged Danish passports, US Navy discharge papers, money, medicines and three types of high-grade secret ink. The group had taken off from Athens and jumped near Jericho, their mission being to sabotage Allied installations, assist in the military training of Arabs, incite revolts, and transmit military information back to Germany by radio. In separate incidents the CIC in Libya apprehended a group of Axis parachutists who landed near Benghazi in June 1943, and a few months later picked up a party of Italian sabotage agents who landed by submarine in the same area with the mission of blowing up Allied aircraft at bases nearby.

The largest percentage of Axis intelligence agents sent into the Middle East came by land, sea and air into the Levant states of Syria and Lebanon. This presented a major counter intelligence problem for the Allied security agencies that was complicated by the large influx of Greek refugees escaping from Nazi occupation in fishing boats, and by local minority nationalist fanatics, including members of Dashnag, an Armenian terrorist group. Quite apart from incoming agents, some 400 agents and informants belonging to networks developed by the Germans and Vichy French prior to the Allied occupation of Lebanon and Syria were still in position and operationally active. The heads of these networks directed their activities from Turkey, a neutral country, via radio links, neutral consuls and a native courier system.

Axis undercover operations met with a sympathetic response from sections of the Levant populations. The strength of the German armed forces in the early years of the war had made a considerable impression. The anti-Jewish policies of the Axis powers were looked upon with favour, as was their enmity with the hated French colonialists, while German and Italian promises to secure the independence of these countries, and improve the living conditions of their peoples, were widely approved. Though security responsibility was shared by the British and the Free French, the CIC maintained a close liaison and provided all possible assistance and advice, especially on political events and intelligence activities. A CIC summary on two agents captured in Syria in 1943 provides an interesting insight into Axis espionage methods at this time:

> George Lividatis and Constantinos Photinos, two agents who were sent to the Middle East by the Germans in this year, have been tried by Tribunal Militaire and executed at Beirut on 29 September.
>
> Lividatis, son of a Greek father and a German mother, came to Turkey in May last on an espionage and sabotage mission in the Middle East. He was not, however, given any sabotage equipment, since part of the plan of action was that he should enlist in the Greek forces and work under cover of his military duties. After three or four months he was to desert, cross into Turkey, and report to the German Consulate in Iskenderon (Alexandretta). He was given certain accommodation addresses in Greece, Turkey and Spain with which he could communicate in secret ink, and was also instructed to listen at specified times to the Athens radio for messages in plain-language code addressed to 'Jean-Jacques'. Lividatis was arrested at Aleppo while attempting to enter the Middle East, and after his interrogation was handed over to the Fighting French authorities.
>
> Constantinos Photinos was recruited as an Axis agent by Lividatis in Greece after the German occupation. In June 1943, he left Piraeus in a caique which, it was intended, should put him ashore some miles south of Latakia. He landed, however, just north of the Turkish frontier and after a few hours was arrested by a Turkish patrol and subsequently handed over to the British authorities in Syria. As in the case of Lividatis, Photinos was expected to enlist in the Greek army in the Middle East and to carry on espionage and, more particularly, sabotage. He also was given an accommodation address and white-headed matches for secret writing, and was told to listen for messages on the Athens radio. Should he meet Lividatis in Syria, he was instructed not to recognize him. Photinos brought some explosive and incendiary material in a metal box with him on the caique, but stated he threw the box into the sea before he landed.

Paradoxically, the biggest catch in which the CIC was ever involved in the Middle East took place in a country where officially they were not operational at all. The CIC's role in what was to become the Persian Gulf Command was narrowly confined to the security of the road and rail supply line along which American Lend-Lease war supplies bound for Russia were transported through Iran and Iraq. But the occupation of Iran by both Britain and the USSR led to such a sensitive political climate that by mutual agreement it was decided that all intelligence activities in the occupied territories should cease. The G-2 division of the Persian Gulf Command was dissolved and the use of CIC credentials was forbidden – though the CIC continued to carry out its security role along the Russian supply route.

This ban on intelligence activities, it goes without saying, only applied to the Allies; Axis intelligence continued as before. Having gained a footing in Iraq and Iran in the pre-war years, Axis agents operated with considerable freedom until the summer of 1941, when the British suppressed a pro-Axis revolt in Iraq and set up a so-called 'protective occupation' in Iran, moving large bodies of troops into both countries. German agents remained in place, however, and continued to maintain contact with Berlin and to assist the Nazis' intensive propaganda programme which as in the Levant exploited the pan-Arab, anti-Semitic, anti-colonial sentiments prevailing among substantial sections of the populace. Even the Iranian government contained Axis sympathizers, and several tribal groups gave active assistance to German agents in the field.

Three names were prominent in secret operations in Iran. Franz Mayr and Ramon Gamotta were officers in the SD, the intelligence service of the SS, while Berthold Schulze-Holthus was an agent of Abwehr I, German Military Intelligence. The SD officers Mayr and Gamotta (of the SS Brandenburg Division) had arrived in Iran in October 1940 in the guise of employees of a transport company called Iran Express. Mayr was a dark-skinned Bavarian with a bushy moustache who was able to pass himself off successfully as an Iranian. Gamotta, by contrast, conformed to the good-looking blond Nazi Aryan ideal, which made it difficult for him to blend in with his environment. Both immediately engaged themselves in intelligence work and political and tribal intrigue on behalf of the Axis powers, but when Soviet troops (following the British lead) crossed the Iranian border in August 1941, the SD men were forced to flee to avoid internment – Gamotta back to Germany by way of Turkey, and Mayr to the provincial Iranian town of Isfahan, where he hid out with an Armenian collaborator and enjoyed the protection of the military commander, General Zahedi (a future Iranian Prime Minister). Mayr had five radio transmitters, given to him by the Japanese Embassy, with which he maintained contact with his intelligence bosses via the main SD communications centre at the Havel Institut in Wannsee, Berlin. He also had the services of a useful and agreeable courier, who had been Gamotta's secretary at Iran Express, and was now Mayr's mistress.

Mayr was now in a position to carry through his plans of building a pro-German political movement which would seize power in Iran, depose the Shah if necessary, and join the Axis once the German Army had broken through the Caucasus. He encouraged a number of prominent Iranians, both civilian and military, to form a new Nationalists of Iran Party, whose members included General Zahedi, along with the head of the military courts, the director of security, the president of the society of Iranian lawyers, a justice of the supreme court, senior army officers, parliamentary deputies and rabidly anti-British, proto-Khomeini clergymen like Ayatollah Kashani, who was every bit as rabid a Jew-hater as his Nazi fellow-conspirators.

All this political activity became meaningless, however, when the crushing German defeat at Stalingrad brought all hope of a break through the Caucasus to an end. German efforts now concentrated on inciting guerrilla warfare as a means of cutting the flow of American Lend-Lease supplies through Iran to the USSR. To this end, Franz Mayr became involved with Abwehr agent Schulze-Holthus in attempts to raise a tribal rebellion in Qashqai tribal territory beyond Shiraz. At least three German special operations teams were parachuted in from Berlin, one of them led by a certain SS Stormtrooper Kurmis, with two SS non-coms and a Persian-Turkish interpreter in support. This team brought with them $150,000 worth of gold bars, together with an even greater amount of counterfeit British currency. But Kurmis proved troublesome to the German intelligence men on the spot, and Mayr offered to solve the problem by shooting Kurmis dead. This proved unnecessary, for the operation seemed hopelessly compromised. The Qashqai interpreter, convinced that Germany was now losing the war, sabotaged the team's radio transmitter and turned the Qashqai tribal chiefs against the Germans. Kurmis, Schulze-Holthus and the others were held in protective custody by the tribesmen and eventually handed over to the British. Kurmis committed suicide by jumping out of a window of the hospital where he was being treated after cutting his wrists, and Schulze-Holthus was exchanged for a British secret service agent and returned to Germany. That left Franz Mayr to battle on alone as head of German espionage and sabotage operations in Iran.

By now, however, Mayr's plans were largely in ruins. He was

already well known to British intelligence as a German spy familiar with the Middle East, but it was not until early in 1943, when his diary was found in a raided house, that the true extent of his operations became known. Ironically, the CIC might have been able to give the lead in Mayr's exposure some while before this, had things gone as they should. For it happened that an American soldier had formed a liaison with Mayr's mistress, who in *her* pillow talk had told him everything that Mayr had told her in *his* pillow talk concerning his espionage operations. But the young American found the story so fantastical that he refused to believe it and failed to disclose what he had learnt to higher authority. It was left to Mayr's Armenian collaborator to betray him to the British in Isfahan. Many of his secret papers were seized and publicized by British intelligence, but Mayr himself managed to escape to Teheran. It was not until August 1944, when counter intelligence agents tracked a parachuted German agent to Mayr's house, that the espionage chief was arrested. Mayr had been warned by a servant that his arrest was imminent and was trying to burn secret papers when Allied agents burst into his headquarters. These papers revealed his identity and contained lists of all his agents and informants in Iran; they also included maps of all the railway tunnels in Iran, with orders for their destruction signed personally by Adolf Hitler.

Mayr turned out to be one of the few Germans who consistently disobeyed his Führer's orders. Though his mission was to interrupt the flow of Lend-Lease matériel along the route to Russia by sabotaging the railroad, and a number of sabotage agents were sent from Germany to help him carry this out, he seems to have unilaterally disagreed with this stratagem and declined to cut any railways or roads between Teheran and the Persian Gulf. In his view the long Nazi march on India and the Gulf was unstoppable. That being so, it was folly to destroy installations which would be necessary to Germany for the further execution of the war. Mayr's alternative plan, therefore, was to rally the tribes and ambush the trains and the truck convoys, and in this way neutralize the aid-to-Russia programme.

Franz Mayr was interned, tried and executed. Some 130 of his Iranian confederates were arrested by British, American and Russian security units. More importantly the greatest threat to the Lend-Lease programme in Iran was removed, and as a result of British disclosures about the extent of Iranian complicity in Mayr's activities, particularly among high officials, the Iranian government declared war on Germany and joined the Allied cause.

*

Duty for CIC agents in the Middle East entailed at times a life of privation. In Palestine, for example, there just wasn't enough food to go around. Agent Elias Hanna lamented: 'For over six weeks this agent hadn't had an egg. Coffee and teas were always served without sugar.' In Iran it was dangerous to drink the water, and since fuel was so expensive it was rare that water was boiled, so agents had to drink wine instead. In most areas the summer weather was oppressive, diseases abounded and 'gyppy tummy' was common. But a predicament peculiar to this region was loneliness. In field posts as remote as Khorram Shahr and Ahwaz in Iran, or strung out along the railway leading from Basra (in Iraq) to the Russian zone, agents could feel desperately cut off and besieged, and it was recommended that no agent should serve more than nine months in these postings before being, in army parlance, rotated.

The general difficulties of life caused by the even more grievous conditions faced by CIC agents in the Pacific war have been vividly described by a Special Agent in New Guinea:

New Guinea was the Fever Coast of the World. Rainfall was well over 300 inches a year and the temperature never got much below 90, even at night. They say your body gets accustomed to the heat. I don't believe it – your brain just gets tired of complaining, that's all. Mosquitos were no problem. We never saw any. DDT had just been invented and it was sprayed around liberally. There was, however, a thing called 'Guinea Crud'. It was a skin infection which was never really analyzed and never, never cured. I had it on my hands and feet. It would start with a few small blisters that would itch something awful. In a few days the skin would peel off and underneath would be more tiny blisters. One doctor would try gentian violet, another would try mercurochrome, the next sulfa ointments, then penicillin ointments. Finally one doctor would say: 'Don't worry about it. Nothing will cure it here. We just don't know what it is.' For 18 months I hardly took a step without my feet going 'squish, squish'. In time I lost three finger nails.

We saw no vegetables in the 11 months I was in New Guinea. Even potatoes would not keep long enough aboard ship to get there. Meat was mostly spam – spam out of the can, baked spam, fried spam, spam baked in raisin sauce, and ways I can't remember. Instead of butter we had a hard yellow grease like coloured vaseline. It wouldn't melt in the sun at 125 degrees. Many a meal I just made on bread and marmalade. My normal weight at home had been 138–140 lb. One day I found a scale and weighed in at 114, soaking wet with boots on.

An agent destined for such horrors of daily existence was Special Agent Arthur Hurlburt, whose description of his prolonged and tortuous journey out to the far-flung thin blue line gives a vivid idea of the violent change of environment to which many hundreds of CIC agents were subjected when they were ejected from the comfortable *alma mater* of their American homeland in the course of their wartime duties.

After he had completed his final CIC training, Special Agent Arthur Hurlburt was sent to Fort Holabird to await overseas shipment. It was at this point that agents were designated for various postings. Some were scheduled for the Manhattan Engineers, which turned out to be the Atom Bomb project at Los Alamos, though none knew it at the time. Some groups were set apart for Europe, others for Alaska, some for the Caribbean, some for the Pacific. Hurlburt learned that he was headed for Brisbane, Australia, along with nearly 100 other CIC personnel. The long journey out, a great adventure for an observant young man, is indelibly etched in his memory:

We left Baltimore during the last few days of February, 1944, on the wildest, hairiest, craziest military train ride ever. At that time soldiers traveled in made-over box cars, sometimes cattle cars with built-in upper and lower bunks. And they ate in a box car, army food, out of mess tins or paper plates. But our train was made just for us. We had four Pullman cars, complete with Pullman porters to make up the beds and clean up. There was a dining car attached, manned by Pullman people, serving railroad food on white linen tablecloths.

Normally military trains traveled under strict discipline. No one got off and no liquor was permitted. But we got off every time the train stopped. There were at least five poker games going continuously, day and night, for the five or six days the trip took. Booze flowed like water. When the train stopped for a couple of hours in Denver, I remember coming back from town with both overcoat pockets filled with whiskey bottles and carrying two cases of beer under my arms.

The best way of viewing the scenery was from the caboose and I rode there for several days. I rode across the plains of Kansas in the locomotive, one of those western plains locomotives with seven-foot-high drive wheels. I recall riding along the causeway at Great Salt Lake in the locomotive. There was not much conversation up there because of the noise. It was late winter then, and most of the broad expanse of the United States was the dead brown of winter grass, with a little scattering of snow here and there. The Rockies was different. In places we went through snow tunnels. These were not underground tunnels but steep-sided wooden sheds, built over the tracks to hold the snow. In some of these high passes the snow was well over twenty feet deep. The most amazing thing of the whole trip was the descent into the valley floor of eastern California, coming from the grip of winter all the way from the East Coast, with snow in the mountains, and suddenly, in a matter of two hours, finding green grass, mud puddles, and children running around barefooted.

Hurlburt's CIC group were accommodated in the concrete cells of Angel's Island in San Francisco Bay, the Ellis Island of the West Coast, where Asian immigrants were processed for admission to the United States. 'And here we were,' noted Hurlburt, 'setting off on a venture across the broad Pacific from whence they had come.' On 11 March the group boarded the *Sea Cat*, a merchant freighter converted into a troop carrier, with five holds and a fast top speed of 18 knots. Some 3000 other troops boarded the ship at Oakland, most of them from an airborne division.

The line of men boarding was snaked down into a hold, and around in the hold until it was filled up, then it was snaked into the next hold, and so on. We each carried a duffle bag, plus a barracks bag of civilian clothes. There was no place to stow your baggage but in your cot. These were pipe cots, made out of canvas laced to a pipe frame, bolted to a single vertical pipe. They were five bunks high. They were so close vertically that if you rolled over in the night, your hip pushed against the man above you; and so close horizontally that we slept head to foot so we wouldn't breathe in each other's faces. The first night one of our lads was deathly seasick. And I mean deathly sick. We all went up on deck at daylight to get some fresh air and were amazed to see we were still tied up at the dock. We all had a good laugh. It was a lesson in how the imagination can make things worse than they actually are.

We left the dock in the early afternoon and as we passed beyond the Golden gate a Navy blimp picked us up and circled the ship until about five. I thought, well, that's why the convoy hasn't shown up yet – he's watching over us until we meet them. Then when he left, I wondered if the convoy would join up during the night. Next morning, bright and clear, not another ship in sight anywhere. And we streaked for 18 days, straight for Brisbane, without seeing another sign of life. No convoy, no nothing. An eerie and helpless feeling. We would have been dead meat for any submarine that happened along at that time.

The airborne soldiers ran the mess. It was a problem. We had millions of eggs and the only way we could prepare them in the quantities needed was hard boiling them. They lasted only about ten days. We also had oatmeal and other kinds of mush. There were two meals a day. Three thousand people had to eat in a space no larger than a one-family house. That meant eating in shifts. Breakfast began about 5.30 am. and ended around 11 am. Dinner began around 1.30 pm. and finished around 8 pm. Two meals were more than enough. Nothing was less conducive to the enjoyment of food than a close area with little ventilation and the odor of hard boiled eggs amid seasickness.

The Americans were glad to reach Brisbane. The Aussies lined the streets to welcome them as they marched up to the tented army camp on the racecourse, and threw them cartons of milk and other goodies. 'Brisbane was altogether a warm, wonderful place,' Arthur Hurlburt recalled, 'inhabited by warm, wonderful people.' Their warmth was not entirely divorced from their situation. 'The Japanese were just to the north of Australia, in southern New Guinea, which was Australian territory. They had the Dutch East Indies, just to the north-west. They were close enough for their bombers to have paid several visits to Darwin. The regular Australian Army had been away since 1940, fighting in Egypt and round the rim of North Africa. All that lay between Brisbane and the Japanese was MacArthur at Port Moresby, and a line of entrenchments called the Brisbane Line twenty miles to the north of the city, the first line of defence.'

Brisbane, it turned out, was not Hurlburt's final destination. He had just enough time to tune his ears to the local vernacular ('Git yer piper here, Diley Mile, tuppence hipe-ney!' the newsboy called out each morning), and to acquire a taste for the local beverage ('tea, all milked and sugared') and french fries ('the national dish'), before he was moved on again. A few American units in New Guinea had crossed the Owen Stanley Mountains and taken a few settlements on the north side of the island from the Japanese – most recently Finschhaffen. This was the war front to which Hurlburt was now destined.

At something like 3.30 am, two other CIC agents and myself were picked up in a black sedan by an Australian WAAC. She drove us to the airport, where we were loaded on to a C-47 in which we hoped to fly 2000 miles before dark. We took off when it was still completely dark. The C-47 had two benches, one on each side, so the passengers sat facing each other, with baggage and mail piled in the middle between them. The plane made two stops, one at

Townsville, the other at Cairns, the locale of the Great Barrier Reef. All I can remember of either is that we got off, emptied our bladders, griped about the heat, got back on the plane and started off again.

Up to that time we had been flying low, probably around 2000 feet. After the second stop we started climbing up, up and out over the Coral Sea. The engines ground and ground, just like a coffee grinder, pulling us up even more. When we crossed over the coast of New Guinea we must have been at about 10,000 feet, and still climbing. It seemed the coast was one huge swamp for miles inland. You could see the glistening of reflected sunshine between the trees, even from that height. In a few short minutes the mountains had come up to meet us and then we could see why the pilot had strained so hard to get up there. And we were still grinding upwards. Soon we were turning and twisting through mountain passes at an altitude of over 12,000 feet. At times we were no more than 50 feet above the ground. As the plane turned and twisted, you could see the aboriginal people looking up and waving. We actually flew through the smoke of their fires. Shortly the plane broke free of the passes and started to descend.

After that we flew close to the water and hugged the coast. The plane snaked along from point to point, never getting within rifle shot of the shore. From time to time we could spot people waving, standing close to rising columns of smoke, but could not tell who they were. There were absolutely no cities, or towns, or even settlements. Never had I seen coastal territory on this earth with fewer signs of human habitation. Even Darkest Africa must have been more populated than this. At 5 pm, well before sunset, we arrived at Finschhaffen, a spot on the fever coast, a place with grass huts for Operations Offices and an airstrip made from coral, not asphalt or concrete. We called the CIC office on a field phone and one of the agents came down with a jeep and picked us up and took us to our quarters on the *Mactan*, an inter-island steamer tied up at the dock. It had been a long day.

Thus one more CIC agent reached his journey's end and Theatre of Operations after the long haul from America's distant East Coast. The nearest Japanese were only 17 miles away. Only 50 miles up the coast there were 70,000 more of them. From now on Arthur Hurlburt was a part of the Pacific war.

Not all the CIC's main tasks lay overseas. A substantial proportion of agents were assigned to counter intelligence duties in the United

States, in military parlance the Zone of the Interior. Of all the missions which CIC agents were called upon to perform at home, none was more sensational or more vital than the Manhattan Project, the code name for the Atomic Energy Programme leading to the development of the world's first atomic bomb. The part played by the CIC in keeping this awesome project absolutely secret and secure was crucial. In the history of World War Two it is rivalled only by the CIC's contribution towards maintaining the secrecy of the build-up and launch of the Normandy invasion armada on D-Day, and it was by far the biggest assignment in CIC's history.

It was in August 1942 that the US Government embarked on the Atomic Energy Programme that was to alter the whole course of the war and profoundly affect the destiny of mankind itself. Obviously the need for the most rigorous security was an absolute requirement, the more so since it was known that the Nazis were also working on a similar programme. The first nation to develop a successful nuclear weapon would clearly possess a war-winning advantage over its enemies.

From the outset, the Manhattan Project had to be guarded against both sabotage and espionage. By the end of the first year, when it became apparent that the American and Allied scientists working on the Project knew that a successful outcome was a practical likelihood, the protection of this fact became no less important than the protection of the actual data about atomic energy. Had the merest breath of suspicion reached the members of the German atom bomb project, they would undoubtedly have done everything to accelerate the development of their own bomb and hinder the development of the Allies'.

The security of the atomic bomb project lay in the hands of the Project's Intelligence and Security Division, which was under the direction of the overall counter intelligence chief, Colonel Boris Pash, G-2 Deputy Chief of Staff. In August 1943 the Project moved from its Manhattan District headquarters in New York to the Clinton Engineer Works at Oak Ridge, Tennessee, the main development centre of the bomb and headquarters of the Manhattan Project throughout the rest of the war – though much of the Project work continued to be done in labs and engineering works all over the States. From the beginning this Division was manned almost entirely by experienced officers and agents of the CIC, whose part in what has been called the war's best-kept secret was therefore paramount. Commanded first by Major Horace K. Calvert, later by Lieutenant Colonel W. B. Parsons, former head of the CIC Advanced School in Chicago, the Division consisted in effect of a special Manhattan

District CIC detachment, which by the end of the war consisted of no less than 148 officers and 161 enlisted men based at Oak Ridge. In January 1944, Lieutenant Colonel John Lansdale Jr was transferred from the Military Intelligence Service to the CIC Detachment at Oak Ridge as a special assistant to General Groves, the army commander of the Project, with full responsibility for all intelligence and security matters affecting it. This included the operation of a positive intelligence programme and direct supervision over the counter intelligence and security programmes of the Manhattan District. From the inception of this security programme in 1942 it was recognized that the goal was two-fold: prevention of unintentional disclosure of information which might find its way to the enemy; and prevention of espionage and sabotage through infiltration of enemy agents.

The physical security of all the many complex plants and facilities involved in developing the bomb became a major preoccupation. Fires and explosions and other major accidents were as much a threat to a successful outcome as deliberate sabotage, so the close control of employees and the meticulous scrutiny of all the lights, towers, gates, fencing, screening, patrol roads and other security features of the atomic plants were daily tasks. In the 12 months between July 1944 and July 1945 agents made more than a thousand security surveys of Manhattan Project installations, and by early 1945 they were averaging 450 such surveys a month. On one occasion CIC Special Agents Norbert I. Gagen and Steve Potter were given the extraordinary assignment of breaking into the atom bomb plant at Oak Ridge in order to test weaknesses in the security system. They succeeded in breaking into this top secret installation not once but several times and their subsequent report enabled the CIC to devise a security-tight system to prevent enemy agents attempting what Gagen and Potter had done so easily.

Security was not an exact science, however. All protection was considered relative, so security measures depended on balancing potential hazards against calculated risks. The gravity of some hazards was difficult to determine. Others become alarmingly urgent. Thus a vital experimental chemical process at Yale University had to be relocated almost overnight when it was found that the explosion hazard was so serious that the operations would have to be otherwise suspended. By the end, the plant protection programme was seen to have been a total success. No leakage of classified information and no damage to installations or equipment could be ascribed to failures in physical safeguards against espionage or sabotage. Much credit was attributed to the 6000 guards and Military

Police who checked the credentials of all personnel passing into the sites. Attempts to crash the gates or run through road blocks were relatively few and only occasionally was it necessary to use firearms to stop a fleeing car or a person ignoring a guard's challenge. Only once was anybody actually shot dead as a result.

As the Project got into full swing it became clear that the transportation of many highly classified or dangerous materials from plant to plant and city to city would require very special handling. Small but vitally important and highly classified items had to be sent by rail in the charge of officer couriers who sat in locked compartments throughout the journey. To attract the least possible attention the officers wore civilian clothes and carried the secret items in their personal baggage. As an increasing proportion of the secret items were radioactive, attention then had to be given to the physical welfare of the couriers who had these medically hazardous materials in their immediate physical possession. Larger items presented different problems for long periods. On two occasions trucks carrying uranium oxide were involved in serious accidents and CIC agents were immediately despatched to the scene until replacement transport could be arranged. In one instance, a container of uranium grindings being shipped by railway express ignited spontaneously while standing at the station platform at Fort Wayne, Indiana, and flames shot 30 feet into the air, much to the alarm of the railway officials and the local population. But as far as is known nobody suffered serious illness as a consequence of exposure to the hazardous materials used in the manufacture of the bomb, and by the end 18 officer couriers had travelled a total of 832,000 miles without ever losing or mislaying a bag, package or document containing classified matter entrusted to them.

Safeguarding of military information was another major task. This involved, among other things, a strict 'need to know' policy. Laboratories, university departments, plants and contractors were denied any information about the overall structure of the work of the Project and were only furnished with the data necessary to carry out their own particular part in it. Equipment was assembled in places other than where it was manufactured, and the processing of raw materials was staggered in such a way that the different stages were done at different, widely scattered locations. The relationship of one Project site to another was kept concealed; even the very existence of other participants in the Project was hidden to prevent persons from acquiring knowledge of its overall scope and nature. Thus the majority of workers did not know what the Project was doing, or what other plants at their own site were doing, or what the other departments in their own plant were doing. All the sites, materials and special items of equipment were given code names. So were many of the scientists, whose specialist background might give a clue to the nature of the Project as a whole.

Since the top scientists were among the few people who did know what the Manhattan Project was all about, a special group of CIC agents was assigned to them as bodyguards. Each agent was matched by personality to the scientist to whom he was to be attached. Thus Special Agent Charles Campbell, the agent who watched Professor Robert Oppenheimer, the scientific head of the Project, was chosen as an able and witty conversationalist, since Oppenheimer was unable to tolerate bores. Fermi, whose English was not of the best, was given an Italian-speaking agent. The agent assigned to Program Chief A. H. Compton had to be ready to recite the latest baseball batting averages. Quick-witted college graduates for the most part, the CIC men could not help but soak up a certain amount of knowledge about nuclear physics in the course of their prolonged daily contact with this scientific élite. Thus it was that Charles Campbell was suddenly asked by the professor one day: 'And where are you studying your theoretical physics these days?'

All in-coming and out-going mail, including official government mail, was screened for leaks, and leading newspapers were scanned by the censorship section of the Manhattan Project for violations of the censorship code whereby any media mention of atomic energy was prohibited. Few possibilities of compromise were overlooked. When one CIC agent noticed that pages concerning uranium in new reference books in a library were showing signs of use, agents were set to reproduce similar signs of wear in other sections of hundreds of other library volumes. Most of the censorship violations were in-advertent ones. Paradoxically, some of them took the form of letters to the editors of well-known newspapers criticizing the Army for their lagardliness in not building an atom bomb. 'Hints point to the earlier realization of the Atomic Bomb,' wrote one prescient reader to the *Toledo Blade* in December 1944. More alarmingly, a Cleveland reporter, having spent a vacation near Los Alamos, New Mexico, wrote a story entitled 'The Forbidden City' which read: 'Mr Big of the city is a college professor, Dr J. Robert Oppenheimer, called a second Einstein. A widespread belief is that he is developing ordnance and explosives. Supporters of this guess argue that it accounts for the number of mechanics working on the production of a single device, and there are others who will tell you tremendous explosions have been heard.' Such near-revelations fell on deaf ears in Hitler's Reich, where German nuclear scientists, bogged down in a morass of technical difficulties, remained convinced to the end that the Allies were getting nowhere in their researches into nuclear weapons.

Between September 1943 and the end of 1945, CIC agents investigated more than 1500 loose talk and leakage of information cases. A number of these involved members of the clergy, who had inadvertently disclosed classified information about uranium and the atom in order to make the spiritual point that God's powers were even greater than the mighty atom. 'We must not overlook the far more vital and assured fact,' wrote one reverend, in a pamphlet entitled *Startling Powers*, distributed by the Moody Bible Institute of Chicago, 'that God has given to Christians the gift of the Holy Spirit with energies far more dynamic than those of exploding atoms.'

More alarming still was a fictional story in the March 1944 issue of *Astounding Science Fiction* magazine which was all about an atomic energy plant and efforts to prevent the explosion of an atomic pile. The details of the atomic plant operations in the story were sufficiently close to those being employed in the Manhattan Project for a veritable posse of CIC investigators to descend on the magazine's premises and thoroughly grill its editor and the writer of the story. Many agents worked on this case for several months before coming to the conclusion that no subversive agency was behind the story, but the Office of Censorship issued a stern warning that no references to atomic energy could be published in future issues of the magazine, and a shipment of the March issue to Sweden was cancelled for fear that German agents would get hold of a copy.

Security investigations of personnel involved in the Manhattan Project were CIC's main task. Access to classified information could only be granted to persons and firms whose loyalty, integrity and discretion had been clearly established. Altogether 400,000 employees and 600 companies were investigated by CIC agents during the course of the Project, and several thousand individuals were barred from participation, including a number whose records showed them to be murderers, arsonists, rapists, drug addicts, escaped convicts, parole violators, deserters and one person who had been convicted 116 times for bootlegging. A CIC undercover office was established in the area of Oak Ridge, ostensibly operating as the office of a magazine subscription company, and later as an insurance agency. Agents worked undercover on a variety of civilian jobs, earning as much as $60,000 over and above their humble army salaries, all of which had to be turned over to the US Treasury. Agents posed as gamblers, contractors, exterminators, electricians, hotel clerks and bell hops – in fact any occupation which might help them to acquire the information they sought.

Surveillances had to be undertaken under any circumstances on a 24-hour round-the-clock basis. CIC agent Don Harley was involved in a surveillance lasting more than a year. The suspect, who worked in the Manhattan Project laboratory in Chicago, was thought to be in contact with Arthur Alexandrovich Adams, long recognized as one of the top Soviet espionage agents in the United States, and was known to be closely associated with Clarence Hiskey, a scientist who was also under suspicion as an informant for Russian intelligence. The suspect was a highly mobile quarry, and during one 30-hour stretch without sleep Harley had to follow him on a bus-trip through up-state New York, much of it during a heavy wind storm approaching hurricane proportions. When it was finally established that Hiskey was in contact with Soviet intelligence, he was removed from the war deferred list, where he had been placed as a research worker on the atom bomb project, and ordered to be drafted into the US Army and posted to a spot so remote that he could do no further harm to his country.

Sensationally, the greatest espionage suspect in the Manhattan Project turned out to be the head of the bomb laboratory and chief scientific co-ordinator of the Project, J. Robert Oppenheimer, who fell under suspicion because of his pre-war Communist and pro-Soviet sympathies and his personal relationship with an American woman well known as a staunch Communist supporter. At the instigation of counter intelligence chief Colonel Boris Pash, Oppenheimer was kept under close surveillance by counter intelligence branch agents, who duly reported their suspicions that the scientific director was passing secrets about the atom bomb to Soviet agents. In fact, an approach *had* been made to Oppenheimer by an intermediary of Soviet intelligence, but Oppenheimer had declined to pass on information, and remained loyal to the Project and his country. Though the scientist remained under the shadow of suspicion, he was totally indispensable to the Project and kept his job. But Colonel Pash's testimony was eventually to bring about Oppenheimer's downfall. At a government hearing in 1954, the father of the American atom bomb was declared to be a security risk, partly because of his pre-war left-wing associations, and partly because of his opposition, on moral grounds, to the development of the even deadlier nuclear weapon – the hydrogen bomb.

When the fateful day loomed for the test explosion of the first atom bomb in the desert at Almogordo Air Base, New Mexico, scheduled for 16 July 1945, CIC Special Agents Norbert Gagen and Len Jamison were assigned the daunting responsibility of conveying the bomb alone to the west coast of America. Thirty CIC agents were then drafted into the test-firing area to make an extensive survey of the local population, hospital facilities, fire-fighting equipment and potential aircraft landing sites, and to monitor local rumours as to the cause of the blast and protect the government from fraudulent claims for damages once the real cause was made known. At 5.30 on the morning of the 16th, when the sky was still dark and heavy rain was falling, the world's first atom bomb was detonated in the desert. The explosion caused a flash that lit up the mountain peaks and was followed by a tremendous, sustained roar and a tornado-like wind. A boiling cloud of many colours rose 40,000 feet into the air and the heat of the explosion, estimated at several million degrees, turned the desert sand into glass. After that historic explosion, no damage was reported, but rumours as to the cause of the blast ranged from earthquakes to falling stars.

Not long afterwards, CIC Major William H. (Bud) Uanna took physical custody of two more atomic bombs from their place of manufacture and transported them on the cruiser *Indianapolis* to Tinian, in the Marianas Islands, Central Pacific, where he turned them over to the Air Corps for delivery to the 21st US Army Air Force. The rest is history. Rightly or wrongly, for good or ill, the culmination of the Manhattan Project was the dropping of two atom bombs on the Japanese cities of Hiroshima and Nagasaki, resulting in the virtual destruction of both places, along with a large proportion of their inhabitants. After Hiroshima, Major General Leslie R. Groves, the head of the Manhattan Project, wrote a letter of appreciation to the CIC Chief, Colonel H. R. Kibler:

> From the date that this Special Detachment was organized to the present time, personnel at the Manhattan District Counter Intelligence Corps Detachment have performed the function of maintaining to the highest degree the secrecy of the work involved and of withholding from enemy agents all knowledge of our progress in this field. The manner in which they carried out this task will survive to the lasting credit of that organization.
>
> The release of publicity concerning the work of this vast undertaking has evoked from the people of the world an expression of amazement that a job of such magnitude and vital interest could have been kept from the public ear. This outstanding success could not have been possible without the work performed by the Counter Intelligence Corps.

Near the end of the war, it should be added, CIC personnel also took part in a series of special operations known as the Alsos Mission, designed to investigate the secrets of the Nazis' own atomic bomb programme and seize the best atomic and chemical warfare experts the Nazis had had. Under the expert direction of Colonel Boris Pash, previously the security chief of the Manhattan Project, teams of scientists and intelligence personnel, including 22 CIC agents, investigated targets in Germany and a number of recently liberated countries, and succeeded brilliantly in their task of seizing top German nuclear scientists, along with valuable uranium and radium products, amounting to 70,000 tons, which were shipped to the USA and subsequently used in the manufacture of America's own nuclear weapons. Described as one of the finest examples of co-operation between civilians and the military, the Alsos Mission ranks in the annals of the CIC among the most important operations ever undertaken by the Corps in World War Two.

3

SAKAKIDA

Of all the unsung heroes of World War Two, Richard Sakakida must
rank as one of the most remarkable. For courage, fortitude and
loyalty to his adopted homeland there were few to rival him. Yet
outside a small circle of veteran CIC agents Sakakida's name is
almost unknown, and his extraordinary story has never been fully
told.

Richard Sakakida was a native of Hawaii, the son of Japanese
parents who had emigrated there from Hiroshima at the beginning
of the century. Most Americans would have described him as a
Japanese-American, but the Japanese had a special word for such
expatriates – Nisei, meaning the firstborn away from the homeland.
Educated at an American high school in Honolulu and brought up as
an American citizen in a Japanese family, Sakakida was a man of two
cultures and two languages. The outbreak of war between America
and Japan might easily have led to a hopeless confusion of loyalties in
a person of his dual background, but it did not. Like the great
majority of Nisei, many of whom were later to distinguish themselves
in action against the Germans in Europe, Sakakida firmly considered
himself to be an American first and last. In March 1941, nine months
before the Japanese attack on Pearl Harbor, this resolute, soft-
voiced, earnest-mannered young man was invited to put his unusual
linguistic and cultural qualifications to practical use by joining the
specialist branch of the US Army best able to take advantage of them
– the CIC. Along with another young Nisei, Arthur Komori, he was
sworn in as a CIC agent in Hawaii with the rank of sergeant. These
were the first Japanese-Americans ever to be recruited into the CIC,
and they were to be among the handful of their detachment to survive
the war against Japan.

After an intensive training course in the use of codes and ciphers
and the recognition of prime targets, Sakakida and Komori were told
to prepare to embark on a secret mission, the nature of which would
be revealed to them later. They were told that their destination was

Manila, the capital city of the Philippines, an American possession on the point of independence, where the United States still maintained a substantial military presence. They were warned that their assignment would certainly be a source of inconvenience and probably of danger. They were to say nothing except to their immediate family – in Sakakida's case his widowed mother.

Less than a month later the two agents set sail for Manila on board a US Army transport, travelling as deck hands in order to conceal their identity as members of the armed forces. In Manila, a city of tropical languor and almost colonial ease, they were met by the Commanding Officer of the CIC Detachment in the Philippines and briefed for the first time about the nature of their mission. The magnitude of their task took their breath away. It involved nothing less than the counter intelligence investigation of the entire Japanese community in Manila, into which they were required to infiltrate themselves as undercover moles in order to target those individuals who had connections with the Japanese military and posed a threat to the security of the United States Army. As a cover story they were to claim that they were crew members of a freighter and had jumped ship after tiring of life at sea – a story Komori enhanced by adding that he was also a draft dodger, a state of affairs which he reported later 'was favourably received by the pro-Emperor sons of Japan.'

Sakakida was instructed to register at a small hotel called the Nishikawa, while Komori checked in at the Toyo Hotel. From these two bases the tyro agents were to start looking around for rôles in keeping with their assumed identities. Their case officers, Major Raymond and Agent Grenfell D. Drisko, were the only members of the CIC Detachment who knew that they were Nisei agents. In order to stay in contact they were given keys to a mailbox at the Central Post Office in Manila under the name of Sixto Borja and told to check the box twice daily for instructions about rendezvous places. Major Raymond or Agent Drisko would then pick them up at a pre-arranged spot and drive them by a roundabout route to the Military Intelligence section in Fort Santiago, where they could submit their report in safety and receive new briefings. For Major Raymond, a long-time Agent, Sakakida and Komori developed tremendous admiration and affection. 'He gradually instilled in us the techniques of subtle investigations and subterfuges in the best traditions of the CIC,' Komori recalled later. To him they owed everything they knew about working as undercover agents amongst the impendingly hostile Japanese.

And so, in the months preceding the outbreak of war, the two young and apprehensive Nisei began the delicate task of burrowing into the warren of the main Japanese community in the Philippines, numbering more than 2000 in all. Sakakida posed as a sales representative of Sears, Roebuck, whose sales brochures he had learnt by heart, and spent most of his evenings in the Japanese Club, where he assiduously ingratiated himself with the Japanese businessmen who frequented this hotbed of Nippon orthodoxy. Meanwhile Komori obtained a post as a teacher of English at the Japanese Cultural Hall in Manila and made use of this respectable position to win the confidence and even the friendship of some of the leading Japanese residents of the city – the Japanese Consul General, the Chief of the Japanese News Agency, the Chief of the Japanese Tourist Bureau, the Chief of the Japanese Cultural Hall and many others. With few exceptions he found the Japanese 'arrogant and expansionist-minded', openly sympathetic to the militaristic ambitions of the Japanese Army generals and increasingly dismissive of the more peaceable and compromising civilian government in Tokyo. War fever had developed to such an extent, Komori reported, that one of his students in his English class, a journalist who wrote for a newspaper in Osaka, even reported the likely route of advance of the Japanese forces once they had launched their attack against the British in Singapore.

Komori had to go along with all this, of course, in order to keep up his cover. He even had to seem to join in the jingoistic euphoria when Japanese planes bombed the American fleet at Pearl Harbor on 7 December and drink toasts to the Emperor when America declared war on Japan the following day. The outbreak of war now put him in grave danger, for it meant that henceforth he would be spying on an enemy people, and would have to face the consequences if he put a foot wrong. The war was only a few hours old when the complexities of Komori's new situation were brutally brought home to him. He was in the Japanese News Agency in Manila, downing yet another sake in yet another toast to the Emperor, when the door burst open and he found himself ringed by a group of Filipino Constabulary with bayonets fixed. To the Filipinos he was just another Japanese. Along with officials of the News Agency, Komori was herded down the stairs and into a waiting bus. He was then driven to the stinking old Bilibid Prison – 'the hell hole', as he recalled, 'of Manila' – and here he languished, an American agent amidst a gaggle of enemy subjects, completely confident that Major Raymond would eventually learn his whereabouts and rescue him.

Meanwhile, in the wake of the rising tide of anti-Japanese feeling in the Philippines that followed the outbreak of hostilities, Sakakida too had been thrown into the Bilibid Prison, though via a much more circuitous chain of events. In the preceding months he had found employment as a clerk in the Nishikawa Hotel in return for his room and board, a job which had given him an ideal opportunity to inspect the passports and other credentials of Japanese visitors to Manila. With the coming of the war Sakakida's information-gathering operation gained much greater momentum. The United States now required all Japanese nationals to file declarations of their bank accounts and assets, and many of them came to Sakakida to seek his help in filling out all the various forms. In this way he was able to interview a considerable portion of the Japanese community in the Philippine capital and obtain a large volume of information which did not go on the forms, particularly about the military background of the people concerned, all of which he passed on to US Military Intelligence.

Sakakida did not, of course, reveal to anyone that he was an American citizen. Since to all outward appearances he was completely Japanese, he was treated as such by the hostile Filipinos, and before long he found himself in such physical danger that he was forced to look to his own survival. When the Manila radio station announced that all aliens should report to their local police station for internment, Sakakida was happy to oblige. Along with three other Japanese he was flung in the back of an open police truck and driven off through the narrow streets of Manila, where crowds of angry, anti-Japanese Filipinos aimed blows and missiles at them, so that they were bruised, bloody and exhausted by the time they reached the sanctuary of the Japanese Club, now an internment centre for Japanese, German and Italian aliens. A few days later he was sent into Manila city to obtain food for the children in the centre, and while he was there he took the opportunity to return to his hotel to pick up his belongings. But he had barely begun to pack his bags when he was seized by three Filipino Secret Service agents on suspicion of being a spy and thrown into Bilibid Prison, where like his fellow agent Komori he languished in hope of rescue by his CIC commander, Major Raymond.

By now the situation on the war front had begun to deteriorate catastrophically. In the first phase of their plans for the military conquest of the Far East, the Japanese had launched an almost simultaneous assault on Hong Kong, Malaya and the Philippines. On the same day as the attack on Pearl Harbor, over half the bombers of the American air force in the Far Eastern Theatre and one-third of the fighters were destroyed in Japanese air attacks on the American air base at Clark Field in the Philippines, and the naval base in Manila Bay was effectively devastated. Without naval support or command in the air, the commander of the Filipino and American forces in the Philippines, General Douglas MacArthur (Commanding General of the US Army Forces, Far East), had no real prospect of holding Manila when the Japanese began landing ground forces in strength on the island of Luzon on 20 December, and he ordered a withdrawal southward to the natural stronghold of the Bataan Peninsula and the island fortress of Corregidor, where he would hold out as best he could till relief arrived from Hawaii, perhaps in six months' time.

Inevitably Sakakida and Komori were swept up in the turmoil of the last few desperate days before the Japanese entry into Manila. Events moved swiftly. First they were snatched from prison by Agent Drisko; then on Christmas Eve, with bombs falling on Manila and the sky over the city a lurid red from the fires of burning buildings and oil tanks, they were bundled on to a tiny steamer bound for Bataan, along with the entire staff of the CIC Detachment and Military Intelligence section and all their documents. Sakakida and Komori were seconded to Corregidor, the tiny overgrown island fortress off the tip of Bataan, popularly known as The Rock, where General MacArthur had established his headquarters after the retreat from Manila. Here Sakakida was assigned as General MacArthur's personal interpreter and translator. So desperate was the general need for Japanese linguists, however, that both Sakakida and Komori were sent to work near the front lines in Bataan in alternating three-day shifts, so that while one was on The Rock the other would be in Bataan until they changed places. In Bataan they operated from makeshift headquarters of bamboo sticks and banana leaves in a clearing in the jungle, where amid the screeching birds and clacking palms they plunged into a frenzy of activity. They went on patrols and scouting expeditions through the lines, interrogated prisoners-of-war, interned collaborators, collected enemy documents and translated them, amassed information of all kinds about Japanese movements and intentions.

On occasion Sakakida travelled to the front to collect personal papers from the bodies of the Japanese dead, for Japanese soldiers kept highly detailed diaries which provided not only useful tactical information but illuminating insights into the morale and outlook of the Japanese soldiery. Once he was summoned from army headquarters to broadcast a surrender appeal in Japanese to diehard Japanese troops fighting a last-ditch battle in the cliff caves at Longoskawayan Point, where the Japanese Army had been trying to build up a pocket to outflank the American defences at the Bataan front. The Japanese responded to Sakakida's appeal with a fusillade of fire and had to be wiped out to a man by pointblank gunnery.

Sakakida was not very popular with American and Filipino front-line troops, because wherever he went he drew a lot of fire from the enraged Japanese. Sitting in his fox hole with his microphone and loudspeaker and an escort of Filipino Scouts, he would broadcast his surrender message across to the Japanese front line, and the Japanese would listen in silence with exquisite politeness until he had finished, and then blast the area to bits with mortars and grenades and anything else they could lay their hands on. At one time Sakakida tried firing little messages at them with a home-made catapult. The messages, which were rolled up in 2-inch lengths of piping, read: 'It is cherry blossom time back in your homeland, and the military have sent you here to the jungles of Bataan. You ought to be at home with your families and loved ones enjoying the cherry blossom. So why continue this futile battle? Come and surrender with this leaflet and your shipment back home will be guaranteed.'

After this bombardment of the Japanese positions with this touching homily, a voice with a strong Japanese accent called out in English from the jungle: 'What the hell are you firing now, Americans? Are you out of ammunition?'

By now many agents found themselves in the thick of intensive and desperate fighting. When Special Agent Lorenzo Alvarado's unit lost all its officers, Alvarado assumed command during a fire fight with the enemy, and for his courage and initiative was subsequently decorated with a gallantry award. Early in March one of Sakakida's colleagues, Special Agent Harry Glass, made history by becoming the first CIC agent to be wounded in World War Two. He was struck in the neck by a .25 calibre rifle bullet fired by a Japanese sniper hidden in a tree along a jungle trail. By a miracle, the bullet entered one side of his neck and exited the other side without piercing the oesophagus or severing any blood vessels, and Glass was back on duty in a couple of days, with only two small plasters, one on each side of his neck, to mark the historic spots.

Back on Corregidor they found The Rock was not a nice place to be. It was now raked daily from dawn to dusk by Japanese air and artillery bombardment, so that the garrison was forced to seek permanent shelter in the tunnel system bored deep inside the hills, where they eked out an acutely uncomfortable troglodytic existence on half rations. Under the hail of Japanese high explosives the two Nisei on Corregidor worked 16 to 20 hours a day helping to decipher Japanese signal codes and monitoring Japanese air force communications, which were broadcast in clear, thus enabling the Americans to warn target areas on the island that a raid was coming. Later they were joined by another Hawaiian-born Nisei, Clarence Yamagata, a

civilian who had practised law in Manila and acted as part-time legal
advisor to the Japanese Consulate until the American withdrawal
from the city.

As time passed the American position became more and more
hopeless and untenable, even on fortress Corregidor. By the beginning of April it was clear that the end was near for the hard-pressed
soldiers on Bataan. After three months of bitter and intensive
combat, malnutrition and disease the men were exhausted. By now
the average daily food intake was down to 800 calories per man; and
90 per cent of the Filipino Army had no shoes. Hope of relief had
faded and most were resigned to the prospect of imminent surrender
to an overwhelming enemy. Few could now escape the tragic fate that
was about to overtake them.

On 9 April Bataan fell in the greatest capitulation in American
history and some 76,000 shattered American and Filipino survivors
were led north into captivity on a notorious death march that killed
over half their number. Many of Sakakida's CIC comrades took part
in this march. Others were transported to the prison camps in
crowded, insufferably hot freight cars, without water or food. Most
were to die at the hands of the Japanese, succumbing to the privation
and brutality of the camps, or drowning in torpedoed prison ships, or
simply disappearing without trace. One agent did manage to escape
after the surrender on Bataan. This was Grenfell D. Drisko, who had
been one of the first CIC contacts that Sakakida and Komori
had made on their arrival in the Philippines. Fleeing to the hills,
Drisko had joined up with a guerrilla group, but unconfirmed reports
indicate that shortly before the Americans recaptured the
Philippines, Drisko's location had been betrayed to the Japanese in
return for a bounty and he was subsequently captured and killed.

By the time of the Bataan surrender General MacArthur had
already removed himself and his headquarters to the security of
distant Australia, leaving his deputy, General Wainwright, to hold
the fort – in a completely literal sense – on doomed Corregidor. Both
generals expressed deep concern over Komori and Sakakida. Since
the Japanese refused to recognize the right of anyone of Japanese
blood to bear loyalty to another country, they would doubtless treat
the two Nisei with even greater harshness in captivity than they
would their Caucasian comrades – especially if they discovered that
the Nisei in question had been undercover agents of American
military intelligence. General MacArthur therefore ordered Komori
and Sakakida to leave the Philippines on the makeshift evacuation
flotilla known as the 'bamboo fleet'. This presented Sakakida with
the most difficult and momentous decision in his life and marked his

transition from an agent of ability to a man of heroic stature – and a master spy.

Sakakida contended that the evacuation plans as they stood entailed leaving Yamagata behind to face his fate as a prisoner of the Japanese. In his view this was unthinkable. Yamagata had openly occupied a position of trust among the Japanese and then voluntarily come over to the American side. Clearly he would be marked out for special treatment by his captors – a fate too dreadful to contemplate. Sakakida was also aware that Yamagata's wife and children were then living in Japan, a situation which made Yamagata even more vulnerable to any pressure the Japanese chose to put on him. Sakakida himself was not in such a vulnerable position. He had never worked openly for the Japanese, he had no wife or family. It was therefore only right and just, he felt, that Yamagata should take his place on the ride to freedom. He put this proposal to his commanding officer, who in turn put it to General Wainwright, who put it to General MacArthur, who agreed. Sakakida would have to survive the Japanese occupation as best he could.

So, early on the morning of 13 April 1942, Sakakida bade Yamagata and fellow agent Komori farewell as they set off on their breakout bid from the beleaguered island of Corregidor. They went not by sea but by air, taking off from the island's tiny airstrip on what was considered a '50–50 attempt' to get out in an army training plane that had been patched up after a previous crash landing, with an American newsman and an emissary from the Chinese leader, Chiang Kai-shek, also on board. The plane flew through the Japanese blockade without incident and landed on the more southerly Philippine island of Panay. Here they were rescued by a B-25 bomber flown, in Komori's recollection, by a legendary pilot by the name of Captain Paul I. ('Pappy') Gunn, an expert in dare-devil low-level flying, who flew them out, Komori later recalled, 'in a flight in broad daylight through enemy territory in a hedge-hopping, canyon-shooting, wave-skipping trip, during which the pilot kept telling us that enemy planes could not see us as we were flying only a few feet above our own shadow.' The B-25 landed on Mindanao, the most southerly of the main Philippine islands, where it took on a maximum fuel load and then took off again on an historic flight of 17 hours to Australia, the longest flight ever made by an aircraft of that type. Komori was later to state that in his view this flight had been a 'test hop' which proved that a B-25 could be flown much farther than had hitherto been believed, and that it set a precedent for the bombing raid on Japan made a few days later by B-25s from the aircraft carrier *Hornet*.

Komori's first task in Australia was to write what turned out to be the definitive American guideline for the handling and interrogation of Japanese POWs, based on the experience that he and Sakakida had had in Bataan. The two CIC Nisei had found that if a Japanese captive was given a drink of water, an American cigarette and immediate medical care if needed, his fear of summary execution evaporated and he was happy to disclose everything he knew or was asked. This 'kindness and understanding' approach was to pay off in huge tactical and strategical intelligence gains throughout the rest of the war in the Pacific area.

Because of his language capability, Komori was next assigned to the newly formed Allied Translation and Interrogation Section under Colonel Sidney Mashbir. ATIS performed an increasingly valuable task in translating captured enemy documents and interrogating captured Japanese soldiers. But Komori was a CIC agent and was in due course assigned to the chief of counter intelligence in MacArthur's South West Pacific command, General Elliott Thorpe. When the tilt of war clearly swung against the Japanese, Komori rejoined the CIC in the field as an agent, first in the Philippines during the American re-conquest, then in Japan, where he was one of the first CIC agents to set foot after the surrender. Komori was to make a career in the CIC after the war, retiring as a colonel to practise law in his native Hawaii.

Sakakida's experience was to prove very different. There was little for him to do now except wait. He joined up with the other members of the CIC detachment on Corregidor preparing for the inevitable surrender and helped them destroy intelligence files and other records. He was then instructed to revert to his former role as an undercover agent and officially listed as a civilian by the American command. It was understood that if the opportunity ever arose he would try to enter the Japanese forces with the object of channelling intelligence material to the guerrilla formations that were already gathering in the hills.

On 6 May the ravaged defenders of Corregidor were overwhelmed by the greatly superior Japanese forces that had fought their way ashore. After sustaining heavy US losses, General Wainright and several of his aides, carrying a white flag, went out of the tunnels in the direction of the enemy lines in order to arrange a surrender. Some four hours later Wainright had not returned – and the Japanese had not ceased their onslaught. Fearing the worst for Wainright's fate, his deputy, General Beebe, decided to take a small leaking harbour craft and try and reach Bataan to contact some higher ranking Japanese. Sakakida went with Beebe to interpret;

Special Agent James Rubard and several others of the headquarters staff volunteered to man the boat for the voyage across.

As the boat came in to Cabcaben Port on the south-east tip of Bataan, a squad of Japanese soldiers appeared, forced the Americans to stand at attention and then proceeded to remove their dogtags, watches and other valuables. The Japanese NCO in charge then spoke to Sakakida in Japanese, and when Sakakida replied the NCO struck him a number of times, breaking his glasses, cutting his face and knocking him to the ground. 'Hold your temper, Kelly,' General Beebe admonished Sakakida, deliberately addressing him by a false name in order to conceal his Nisei identity. Rubard feared they were going to kill Sakakida on the spot, but instead they refused to allow him to accompany General Beebe as an interpreter and returned all but General Beebe and his aides by Japanese landing craft to the area of Corregidor where American forces were being held captive.

For CIC men like Rubard and Sakakida this was a highly volatile and dangerous time, especially when the Japanese began calling members of Wainright's headquarters staff to Malinta Tunnel for interrogation. Along with other members of G-2 staff, Agent Rubard had been engaged in despatching Filipino natives in small boats to Bataan and to the mainland to observe and report on Japanese military dispositions and movements. Being aware of the identity of these Filipinos, he feared that under intense physical abuse and torture he might be compelled to reveal their names. For that reason he intended concealing his identity from his captors, at least until the interrogations had ceased and prisoners had been transferred to other locations.

But Rubard's plan was foiled, and his life and that of his CIC colleague Sakakida put in jeopardy, by the activities of a certain John David Provoo, a former G-2 clerk from army headquarters in Manila, who as a Japanese linguist had at one time been considered as a potential recruit for the CIC Philippines Detachment. Provoo had never been accepted into CIC because his background investigation revealed that he was a suspected homosexual and Japanese sympathizer who had spent several years in Japan learning the Japanese language and studying to be a Buddhist monk. Immediately after the surrender of Corregidor, Provoo began acting as an interpreter for the Japanese occupiers. He went with Japanese troops to the hospital wing of Malinta Tunnel and relayed their orders that all sick and wounded Americans should be moved out at once so that Japanese wounded could be hospitalized there. When he heard this order Captain Thompson of the Medical Service Corps told Provoo: 'Tell them to go to hell, the men are too sick to be moved.' When Provoo interpreted this response to the enemy, they immediately dragged Thompson out of the tunnel and executed him on the spot.

This same John David Provoo now brought a squad of Japanese soldiers down to the prisoner enclosure and pointed out Rubard and several other headquarters staff members. Three gruelling, intensive days of ceaseless interrogation then befell the helpless Rubard as his captors demanded information on codes, Filipino agents and much else besides. At each interrogation the Japanese became increasingly angry and abusive. But they were not very skilled in the art of interrogation and were further hampered by their very limited knowledge of English. By the third day of questioning Rubard's interrogators were slapping him about and swinging their swords to demonstrate how they would behead him if he did not co-operate. But he was able to maintain a consistent story throughout his interrogation. He claimed that his only duty had been to keep the G-2 situation map up to date, that codes were kept by the Signal Corps (which was true), and that Filipino agents had been handled by two G-2 officers who had been evacuated to Australia by submarine shortly before the fall of the island. At the end of the third day Rubard was returned to the prisoner compound with his head still intact. The next day he joined the main body of American prisoners leaving Corregidor for a prison camp in Central Luzon. He was never interrogated again. (After his liberation, Rubard learned that Provoo had worked for Japanese propaganda radio in Tokyo during the war. He was never charged as a traitor, however, and his trial in a US court on charges of complicity in the murder of Captain Thompson was dismissed on the grounds that he had been denied a right to a fair and speedy trial. So Provoo went unpunished for his actions against his fellow countrymen, though some years later he was reportedly imprisoned for different criminal offences.)

Like the surrendered troops on Bataan, the American defenders of Corregidor were herded into captivity on a death march which left many dead or dying, and some of those who survived this grim ordeal then had to endure an even grimmer one in the hands of the Japanese military police – the dreaded Kempei Tai.

Sakakida was one of those in whom the Kempei Tai took a special interest. He did not take part in the death march but was kept on Corregidor for six months – the only American left on this tragic rock. He had originally come to the attention of the Japanese military on the very first day of the surrender, when he had accompanied General Wainwright to Bataan to act as interpreter at the surrender conference. From that day his life had followed a steep decline into hell. He told the Japanese that he had been taken by the Americans from internment camp and made to work for them under duress, but the Japanese did not believe this cover story and produced several liberated Japanese prisoners-of-war who testified that Sakakida had worked for the United States Army as an interrogator on a completely voluntary basis. He was kept in one of the side tunnels in Corregidor's honeycomb of tunnel installations and interrogated over a period of several months. As Sakakida was not very co-operative the method of interrogation grew daily more severe. Sakakida was tortured, often severely. Sometimes he was burned all over his body with lighted cigarettes, sometimes he was beaten. He was slung with his back over a wooden beam, his feet dangling free of the floor, and he had water pumped into his stomach and was then jumped on by his Japanese guards.

It was never entirely clear whether the torture was meted out as a punishment for being a Nisei, as a means of extracting information, or both. The Kempei Tai not unreasonably believed that any Japanese who had suddenly appeared in their midst at the side of the American C-in-C in the Philippines, as Sakakida had done, ought to have something interesting to divulge to them, though they were not sure what. So every so often they beat him and burned him some more, but he still would not talk. He was taken to the former School of Artillery at Fort Stotsenberg and tortured, and sometimes he was hauled off to the Judge Advocate General's section at Fourteenth Army Headquarters in Manila, where the view and the faces were different but the general ambience much the same as before. Throughout all this unpleasantness Sakakida held out and stuck to his original story. He claimed that he was a victim of circumstances and that the Americans had taken him to Corregidor and Bataan as an interpreter and nothing more. He maintained that he was an American citizen (which was true) and a civilian (which was not). Never once, burnt and bloody though he was, did he so much as breathe a hint that he was an agent of enemy intelligence.

In December 1942 Sakakida was removed to Bilibid Prison. Here he shared the same cell block as Japanese soldiers serving life sentences for surrendering to the Americans during the battle for Bataan. Some of these soldiers had been interrogated by Sakakida after their surrender and they now relished the opportunity of getting their own back. Sakakida was now informed that he was to stand trial for treason, since anyone of Japanese ancestry was of necessity a Japanese citizen, and it was therefore as a Japanese citizen that he had given his services to his country's enemies, the Americans. If this charge was continued with, Sakakida faced the death sentence. But towards the end of the year Fourteenth Army Headquarters received word from the Japanese Foreign Ministry in Tokyo that, although Sakakida had indeed been registered with the Japanese Consul in Hawaii at birth, his Japanese citizenship had been officially made void in August 1941 by his mother. She had the foresight to take this action after her son had left for the Philippines – an action which even the Japanese recognized made the charge of treason illegal. The charge against Sakakida was therefore reduced to one of disturbing the peace and order of the Japanese Imperial Forces in Japan, and the interrogation continued, and the torture too, though on an appropriately reduced scale. Then this luckless Nisei was put in solitary confinement and left to rot.

Altogether Sakakida spent nearly a year in the hands of the Kempei Tai. Finally, in February 1943, he was taken from Bilibid Prison to the office of Colonel Nishiharu, Chief Judge Advocate of Fourteenth Army Headquarters, who had evidently reviewed the case and come to the conclusion that the story which Sakakida had continued to tell without a single variation was in all probability genuine. The Colonel told Sakakida that he would now be released from custody and taken into his, the Colonel's, employ. He was to work in the office as an English translator, run a mimeograph machine, make tea and help out generally, and in his off-duty time he would serve as a houseboy at the Colonel's home. Sakakida was soon to discover that security was not the Japanese military's strongest virtue. Often he found himself alone in the office with countless sensitive documents lying untended in unlocked filing cases. Some of these documents he proceeded to memorize or purloin, though as yet he had no means of communicating their contents to the Allied cause.

Sakakida's rehabilitation was only probationary, however. At various times and in devious ways the Japanese tried to trap him into an admission that he was a serving member of the United States Army. One day someone threw him a .45 pistol to clean, just to see how he handled it. Sakakida realized that to disassemble the weapon properly would demonstrate an embarrassing military expertise on his part, so he merely wiped it with an oily rag and handed it back. On another occasion a Japanese officer, a graduate of Harvard with a disarmingly sympathetic manner, quietly asked him how much the US Army paid him as an interpreter. Sakakida saw through this ruse at once, of course – it was a common method of finding out a prisoner's rank – and replied that he had received no pay at all, only food and accommodation. Once he was alarmed to hear the counter-espionage chief at Fourteenth Army suddenly accuse him out of the blue of being a sergeant in the American Army, a charge he denied with sufficient vehemence for the officer to turn to other things. All these ruses he survived, only to be caught dipping into Colonel Nishiharu's precious stock of American cigarettes, an outrage which earned him the sack as houseboy at the Colonel's house (though he was kept on in his job at the Colonel's office).

As it turned out, this was the best thing that could have happened to him. He was now sent to live in the civilian barracks in the former English Club in Manila city. Even under its new managers, the English Club could hardly be described as a penitentiary. Though the Japanese warrant officer in charge kept strict discipline – roll call at six in the morning and 11.30 at night, bed check at midnight – he overlooked the hours between midnight and the morning roll call. Sakakida thus found that he had several hours of the night at his disposal to resume his role as a CIC agent deep behind enemy lines. During those hours of darkness he had the opportunity to pass on valuable intelligence information gained at Fourteenth Army Head-quarters during the day. He knew that by this time the Filipino resistance had built up a well-organized guerrilla movement in the mountains and possibly had established radio contact with General MacArthur's headquarters in Australia. If Sakakida could find a suitable go-between he might be in a position to make an important contribution to the intelligence war against Japan. The risks he ran were appalling, but at no time did he see himself as heroic – it was simply something he felt he had to do, and was glad to do.

Sakakida's lucky break came not long afterwards, when the wife of an imprisoned guerrilla leader, Ernest Tupas, who was serving a 15-year sentence for anti-Japanese activities, walked into the Judge Advocate General's office to apply for a pass to visit her husband in Muntinglupa prison. Sakakida was required to translate her request into Japanese, and during this initial contact he not only revealed his identity as a US Army Nisei to her, but was able to fill out a number of bogus passes for her and other guerrillas' wives, and also hand over several intelligence documents concerning Japanese military plans. In return, Mrs Tupas was able to arrange meetings between Sakakida and many of her husband's guerrilla comrades who were still at large in the Filipino resistance. In his free hours Sakakida was able to pass on tactical information to them and to hatch a daring plan to spring Tupas and as many as 500 of his fellow guerrillas from prison.

Sakakida's plan was simple in concept. All that was required was for Sakakida himself and a small group of guerrillas disguised as Japanese officers to overcome the prison guards and release the inmates. In practice, of course, it was a rather more complex business. There were three essential components to Sakakida's plan. The first was that Tupas himself should somehow wangle himself a job in the prison's electrical department, so that at an appropriate moment he would be in a position to short-circuit the prison electrical facilities. The second was that the guerrillas should keep a meticulous watch on the prison in order to determine the precise movements and time-keeping of the prison guards. The third was that somehow they should get hold of five or six Japanese officers' uniforms, preferably without knife-holes in the back of the tunics.

All this was done and by October 1943 everything was arranged. Immediately after the midnight bed check in the barracks at the English Club, Sakakida stole out into the darkened, deserted streets of Manila and made his way to his rendezvous with the guerrilla raiding party. Along with four of the guerrillas he changed into Japanese officer's uniform, complete with medal ribbons and a clanking sword at his side, and spent a few moments rehearsing army salutes and formal Japanese bows. Then, with military precision and a haughty imperial swagger to their stride, the group strutted off down the road to the Muntinglupa prison, backs straight, chests puffed out, faces grim and set, polished boots echoing click clack on the paving stones. Sakakida, as the only ethnic Japanese and linguist in the group, marched at their head as they approached the main gate of the prison. It was he who addressed the soldiers of the guard at the prison entrance, barking at them in harsh, guttural commands which compelled their confidence and respect. Thinking that the guerrillas were officers from the Japanese garrison making their nightly security inspection of the prison – which the guerrillas had already established took place regularly between midnight and 2 am – the guards bowed low in respect for their superiors, in accordance with Japanese custom. And as they bowed, eyes firmly fixed on the ground at their feet, Sakakida and his partisan comrades tapped each one on the back of the head with the weighted butt of a .45 revolver.

With precision timing the lights in the prison were suddenly extinguished – Tupas had done his job well. Sakakida was now joined by a second, much larger guerrilla group of some 25 men, and under cover of the darkness and confusion the reinforced guerrilla force broke into the prison, rapidly overpowered the guards inside and began opening the cell doors. Altogether nearly 500 Filipino prisoners escaped from Japanese captivity that night in one of the biggest gaol-breaks of the war. Most of them got clean away, scampering as fast as their legs would carry them out to the city outskirts and the friendlier countryside before dawn could reveal their whereabouts to the enemy. By then Sakakida was safely back in the English Club in time for morning roll call, and later in the morning he had the gratification of witnessing the hysterical Prison Superintendent report to the barely less hysterical Judge Advocate General the inexplicable loss of his entire contingent of prisoners – only to be dismissed on the spot for his pains.

Among those who got away was the biggest prize of them all, the guerrilla leader Tupas. With the other escapees, Tupas made for the mountains of Rizal, where he set up new partisan headquarters and – most crucially – established radio communications with the Australian headquarters of General MacArthur, who was now C-in-C of United States land and air forces in the Pacific Theatre. At last Sakakida had a means of relaying to the Americans the vast amount of information he had acquired while he was working in Colonel Nishiharu's office at Fourteenth Army Headquarters. In effect, Sakakida had become one of that exotic band of makeshift intelligence agents known as the 'coast watchers of the islands', a fifth column of traders, telegraphists, anthropologists, civil servants and others who were left behind when the islands were overrun by the Japanese but managed to evade captivity and to communicate information about Japanese movements and forces by radio to MacArthur's headquarters throughout the course of the war.

Sakakida's position was almost unique, however, for it was a rare event in the history of World War Two for the Army headquarters of one belligerent nation to have one of their serving soldiers and intelligence agents reporting back from the very heart of the Army headquarters of an enemy belligerent nation. But this was the case with CIC Agent Richard Sakakida. Moreover, much of the information he now transmitted was priceless. Much of it concerned Japanese troop movements and shipping activities, all of which was of vital significance in the day-to-day conduct of the campaigns in the Pacific Theatre. But probably his single most devastating contribution to the American military cause was a portion of the invasion plans of a Japanese Expeditionary Force of the Thirty-Fifth Army which was to be sent to Australia. Just how important these plans were Sakakida was able to glean a few months later from a Japanese officer in the Judge Advocate General's office who had taken part in the ill-fated mission. The officer in question had been on board one of the navy ships that had left the Philippines, ostensibly with plans to land invasion forces at Port Darwin in Northern Australia. The officer returned to the Philippines on the only ship that got back. American submarines had taken care of the rest.*

With the tide of war now beginning to run against the Japanese,

---

* Since there is no record of any Japanese invasion of Australia, it must be assumed that what Sakakida had in mind here was the engagement known as the Battle of the Bismarck Sea.

and the dream of imperial conquest cracking and crumbling away, Sakakida's position at Fourteenth Army Headquarters grew steadily more precarious. It was not that he was under any direct suspicion, only that as a Nisei he was viewed with increasing opprobrium by any member of the Japanese military who came into contact with him. Once Japanese headquarters came under direct American attack the mutterings against him deteriorated into outright hostility. In December 1944, because of heavy air raids on Manila, the Japanese commander in the Philippines, General Yamashita, the legendary conqueror of Singapore, was forced to move his headquarters to Baguio in the mountainous north of Luzon, and then even farther into the mountains, to Bontoc, a few months later. The time had come, Sakakida reckoned, to make a break for it and hide out through the final phase of the war in the security of the hills.

It was not the first time he had considered escape. More than a year previously General MacArthur's headquarters had ordered Anderson's Guerrillas – a guerrilla unit led by an American officer who had escaped from Bataan – to try and extricate Sakakida from the Philippines, but Sakakida had feared a trap, Anderson's messages to headquarters had got garbled, and the whole operation had broken up in confusion. This time he would make no mistake. Early in June 1945 he escaped into the mountains and a week later joined up with a small band of guerrillas in the vicinity of Farmschol. Ten days later they came under heavy Japanese shelling during which Sakakida was so badly wounded that he had to be left behind when the guerrillas made good their escape. He was now on his own and would remain so to the finish, wandering between the lines for weeks and months on end.

In the remotest reaches of the jungle Sakakida lived more like an animal than a man. Though the jungle was luxuriant it offered little enough to eat beyond grass and wild fruits. With a razor blade he removed shrapnel fragments embedded in his abdomen, but his wounds festered and he was drenched by tropical cloudbursts, for it was now the rainy season, and bitten to within an inch of his life by the hordes of tropical insects. For months he endured semi-starvation and the ravages of malaria, dysentery and beriberi. His hair and beard grew long and wild, his skin was covered in sores and scratches, his voice grew cracked and feeble, his eyes burned fever-bright, his clothes hung in tatters. He had no means of knowing what was happening in the outside world, no knowledge of the course of the war, of the liberation of the Philippines, the bombing of Hiroshima and Nagasaki, the American landings in Japan, the Japanese surrender to General MacArthur on board the battleship

Missouri. But he did notice that no more American P-38 fighter-bomber planes were coming over dropping napalm, and that there seemed to be a lot of trigger-happy Filipinos about, whom he was careful to avoid.

World War Two had been over for weeks when Sakakida decided his condition was so desperate that he ought to attempt to reach help. Finding himself close to the Asing River, he resolved to follow it downstream, hoping to reach the sea, but he was so ill he could only make painfully slow progress, and sometimes he blacked out. Then one day he spotted some movement among the trees ahead, a group of soldiers coming up the hill, and he drew as close to them as he dared. The soldiers carried equipment and wore helmets and uniforms which were strange to him. They were clearly not Japanese, nor obviously American, and his first thought was: 'God! Now they've got Germans out here!' Not until he was within earshot of the men and could hear snatches of their conversation did he suddenly, ecstatically, realize that they were Americans after all. At first he was afraid to come out of hiding for fear they would take one look at his wild Japanese appearance and shoot first and ask questions later. But eventually euphoria overcame his caution, and madly waving his arms and yelling as loudly as he could, he stepped out of the jungle for the first time in months.

'Don't shoot!' he yelled. 'I'm an American! Can't you see? An American!'

The soldiers were extremely sceptical. Sakakida hardly looked human, and certainly not American. They took him to their battalion headquarters, an outfit which turned out to be a medical evacuation unit posted in the forward areas to collect stragglers. To the CO of this unit Sakakida identified himself as an intelligence agent captured by the Japanese at the outbreak of the war, and he gave his serial number (10100022) and other pertinent data to back up his claim. The officer was also extremely doubtful about all this but agreed to put through a telephone call to the CIC Field Office, and two hours later two CIC lieutenants drove up in a jeep, leapt out and identified the weary agent as one of the men they had been ordered by General MacArthur's headquarters to look for. Then they bundled Richard Sakakida into the jeep and drove him to the Bagadec Field Office of the First CIC Region of the 441st CIC Detachment. He had come home at last. An uproarious welcome engulfed this lone survivor and a festive banquet was laid out in his honour, with fried chicken and beer and white bread and fresh butter and other good things. Having lived for months on nothing but herbs and grasses, such sumptuous fare proved too rich for him and it took him a week to recover from the effects of the most memorable binge in his life.

Sakakida was hospitalized for a week, then sent to Manila for de-briefing. His story was so extraordinary that he found people needed a lot of convincing he had not been a collaborator with the Japanese. At Christmas 1945 he was at last sent home to Hawaii for two weeks' leave, one of which he spent in hospital with malaria and a high white corpuscle blood count. Then it was back to Manila, where he was assigned to the War Crimes Investigation team, locating and identifying guilty parties, aided by the Japanese pre-dilection for keeping records and diaries. He testified in the trial of General Yamashita and later in the trial of the American traitor of Corregidor, Sergeant John David Provoo. Commissioned in 1947, he sought a transfer to the air force and was subsequently posted to Japan, finally retiring in 1975 as a lieutenant colonel in the US Air Force. Today Richard Sakakida is alive and well and living in California – and happy to avoid the ballyhoo that attends most national heroes.

Richard Sakakida and Arthur Komori were among the only members of the CIC Detachment in the Philippines – the 'Lost Detachment' – to survive the war. Others known to have survived included Special Agents Lorenzo Alvarado, John Lynch, Ralph Montgomery, James Rubard and Clyde Teske. Most of the rest died in Japanese hands. Both these brave Nisei were awarded Bronze Stars for their work which, in the words of their commendation, 'they performed with complete disregard to the danger in which they found themselves.' These two Nisei, the citation continued, 'are a credit to their people and to the United States Army.' Of Sakakida's exploits over and above the call of duty, his friend Komori had this to say: 'His successful duping of the Japs is the finest story of counter intelligence within enemy lines. His recovery was considered even more important than the capture of General Yamashita, the conqueror of Singapore.'

4

THE CIC GOES TO WAR

No one in the military high command had ever seriously considered throwing CIC agents into the front line with guns. Whatever else they might be – and in the early stages of the war few tactical commanders had much idea what they were – the CIC were not combat troops. They were uneasy in the company of a grenade, or a bazooka, or a bayonet. They did not care for gunsmoke or blood. In these early years at least their infantry training had been basic rather than exhaustive. For a few of them, thrown into the deep end at the last minute, their longest hike had been from the bus stop to the office. For the CIC were intellectual warriors rather than physical ones. Their job was to sniff out, not rub out. Their usual weapons were the familiar apparatus of counter espionage. Their most common martial emotion was curiosity rather than aggression. It came as a great shock, therefore, when they were told that they were to hit the beaches alongside the infantry in the first combat action in the history of the CIC and the biggest invasion in the history of the world to that date – the Allied invasion of North Africa, codenamed Operation Torch.

It was Operation Torch that was credited with the addition of the word SNAFU – Situation Normal, All Fucked Up – to the Army's vocabulary. Like many great and complex enterprises in their re-hearsal stages, Torch was SNAFU from top to bottom during the hectic period of preparations in London and Washington. This is not surprising, for Torch was not conceived until July, and only three months was allowed for the complex planning of that most difficult of military operations, an amphibious landing, using no less than 650 ships. The code name was changed three times. The date of the landings was changed six times before it was fixed for 8 November 1942. The Supreme Commander was not designated until August – it turned out to be Lieutenant General Dwight D. Eisenhower, then commanding the US forces in Britain – and the debating phase of the organization did not end until late in September, barely 60 days before D-Day. The first the CIC heard about it was towards the end of August 1942, two months before the Allied armada was due to assault the African continent; but some units were not informed until September, and official authority for their participation was only established as late as 20 October, less than three weeks before they were due to go into action. To say that plans for the CIC's role during the invasion were not very complete is to utter an heroic understatement. It is to the credit of the many dedicated, even brilliant men who took part that they acquitted themselves as well as they did in a venture that was wholly new for all concerned.

Torch was originally conceived as a means whereby Great Britain and the United States could relieve German pressure on the Soviet Union, which by the spring of 1942 was in danger of collapse. An American plan for a cross-Channel invasion of Europe in the spring of 1943 was rejected on the grounds that it would be too difficult, too late and too costly in lives. As an alternative, more indirect way of striking back at the Germans, it was decided to launch the North African invasion, the object of which was to clear the northern coast of Africa of Axis forces, thereby securing a base from which a subsequent attack on Italy could be launched (via the stepping stone of Sicily). The North African campaign would also have the effects of opening up the short sea route through the Mediterranean to the Far Eastern Theatre of Operations and of relieving the British forces in Libya, which in June had suffered a major defeat at the hands of General Erwin Rommel's Afrika Korps and been driven all the way back to El Alamein, on the edge of the Nile delta.

To achieve its objective the invasion necessitated the occupation of Morocco and Algeria, which were the most accessible of the French colonial possessions in North Africa, followed by a rapid advance into French-ruled Tunisia in order to occupy as much of the area as possible before the Axis reinforced it in strength. Tunisia was the real prize, therefore, for its proximity to Italy gave it considerable strategic importance, while the facilities at the modern ports of Tunis and Bizerta would be ideal for the subsequent Allied jump-off to Sicily and Italy. The one imponderable complication in this plan was the position of the French. The pro-German Vichy Government still controlled French North Africa and would probably oppose any Allied attempt to occupy it; and though there was considerable opposition to the Vichy regime among the local populace, it was difficult to gauge its strength or effectiveness. One thing was certain – the Vichy Government was so violently antagonistic to Great Britain that it was considered tactful to make the invasion predominantly American in character.

The task of the Operation Torch invasion was thus a daunting one. An amphibious landing on such a scale was new in the experience of planners and combat troops alike; and the beachhead was enormous, stretching for 800 miles from Safi on the Atlantic coast of Morocco in the west to Algiers on the Mediterranean coast of Algeria in the east, and bounding a vast area of French colonial Africa where French allegiances were obtuse and contradictory and deep-rooted religious and racial hatreds posed political problems that could not be assessed in advance. The invasion armada was to be divided into three task forces. The Western Task Force under the command of Major General George S. Patton was to sail from the United States and invade French Morocco. The Center Task Force, consisting of the American II Corps and British air and navy components, was to sail from the United Kingdom and capture Oran on the western Algerian coast. The Eastern Task Force, a combined Anglo-American force under a British commander, Lieutenant General K. A. N. Anderson, was to sail from the United Kingdom, capture Algiers and advance immediately into Tunisia. In all 112,000 men were due to land on a potentially hostile shore in an exotic and alien continent – among them 75 CIC agents equipped with Tommy-guns and Colt .45s and a few weeks of rudimentary infantry training.

So it was decreed. Late in August 1942 the Chief of the CIC was ordered by the Director of Intelligence of the General Staff to procure immediately approximately 100 CIC agents for tactical employment in the invasion. By the middle of September he had managed to assemble 58 enlisted men and 13 officers from the various active service commands. Soon 71 CIC agents, fresh from the warm rooms and soft beds of ordinary urban life, were camping rough with the hardened troopers of the 2nd Armored and 3rd and 9th Infantry Divisions and calling the harassed Chief of the CIC harder names than the ground they slept on. They couldn't understand it, and their Chief was in no position to argue or explain.

This unusual assemblage of counter intelligence agents came from highly diverse backgrounds and included a journalist from Paris, a Rhodes scholar from Oxford, a lecturer at the Sorbonne, a Swiss motor-racing driver, a deputy sheriff from Nevada, a seasoned lawyer from Chicago, an ex-Yale athlete and Jimmy Stewart look-alike with whom lady suspects kept falling in love, and a bespectacled linguist from Harvard who went through the war carrying a Sanskrit-Flemish dictionary which he read for pleasure. What they had in common was a high IQ, a minimum age of 25 (later reduced to 22), and a working knowledge of at least one foreign language – in one group, for example, seven of them spoke French fluently, two spoke German, two Spanish and Norwegian, others Italian, Danish or Dutch. General Bradley described them as 'a group of brilliant and versatile young officers' who sometimes displayed a zany, non-conformist independence of spirit which could be disconcerting to the conventional regimental mind. Thus Crosby Lewis, an agent who was added to the CIC roster of II Corps at the last moment, started out as an American rector's son who volunteered for the Canadian Army soon after Britain declared war on Germany in 1939, then left the Canadian Army with the rank of sergeant major and joined the American Army with the rank of private soon after the United States declared war on Germany in 1942, only to be promoted to officer rank with a battlefield commission soon after landing in North Africa.

Shortly before this motley band was due to embark on the invasion flotillas, their Chief had arranged for them to undergo a week or two of seasoning with combat troops, so that they could at least discover what a machine-gun and a mortar burst sounded like. In London the Center Task Force, better known as II Corps, had set up its headquarters behind the three-foot-thick walls of ancient Longford Castle, where the Corps' intelligence chief, Colonel Benjamin A. Dickson, known in the Army as Monk, a brilliant but temperamental veteran of World War One on the Siberian front, turned in feverish haste to planning the mission of the newly adopted child of the combat arms. In this complex task he was able to lean heavily upon the British Intelligence officers at Allied Force Headquarters, who had had several years' experience of this sort of thing and offered many recommendations which were forwarded almost verbatim to the US War Department.

The five agents who were to sail with Center Task Force were already in England being trained and briefed for their mission. Those assigned to Western Task Force, which was to sail direct from the United States, were summoned to Washington for orientation, an experience recalled with amusement by the commander of the 3rd Infantry Division Detachment, Lieutenant (later Lt Colonel) Jack Cameron:

After being shuttled from office to office for several hours, we were finally herded into a small room whose walls were covered with newspapers hiding maps of various European areas. Then a Colonel was ushered in. His address was simple and straight-forward. It was a command for the Counter Intelligence Corps to go out and 'KILL, KILL, KILL!' With these words rebounding in the small room and blanching the faces of the entire group, he was rushed out and extensive orientation ended.

We were then returned to CIC Headquarters where we were addressed by key personnel who told us that we were 'the pick of the bunch'. As if to accent this point, we were further told that there wasn't a man at CIC HQ 'who wouldn't give his right arm to be in our shoes!' A huge map dotted with pins with names attached was uncovered for a brief moment – but not long enough for any of the agents to identify themselves with their pins!

As D-Day for the North African landings drew near the CIC agents who were to sail began to be assigned to their tactical units for orientation and brief training. This was a variable experience, often frustrating, sometimes downright comical. Some unit commanders understood what manner of people the agents were and what their proper role was. Many didn't. The first CIC agents to report to Western Task Force HQ were put to cleaning petroleum jelly from the weapons because the HQ Commandant could see no reason for carrying out training for special security missions about which he understood next to nothing. The CIC agents, he declared, were 'a citizens' army of misfits', and he claimed the right to use them as he saw fit. His disdain was not entirely inexcusable. The first CIC group got off to a bad start in the eyes of the tactical troops. When the group arrived and were issued with standard-issue pyramidal army tents in which to house themselves like the rest of the soldiery in the camp, one of the CIC officers plaintively asked: 'What shall we do with these?' Amid hoots of derision the new boys squeezed their tents in uneven ranks between two lines of existing tents, where they were immediately adopted by the neighbouring soldiery as trash repositories. 'That they became excellent soldiers never erased the Gilbert and Sullivan operatic classification initially given the group,' Lieutenant Cameron recalled.

At invasion headquarters the security of the entire planning, including the physical security for the Task Force Headquarters in the Ports of Embarkation, fell on the CIC sub-section. Almost every day brought a new security problem. Maps were one. It was discovered that only a few of the 800 civilians employed in the plant that produced the invasion maps had ever been given security screening. The only solution was to set up a careful watch over the maps as they were prepared, sorted, packaged and taken aboard the ships for distribution by the CIC after sailing. For those commanders who required to work out tactical plans special beachhead maps were made with all the names blanked out and a false North provided to disorientate any potential snoop or spy.

The field orders outlining the general mission for the CIC during the invasion, drawn up with little or no precedent for guidance, revealed a deep-seated insight into the CIC's eventual role in combat, as well as the difficulties these agents would encounter through lack of understanding of their mission by commanders of other units. The CIC mission was defined as providing effective counter-espionage, counter-sabotage and counter-subversive activity, and the detection and investigation of all cases of positive or suspected espionage, sabotage, subversion or disaffection within or affecting the military service. The field orders spelled out the need for CIC personnel to exercise their initiative to the fullest possible extent, and required 'that they be permitted to operate without restrictions upon their movements or channels of communication' – agents were not to be delayed by observance of 'standard customs and prohibitions'. This was a directive which many tactical commanders could only swallow with a large gulp.

The topmost priority task for the CIC teams in the North African invasion was to be the capture of the personnel and records of the German Armistice Commission, an organization with an innocent-sounding name but a profoundly sinister function – that of re-organizing the economy and industry of French North Africa to deliver all available raw materials and foodstuffs to the Nazi war machine. The control of the Commission extended over all aviation, shipping, port, railway, storage and merchandising facilities and related utilities, and it was expected that they would make every effort to destroy these facilities rather than allow them to fall into the hands of the invasion forces intact. All CIC detachments were therefore to proceed immediately to key rendezvous points designated in secret orders issued just prior to embarkation, for it was essential to neutralize the functioning of the Commission at the earliest possible moment after the landings. Thus the small CIC detachment attached to II Corps of the Center Task Force landing near Oran was given the following specific targets: the immediate arrest of the German Armistice Commission, the Italian Armistice Commission (a similar but less significant organization), all German, Italian and Japanese consular personnel, and all enemy agents located on the roads out of Oran. In addition, with the help of 'specially trained personnel' seconded from the tactical units they were to seize all hotels in use by Axis personnel, take control of the railways, and establish means of controlling the civil population in the event of prolonged French opposition to the Allied occupation. Similar specific targets were pinpointed for CIC agents with the Western Task Force, though such was the feverish pressure of time that the plan was not completed and rushed to the troops until 48 hours before sailing time.

The Western Task Force, assembled in ports on the Atlantic seabord of America, was the first to set sail, since it had the greatest distance to cover. Seventy CIC agents under Detachment Commander Major Charles Ellis sailed with it, along with Lieutenant Colonel William Parsons in command of the Counter Intelligence Section of the entire invasion. Few day-to-day records are available for this period, but a war diary kept by the 2nd Armored Division CIC Detachment gives some insight into CIC activities on the voyage to the invasion beaches of Africa. The Detachment embarked on board the USS *Harris*, formerly a Dollar Line steamer, at Newport News, Virginia, on 18 October 1942, and by next day they were at sea. The skeletal diary entries kept during the three weeks' voyage baldly recorded the bread-and-butter duties of a CIC outfit at war:

Arranged for housing men on hurricane deck – holds too crowded . . . Surveillance . . . Made ship survey of location of explosives . . . Army mail stopped from going ashore . . . Obtained ammunition issue . . . Study of Intelligence Plan . . . Surveillance, 24 hours . . . Discussed Prisoner of War Plan . . . Shot Tommy-gun and .45 . . . Acquainted men with tactical situation . . . 2 hours tour of deck after dark – ship's guard on its toes . . . Lecture on booby traps . . . French lessons . . . Studied German . . . Studied Arabic from scratchy phonograph record . . . Set up card index systems of known subversives likely to be encountered . . . Discovered fire in pantry . . . Conference with General Officer Commanding . . . Conference with Chief of Staff . . . Conference with Chief Signal Officer . . . Conference to arrange landing . . . Report that radio was sending from some ship in convoy – messages on 500 to 600 frequency . . . Baggage search of Major X, Task Force suspect . . . Surveillance, Major X, 24 hours . . . Subject kept under surveillance at all times – to be prevented from leaving ship at H-Hour . . . 8 November: CIC Detachment arrived at Safi; hit beach at 1000.

Such cryptic entries represent no more than some of the nuts and bolts of this great military adventure; of the structure of the edifice as a whole, the excitement and atmosphere of life on board the 110 Army transports and 127 warships converging on the north-western corner of Africa, they convey little, nor were they meant to. There is nothing here of shipboard life and chow-line rumour and banter on the convoys of heaving ships jammed to the gunwales with armed men; nothing of the dark and silent ship routine in ocean waters threaded with invisible German submarines, of alerts and alarms and false sightings, the nightmares and secret dreads that each man carried within himself towards the foreign shore of Africa; nothing of the secretive landfall off the British rock fortress of Gibraltar, where one by one the ships destined for the Algerian assault slipped silently through the narrow straits in the dark, watched by the unseen, invisible figure of their expeditionary commander, Eisenhower, standing on a headland under cover of the night; nothing of the hushed expectancy, the icy sliver of apprehension, when daybreak at last revealed the enemy coast ahead, with its hazy palms, its innocent, limewashed houses lining the land horizon, its hidden guns and infinite promise of retribution.

The invasion of North West Africa has been described as an essay in military co-operation with political complications. The complications were due to the fact that there were two French authorities in existence – that of Pétain and Laval based at Vichy in southern France and that of de Gaulle and the Free French based in London. The rulers of France's North African possessions – though not all the ruled – were in the main loyal to the pro-German government at Vichy, not so much out of political sentiment as due to a feeling that Vichy was the only legal French authority in existence. This being the case, it was imperative that the Allies should somehow secure at least the neutrality of the 120,000 strong French forces in North West Africa if the landings were to succeed and be followed by an eastward advance along the coast into Tunisia. Surprise was the essence of the invasion plan, for though it might rob the Allies of the help of French units sympathetic to their cause, it would go a long way towards precluding concerted opposition at the spot where the Allies would be at their weakest, on the invasion beaches. In the event, the element of surprise was considerable, though the landings were by no means unopposed. On the Atlantic coast French batteries opened up on the American forces of the Western Task Force, and a fierce naval battle, in which several ships and submarines were sunk, was fought out off shore. Fighting stiffened as American troops advanced inland and it was not until 10 November that the French in the west lay down their arms. In the meantime the Center Task Force landed near Oran, encountering moderate opposition which struggled on until 11 November, while at Algiers, where the surprise was total, the French surrendered to the British and American forces of the Eastern Task Force on the afternoon of the landings.

CIC agents' reports are understandably sparse for those first few hectic hours and days after the landing; there was no time to write or reflect, only to act, as speedily and positively as the circumstances allowed. The agents landing with the Western Task Force on the Safi–Casablanca stretch of the Moroccan coast had the roughest time. Some of them landed under the fire of the French shore batteries. The Headquarters Detachment commanded by Major Charles Ellis and the 3rd Division Detachment commanded by Lieutenant Jack Cameron hit the beach at Fedala amid shellfire so intense that several landing craft were hit and Ellis had to return from the shore to save the lives of two men who had been wounded and thrown into the sea by French shellfire – an act of courage for which he received the Silver Star, the CIC's first citation in the campaign. Shortly afterwards the HQ CIC's mother ship was torpedoed and sunk by a German submarine.

The situation was so difficult and fraught with peril that it took two of Cameron's men – Richard Ryan and John Humphreys – two hours to work their way through French roadblocks to the Miramar Hotel in Casablanca, the headquarters of the German Armistice Commission. By the time they got there the German members of the Commission had fled, but all the remaining personnel were captured, along with all the official Commission papers; in addition nine of the Commission members were arrested later that day as they tried to flee north to Rabat, and three more were shot dead and another wounded. Ryan and Humphreys made another interesting discovery in the Miramar Hotel, which had been taken over as US Headquarters. It seemed that during the Germans' occupation French Intelligence had bugged the hotel rooms with an electronic listening system which they had left in working order when the Americans took over. The CIC also discovered that the French had an elaborate system which enabled them to monitor any telephone in the area. In four other targeted buildings in Casablanca the CIC agents located additional Armistice Commission papers, which included a list of the names and aliases of the French Intelligence Service compiled by the Italian Secret Service, together with a German list of French collaborators. They had thus at a stroke uncovered most of the crucial intelligence relating to German and pro-Nazi French undercover agents and their activities in French Morocco – a priceless intelligence coup for which Ryan received the Silver Star and a battlefield commission and Cameron the Legion of Merit.

The CIC Intelligence Plan, compiled shortly before the Western Task Force sailed from America, listed an almost phenomenal number of counter intelligence missions to be accomplished by the agents on the ground along the Moroccan coast. It is a measure of the dedication and resourcefulness of these men that they accomplished every mission that was required of them, often against all odds. Some of these odds were self-inflicted ones, or at any rate inflicted as the consequence of their own side's confusion and inexperience in CIC affairs. Unlike most other units in the US Army, the CIC had not been provided with what Staff parlance described as a Table of Organization and a Table of Equipment. In practice this meant they were not assigned certain vital items, including (most notably) vehicles of their own and radio monitoring equipment and direction finders. These were grievous and inexcusable deficiencies. Thus, when it seemed very probable that radio messages were being transmitted to the pro-Nazi Vichy régime in France from the French battleship *Jean Bart*, no investigation or interception could be attempted because of the lack of special detection equipment, and many other clandestine radio transmitters had to be left *in situ* undetected. The lack of vehicles was partly compensated for by the practice of 'liberating' civilian cars from their French or Moroccan owners. Even then, care had to be taken that such 'liberated' cars were not 'reliberated' by other military personnel with higher authority. As always, the CIC were able to go about their complex tasks in spite of – rather than with the co-operation of – their comrades-in-arms.

Surviving reports give a picture of manic activity along a broad front as the CIC agents roamed far and wide along the coast and into the desert in their hunt for suspected agents and sympathizers of the Axis powers, exploring a dream-like landscape of great plains and jagged hills where camels growled among the melon patches and mud-walled kasbahs perched precariously on the edges of the wadis, and where bearded Arabs in long jellabahs stood and stared at the new breed of white men in their midst. At Casablanca Airport a radio navigation beam was found to have been left open on the night of a heavy German air-raid, thus enabling the German bombers to fly straight to their target. The individual responsible for this deliberate act of subversion was still being investigated when he was killed in an aeroplane accident. In the Fedala area Captain Stephen Spingarn led a team which quickly rounded up 77 Italians who in the light of advance intelligence reports were considered a danger to the security of the US Army. In the Safi area teams led by Lieutenants Paul Heegaard-Jensen and Robert LaBranche landed under fire from pro-Vichy French forces and immediately took over the postal, telephone and telegraph offices and cut all the wires leading out of the city. On D+3 Heegaard-Jensen, with Alfred Benjamin and two other agents, ventured through enemy lines some 70 miles north-east of Safi to pick up a wanted German agent named Van Ruyn, who had great influence with some 300 Arab *caids* (or chiefs) in the area, and was on close personal terms with the German Consul and the members of the German Armistice Commission. On the return trip the CIC team detoured to Oulidia, where they disarmed the fortress, captured eight prisoners and took away a haul of automatic rifles and machine-guns which would otherwise have been turned against the American forces. For this action, which went far beyond the expected duties of a counter intelligence agent, Heegaard-Jensen was awarded the Silver Star and Benjamin the Legion of Merit (posthumously, for he was killed in an accident a few months later).

Elsewhere other Moroccan towns and cities – Mazagan, Mogador, Marrakech, Port Lyautey – were one by one cleared out and cleaned up by the enthusiastic CIC hit teams. There were arrests, confiscations, investigations, interrogations. The deeper they burrowed into the infinitely complex and impenetrably murky and cloacal ebb and flow of French colonial politics, the more arcane and elusive the counter intelligence reports became:

> Contacted Spanish refugee, deserted soldier, who gave dope on Spanish and Italian situation for 200 francs [ran the war diary of the 2nd Armored Division CIC Detachment]. Bombing at 0600. No agents killed but two soldiers less than 100 yards away killed. Planes shot down . . . Spanish Consul at Mazagan suspected of espionage . . . Phoned General Martin, Governor of Marrakech, and insisted we parlez with him . . . Agents spent day checking on cause of radio interference that did not exist prior to invasion. Leads developed re Van Cotten, alias Kotten, secretary to Baldovini, Chief of Police. Report that Cotten is German SS agent . . . Radio interceptor located on top floor Municipal Service building behind skull and X-bone insignia . . . Met General Martin in Marrakech and apprised his G-2 officer, Deuxième Bureau and our Intelligence re Safi sector. Advised that De Gaullists were going to paint V for Victory signs all over Safi . . . Interview with Governor of Safi. The painting of Safi, as previously we were advised, took place. Van Cotten arrested and put in enforced residence at Marrakech. Douard (pro-Axis) given 24 hours to leave town . . . Obtained new list of suspects; check with old intelligence. Located 13 deserters from French Army. Attempted to get orders to prevent execution; no luck yet. Guards stationed power company, dock, phosphate buildings, water plant and three bridges . . .

Meanwhile the CIC agents who had landed with the Center Task Force near Oran on the Mediterranean coast of Algeria had accomplished the missions required of them, though under less bellicose circumstances than those experienced by their colleagues with the Western Task Force. In the Grand Hotel at Oran they had arrested 20 members of the German and Italian Armistice Commissions and seized a wealth of documents of immense value to later counter intelligence operations. But their moment of glory was yet to come. The CIC agents who had landed at Oran with II Corps were destined to go on through the sand and mud and blood of General Patton's campaign against Rommel's Afrika Korps in Tunisia; while their comrades who had sniffed a brief whiff of gunsmoke with the Western Task Force in Morocco were to settle down to the anomalous role of a counter intelligence agency in a liberated country where the strange and highly devious twists and turns of political fate made it necessary sometimes to treat with respect enemies who should have been friends, and deny help to those who were really friends.

CIC Agent John Schwarzwalder, who was based in Casablanca, has described something of the Machiavellian atmosphere in which he and his colleagues had to work – a world somewhat akin to that which Humphrey Bogart and Ingrid Bergman made famous in their classic film *Casablanca*. 'There were literally thousands of agents, informants, hangers-on and garden-variety spies all over town,' he recalled. 'No one trusted anyone else and with the best of reasons. Casablanca, both before and after the invasion, was as torrid a hotbed of espionage as has ever existed on the face of the earth.' Many of the spies were double agents, most were agents of opportunity, but few surpassed in versatility two unnamed deserters from the French Foreign Legion, one Bulgarian, the other Austrian, both conversant in all the European languages, including the Scandinavian and Turkish, who worked simultaneously for the Germans, the Vichy French, the Gaullist French, the British and the American State Department. 'They had more aliases than were ever dreamed of,' Schwarzwalder reported, 'and collected pay from their various governmental employers with the greatest aplomb. They were, certainly, the finest spies I have ever known. Their information was always reliable and precise. The only trouble one had in employing them was in trying to guess where their sympathies and principles really lay. I never found out and neither did anyone else.'

Special Agent Schwarzwalder did not hesitate to meet skullduggery with skullduggery, sometimes in a manner that anticipated the ruthless spy games of a later generation of Cold War agents. When the French Navy refused to supply Schwarzwalder with the charts of a Mediterranean harbour which official channels had been unable to procure, the CIC agent enlisted the help of a Gaullist French naval officer whom he described as 'really one of the most astonishing characters of this or any other war, highly regarded in his own Navy as a most brilliant young officer, and the bravest man I ever personally knew.' To get hold of the charts the officer broke into a closely guarded headquarters, killed a sentry, rifled a safe and walked out with the charts, which he handed over to Schwarzwalder next morning.

On another occasion, when it became apparent that secret agents were beginning to filter across the long, tortuous border with Fascist-ruled pro-Nazi Spanish Morocco, some of them on sabotage missions directed against the Port of Casablanca, Schwarzwalder sought the co-operation of the CIC Border Control Detachment and soon discovered that the whole system of infiltration was being run by a bizarre German character called Hans Richter, who lived at a place called Richter's Mill in Spanish Morocco – 'as capable an organizer as has ever been seen in the field of Arab espionage, not excepting such masters of the art as von Papen and von Oppenheim.'

Richter was more than 80 years old and though he had lived in French or Spanish Morocco for more than 50 years he had never given up his German nationality, and it seems that he and his son, who both went by the alias of Archibald, had worked for the German espionage system since 1910 – irrespective of what kind of government was in power. The elder Richter had been the brains behind the rebellion of Abd-el-Krim, which had very nearly succeeded in throwing the French and Spanish out of Morocco in the 1920s, and had long been a friend of most of the Arabs in the north. Both father and son spoke fluent Moroccan Arabic, passed as native Arabs, and in all probability were converts to Islam.

Schwarzwalder finally decided that the risks of a successful sabotage attempt in the Port of Casablanca were so great – bearing in mind the daily cargo of munitions, gasoline and other explosive and incendiary war matériel that was offloaded there for the great desert war then in progress in Tunisia – that it would have to be nipped off at source. In other words, he would have to put Hans Richter out of the way.

This was not a particularly straightforward thing to do. For one thing, the old man had given up venturing into French Morocco because of his age and infirmities. For another, he was always surrounded by a bodyguard of well-trained and devoted Arab henchmen. In the end Schwarzwalder decided to employ three professional murderers whom he hired through a group of anti-Fascist French-men. 'Payment for this was made in the traditional manner,' Schwarzwalder recorded later. 'A roll of bills was cut in two exactly in the middle and one half given to the agents. Upon receipt of the news that the job had been accomplished, they were to receive the rest. It is an old method but almost a foolproof one if the bills are stacked all face down or all face up to prevent matching of different halves.'

The three cut-throats never returned to claim their halves. All were killed by Richter's bodyguard in the course of the assassination attempt; but Richter himself was so seriously injured that he feared he would die and begged to be allowed to return to Germany for one last sight of his beloved Fatherland. A German plane flew him and his son to a resort in the Harz Mountains where it is said that Hitler himself came to pay his respects to the old diehard. Hans Richter eventually recovered, but he never returned to Morocco, and for a long time no further saboteurs were reported in Casablanca.

Sometimes the CIC's duty was to preserve life rather than despatch it. When the Free French leader, General de Gaulle, visited Morocco, Schwarzwalder was one of the CIC team detailed to look after the general's personal security. This was a thankless task, for de Gaulle clearly paid scant regard to his own safety in public. When the general arrived by car at the Monument to the Unknown Soldier in Casablanca, Schwarzwalder was horrified to see that instead of simply laying a wreath and then returning to the safety of the car, de Gaulle plunged into the huge and near-hysterical crowd of well-wishers which had gathered to greet him, gravely saluting to right and left. 'His tremendous height made him the easiest mark in the world,' Schwarzwalder related, thereby portending actual plans for the General's death in the post-war Algerian revolution and the fictional assassination plot recounted in the best-selling book and film, *The Day of the Jackal*, 'and my worry was not allayed by the fact that only ten minutes before his arrival the French police had arrested two French sailors, armed with pistols but dressed in civilian clothes.' The situation was even worse at the town hall. The General was presenting decorations to French soldiers wounded in Tunisia, when another French soldier stepped forward and struck one of the wounded in the face, calling him a traitor for shaking the hand of de Gaulle. In the tumult that ensued before the CIC agents managed to manhandle the aggressor out of the salon, by far the calmest person present was de Gaulle himself. Later a French detective remarked to Schwarzwalder that the general was a brave and true Frenchman but if he continued to conduct himself elsewhere as he had in Casablanca 'the French nation would have to look around for a successor, since it was doubtful if de Gaulle had long to live.'

Even more difficult to protect was the much hated French Resident General in Morocco, General Auguste Noguès, a staunch Vichyite. Along with five other CIC agents, John Schwarzwalder was assigned to provide a bodyguard for General Noguès and General Mark Clark, acting as Eisenhower's personal deputy, when they visited Casablanca to review a new delivery of French and American army tanks. 'I have never been so frightened in my life,' Schwarzwalder related afterwards. 'For at least twenty minutes before the generals arrived, a crowd of almost thirty thousand people had been shouting for Noguès' immediate death. "*Au poteau Noguès!*" was the cry. It was chanted, "AU PO – TEAU – NO – GUES," with the two O sounds long drawn out like a wail and the "guès" cut off short. Translated literally it means, "To the lamp post with Noguès," and the American equivalent is "String him up." It is a rather terrifying thing to hear thirty thousand people calling for the death of a man in whole-souled unison, even when the proposed human sacrifice is as doubtful a character as Noguès.'

When the generals arrived the crowd burst into a passionate rendering of 'The Marseillaise', then surged forward against the line of French police and Senegalese troops as Noguès took the reviewing stand with Clark. 'Our pitifully small protection guard manoeuvred closer to the reviewing stand,' Schwarzwalder continued, 'resolved that Clark was not going to get killed regardless of what else happened. Then General Clark did a quite remarkable thing. He realized what the fuss was all about and he stopped it there and then. He stopped it without saying a word. All he did was stand up, all six feet two of him, and look at the crowd. They saw him there and they realized that whatever Noguès' deserts might be, now was not the proper time to kill him. They quieted down rapidly.' Noguès was destined to survive and find eventual asylum in the Fascist Portugal of Salazar.

The daily Counter Intelligence Summaries of the Western Task Force at this time are full of the machinations of General Noguès and the deceitful intrigues and internecine conflicts of French colonial politics that followed the trauma of invasion. Though these may seem obscure and arcane matters today, they were deadly earnest then:

Information from a reliable source indicated that General Béthouard, pro-Ally, arrested because of his intervention in favor of the Americans, is held in prison in Meknès . . . Lists of French political prisoners are being compiled and the possibility of detrimental action by General Noguès is under investigation in co-operation with the Deuxième Bureau . . . French officials have provided this office with documentary evidence of the anti-American activities of General Noguès and his cabinet . . . A French intercept station at Rabat is reported to be intercepting all American and British wireless messages and attempting to break the codes . . . German and Italian activity in Spanish Morocco, especially in regard to the activities of the German and Italian Armistice Commissions and the German Intelligence Service, is being intensified . . . Attempts by French civilians to cause American soldiers to adopt the German attitude towards the Jews have been noted. These seek to make the soldier ask himself, 'What am I fighting for, and what am I getting out of it?' Information from a source indicates that German propagandists are leading the Arabs to believe that all Americans are Jews and later will take away what they have given to the country . . . Information from a source believed reliable indicates that a large number, possibly 25 per cent, of the Arab population of Casablanca have left the city as a result of fear induced by German propaganda . . . Pro-American Frenchmen cannot understand why collaborationist French leaders have been left in power in North Africa. Pro-American citizens are afraid to show their sympathies because of their leaders, and pro-Axis sympathizers see no reason to change their beliefs in view of the acceptance by the Americans of French leaders with pro-Axis views. In many cases French civilians favouring the Allied cause have suffered more since the landing of the American troops in French Morocco than they did before. Persecution by the French authorities has taken the form of imprisonment or eviction from dwelling places . . . The drunkenness of American soldiers is being used as a basis for anti-Allied propaganda in the form of a whispering campaign conducted by members of the Légion Française des Combattants in bars, stores and private homes, with statements such as, 'These are the men who will be fighting the Germans in Tunisia' . . . The German Intelligence Service at Melilla, Spanish Morocco, has received a supply of American Army uniforms . . .

The Americans were new to this world of old-fashioned intrigue and they learnt a lot. According to Colonel Parsons:

Perhaps the biggest lesson we learned in North Africa was that the United States must not rely upon other countries to furnish intelligence. Americans were unprepared to evaluate information from Old World sources, long schooled in double-dealing and professional spying, and we made some errors because of our lack of training and experience. Some friction developed with the British, who doubted our ability to handle intelligence situations and wanted to have all information channelled through them, even in the Western Task Force area where the British had no troops. We were unwilling to give up this control: this was a testing ground for the rest of the war, and we had to learn to deal with the complex situations to be met in a field that was new to us.

Meanwhile, over on the Tunisian front the Intelligence Chief of II Corps in December 1942 reorganized all available CIC agents within his command into a new Detachment which was to move from Algeria eastwards into Tunisia, where Allied forces had been bogged down by the winter rains after racing there almost immediately after the November landings. He placed the new Detachment under the command of a remarkable officer by the name of Horace Miner, whom General Bradley, who was eventually to command II Corps, described as a 'quiet, pipe-smoking Professor of Anthropology from Ann Arbor University, Michigan, who had trekked across the Sahara from a native hut in Timbuktu to get into the war.'

Under Miner's command the CIC in Tunisia metamorphosed into a dazzlingly bold and eccentric organization whose exploits behind Rommel's lines in the desert war owed more to Lawrence of Arabia and the French *méharistes* of the Saharan Camel Corps than the routine plod of more regular military outfits. Three agents were lost at the hands of the Afrika Korps during this campaign, and some activities were deleted from the CIC's future combat role as being too far removed from its basic mission; but these activities nevertheless provided the basis upon which future combat missions were planned. Agents roved the battlefront, sometimes ahead of the forward reconnaissance elements, collecting combat intelligence, penetrating enemy lines to organize Arab nets, arresting enemy agents, directing psychological warfare operations, as well as fulfilling the more routine tasks of CIC security, including supervision of the password system, handling of classified documents, security of Arab civilians, organization of camouflage security and arrangements with the French authorities for the trial and execution of spies. Still regarded with incomprehension and suspicion by the regular military, the CIC lived on its not inconsiderable wits; so as not to be tied down with headquarters duties, agents were detailed to lower echelons in the field, so that Division Detachments became an integral part of all combat units from then on; and to establish their own independence of movement and mobility, they continued to liberate trucks, jeeps and motor-bikes wherever they found them.

The story of II Corps' early setbacks in Tunisia, its ill-fated attempt to push through to Sfax on the Gulf of Gabès, its shattering defeat by Rommel's more experienced forces at Faid and the Kasserine Pass in February 1943, is one of the bleaker episodes in the history of Allied fortunes in the desert war. It was when the German Panzers overran the inexperienced forces of the US 1st Armored Division at the Faid Pass, and raced through the Kasserine Pass and on through the flat bowl that leads towards Tebessa and Thala, that the CIC suffered its first serious casualties in combat. CIC teams were operating with the 1st Armored Division and the attached infantry units which bore the brunt of the slaughter in this sector. Agents Harold Murphy and Rudolph Gollumb were up front with combat command 'A' of the 1st Armored when the German Tiger tanks broke through. On 18 February Murphy was killed and Gollumb taken prisoner.

Undeterred, Agents Horace Miner and Lennie Bessman – a lawyer from Milwaukee and Marine Corps veteran of the 1929 Nicaraguan campaign – joined combat command 'B' of the 1st Armored when it moved secretly to the west of the Kasserine Pass, and took up a position where they could intercept all Arabs who tried to by-pass the army roadblock and hold them in custody until the American counter attack had been launched. The Arabs were a peculiar problem in this particular war. Muddled up in a pitched battle between two foreign armies that had both invaded their homeland without invitation, they could be excused if they cared for neither and took advantage of each as opportunity offered. One Arab arrested by Bessman was found to have stripped and abandoned an RAF officer who had been shot down behind enemy lines. An Arab line-crosser interrogated by Miner was found to be a radio agent trained at a German espionage centre in Tunis, and Miner was able to extract from him the details of his mission, his code and the signal he was to use to indicate if he was operating under American control. During the course of II Corps' attack against the German positions Miner and Bessman took their three-quarter-ton truck up to the forward infantry line, then went forward into no-man's-land on foot, taking prisoners as they went, making unit identifications for Order of Battle intelligence and searching captured positions for documents. It then became almost usual practice for a CIC agent to accompany every divisional reconnaissance platoon, to ensure deeper probing and more accurate and detailed observations than were normally collected by the platoons alone.

Enemy Order of Battle intelligence – enemy command posts, observation posts, communication centres, bivouacs, gun positions, minefields, trenches, fuel and arms dumps, strength, dispositions, intentions, espionage – was life blood to Colonel Dickson, II Corps' Intelligence Chief, especially after General Patton took over command of a rejuvenated II Corps early in March and resumed the American offensive against the Afrika Korps in support of the knock-out blow to be delivered by Montgomery's Eighth Army on the Mareth Line. To get the information he needed, Dickson organized a network of small, self-contained CIC field parties, each composed of two agents carrying their own rations and bedding, who often operated under his own direction and were shifted around the battlefront as required like knights in a chess game. One field party, working closely with a British infantry battalion, the Derbyshire Yeomanry, had the specific task of recruiting Arabs through *caids* and caliphs with known anti-Axis sympathies to assist reconnaissance units and undertake espionage in the German lines. Another field party, consisting of an Arab and CIC agent Lieutenant Crosby Lewis, who used to darken his skin with shoe polish and garb himself in dirty Arab costume, distinguished itself by disappearing for days behind the enemy lines, out amid the barren, rocky mountains and the flies, whence he would send reports like the following: 'To Colonel Dickson from HECTOR. Will confirm tomorrow reliable report enemy holding line J-324853 to J-335867 behind two separate minefields. According to local Arabs no enemy patrols in valley of Oued Sedjenane. Reconnaissance confirms only two possible crossings at Oued Sedjenane east of J-2083 are bridge at J-2383 and stone ford at J-3386, latter impassable 48 hours after heavy rain. Am in liaison with SLIPPERY.'

Once Lewis came back not just with the requisite military reconnaissance report and enemy Order of Battle intelligence but an agreement with the Caid of Sidi Bou Zid guaranteeing the loyalty of the Arabs in the desert in the no-man's-land between the Faid and Kasserine Passes – an exploit for which Crosby Lewis was rewarded by Colonel Dickson with a reprimand for going AWOL and a Silver Star for being brave. Another field party, aided by a soldier from the 1st Armored who could speak Arabic, specialized in plotting the lay-out of enemy minefields using information gleaned from local Arabs.

On missions like these the CIC were living dangerously, none more so than Lieutenant Leonard Bessman. At some point a price would have to be paid for such audacity and on 7 April the inevitable happened. On that day Bessman was ordered forward by his G-2,

Colonel Dickson, to search for documents at Bordj El Hafey, which was scheduled to be taken during the course of II Corps' southern thrust. Bessman set off with his jeep and driver, bouncing over a track which the map indicated as a road, but which bore about as much resemblance to an American highway as a goat does to a mule. His only consolation was that about thirty minutes behind, leading a regimental combat team over the same dusty track, rode the very same G-2. At least, thought Bessman, the old buzzard has to eat my dust.

Thinking along these faintly disaffected lines, Bessman, his jeep and his driver drove up out of a wadi onto a point of high ground on the Gafsa to Gabès road. Whatever his thoughts, they were suddenly erased from his mind by the sudden staccato bursts of two machine-guns – one on his right, the other on his left. Then the jeep was drilled through by an armour-piercing shell. Ordering his driver to take cover, Bessman grabbed his rifle and ducked behind a tree. After exchanging a couple of shots at two hidden machine-gun nests, he stuck his head out around the tree. He could see nothing.

'Come on out, you bastards!' he shouted to his assailants. 'We won't shoot!'

Bessman took it for granted that his ambushers were Italians. In his experience they generally required little encouragement to proffer their surrender.

The sharp crack of a rifle and the whine of a bullet ricocheting off the tree just above his head was the only answer he got.

'Goddamn – these guys aren't Italians!' he yelled at his driver. 'These guys are Krauts! See if you can get out of here and warn the column.'

That was all the word his driver needed. He leaped into his jeep, whirled it around and sped back towards the regiment.

Bessman had ridden straight into an overwhelming German force which, unknown to him, had been by-passed by Patton at the last minute. The Germans occupied a strong natural position which they held with an armoury which included machine-guns, two field guns and a tank. For two and a half hours the defiant CIC officer, alone and lightly armed, lay behind his tree exchanging shots with the Germans. But it was an uneven fire fight and at length the inevitable came. An enemy patrol crawled round him and jumped him from the rear. These facts were verified several days later by two German prisoners who had taken part in the ambush. They had no knowledge, however, of what had happened to Bessman, or whether he had been killed or captured. Some days after the incident, the CIC commanding officer carefully examined the ground where the action occurred but could not find any traces of blood. The whereabouts of Bessman became an unsolved mystery, and he was eventually reported as missing in action.

At least one American found it difficult to believe that this indomitable warrior could be no more. Filing by cable from the war front in Northern Tunisia, star war correspondent Ernie Pyle sent this despatch to the American papers concerning the fate of his CIC friend: 'As is bound to happen in war time, your close friends sometimes disappear. The closest friend I've got so far is Lieutenant Bessman, a lawyer from Milwaukee. His bravery was based upon idealism – the invulnerable kind of bravery – and it was inevitable that sooner or later he would die or fall prisoner.'

The incident remained buried in military files for over a year until in 1944 a man slipped through the German lines in Italy and dramatically re-opened the whole affair. The man was Bessman.

As Pyle had rightly surmised, Bessman had not been killed but taken prisoner. Fortunately he had left his CIC badge and credentials behind at headquarters, so his captors treated him as an ordinary infantry officer, not a spy, and had him flown out to Italy as a prisoner-of-war. In September, nearly five and a half months after his capture, he learned that the Germans were preparing to move him to Germany, so in the company of two other lieutenants he made good his escape from his PW cage, spending the next six months hiding in caves in the hills. Eventually he was passed down an escape line run by the Italian underground movement, reaching the Allied lines in a party that had grown to number twelve British and American soldiers.

Bessman was then sent back to the United States, where the War Department ruled that under no circumstances would he be permitted to return to the European front, where the danger of recapture was considered to be too great a risk. Yet within a few months this indomitable spirit had worked his way back to Europe with the First Army CIC Detachment, where he specialized in testing German escape routes near the front line. For saving an American Regiment from heavy casualties through what was officially described as 'extraordinary heroism against an armed enemy' and 'conduct in accordance with the highest standards of the military service' Bessman was awarded the Distinguished Service Cross.

By the end of the first week in May the Tunisian campaign had reached its final phase, with the American attack developing into the fast-moving, open warfare the desert allowed. For the CIC this was a hectic period, doubly complicated by the political confusion and internecine bitterness verging on civil war among the French civil and military population in the wake of the German collapse. It was still a dangerous and difficult time. On 8 May Agent James Gardner entered Bizerta at the head of the field party sent on ahead of the 9th Infantry Division to check out the town before the arrival of the regular troops. While still under machine-gun and sniper fire, Gardner secured valuable records of pro-Axis organizations, seized all civilian mail and established contact with the French government authorities. This action was considered so valiant and so valuable to the Allied cause that Gardner was awarded the Bronze Star and Purple Heart for his pains.

The next day, 182 days after the Allied landings in North Africa, the Germans surrendered throughout the II Corps sector, followed by all remaining Axis forces in Tunisia on 13 May. On 10 May Lieutenant Horace Miner, like most CIC officers unjustifiably low-ranking in relation to his responsibilities and duties, had found himself in head-on conflict with the French Admiral La Flèche, who had collaborated in the suppression of Free French activity through-out the entire period of the German occupation. Miner had headed a CIC team which had entered the French Naval Post of Ferryville with an armoured reconnaissance unit a few days previously in order to reduce various key targets, including the naval headquarters, the post and telegraph offices, the police headquarters and the prison where Free French activists were being held in custody. When the Admiral returned to the city to take command of the Naval Post the day after the German surrender, his first act was to order the lowering of Free French flags from public buildings, and to threaten the loyal Chief of Police with dimissal. The reappearance of this paragon of Fascist virtues brought the dock workers and civil popu-lace of Ferryville to the verge of revolt, and since the dock workers were responsible for maintaining the Allied supply lines the situation amounted to subversion of the Allied war effort. Horace Miner felt he had no alternative but to place the Admiral under arrest. This he did, avoiding resistance from the Admiral's staff by seizing the Admiral as he left his mistress's apartment in the early hours of the morning. A few hours later Miner was able to persuade the dock workers to return to their crucial task of unloading war supplies. For this decisive and vital action Miner was awarded the Legion of Merit.

The euphoria was soured by an unfortunate incident which occurred after the fighting in Tunisia had ended. Though the case was a brilliantly successful one for the CIC, it proved a bad business for the US Army, for it involved the investigation and exposure of the first traitor to be uncovered in the army's ranks in World War Two. The true name of the soldier concerned was not publicly revealed and reports merely referred to him as Private John Smith, a member of a supply unit which had been engaged in trucking ammunition to the front line during the Tunisian campaign. In fact, we can now reveal for the first time that the real name of the man in question was Private Dale S. Lipps, of Company C, 389th Port Battalion, who was apprehended on 7 April 1944.

According to Schwarzwalder, at the end of the Tunisian campaign Private Lipps contracted a severe bout of influenza, probably as a consequence of all the cold Tunisian winter nights he had had to spend in the scanty shelter of his cab. He was sent to a military hospital near Tunis to recover, and afterwards put in a convalescent ward which happened to be adjacent to a ward where sick German prisoners-of-war were also convalescing. During a routine check of the German ward during the prisoners' absence a CIC Special Agent was surprised to discover a hidden German Army bayonet, along with knives, ropes, metal files, charts showing the American guard posts, and other useful items. The signs were that the prisoners were planning an armed break-out and that they were receiving help from outside – almost certainly from an American. An exhaustive investigation narrowed the list of suspects down to one – Dale Lipps.

Posing as a hospital orderly, the CIC Special Agent ingratiated himself with Lipps and found that almost the only subject he talked about with any particular enthusiasm was that of German Army souvenirs. The Special Agent now set a trap for him. He told Lipps that the one thing in life he wanted above all was a German officer's Luger or P-38 pistol. Lipps fell for the bait. He told the CIC investigator exactly where and how such a weapon could be obtained. He gave the address of an Arab store in a nearby town and handed over a piece of paper with three strange-looking triangles drawn on it – the guarantee of his personal authority. The Arab would hand over a parcel, Lipps said, and if this was delivered to him in the hospital compound before midnight – which was apparently the start-time planned for the prisoners' break-out – he would be able to hand the Luger over.

The Special Agent picked up three more CIC agents and drove out to the Arab store. He handed over the piece of paper with the triangles on it and in return received a large box which was found to contain four pistols (including one Luger), all fully loaded, a quantity of extra ammunition, a 50-foot length of rope, two wire cutters, and two German compasses. Possession of such equipment was against military law and the penalty was death. In an attempt to save his skin the Arab implicated others in a ring of illicit blackmarket dealers trading in German Army war loot, including three other Arabs and two Italians. At eight that evening the Special Agent handed the box over to Lipps in the unlit exercise compound at the hospital, then went back inside the hospital building. In fact, Lipps remained under covert CIC observation, and a short while later was seen to be passing the dismantled weapons to two German prisoners through the barbed wire fence which separated the American exercise compound from their own. At this point a searchlight was suddenly switched on and the men were arrested at gunpoint by CIC agents and Military Police with Tommy-guns.

After arrest Private Lipps was found to be armed with a .45 pistol and in possession of a large quantity of occupation currency. The Germans, who were entitled to try and escape, were given exemplary light sentences. The Arab storekeeper and his confederates were tried by a French court and shot. On 19 April 1944 Private Lipps was tried by American court martial and sentenced to dishonourable discharge from the Army, to various forfeitures of pay and allowances, and to death by hanging. He thus became the first and only US serviceman to be sentenced to death for treasonable offences, namely Article of War 81 (aiding the enemy) and Article of War 96 (fraternizing with enemy prisoners). According to John Schwarzwalder, the sentence was reviewed by the Commander-in-Chief and confirmed, and the Special Agent was present to witness the hanging, which duly took place, Schwarzwalder wrote shortly after the war, one grey morning a few weeks later. In fact, US records shown to us reveal that there was no hanging and that Lipps' sentence was commuted to 10 years' imprisonment. It would also appear that Schwarzwalder was either badly misinformed about the case or privy to information not disclosed at Lipps' court martial, for the court records show that Lipps was in fact tried and sentenced to death for providing supplies (to wit, one compass worth one dollar) to help enemy prisoners escape, and fraternizing with enemy prisoners by furnishing them with food, money and medicines.

With the cessation of hostilities in North Africa, the CIC had completed its first trial in a long and increasingly responsible combat role. Official reports agree that these first agents were inadequately trained for military combat action, their missions ill-defined, their role a subject of misunderstanding and confusion between the War Department and Theatre HQ. But thrown into their task in the last moments of invasion planning, they had substituted courage and audacity for the combat training they had not received, intuition and initiative for missions no one had anticipated, and resourcefulness for a Table of Basic Allowances. And in spite of all its organizational difficulties and frustrations, the Counter Intelligence Corps in

North Africa had won numerous decorations and warm commendations from most of the combat commanders and intelligence chiefs under whom they had served.

But in the summer of 1943 there was little time to think of honours, for ahead lay Sicily and Italy, new landings, new campaigns, new worlds to conquer.

5

THE INVASIONS OF EUROPE

For many of the Americans who had crossed the Atlantic to fight the Axis Powers in Africa and Europe, the Old World seemed a sometimes incomprehensible and quite often reprehensible kind of place: exotic in an antique and charmingly faded sort of way, but also wickedly devious, a vipers' nest of whispering factions, plots and counter-plots, alliances of convenience and stabs in the back – everything, in fact, that the boys from home liked to think they had expunged from their own country long ago. Colonial politics, schisms of race, colour and creed, class war, regional conflicts, historic hatreds, ideological polarities, revolutions and *coups d'état* – the Old World was a can of worms where a decent Joe never knew what was what or who was who.

Such problems did not affect the main body of the military, who carried out their orders within a tactical framework which limited their role to letting off various kinds of explosive devices and, on rare occasions, wielding various kinds of sharpened implements. The people who *were* affected by the crazy-paving politics of the Europeans were those who functioned at opposite ends of the fighting forces – at one end the political leaders of the Grand Alliance who decided the strategy by which the war was conducted; and at the other end the various small groups of clever and dedicated men (and women) in the field who burrowed and bored and ferreted for the intelligence data on which the military and political leaders in part based their command decisions. Among the latter could be counted the CIC, a Cinderella organization which, having successfully survived its baptism of fire in the invasion of Africa, was now required to wade ashore on a whole string of picturesque but deadly invasion beaches in Europe, reaching all the way from Sicily to Salerno and Anzio in Italy and on to the D-Day beaches of Normandy and the Côte d'Azur in France.

Not all these invasion campaigns were of equal danger and difficulty and some departed more dramatically from routine than others. The invasion of Sicily which began on 9 July 1943 – an even bigger amphibious landing than the North African one – was over in a few weeks, with advance patrols of Montgomery's Eighth Army, advancing from the east, entering Messina on 17 August almost simultaneously with advance patrols of Patton's Seventh Army, advancing from the west. During those few weeks the Germans and their aeroplanes were driven off the island, the Mafia was reinstated by the Americans as a viable anti-Fascist organization after its ruthless suppression by Mussolini, and the CIC, by applying the lessons it had learnt in North Africa, had an invaluable workout – they caught nearly 100 enemy spies, all of them Sicilians recruited by the Abwehr – for the infinitely greater task of counter intelligence operations that lay ahead.

During the Sicilian campaign a war photographer for *Look* magazine, Robert Holm Hansen, was attached for a while to the 45th Division CIC Detachment of the Seventh Army. The CIC team made a considerable impact on him. He reported later that he had been deeply impressed by the calibre of the men in the Detachment. It was the only military organization he had ever been in in which college graduates of unusual background were serving as privates, corporals and sergeants. For example, Staff Sergeant Lansing Robinson and Sergeant George Moseley were graduates of Harvard University, the former having an MA and a Ph.D, while Lieutenant Rupert Gunther, the Detachment Commander, was a college and law school graduate who had previous investigative experience with the Civil Service Commission in Washington. Although the agents were poor field soldiers in Hansen's view, they did a terrific job getting their intelligence information, and the Division G-2 was highly enthusiastic about the work the Detachment was doing. The men were viewed with suspicion by other officers in the Division, however, principally because they did not understand what it was the Detachment was actually supposed to be doing – an incomprehension exacerbated by the fact that the Detachment operated as lone rangers, living and working on their own, remote from the rest of the Division.

Wherever they went the presence of CIC agents in American uniforms drew large crowds who posed the agents problems of every conceivable description. On one occasion Corporal Frank Messina and another agent entered a town at the moment when a mob of Sicilians were about to hang the former Mayor because of his Fascist sympathies. Agent Messina advised the crowd in Italian that he was acting for the United States Government and restored order until such time as the Military Police arrived in the area. On another occasion the Detachment inadvertently made its way ahead of the Division Infantry into a town which had but recently been vacated by the enemy and was welcomed by the Mayor as the advance guard of the liberating army. In this campaign, Hansen reported, the CIC agents were frequently the recipients of large quantities of excellent vintage wine and other tangible expressions of civilian generosity and appreciation. They therefore not only worked hard, but lived well.

For the Italians, even more than for the Germans, the shock of the invasion, the trauma of defeat and the loss of an entire province of the Italian nation had been devastating. The Axis armies had suffered 165,000 casualties. The civil populace had welcomed the Allies as liberators. The political repercussions were immense. Mussolini, the Fascist dictator of Italy, had been forced to resign and was succeeded by Marshal Badoglio. On 19 August two days after the conquest of Sicily, Badoglio contacted Eisenhower to negotiate the surrender of the rest of Italy without the knowledge of the Germans, and on 3 September he signed the Italian unconditional surrender. The Italian fleet surrendered to the Allies, but the Germans disarmed the Italian Army and occupied Rome. The Allies, poised to launch an invasion of southern Italy from the stepping stone of Sicily, were now confronted by the German Army alone. In Italy, with its great cities, its rugged terrain, its divided loyalties and extremist politics, above all its Germans, arrayed in strength with their backs to the Alps and their Fatherland, the CIC were to endure a dour campaign up the long, narrow, mountainous and easily defended peninsula that was to last the rest of the war.

On the morning of 9 September 1943, a year and a day after the North African landings, Counter Intelligence Corps agents disembarked with combat troops of the US Fifth Army onto the beaches along the Gulf of Salerno, south of Naples, in an operation code-named Avalanche. Though doubts had consistently been raised about the usefulness of landing CIC personnel at the sharp end of such operations, Avalanche was the third time that the CIC had been involved in such combat experience, but this was an experience like none other. The evening before, Marshal Badoglio had publicly announced over the radio the news of the armistice that Eisenhower had agreed to a week previously. This meant that the beaches on which the Allies now landed were officially classified as co-belligerent and not enemy territory. But any hope that the Marshal's announcement would abate the fury of the defenders' guns was soon dashed. From the shore a German voice could be heard shouting in English through a loud-hailer: 'Come on in and give up! You're covered!' Most of the CIC agents had to wade ashore from the landing craft through a sea littered with torn and floating bodies and wrecked and disabled vehicles. In the din of battle they gave little thought to the business of catching spies; their one thought was to save their skins. This time they had had some training in amphibious assault and knew the best course to take under fire. The first CIC agents to hug the soil of Italy – John Hammond and his four men in the 36th CIC, and Kenneth Crowell and the members of the 206th CIC (VI Corps) – rushed for the scanty cover bordering the head of the beach, nestling inside the protective sanctuary of their helmets while the lead and shrapnel flew all around them. By the evening of D-Day these two Detachments had managed to filter inland a little and link up and establish a joint command post at a farmhouse near Paestum.

In the next few days other CIC Detachments, including the Fifth Army Detachment under Major Stephen Spingarn, began pouring into the beachhead and going immediately into action. As the demand for combat intelligence often outstripped counter intelligence requirements during these first weeks, CIC agents liberated towns with the first infantry troops and sometimes found themselves ahead of the combat units or even behind enemy lines. On one occasion Major Spingarn and two agents drove their jeep ahead of the combat troops to the outskirts of the town of Battipaglia, where they found themselves cut off by superior German forces. Spingarn's terse report reveals how near they came to catastrophe: 'The Infantry had not yet come up. German tanks were discernible just ahead. At this point two German tanks came forward, reaching a point about 400 yards from us, one on the road, the other on the left. They had spotted us and opened fire on us with machine-guns and 88 mm cannon. A slight hummock, perhaps a foot high, saved us from the machine-gunning, but the bullets were only eight or ten inches above us as we flattened out, and we did our best to bite our way into the ground.'

It was only with considerable difficulty that Spingarn and his comrades wriggled – literally – out of this unpleasant predicament and made their way into the town, which they found totally destroyed and evacuated.

Spingarn survived to enjoy a jollier assignment on the incomparable islands of Capri, Ischia and Procida in the Bay of Naples. It was on Capri that he was able to make contact with the leading spirit of the anti-Fascist movement in Italy, Senator Benedetto Croce, the country's greatest living writer and philosopher, and now a minister in the new Badoglio government. Spingarn spent a night as a guest at

Croce's villa on the island, discussing the Italian political situation and the anti-Fascist groups in Italy. It was a constructive connection. So too was the CIC's liaison with the leader of the anti-Fascist movement in Southern Italy, General Giuseppe Pavone, who worked as closely with the CIC as if he had been a member. With his help the CIC were able to install successful counter intelligence measures in more than 50 towns and cities along the beachhead within the first two weeks. So the long, agonizing, controversial but utterly memorable campaign began.

It was a campaign that for the CIC was to culminate, eventually, in a counter espionage campaign without parallel in history – an exploit that merits a later chapter of its own. But for their first months in Italy – first year even – the CIC were to share the experience common to all the Allied troops inching their way up the rugged, resistant spine of Italy: frustration and slog in a protracted war of attrition, dismay at a climate which belied its reputation and turned to rain, cold and snow at the first touch of autumn, affection for its badly used and hard-pressed people, admiration for its women.

In that first year, before the German intelligence services launched their sabotage and espionage blitz against the Allied lines, the CIC rôle entailed the exercise of a set of routine but necessary tasks which not only established the military security of the area into which they moved but laid the groundwork of military government for the Civil Affairs teams that would follow up from the rear: collecting arms; the burial or burning of the dead; closing down communications; impounding official provincial and municipal records; imposing curfews; the prohibition of meetings; establishing informant nets; searching German military installations and Italian Fascist head-quarters; the interrogation and internment of known Fascists; investigating local officials' reliability, especially the mayor and chief of police, so that local government could be re-established and public order restored; the proclamation of orders and penalties for sab-otage, espionage, looting and aiding enemy soldiers, often using the services of the village priests and town criers. As one CIC Detach-ment commander put it when he addressed the local officials of a recently occupied town: 'We have come here as friends of the Italian people. We do not intend to interfere with your lives or affairs in any manner except in the suppression of Fascism and the protection of our troops from enemy activity. But the placing of any obstacle in the way of Allied military operations will be severely dealt with.'

In some of the towns the CIC found they had to deal with people who were distasteful to them – Fascist local officials who often had to be left in place because there was no one else available who knew how to run the administration. CIC units were continually bedevilled by a shortage of interpreters for this sort of work. At one point Major Spingarn was forced to complain: 'I continue to press my urgent request to you for that Italian speaking group *with* jeeps. I honestly believe that if we can get them we can really put the CIC on the map over here. OSS [the Office of Strategic Services] is bringing in Italian agents by the droves and, frankly, the competition is pretty tough. I *NEED* THOSE ITALIAN AGENTS.' Later Spingarn reported: 'I am frankly at my wit's end. I have absolutely no use for men who don't speak Italian.' Offers from friendly Italians did not altogether solve the problem. One of them wrote: 'I, Alfred de Gennaro, son of American citizen, born in 1924, expose you as follows: From four years ago I fight against Germany and Fascismo. From four years ago I have organised any men, I have throwed messages to Italian people, I have pushed the Naples people against the Germany and Fascismo. Now, as I already have given to you some information of value, I ask you of lend my work in the Allied Services. Moreover, I inform you what a my brother, american citizen, is officer of American Army.'

During this period of assiduous attention to detail, three events stood emblazoned in the memory of every CIC agent involved: the fall of Naples, the landing at Anzio, and the entry into the Italian capital, the Eternal City of Rome.

Naples, a city of a million people ranged round a bay beneath the soaring volcano of Mount Vesuvius, was the first important prize of the Allied landings at Salerno. After the link-up of General Mark Clark's US Fifth Army and General Montgomery's Eighth Army on 18 September, the two armies began to advance up the Italian peninsula abreast, with Rome as their great objective and Naples as the most important city on the way. On 1 October the British and Americans entered Naples, 16 agents of Stephen Spingarn's 305th CIC arriving with advance elements of the 82nd Airborne Division in a convoy of jeeps, trucks and motor-bikes. 'The reception by the residents of the city was tumultuous,' Spingarn recalled. 'At every stop the group was virtually mobbed by people with fruit, flowers, cheers and kisses.' But after the destruction wrought by Allied planes and German troops the city lay in ruins. Everywhere was débris and wreckage, burnt-out houses and sunken ships, the stench of the dead and dying. For three weeks Spingarn and his men were in charge of counter intelligence operations in Naples – up to that time the largest city ever handled by a CIC Detachment.

On 24 October the Fifth Army CIC was once again on the move – this time with the combat forces advancing towards Rome. But as the Fifth Army pushed forward in pursuit, resistance by the retreating

Germans stiffened and Allied progress became painful and slow. As winter approached the Germans withdrew to their winter line, known as the Gustav Line, which guarded the Liri and Rapido valleys from the south. By mid-November rain, sleet and snow transformed this line into a formidable defensive position, or so it seemed to the tired, muddy, frozen men of the Fifth Army as they hauled themselves over the rugged terrain. By mid-January, fighting step by step, the Allied armies had reached the edge of the Liri valley, the main corridor for the advance to Rome. But there seemed no way of passing the town of Cassino and the mountains surrounding it, where strong German defences, which included crack units like the 1st Parachute Division – 'the best German division on any front' according to General Alexander – blocked the main route north through the mountains. The Allied advance petrified into stalemate, with the bitterest fighting of the whole campaign raging without avail around the besieged monastery that topped Monte Cassino. On Christmas Day 1943, therefore, the Allies decided to launch an amphibious landing to the rear of the German forces at Anzio with the purpose of disrupting German communications in the area of the nodal battle around Cassino.

Once again the CIC were required to land with the combat troops in a new amphibious assault. On 21 January 1944 the CIC Detachments of the VI Corps and 1st Armored Division boarded the landing craft with the fighting troops and headed out of Naples harbour for the Anzio beaches. The landing was a complete surprise and troops came ashore unopposed, but instead of making a drive to seize the Alban Hills, which dominated the German line of communications, the invasion force concentrated on consolidating its bridgehead, allowing the German commander time to counterattack with reinforcements and seal the bridgehead off. For four months 50,000 American troops were pinned down at Anzio under extreme combat conditions. The Allied campaign was now at a standstill. In March attempts to capture Cassino were given up and the Allies settled down to await the spring and the start of a new offensive against the impregnable Gustav Line.

CIC agents who were hemmed in at Anzio are in universal accord that life on the edge of the picturesque Tyrrhenian Sea was vile. German counter-attacks were frequent and severely testing and at one point threatened to split the invasion force in two. Life, the agents reported, was one long explosion. This was especially true after the Germans introduced an outsize gun called the 'Anzio Express', a mobile cannon of enormous calibre which was mounted on a railroad car and could be moved about with impunity from one location to another. With each colossal round it fired this monstrous device wrought devastating destruction. The situation was not without occasional light relief, however. When messages relayed back to the commander of the Fifth Army CIC spoke of the 'living hell' on the beaches, Major Stephen Spingarn decided that duty demanded he visit the battle area to see for himself the conditions to which his luckless men had been consigned.

The day Spingarn was due to arrive the Tyrrhenian Sea glittered in the bright, warm sunshine of early spring, and over the land all around a profound silence reigned, unbroken by the sound of a single enemy plane, rattle of gunfire or shellburst from the dreadful 'Anzio Express'. The men decided to take advantage of this paradisaical lull in the fighting as best they could, so that when Spingarn at last arrived, his helmet tightly strapped, he found his hard-pressed agents had emerged from their foxholes and were happily at play on the sands, sun-bathing and paddling and pitching horseshoes, for all the world as if they were on Malibu Beach, or Hampton Beach, New Hampshire, in the laughing days of peace. 'So this is the living hell you're all talking about!' Spingarn snorted as he strode about the fun-loving CIC combat zone. For a while it seemed credibility was severely strained; but when the time came for Major Spingarn to leave, the Germans resumed their deadly unpleasantness, plastering the bridgehead with projectiles from the 'Anzio Express' and dive-bombing the beach in their time-hallowed way. Spingarn was impressed. When he got back to CIC headquarters he reported: 'It's a living hell for our boys out there.'

The siege at Anzio was complicated by the refugee problem in the area. The Germans had moved the 12,000 civilian inhabitants of the neighbouring towns of Anzio and Nettuno out into the surrounding countryside, where the population pressure that their presence produced in the militarized zone almost threatened to push the Allied forces into the sea. In other sectors of the front refugees could cause a significant counter-espionage crisis for the CIC. In early March, for example, large numbers of refugees began arriving by rowing-boat along the Allied-held coast from the town of Gaeta, then in enemy hands. Among them were the first German espionage agents encountered by the CIC in Italy. Seven enemy agents carrying three radio transmitters landed on a stretch of the coast near Mondragone, north of Naples, not covered by the CIC observation post network or foot patrols. One of the agents was apprehended by an Italian guard who turned him over to the 88th CIC Detachment which was responsible for 15 miles of coast in this sector under the command of agent Harry Riback. The captured agent soon broke

Above: Camp Ritchie, the Military Intelligence Training Center in the Blue Ridge Mountains of Maryland – 'a finishing school for outdoor, rough and tumble, last minute cramming before going overseas'. This is the old headquarters building, built in a style known as National Guard Gothic. *(National Archives)*

Below: Following Pearl Harbor, CIC students learn to recognize enemy Japanese insignia of rank during combat intelligence training at Fort Sheridan, Illinois, in 1942. *(Defense Audiovisual Agency)*

Closing in on the spoor of the Führer:

Above: Special Agent Victor de Guinzbourg takes a triumphal ride in the back of Hitler's limousine after its liberation by the US Army. *(Robert R. Richards)*

Below: Inside Hitler's favourite Alpine haunt, Victor de Guinzbourg and Robert R. Richards at the Eagle's Nest, Obersalzberg, 1945. *(Robert R. Richards)*

Right: Oxford historian and British agent, Hugh Trevor-Roper (right), looking for clues to Hitler's fate with CIC Special Agent Arnold Weiss in Seefeld, Austria, Christmas Eve, 1945. Two days later they discovered Hitler's last will and testament. *(Arnold Weiss)*

In the field in the Japanese war:

Above: CIC agent Leroy T. Newland Jr in Burma
interviews a village headman and his assistant through an
interpreter. 'We had to go sit in the grass because there
were too many listening in.' *(Leroy T. Newland Jr)*

Below: Leroy T. Newland Jr in Assam with his jeep. To meet all
contingencies the name 'CIC' is inscribed in English, Chinese and
Burmese. *(Leroy T. Newland Jr)*

Left: Special Agent Arthur S. Hurlburt at the CIC's palm thatch office at Finschaffen, New Guinea, April 1944. *(Arthur Hurlburt)*

Below: Night in the jungle at Buna, New Guinea. Japanese-speaking interpreters from the ATIS interrogate a Japanese prisoner captured in the fighting. Few Japanese surrendered; most who did talked. *(Defense Audiovisual Agency)*

Opposite above: Okinawa, 1945. CIC agents screen native Ryukyuans with the help of locally recruited CIC assistants. *(US Army Intelligence and Security Command)*

CIC in the Japanese home islands: *Opposite below:* Filipino collaborators captured in Japan are escorted back to the Philippines by CIC agents to stand trial. *(Defense Audiovisual Agency)*

CIC Headquarters in Bad Nauheim, American Zone of Germany, at the height of the Cold War. *(Colonel Ted Girouard)*

Right: The 'Butcher of Lyons', Klaus Barbie, photographed at Gestapo Headquarters in Lyons during the war. *(Topham Picture Library)*

Below: A CIC column takes to the German backwoods during operations at the height of the intelligence Cold War against Soviet espionage agents. The 43rd CIC Detachment in Staging Area Y-79. *(Colonel Ted Girouard)*

Above: 'In any confrontation between Victor de Guinzbourg and Otto Skorzeny, Germany's super-spy, I would have put my money on Victor.' (Agent Nelson Dungan). Interrogation of Skorzeny by CIC agents de Guinzbourg and George Perper, 1945. *(Robert R. Richards)*

Left: Wartime head of Hitler's special operations commandos, Obersturmbannführer Otto Skorzeny. *(Robert R. Richards)*

office, and impound all mail for censorship. By the end of the first day the two CIC teams had made the town militarily secure and established a temporary local government composed of officials to whom they had granted provisional approval.

The following morning the teams began the investigation and interrogation of political prisoners brought in by the Partisans. Among them were Republican Fascists, collaborators, German soldiers, and Polish and Russian soldiers suspected of fighting on the German side. Finally, after completing their preliminary investigations, the four Divisional agents handed over responsibility for the town to back-up agents from Corps and moved on to other towns that lay in the path of the northward advance.

So fast was the pursuit that by mid-June Leghorn had fallen and Allied soldiers stood at the River Arno, threatening Florence and Rimini. Hopes were high that the war would soon be over. 'The Fifth Army had become a tremendous fighting machine,' recalled its commander, General Mark Clark, 'and its horizons were unlimited.' But by then the success of the British and American armies in Italy had been eclipsed by an event of even greater magnitude and importance for the course of the war in Europe. For a few days previously, on 6 June 1944, Allied forces had begun landing in strength on the Normandy beaches of France in the greatest D-Day of them all.

The long-awaited Second Front, the invasion of France – code-named OVERLORD in its planning stage and NEPTUNE in its assault stage – was conceived as a frontal attack upon the Third Reich by Allied ground forces launched from England by the shortest and most direct feasible route. In this it was expected to succeed where the Italian campaign – an oblique attack at what Churchill called 'the soft under-belly of the enemy' – had clearly failed. The directive issued to General Dwight D. Eisenhower, the Supreme Commander of the Allied Expeditionary Force, made this plain: 'Enter the Continent of Europe, and, in conjunction with other United Nations, undertake operations aimed at the heart of Germany, and the destruction of her armed forces.' Intensive planning and a massive build-up of troops and matériel were necessary before the invasion could be in a position to win a beachhead in Normandy by D-Day in June 1944, or secure a lodgment against a powerful German field force of 60 Divisions under the redoubtable Field Marshal von Rundstedt and army commanders like Rommel. It was during the planning for this historic operation that the CIC finally came into its own.

Nobody in the CIC this time could claim that their special interests were neglected. Gone was all the confusion and uncertainty about the Corps' role that had preceded the invasions of North Africa, Sicily and Italy. Through the trial and error of these campaigns CIC agents in the field had demonstrated their courage, initiative and special abilities to Intelligence chiefs who were now key men in the planning of Overlord – men like Lieutenant Colonel Gordon Sheen, who was now Chief of the Counter Intelligence Branch at the Supreme Headquarters of the Allied Expeditionary Force (SHAEF); Colonel Oscar Koch, now G-2 of General Patton's Third Army, who had known the CIC in Tunisia and Italy; Colonel Benjamin Dickson, G-2 of First Army, who had directed the CIC in the invasion of North Africa and the fighting in Tunisia, and who now chose as his CIC Chief the Michigan professor, Horace Miner, who had guided II Corps CIC through the Tunisian and Sicilian operations. With such men as these in charge of counter intelligence in the American invasion army, planning for the CIC in combat was for the first time done from the top down rather than from the bottom up. The CIC's assigned part in the liberation of Europe was clearly and exhaustively spelled out in SHAEF Directive No. 7, which left no army commander in any doubt as to what the CIC was about, and marked a milestone in CIC history.

Directive No. 7 reaffirmed that the CIC's mission was 'to provide effective counter-espionage, counter-sabotage, counter-subversive and other necessary forms of security for all military and civilian organizations within the jurisdiction of the Commanding General, European Theater of Operations' and that their efforts were to be 'directed against the enemy's efforts to gain information about, or do damage to, the Allied forces, their installations, personnel and equipment.' Prior to the invasion the CIC was to devote itself to the total security of all units involved in the operation. After the invasion was launched the CIC would have three main targets in the assault phase: known and suspect enemy agents; other persons whose presence menaced the security of the Allied forces; buildings and installations known or suspected to contain documents of counter intelligence value.

CIC agents were given great leeway in using their own judgement to make decisions that were normally considered the sole prerogative of combat command, and they were empowered to call upon other troops for assistance in executing their counter intelligence duties, including the seizure of target installations. Tactical commanders were left in no doubt that they hindered CIC personnel at their peril. 'CIC personnel attached to Corps or Divisions,' ordered the SHAEF

Directive, 'will not be diverted to duties which may retard or interfere with their proper employment.' For the first time in its history the CIC was allocated a proper establishment of men, vehicles and equipment, and a normal provision for the promotion or commissioning of qualified agents. For the first time the CIC was recognized as an integral component of the American military machine and an essential part of the grand design to liberate the continent of Europe from Nazi domination.

The SHAEF directive also recognized that the CIC was not the only intelligence organization embarking for France and that some clarification would be necessary if they were not all to get their lines tangled:

> Information relating to enemy secret intelligence services in enemy, enemy-occupied and neutral territory is available in London, mainly in Section V of MI6, X2 Branch of OSS, but also in other departments such as MI5 and MI14(d), War Office, but owing to the special nature of this information and the great discretion required in its use, it is not suitable for passing to the CI Staffs through normal Intelligence channels. Special CI Units will therefore be supplied by Section V of MI6 for attachment to British Army Group and Army Headquarters and by X2 Branch of OSS for attachment to US Army Group and Army Headquarters. These units will act as a channel for passing information to CI Staffs about enemy secret intelligence services and will advise them as to its use.

The chances of CIC becoming ensnarled with MI6 operatives in the field were relatively slight, since MI6 tended to operate through the British lines. But it was almost inevitable that they would run foul of the American OSS, since in some respects their missions were almost identical. The Office of Strategic Services had moved into London during the planning stage of the invasion with a large staff of officers, unlimited funds, and a directive outlining the function of their Special Counter Intelligence (SCI) unit, which threatened to nullify that of the CIC. Since the CIC and OSS had at that time a low and terrier-like regard for each other, the omens for harmonious relations under the stress of operations at the front seemed poor. Fortunately, Directive No. 7 was able to redefine the missions of the two counter intelligence organizations. The detection and apprehension of enemy agents crossing into Allied lines was to be the prime responsibility of the CIC, and the OSS was directed to pass on to the CIC any information they obtained of a counter intelligence nature. In return, the CIC was directed to give similar assistance to the OSS in its primary mission of gathering positive intelligence behind enemy lines.

During the months of preparations for the invasion, the CIC continued to fulfil a dual assignment: firstly, getting ready for their combat mission in France, and secondly, coping with their awesome responsibility for the security of the invasion forces in England – perhaps the greatest security assignment of all time. As far back as a year before D-Day the CIC had launched their first co-ordinated security campaign, checking out some 450 service clubs, bars and restaurants in 150 towns throughout the British Isles during the last two weeks of May 1943 to ascertain the extent of loose talk and gain knowledge to be used in formulating final security plans. In the tense atmosphere of the months preceding the invasion, it was considered impossible to hide from the Germans the knowledge that an attack was coming – all the Allies could hope to do was to confuse the waiting enemy as to the place and time. Since these pertinent facts were inevitably known to an increasing number of personnel, the CIC's task in preventing leaks was endless. As General Omar Bradley, commanding Twelfth US Army Group, recalled: 'Although our commands were carefully seeded with CIC agents who rifled the desks nightly and rattled safes in search of security violations, only one serious breach was uncovered during the life of the big secret.' Bradley was referring to an incident at a cocktail party in April 1944 when an American Major General talked too explicitly about the invasion date. He was reduced to the rank of Colonel and banished from the Theatre within 24 hours. 'All those who had heard his indiscreet remarks were visited by CIC agents and cautioned to forget the conversation. The prompting was probably unnecessary; by that time all of them had been too badly frightened.'

As the hundreds of thousands of combat troops began to move to the campsites (or 'sausages') in southern England from which they would make the final journey to the waiting invasion ships, the CIC agents were faced with the complex task of segregating the American troops from the English populace which lived and worked in the surrounding area, and keeping briefed troops apart from unbriefed ones. Sentries were posted and barbed wire strung up to hem the troops in, but even so security was breached. On one occasion the CIC had to arrest a number of amorous Devon lassies who managed to break into the 'sausages' where briefed men were bivouacked. Later they were forced to apprehend a group of British 'Wrens' who had attended a cocktail party in the Chart Room of the lead American ship where the walls were hung with the invasion maps of OMAHA and UTAH beaches. It was a time of extreme anxiety, as one CIC agent recalled:

Few know how unusual was the briefing, the need for security. For the first time perhaps in military history, ordinary private soldiers knew in advance exactly where they were going, a secret the whole world speculated upon. These tiny 'sausage' camps, sprawled systematically along every little road in southern England, saw the 'bigoting' of every GI and Tommy with his secret town targets. After the 'bigoting' the coming invaders could not even talk to the mess men who served them, or stray from the steel airfield mats leading from tent to tent, for fear enemy aerial surveillance would pick up paths in the earth. The security was so intense that walking along the roads of our own 'sausages' in Cornwall in broad daylight we would sometimes be picked up by sentries who shoved real rounds into the chambers of their rifles and grimly took us to their leaders. Then even the Company CO in his tent would have to shout to get the sentry to take his finger off the trigger and explain that we were the guys in charge of the security that they were certainly enforcing.

Then came the convoys of infantry down to the ships. We did escort duty to prevent any conversation between troops and civilians. We went straight through towns, escorting the invasion troops for miles to the 'hards', the concrete loading docks for the landing craft, then raced back to pick up more. Finally we were escorting them down to the ships for up to 27 consecutive hours. We had been given brand new motor cycles for escort duty and I didn't leave the saddle for the whole of that time. Then we went down to check the ships, still there from first loading Thursday night until Tuesday, June 6. Loading went on night and day, and coming back on those narrow roads we had to throw the cycle up on side banks to avoid big engineering trucks with only blackout slits. The tight security would have to go on after D-Day because the wounded would be coming back from Normandy – and they'd know too much.

6

GUARDIANS OF
THE LIBERATION

First came the airborne landings. At about 0130 on 6 June the US
101st Airborne Division began dropping south-east of the town of
Ste Mère-Église, behind Utah beach, followed by the British 6th
Airborne Division at 0200 on the eastern flank of the invasion area
and the US 82nd Airborne Division in an area north-west of the
101st at 0230. CIC agents jumped with the first wave of paratroopers
from both US divisions and paid the price for doing so. The 101st
CIC Detachment was the first to be thrown into the battle for the
liberation of Europe, and suffered heavier casualties than any detachment in the entire European Theatre. Of the 25 men in the detachment, 17 were to arrive by landing craft later on D-Day, and eight
were to land by parachute under the command of Captain Martin
McGuire, who had only joined the team three days previously and
had had no time to make even a practice jump – the jump on D-Day
was to be his first.

As the summer dusk slowly darkened over the airfields of southern
England on the evening of 5 June 1944, the eight agents joined up
with small groups of combat troops of the 101st Airborne to make
final checks on their weapons and other last-minute preparations. In
the hope of keeping casualties to a minimum, each agent had been
assigned to a different plane, for it would be difficult to replace men
with such specialized training. At last, after what seemed an eternity
of waiting, the men boarded the DC-6s, their faces blackened and
their bodies burdened under eighty pounds of equipment. Accompanied by a heavy fighter escort the air armada headed out across the
Channel in the direction of Normandy, the occasional breaks in the
dense cloud cover sometimes allowing them a brief glimpse of the
huge seaborne armada heading in the same direction below them. As
the planes neared the enemy coast, German flak forced them to
scatter, and in the heavy cloud banks many of them were soon
disorientated and unable to find the drop zones, so that the 101st
tumbled out in confusion over a huge area measuring some 25 miles

by 15, and lost all coherence as a fighting force. In this nightmare chaos, the eight-man CIC team was reduced to three on landing. Three agents were killed, one was seriously wounded, and another – Second Lieutenant Bradley McKennon – was wounded and taken prisoner when he landed directly on top of a German command post. In those first desperate hours there was little time for counter intelligence work, only the struggle to stay alive as the men of the 101st fought to link up with the forces landing on the beaches at dawn.

CIC agents who dropped with the 82nd Airborne fared less grievously, suffering only one wounded, and managing to re-group after landing and carry out some of the D-Day counter intelligence tasks to which they were assigned. Under the command of Lieutenant Jacobi they entered the enemy-held town of Ste Mère-Église, where they established contact with the Mayor and members of the Resistance and seized classified documents in the former German headquarters. Three members of the 82nd Detachment were mentioned in dispatches as performing outstandings services on D-Day. Lieutenant Salstrom and Agent Whalen 'seized the post office, cut communications and impounded all mail while under extremely heavy enemy shell fire,' while Agent Graves Gladney was sent on 'numerous hazardous missions outside his regular duties, such as manning observation posts under heavy shell fire' and had shown 'an untiring devotion to duty'.

Meanwhile other CIC detachments were landing with the combat divisions in the amphibious assaults on the invasion beaches. The 4th CIC went in with the 4th Infantry Division when it stormed Utah beach at 0645 against relatively light opposition. CIC detachments with the 1st and 29th Divisions landing at Omaha had a more difficult time. Underwater obstacles, heavily mined beaches and intense and deadly fire from well-defended German positions on the high ground backing the beach wrought a terrible slaughter among the first waves of American assault troops, but CIC agents were hard on their heels as they fought their way ashore, and more agents from V Corps landed later in the day and set up their HQ on the bluffs seized by the infantry as they battled inland. In the chaos and carnage of that terrible place CIC activities were fragmentary and unco-ordinated, and reports from the field are few. But in the subsequent days, as Allied forces continued to pour men and supplies into the beachhead in an unending stream, CIC detachments attached to divisions, corps and First Army – the latter detachment under the command of Tunisian veteran Horace Miner – continued to land in this expanding pocket of liberated Europe and fanned out into the Normandy countryside in the wake of the tactical units. Here the Allied Army of Liberation prepared to break out and begin the long drive towards Berlin.

By the end of the first week 200 CIC agents had landed in Normandy in a beachhead which had been consolidated and broadened into a zone extending up to 20 miles inland and 42 miles across, and the number increased to 300 as the build-up progressed. With intelligence and enthusiasm they went about their assigned missions of guarding military security, searching for enemy documents and establishing rapport with the French, especially the Resistance and the local officials. Increasingly, to fulfil their mission more effectively, they adopted a self-contained kind of lifestyle a little apart from the regular military outfits. A Special Agent who had come ashore at UTAH beach in an amphibious jeep recalled those early days in Normandy:

> After two days sleeping in fox holes and bathing in cow ponds, we commandeered a small country château, hired a Norman cook, and spent the balance of the war living independently, reporting only what we accomplished to the division who borrowed us, our Army HQ, and Bradley's remote HQ. We seized upon our freedom, not to be Big Time Operators but to better get the job done. Thus we commandeered civilian Mercedes, and I was one of the few to take entire civilian clothing in my duffel bag, so I could go undercover. I fooled more GIs than I did Germans, although no one ever suspected my identity. You showed either one your credentials and neither side could comprehend them. Most of all you needed only a brisk air of authority.

One after the other the CIC teams reduced the beachhead towns – Le Grand Chemin, Ste Marie du Mont, St Martin de Varville, Foucarville and many more. The first complete target reduction report on file was from the 29th CIC in Isigny, which the 29th Infantry Division occupied on 9 June. The CIC agents came in right behind the first combat troops and found the residents confused and restless, which was not surprising, for many of their homes had been destroyed by bombardment, street fighting and fire, and a German unit was still dug in just outside the town. Counter intelligence procedures employed by the agents in this town – the establishment of a curfew, co-operation with resistance leaders, seizure of enemy documents – followed a pattern that was to be tried and tested by many CIC detachments. First they made contact with Isigny's Resistance leader, a Monsieur Charles, the director of the local bank. With Charles' help they arranged an immediate meeting with all the other local Resistance leaders in order to determine the current counter intelligence situation, check White (loyal pro-Ally) and Black (suspect pro-German) lists and the reliability of the town officials, and discuss plans for an interim government.

Sometimes there were exceptional rewards. On D+3 agents of the 207th CIC found the German Order of Battle maps covering the US V and VII Corps combat zones, together with an artillery map of the zones of fire in the eastern part of the Cotentin Peninsula. On the body of a dead German soldier CIC agents found a document indicating the Order of Battle of German units opposing the Americans, and in the abandoned headquarters of the Nazi forced-labour construction organization, Organization Todt, they found boxes of plans and documents relating to the German defensive installations – pill-boxes, road-blocks, supply dumps and heavy gun emplacements – on the Cotentin Peninsula, together with the names and pay records of French civilian employees. From a French resistance leader the CIC team obtained the locations of German army ammunition dumps, the names of key resistance leaders, and movements of enemy troops ahead.

Such work was often fraught with difficulties which required ingenious solutions. On one occasion the 101st CIC were obliged to carry out a kidnapping under the very noses of the Germans after a tip-off that the widow of a French underground leader, who had been murdered by the Nazis, was hiding in a villa just inside the German lines. Realizing that the lady would be in possession of a great deal of extremely valuable counter intelligence information, Lieutenant Martin McGuire and Agent Curtis Foster organized an expedition to rescue her. Using an old French truck as cover, and accompanied by the French woman who had first tipped them off, the CIC men bounced and weaved their truck across no-man's-land under constant German observation. They reached the villa, picked up the widow, and successfully returned to the American lines, where the woman filled their notebooks with the names and addresses of many Black List personalities who would be rounded up later.

Sometimes counter intelligence activities took an unexpectedly hilarious turn. Shortly after the 79th CIC entered the town of Brix during the advance across the Cotentin Peninsula to the port of Cherbourg, detachment members had an unprofitable but instructive encounter with a safe found in one of the headquarters of Organization Todt. The safe was deemed a prime CIC target but had resisted all efforts to open it by agents from Corps CIC, who had passed through Brix earlier, and it bore the scars of previous attempts to blast it open with hand grenades. Realizing that the safe was an unusually strong one – an indication perhaps of the extreme sensitivity and value of its contents – the agents of the 79th brought in a master sergeant, an amateur blasting expert they borrowed from Division, to try and crack it on their behalf. The sergeant arrived, examined the safe with an appraising eye, and decided that five pounds of dynamite should succeed where all else had failed. And he was absolutely right. He put the dynamite in place against the safe door, lit the fuse, and took cover. The resulting blast has remained in the memories of all those who were privileged to witness it. It not only removed the door of the safe but demolished the rest of the safe as well, together with the room in which it stood, as well as all the other rooms in the eight-room house; indeed it demolished the house in entirety, scattering money and documents and unidentified objects all over the Normandy countryside, starting numerous small fires, and bringing up a whole battalion from a nearby infantry regiment, who thought the Germans had begun a new offensive in the area and required some persuasion before they accepted that some of their colleagues in cloaks-and-daggers were indulging in a little perfectly routine, absolutely legitimate safe-breaking.

The matter did not end there. When Colonel Dickson, the First Army G-2, got to hear of it he issued a directive, entitled 'Opening of Safes and Strong Boxes', in which he recommended that next time the CIC came across something of the sort they ask his permission before opening it up 'by destructive means' – or even try to find the owner with the key.

In general the CIC found the French populace almost 100 per cent pro-Allied. There were, of course, exceptions. These could be roughly divided into two categories – past and present. People in the first category were those who had collaborated with the Germans during the German occupation and now had to answer for their actions – these were mainly the responsibility of the French. People in the second category were those who were still collaborating with the Germans, usually as low-level espionage agents – and these were very much the concern of the CIC. Sometimes a person could belong to both categories, though in the main local awareness of their past negated their usefulness in any present rôle. The CIC were ever vigilant and instinctively suspicious, arresting line-crossers and often interrogating up to 200 suspects day, a task which would take an average CIC team up to 18 hours of the 24.

The CIC were helped in these manifold duties by the co-operation of other intelligence organizations in the field, including the Office of Strategic Services (OSS), Office of Naval Intelligence (ONI), Military Intelligence Interpreter Teams, Censorship Teams and the

French Sécurité Militaire. The OSS proved the most awkward partners. In previous campaigns the CIC had looked down on this glamorous outfit of high-level positive intelligence gatherers as, in their words, 'unscrupulous, befuddled amateurs, with an inexhaustible supply of funds and veil of mysticism, but wrong 90 per cent of the time'. According to Agent Alfred Bowen, when the OSS representatives first arrived in Normandy, they came 'with just about everything' – linguists, radio men, interpreters – and adopted a rather mysterious attitude. In the beginning the OSS men looked down on the CIC, but this soon changed when CIC agents began to catch OSS civilian agents who were attempting to cross the line into German-held territory. After that the OSS became extremely cooperative, and a codeword system was set up so that CIC would not interfere with OSS agents on positive intelligence missions; in return OSS personnel would assist the CIC in counter intelligence operations by contributing their language and technical skills.

On 20 June 1944, outside Carentan, Agent David Wright of the 207th CIC, captured the first two enemy agents to fall into American hands after the invasion.

> While driving along the dusty highway towards Carentan [he wrote], filled with refugees and allied military movement, I noticed two persons who stood out amid the dirty and unkempt people walking along the roadway. My attention was attracted towards these two persons because they had relatively clean clothing and their bicycles were clean and appeared to be new. When I searched them, I found they had brand new franc notes pinned to their inner shirts. I therefore apprehended them on suspicion and took them to our CIC office where they were interrogated by Fenton Moran, a 207th CIC agent. Both then confessed that they had attended a German espionage school in Paris and their assignment was to go behind the allied lines and carry out sabotage operations against ammunition, fuel and equipment, etc. As a result of this case, an enemy sabotage network was dissolved. As the two agents were French nationals, they were turned over to the French, who tried and convicted them with life sentence terms. The US Congress was so incensed about the French giving only life sentences for such offences in wartime that the French later executed them.

Controlling the flood of civilian refugees and processing the hundreds of denunciations against suspected French collaborators proved to be among the CIC's greatest problems. There were often times when the CIC agents in the field felt they were wasting their

time. This was because people they arrested on suspicion of espionage and sent to the rear were later released by higher authorities
without investigation or even explanation, with the result that the
suspected spies reappeared in the area where they had first been
arrested. This caused a particularly difficult situation when the
original arrest had been made on the basis of informed local de-
nunciation. For the 29th CIC at St Clair there was no more irritating
case than that of Annette.

Annette was not her real name, but since she was ultimately never
charged with an offence her real name cannot be used. Annette struck
the CIC agents who handled her as extraordinarily odd. Not only was
she the most incredible liar – meaning the most inventive and the
most inconsistent liar they had ever come across – but she behaved in
a curious, not entirely rational manner. Her original arrest had been
made at the request of both the 115th US Infantry and the local
townspeople of St Clair, who felt that her activities in riding around
the battle area on a bicycle in the thick of the fighting 'gave cause for
suspicion'. Annette was duly apprehended by the French authorities
and turned over to the CIC, who found among her few possessions
some torn pieces from a ration book. Preliminary questioning
produced an incredible story to explain the ration book and a
succession of extravagant stories about her various German ac-
quaintances, each story differing considerably from the last. A report
of the preliminary interrogation and of interviews with the woman's
denunciators was sent along with the prisoner to the First Army
Civilian Cage.

On the day following Annette's internment the CIC searched her
home and found 21,000 francs, two silver fox furs and a receipt
showing they had been purchased in Paris for 30,000 francs (about
$6000), several ration books, various papers of a personal nature, and
a small notebook containing highly complicated formulas which
seemed to relate to electrical, radio and chemical matters. These too
were sent down the line to the Cage.

Barely a week later, to the 29th CIC's complete surprise, the Chief
of Police of St Clair came to report that Annette was again free in the
area. The CIC were incensed. The 29th's CO, Lieutenant Mayfield,
went at once to the First Army Civilian Cage to try and find out what
had been going on. In a lengthy, hotly-worded report to Division he
complained 'that none of the witnesses listed had been interviewed;
that Subject had not been questioned regarding the notebook with
electrical and radio formulas; that Subject's story about the ration
book had been accepted; that none of Subject's personal papers were
used in the interrogation. Subject has been released upon the

strength of her own story against the word of known and reliable informants who had been on the ground and who had Subject under observation for more than a year.'

With two fellow agents Lieutenant Mayfield went straight to Annette's home. Another search uncovered a note which indicated that in the short space of time since her return from the Cage she had had a visit from a hunted German officer. The agents also found a radio, a pair of ten-power binoculars and a map showing German installations in Paris. They began to question Annette all over again. After hours of interrogation, during which she changed her story repeatedly and never gave a credible answer to anything, she threw a fit of hysterics and screamed that she would admit to anything they wanted and that all she wanted was to be shot as a spy. The agents gave up. All they could do was send her back to the Cage with the strong recommendation that they at least keep her there until American troops had moved out of the St Clair area. It was impossible to prove that she had committed an overt act of espionage, although, as Mayfield reported, 'the very unusual circumstances of this case render this woman highly suspect of being an enemy agent.'

Fortunately days of frustrating, unrewarding endeavour could be followed by unexpected, richly rewarding windfalls. A great deal of positive intelligence was obtained by CIC agents in the course of their normal counter intelligence operations in forward areas, not all of it solicited or sought for. One of the most rewarding hauls was made by the 35th CIC on their first day in St Lô and was known for ever after as 'The Case of the Fabulous Fountain Pen'.

An old, dishevelled, destitute Frenchman with bruised and bleeding feet hobbled into the CIC office and offered to give the CIC some information in return for a new pair of shoes. The agents in the office were incredulous. While it was quite evident that the old man needed the shoes, it was less evident that he could offer any information of value. However, to humour him they went along with the arrangement, whereupon the old man produced from his pocket a fountain pen. Slowly, with fumbling hands, he took the pen apart, unscrewing the pieces until he reached the plunger, which was hollow. Out of the hollow plunger the old man teased a tightly rolled piece of tissue paper which measured about one foot long and four inches wide when it was straightened out.

The agents peered at the piece of paper and were amazed by what they saw on it. For inscribed in a minute hand was a complete inventory of the position and deployment of every German unit for up to 200 miles in front of the Allied armies – every enemy road block, observation post, mine field, ammunition dump, radio station, machine-gun nest, everything. The sharp-eyed, keen-eared old Frenchman had even jotted down details about resistance groups, key figures in the major towns, location of air fields and reports about a woman spy. The CIC agents happily searched about for a pair of Army-issue GI shoes of the old man's size and bade him a cheery farewell as he hobbled away in them. Never had they struck a better bargain or been given so much for so little.

Like the invasion itself, the story of the break-out from Normandy and the massive thrust of the Allied armies eastward past Paris to the Rhine has become one of the great sagas in the history of the western world. Certain key episodes mark the major stages in the grand sweep of the campaign to liberate France and the rest of North West Europe and conquer and occupy the Third Reich. On 27 June the Americans took Cherbourg, the Allies' first port, by which time nearly a million men and over half a million tons of supplies had been landed in Normandy, mostly over open beaches. By 25 July the Allied build-up had achieved a momentum sufficient to permit the launching of Operation COBRA, the break-out from the Normandy lodgement into the countryside of Northern France in the direction of the Seine – probably the most decisive battle of the war in Western Europe. In the course of the next seven weeks the Allied Armies overran the Britanny peninsula; annihilated the German Seventh Army, which on 15 August was caught in the Falaise Pocket, and systematically destroyed, with the loss of 19 divisions, most of its equipment and half a million men, including 100,000 dead; rolled north and east at great speed, sometimes 50 miles in a day, hard on the heels of the retreating Germans, taking many of the towns and cities of Northern France; crossed the Seine and finally received the surrender of Paris on 25 August, the Free French Armoured Division under General LeClerc being given the honour of this tactically meaningless but psychologically important prize.

Paris was also a major counter intelligence target. At the outset of the campaign in North West Europe planners at SHAEF had recognized that army intelligence units alone would be insufficient to reduce all the targets to be found in the great cities now lying in the path of the Allied armies, the first of which was Paris. They therefore decided to organize composite intelligence collecting units known as 'Target' or 'T' Forces, which were made up of a number of specialist teams with the mission of 'seizing, safeguarding and facilitating the exploitation of important intelligence and counter intelligence targets in the larger cities'. Since the first 'T' Force was to move into Paris within a few hours of the end of the fighting it was necessary for it to be a self-contained mobile force with sufficient combat troops to guard buildings, remove mines, booby traps and explosives, man a detention centre and provide physical security for intelligence personnel. A total of 1805 men made up the force, of whom 1057 were combat troops (comprising a cavalry squadron of 900 men, a naval assault force of 77 and a French special services unit of 80); 200 were headquarters personnel, and the remaining 548 represented various branches of ten Allied intelligence agencies (British, French and American), spearheaded by the CIC, as follows:

CIC (including antisabotage teams)	114
Propaganda & Psychological Warfare specialists	108
Scientific & Economic specialists (known as the Combined Intelligence Priorities Committee)	63
OSS: Espionage & Special Counter Intelligence (SCI)	62
Escape & Evasion Interrogators	47
Air Intelligence: Strategic, Tactical & Technical	43
Army & Navy Technical Intelligence Teams (Chemical Warfare, Signal Intelligence, Medical, ONI, etc.)	35
Military Intelligence	34
French Army Intelligence Service (SSM)	24
Atomic Research & Development (ALSOS)	18

At 2200 hours on 25 August this huge and motley force of intelligence gatherers sped into Paris in a convoy of 216 vehicles. Among them, one of a CIC team of twelve, was a 23-year-old Czech-speaking CIC agent by the name of Edward Koudelka, who years later still vividly recalled that heady time: 'The excitement among our little group could not be disguised, all twelve of us moving toward a new and historic happening, the liberation of a great city. Some of the initial euphoria had died down, but the city was still on a high. People were smiling and waving. There were shouts of "*Merci, merci!*" and "*Vive l'Amérique!*" . . . The Vichy Government had died, unwept, unhonoured, and unsung.'

Koudelka and the rest of the CIC set up their headquarters in one of the grandest of the city's historic buildings, the Petit Palais on the banks of the Seine. In the next two weeks the Paris 'T' Force reduced 382 building targets and 514 personality targets, 64 of whom were arrested and processed through the Interrogation Centre in the Maison Rothschild in the Avenue Foch, and another 181 kept in detention – among them Gestapo agents, German military personnel in civilian clothes, miscellaneous German nationals, French collaborators and even British and American citizens who were under suspicion because they had survived the German occupation without being interned. Few high-ranking Nazis were found in the city, however, since most of them had fled before its liberation. In the end, according to one estimate, some 7000 collaborators had been rounded up, including industrialists, journalists, businessmen, well-known actors and actresses – the best known was Maurice Chevalier – and former Vichy-French officials. CIC Agent Koudelka was one of those involved in this massive search and arrest operation in Paris. As he recalled:

> I felt like some old revolutionary during the French Revolution, rounding up suspects for some future execution. At least there would not be a guillotine. It all seemed very impersonal. The operation was decentralized in this manner because of the large scale nature of the total intelligence task, and the significance the French then gave to their renegade citizens of the occupation years. Quite a few theatre and entertainment people were on our suspect list. Some individuals, male and female, based on their initial records, looked interesting. I can still vividly recall some of their facial expressions; mostly sad, worried; then there were looks of disbelief and some of anger; there were the cool and confident, and the apparently resigned. I thought of what sort of future they had to face, what indignity they would have to endure for the decisions they had made during the occupation.

Among the important items of intelligence uncovered during the operation were the key to a rare cipher system, plans of the V-1 rocket bomb, a map showing plans of the mining, booby trapping and demolitions of Dunkirk (which had not yet been taken by the Allies), together with valuable operational maps of the eastern part of France through which the Allied armies were about to advance, and much highly sensitive material of a specialist nature.

All this had been accomplished in circumstances which at least initially verged on chaos. When the 'T' Force first moved in there was still some fighting between remnants of the German Army and the French Forces of the Interior, the ill-disciplined and somewhat vengeful Resistance army, and some French units were so drunk with victory and strong liquor that from time to time they opened fire on one another by mistake. Two members of the 'T' Force were wounded in the general mêlée, and on one occasion one of General LeClerc's tanks opened up on the Petit Palais when a gunner mistook a CIC agent looking out of a window for a sniper. There were also many far pleasanter distractions. Agent Koudelka never forgot some of them:

One day, a small group of girls found me sitting in my jeep just outside our office at the Petit Palais. These were clearly nice girls and we became very good friends. They were exuberant, cheerful and just wonderfully delightful, to say nothing of their beauty. I was proud to be in their company. As a group, these four charming Parisiennes accompanied me to my hotel room where I dispensed the much desired chocolate and soap. They each gave me a vigorous hug and kisses in appreciation. I joked that I enjoyed that kind of torture. They soon began calling my room *la chambre de torture de la Rue Madaleine*. Such torture I had no trouble enduring . . . I lost fifteen pounds while in Paris, all attributable to long days of work and long nights of pleasure. My colleagues informed me that I was wasting away to a shadow. The Paris adventure had taken its toll.

Meanwhile the millions of soldiers in the main body of the Allied thrust by-passed the capital and raced on towards the Siegfried Line and the Rhine. With Hodge's US First Army and Patton's newly formed Third on this irresistible rout went the CIC, assiduously busy in their terrier-like concern for the security of the American ground forces. In the early days of the offensive they apprehended relatively few German espionage agents – probably because the speed of the Allied advance and the chaos of the German retreat gave German intelligence organizations little opportunity to plant stay-behind agents. But as the Allied armies relentlessly closed on the Siegfried Line, enemy intelligence activity increased sharply.

German agents in France were of various kinds. Considerable use was made of untrained line-crossers, who were for the most part recruited from members of the French collaborationist parties or people who wished to avoid forced labour. Many of the former category were collaborationists against their will, for the Germans often gave a Frenchman who had been apprehended in a crime a choice of joining a collaborationist party or facing a death sentence. Thus a certain Monsieur Rougeray, of St Hilaire, who was apprehended as a line-crosser by the CIC, had been forced to join the LVF (La Volonté Française) or face a firing squad as punishment for killing a German in a fight over a girl. Such short-range agents enjoyed little success, for their training was inadequate, their cover was poor, and their incentive to accomplish their mission and return to the German fold was weak. In any case, so rapid was the Allied advance that after a few days an agent would find himself deep in the Allied rear, from which it was virtually impossible to get back to the German lines. Long-range or deep-penetration agents, who only became active after the initial phase of the Allied occupation, often found the prospect of German defeat so certain that they abandoned their mission almost as soon as they surfaced.

Somewhat more successful was a more sophisticated category of German intelligence agent – specially selected and trained personnel, both French and German, recruited for both low-level and high-level missions by higher-level agents of the Abwehr and the German Security Service (the SD). Many potential agents recruited from among the French were genuine, ideologically motivated members of the collaborationist youth movements, all of which were affiliated with various German intelligence agencies. Training of agents took place at three espionage centres – one run by the Abwehr at the Château Antoignet, near Le Mans; and two run by the SD, one for saboteurs at La Montagnette and another for low-level intelligence agents at the Château de Maulny, both of them disguised as training camps for the Organization Todt. At Maulny the training course included the use of maps, radios, explosives, small arms, night reconnaissance, ambushes and sentry killing – a course not substantially different from that provided by SOE schools in Britain for agents operating behind German lines in occupied Europe, but even briefer. After they had completed the course at Maulny, qualified agents were paid a retainer of 3000 francs a month (equivalent to about $60), plus rations and quarters, and extra pay up to 15,000 francs for each mission. Usually the agents were sent through the lines in pairs with the broad mission of observing Allied troop and vehicle identifications, location of airfields, ammunition dumps and tactical headquarters, the reception given Allied troops by French civilians, the degree of co-operation given by French officials and Resistance groups, and the sabotage of small-scale targets. These agents usually used one of various covers – as Organization Todt workers, Resistance members or voluntary informers, sometimes Red Cross workers – and were usually sufficiently of a type for the CIC to compile a composite profile of a typical short-range agent which was circulated to all detachments:

Age 20, height 5'7", curly brown hair, tortoise shell glasses, slender to medium build, member of Jeunesse de l'Europe Nouvelle, aliases beginning with same letters as real initials, *carte d'identité* issued from the Paris area, student dress – light trousers, darker coat or sport jacket.

According to Twelfth Army Group reports, the first *bona fide* German spy to be tried by the US Military Commission in the European Theatre of Operations was Guenther Ohletz, captured by

the CIC on 14 August while making a reconnaissance of US Army
military positions. He was taken to First Army Interrogation Center,
tried by the US Military Commission and sentenced to death by
hanging. This sentence was duly executed by Seine Base Section on 7
October 1944. Not long afterwards the 220th CIC apprehended two
German espionage agents who had crossed the American lines in
civilian clothes. They were taken to the Third Army Interrogation
Center at Toul, tried, and shot. On numerous occasions
apprehended agents were women, one of them the mistress of a
Gestapo officer in Brest, whom the CIC sent to the concentration
camp run by the FFI (French Forces of the Interior) at St Pabu.

In the meantime, more CIC detachments swept through France
from the south in the vanguard of Patch's US Seventh Army, which
on 15 August had landed with French and British forces in the last of
the war's great amphibious assaults, the invasion of Southern France,
codenamed Operation DRAGOON.

Because of the demands made by the Normandy landings and the
operations in Italy, Dragoon had been repeatedly postponed, but the
Allies' need for additional port capacity through which to feed their
ever-extending supply line made it clearly undesirable to delay any
longer the capture of Marseilles. The invasion – by over 155,000
troops carried in 500 ships on a voyage of more than 400 miles – took
the Germans by surprise, like most Allied actions in France, and the
landings were only weakly opposed. By the end of August the
Seventh Army was moving up the Rhône valley and both Toulon and
Marseilles were in Allied hands. Marseilles was a special concern of
the CIC, and of one Special Agent in particular.

Generally acknowledged as one of the more remarkable of the
CIC agents in France, Victor de Guinzbourg of the 307th Detachment, Seventh Army, was what was known as a 'two character' agent
– an unofficial assessment rating based on a combination of merit,
personality and achievement, and prized more highly than a cap-
taincy by most agents. In fact, it was so highly prized that at the time
of the Allied advance through southern France in the late summer of
1944, there were only two other CIC agents in the whole of the
European Theatre who had a 'two character' rating.

De Guinzbourg's background, as befitted a CIC agent operating
amid the cultural complexities of continental Europe, was highly
cosmopolitan, and courtly and cultured too. He had been born in
Russia but left during the Revolution, seeking asylum first in one and
then in another Balkan or Slavic state before coming to rest for a
while in Weimar Germany, where he completed his university
education. From Germany de Guinzbourg moved on to France,

where he became highly successful in business and acquired – exactly how is not known – the rank of Honorary Private in the French Foreign Legion. By the time he emigrated to the United States a year or two before the outbreak of the war in Europe, this rather larger than life rolling stone had become fluent in almost every European language except Finnish and Swedish – but including Yiddish and some of the Albanian dialects.

Soon after Pearl Harbor, de Guinzbourg volunteered for service in the US Army, which decided, with commendable acumen, that the best place for this many-sided peg was the many-sided hole of the CIC. In due course Agent de Guinzbourg was sent to invade North Africa, where he displayed such nonchalance under fire and such dash and invention on counter intelligence assignment that his reputation grew to legendary proportions. Then came Operation Dragoon. Three or four days after the American landings in Southern France, a team from the 307th CIC was despatched in a cavalcade of twelve jeeps to the logistically vital but politically unstable city port of Marseilles. The agents had barely got beyond the outskirts before they realized that the city was still very much in Nazi hands and they all hurriedly vacated the area – all, that is, except de Guinzbourg, who was left there under cover in enemy territory, garbed in nondescript oddments of American Army uniform, just like scores of French civilians out in the city streets.

Generally speaking, the ideal undercover agent is one who can, by virtue of his or her apparent ordinariness of appearance and behaviour, blend in with the local populace, or even submerge beneath it, so as to attract the least unwelcome attention. De Guinzbourg was the exact opposite, for his imposing physical qualities served to make him the most overt agent imaginable. For a start, he did not blend in with the Latinate people of Marseilles; he towered over them, standing a full six foot three in his socks and weighing well over 14 stone. Then again, his head was as bald as an ostrich egg, and his magnificent moustache rivalled that of any British sergeant-major. Victor de Guinzbourg was an unmistakeable figure in Nazi-occupied Marseilles, a fact which merely redoubled the awe with which his legendary feats were perceived by his fellow agents within the CIC.

In order to discover the whereabouts of Japanese nationals who had gone to ground after the American landings, de Guinzbourg took to bed a young half-Japanese girl who became so impassioned of his burly charms that she told him all she knew about her compatriots. The Germans fared little better. Fifteen minutes after taking a fully-fledged German agent out for a ride, de Guinzbourg had cajoled a full confession from him. The French Army and the

French police were as easily beguiled. The French police co-operated with him with such enthusiasm that between them they were able to make arrests that French Army Intelligence had been unable to make. The French Army invested him with the rank of colonel and gave him access to all their files. And when de Guinzbourg acquired secret information that French Communist agitators, as part of a revolutionary bid to take over government, were about to call on the dockers to strike in the port, through which most of the war matériel for the southern front was being unloaded from American ships, it was he who single-handedly organized the means to intervene peacefully – not so much to save France for democracy as to protect the Seventh Army supply line, where gasoline was down to less than three days' reserves.

Since the French police were undecided what action to take to avert this dire emergency, and the regular French Army was reluctant to maintain order by firing on their fellow countrymen, de Guinzbourg hit on the idea of mobilizing the French Foreign Legion, an organization which would fire on anyone anywhere at any time, and of which as we have seen he was himself an Honorary Private. Some ten thousand battle-hardened Legionnaires had disembarked in Marseilles a few days previously and were camped ten miles out of town awaiting supplies. On the day before the strike was scheduled to begin, therefore, de Guinzbourg went to the Legion's commander and suggested that it might be a good thing to celebrate some French military victory – the Liberation of Southern France, perhaps – with a great parade through the streets of Marseilles the next day. The commander agreed and on the day of the strike the Foreign Legion marched its famous slow-step down the central avenue of Marseilles in front of an enormous and wildly enthusiastic crowd, past a reviewing stand stuffed with French and American generals, behind whom might be glimpsed the imposing figure of the mysterious Monsieur de Guinzbourg, the strange American who thought like a European and looked like a bear and wore no insignia of rank. So the parade marched by, the white desert caps of the men and the sky blue caps of the officers in perfect alignment, bayonets glinting in the sun.

Bayonets glinting in the sun! It was not customary for the Legion to perform ceremonial parades with bayonets fixed. A closer glance revealed that the Legionnaires' rifles were also loaded, and that a round was in the chamber of each gun. This state of armed readiness was not lost on the organizers of the strike. Nor was the fact the Legion did not return to camp but bivouacked in the town. There was no strike that day, nor on the days that followed. The dockers continued unloading the ships, the Communists published a disclaimer of any intention to wreck the war against the Nazis, and de Guinzbourg, having secured the house of a French admiral as a base for the CIC, went on to achieve one final triumph in Marseilles – by obtaining from one of the city's finest restaurants, the Normandie, the services of one of the great *cordon bleu* chefs of France.

The legendary de Guinzbourg died some years back, after a distinguished post-war career in the United Nations Organization in New York. But his many CIC colleagues still remember him with immense affection and respect. 'We did have some outstanding agents,' writes Nelson Dungan, who also served in Seventh Army CIC, 'such as a friend of mine, Victor S. M. de Guinzbourg. He spoke many languages, was an excellent interrogator, a true diplomat and a fine person. Of all the CIC agents that I encountered, excellent as they were, Victor stands alone. In any confrontation between him and Skorzeny, Germany's super-spy, I would have put my money on Victor. Any special jobs that had to be done, whether they were counter intelligence or almost anything else, Victor was called on and did well. He was truly a giant among us. A good friend and a great man.' (In fact, de Guinzbourg did eventually confront Skorzeny when the arch saboteur was brought into 7th Army CIC headquarters in Augsburg for interrogation on 17 May 1945. Skorzeny loudly complained that his agents were never adequately paid or promoted – a complaint that had a familiar ring to de Guinzbourg and his long-suffering CIC colleagues.)

In the meantime the Allied advance rolled on through eastern France and into the Lowland countries to the north, with CIC detachments and various 'T' forces following breathlessly on the heels of the front-line units. In the speed and confusion of the advance, there was little time for coherent counter intelligence work, and the nearer the Allies drew to the German frontier the greater the number of collaborators they found swarming in the towns and the less useful and reliable they found the various organizations of the Resistance.

An unexpected counter intelligence problem developed when CIC detachments moved into Belgium, a politically ambivalent country with an historically built-in double agent mentality, the consequence of being sandwiched between two traditional foes, Germany and France. Throughout the French campaign the CIC had found that carrier pigeons posed a problem as potential espionage couriers. The problem grew considerably more acute once the Allies had moved into Belgium, where pigeon breeding was a national pastime and there were some 18,000 registered birds. The Germans had ordered all pigeon lofts to be padlocked, but in fact pigeons had been known to carry intelligence information between Belgium and England during the Nazi occupation, and the CIC, fearful that the birds could perform the same services between Belgium and Germany, renewed the German order for the closure of pigeon lofts, and fined and even imprisoned violators of this order. Many American front-line units reported seeing pigeons flying towards the enemy lines, but none of these birds were brought down during their headlong scurry above the battlefield, and it was never ascertained whether German Intelligence ever profited from their use. The problem cropped up again as the armies neared the German frontier, and an order was issued that all carrier pigeons found in Germany were to be destroyed.

The campaigns in Northern and Southern France drew rapidly to their end. On 3 September Lyons fell, on 11 September Luxembourg – and with it Radio Luxembourg, which was taken over by Psychological Warfare personnel to beam Allied propaganda at the Germans. Four days later the city of Nancy was captured and Patch's Seventh Army, advancing from the south, effected a junction with Patton's Third and de Tassigny's French First Army to the northwest of Dijon. Allied forces now formed a continuous front that stretched from Holland and the Channel all the way along the French frontier to Switzerland and down to the Mediterranean. As the Germans retreated behind the Siegfried Line, the so-called West Wall, which was their outer line of defence in the west, their resistance stiffened. But on 11 September units of the US First Army set foot on Third Reich soil for the first time near Trier, and on 13 September, one hundred days after the invasion of Normandy, the lead tanks of the 3rd Armored Division breached the Siegfried Line just ten miles south of the German city of Aachen. The battle for France was virtually at an end. The battle for Germany was about to begin. The battle for Italy, meanwhile, continued.

7

SPY HIGHWAY ITALY

The last six months of the war in Italy were the most productive period in the history of the CIC – and perhaps one of the most remarkable in the annals of espionage in wartime. In September 1944 the Allied advance which had forged across the River Arno and taken the towns of Pisa and Lucca came up against stiffening German resistance along the Gothic Line high up in the Apennine Mountains and slowly ground to a halt. From October 1944, when the Allied advance began to falter and finally bog down in the grim winter weather of northern Italy, the Germans launched a flood of espionage and sabotage agents against the Allied lines on a scale that was without precedent. The task of preventing this undercover army from insinuating itself behind the static winter positions of the United States Fifth Army fell squarely on the shoulders of the CIC.

Up to this point the CIC had been largely in the dark concerning German intelligence activities in Italy, mainly because the drive to the Arno had been too rapid to allow effective counter intelligence. Relatively little was known, therefore, about units and personalities, agents and recruiters, methods and techniques. Allied counter intelligence were soon to find out the hard way under the almost continuous barrage of German agents heading for Allied occupied territory. From those who were captured and interrogated, and from other sources of intelligence information, including Most Secret sources (probably involving some input from Ultra decrypts of German secret communication codes), the intelligence staff at the headquarters of the Allied Armies in Europe was gradually able to build up a clearer profile of their German opposition. They gave to this opposition the convenient generic name of the German Intelligence Services, or GIS for short, an abbreviation used by Allied intelligence throughout the remainder of the war in Europe.

The GIS consisted of three elements. One element was the Abwehr, the military espionage agency of the German General Staff, which until February 1944 was run by the almost legendary Admiral

Canaris. A second element was the SD, or Sicherheitsdienst (Security Service), which, like the Gestapo, was part of Himmler's RSHA, or Reichsicherheitshauptamt (Reich Security Administration). Department VI of the RSHA was the SD foreign intelligence organization under Walter Schellenberg, and was largely concerned with political espionage. In June 1944, following Canaris's dismissal, the Abwehr became absorbed by the SD, and the foreign sections of the Abwehr came under Schellenberg's command, who thus came to control all German espionage, military as well as political. In Italy, however, Allied counter intelligence continued to see itself confronted to all intents and purposes by two distinct German intelligence organizations. In addition, a third enemy intelligence element began to emerge. This consisted of espionage networks organized by the Corps intelligence staffs of the German Army in Italy, who resorted to recruiting their own agents and sending them across the lines on espionage and sabotage missions because they felt they were not getting what they needed from the Abwehr and the SD.

In course of time Allied intelligence was able to draw a reasonably detailed picture of the GIS in Italy, particularly of the Abwehr element. Abwehr Kommandos 150 and 190 ran the espionage operations, while Abwehr Kommando II, whose six officers and eight warrant officers were listed by Allied counter intelligence, looked after sabotage from its HQ near Alto Adige in northern Italy, with dumps of sabotage materials in the Parma area and elsewhere. In Milan the Abwehr was headed by Lieutenant Colonel Werner, 20 of whose agents were known and named by the Allies. By early 1944 the Allies were in possession of 250 names of Abwehr personalities, including those of the directing staff in Bolzano, Merano, Milan, Genoa and Garda. In Genoa the Abwehr was run by Riccardo Wappner, four of whose men were listed, along with three in Trieste.

Though the enemy intelligence organizations confronting the Allies in Italy were German, virtually all the espionage and sabotage agents put in the field by them were Italian. Whichever service they represented, most of them were short-term tactical agents, the so-called front agents, whose task was to attack targets or gather intelligence details up to a maximum of 30 miles behind the enemy front on missions generally lasting only a week or two. Unlike long-term strategic agents, who were always very few in number, the front agents were despatched *en masse*, sown like dandelion seeds in the hope that at least a few might get through and produce results. Some of the German agents were parachuted in and some landed by boat; some were left behind by the retreating Wehrmacht and were thus already in place when their towns or cities were occupied by

Allied forces; but the overwhelming majority were line-crossers or infiltrators who came over the mountains from the German-held north. They came in all sorts of guises and with all sorts of excuses. Some crossed the lines dressed as priests or nuns, or purporting to be Partisan officers or members of the Committee of National Liberation or on occasion officers in the Royal Italian Army or Polish deserters from the Wehrmacht, seeking to enlist in the Polish Corps. One was instructed to pose as a doctor so that his 'surgery' could serve as a port of call for other agents and couriers. Others were instructed to obtain employment with Allied units – one of these actually worked for a week in a British officers' mess before he was caught. A few even came driving flocks of sheep. One such shepherd spy was one of the few Germans known to have taken part in field operations. His name was Lieutenant Pfannenstiel, of Abwehrtruppe 257, who made his way to the Allied lines complete with a few score baaing sheep in order to see how things were with his own eyes, and then returned to the safety of his own lines with the loss of only a handful of his sheep along the way.

The motives of the young men and women who risked their lives as spies behind the American and British lines tended to be pragmatic rather than ideological. For younger men it was a means of avoiding being sent to Germany for forced labour. For those from the south it was a way of getting back home. Above all, perhaps, the pay was princely, amounting to £1000 to £2000 per mission, a fortune in those days. Most agents were espionage agents looking for tactical military information, though some also had naval, economic or political missions – and at least two agents were under instructions to get hold of the Counter Intelligence List of suspects held by the CIC. If they were unable to remember all the tactical information they had collected, they were instructed to buy something from a shop and add fictitious purchases, standing for items of information, to the bill.

In August 1944 Allied Armies in Italy issued a stocktaking report entitled 'Notes on counterintelligence in Italy' which warned about the magnitude of the task posed by the GIS campaign. 'The enemy has made use of agents on a scale far exceeding that experienced in any other theatre either in this war or the last,' the report ran. For the Allies the onslaught of enemy agents produced a situation so desperate that the commander of the CIC Detachment attached to the 10th Mountain Division felt bound to advise a reverse of normal law measures. 'A good practice for men on the front,' he wrote in a memorandum, 'is to consider all persons suspect until they are able to prove their innocence.'

Arrayed against the serried phalanxes of invasive pawns sent over by GIS in this gigantic chess game was a whole army of pieces representing a wide range of Allied counter intelligence agencies. The CIC and their British counterpart, the Field Security Services, formed the backbone of the Allied defence. Other agencies included the Security Branch of the Allied Control Commission (the supreme Military Government body); No. 1 Intelligence Unit (which handled the counter intelligence exploitation of newly captured cities); the Refugee Interrogation Points; the Sécurité Militaire of the French Corps; the SIM, or Italian military intelligence agency; the Questure (the civilian police forces in the towns); and a back-up of Military Police, Carabinieri and Italian troops at checkpoints controlled by the CIC and Field Security.

Significant components of the Allied security system were the Special Counter Intelligence (or SCI) Units, of which there were four in Italy. Their function was 'to receive, record and use certain information emanating from specially secret [meaning probably Ultra secret] sources.' The Units were 'responsible for undertaking the penetration of enemy intelligence services and for the special exploitation of captured enemy agents.' The SCI worked closely with the CIC and on occasions they pulled off remarkable coups together. One such was the successful turn-round of the Italian spy, Alpha Primo, who in May 1944 flashed word to his former bosses that the British Eighth Army was preparing to attack Italy's east coast. As a result, the Germans massed their reserves there, only to discover a few days later that the American Fifth Army, reinforced by British troops, staged its all-out offensive in the west-coast sector, later driving through to Rome.

The Nazi espionage assault was concentrated on the zones where American (and British) troops were most thinly spread and most vulnerable. In the American area these were mainly the static positions of IV Corps and the 92nd Division. The 92nd Division, a unit composed entirely of black soldiers, was perhaps the most vulnerable of all, for it had arrived at the front without a CIC detachment and experienced some difficulty in acquiring one. The Division had had a chequered history in the Italian campaign and performed very badly under fire – a fact generally attributed to the black soldiers' perception that they were fighting a white man's war for a white man's society. White officers resented being posted to this Division, which only served to worsen morale, and in its wisdom the War Department had therefore decreed that no CIC personnel could be spared for the 92nd since under no circumstances would a detachment of white personnel be allowed to serve with a coloured Division – the

CIC role would have to be carried out by coloured personnel already in the Division. In vain it was pointed out to the War Department that for black soldiers to undertake discreet or undercover counter intelligence work amongst the white native Italian populace or against agents of the fanatically Aryan German Abwehr or SD would require powers of disguise far beyond the call of duty. Eventually a 92nd CIC was formed from agents on detached service from other units, with Agent Ramon Arrizabalaga, of Hispanic American back- ground, in command. It was upon this scratch detachment that the full weight of the Abwehr fell.

Arrizabalaga had barely arrived at the 92nd's front-line position at Viareggio, on the coast road north of Pisa, when a suspect named Santo Santagati was brought in and under intensive interrogation admitted that he had been recruited as a spy by the Germans in Sicily and that his contact was the stay-behind spy chairman in Pisa. Arrizabalaga promptly led a team into Pisa and had the chairman arrested. At the same time he opened a detention cage in Viareggio and drew up a plan of campaign. It was apparent that the spy trail used by a large number of GIS agents was the route over the Mount Altissimo Pass taken by 90 per cent of the refugees filtering down into the valley from the German-occupied territory in the north. An extensive road-block system manned by Italian Carabinieri was therefore established in Allied-occupied territory, and by working in collaboration with the Italian Partisans up in the mountains, CIC agents were also able to set up road-blocks right up at the head of the spy trail inside the enemy-held area. Refugees coming through were held by the Partisans and sent down to Viareggio in groups of 25 to 30 for interrogation at the CIC cage. By the end of the winter the 92nd CIC had screened more than 18,000 civilians in this way and arrested more than 25 confirmed enemy agents.

The captured GIS agents proved to be a curiously motley bunch. The youngest was a boy aged 13. The oddest was a certain Rosario Tripodi who aroused suspicion when it was found he had a forged French identity card and 'was carrying a Beretta pistol attached to his private parts.' One was a South African POW who had agreed to be recruited as an agent by the Germans as a way of getting back to the Allied side of the lines. A quarter or more were women. One of them, according to a CIC report, was a woman by the name of Leonia Celli, who 'was made up to look as unattractive as possible, including wearing red ankle-length drawers and horn-rimmed glasses.' She claimed she was an actress of some renown. She admitted she had been assisting her husband in writing Fascist propaganda in Milan and had called personally upon Mussolini – who after his rescue from imprisonment in the Apennine mountains in September 1943 had established a new Republican-Fascist government in German-occupied Northern Italy – and had received his blessing. She also admitted that her present mission had been to gather information in Florence, Venice and Rome to be used in propaganda work on her return to Milan. Unlike most arrested agents she proved such an ardent Fascist that she resolutely refused to divulge the name of other Nazi agents.

Under interrogation it seemed that on the whole the women were tougher than the men. This was highlighted by a case which proved to be the most colourful in the whole history of the 305th CIC Detachment. The case opened towards the end of September with a report from Allied Forces Headquarters concerning a young woman who was believed to have crossed into Allied occupied territory during the previous month. At this time she was known simply as Carla. Her description read: 'Age 18, height 5′1½″, thick set, black hair, dark complexion, Roman accent, claims to be skating champion. Details of her mission are unknown except that she was to carry back copies of extreme left-wing newspapers.'

All Fifth Army CIC Detachments were alerted, as were the Military Police and Carabinieri checkpoints. The breakthrough came towards the end of October, when an Italian by the name of Martinelli, held by the CIC in Florence on suspicion of being an enemy agent, broke down and confessed that he had come through the lines on an espionage mission for Abwehr Kommando 190 in the company of a young woman called Carla Costa, whom he described as 'the No. 1 female espionage agent'. From details supplied by Martinelli and leads picked up by agents in Florence it was possible to work out the route of Carla's planned return to German territory and all check-posts were alerted. On 23 October a CIC Special Agent apprehended Carla as she was making her way through a thinly held sector of the lines near Pontepetri and she was taken to the rear for interrogation.

Carla Costa made an indelible impression on the CIC agents who handled her case. For one thing, she was very attractive and, at 17, even younger than they had been led to believe, so that they found it difficult to imagine she could be the No. 1 woman agent. For another she proved a tough and professional operator and a fanatical Fascist. During the days that followed her arrest the CIC came to appreciate Carla's high standing, for this young girl turned out to be the stubbornest and most tenacious enemy agent they had ever dealt with. Carla simply refused to answer CIC interrogators' questions although, as Lieutenant Colonel Stephen Spingarn, commanding the 305th Detachment, reported: 'Various devices have been employed without success, including confronting her with Martinelli, who crossed the lines with her. I have virtually arrived at the conclusion that no short-term psychological treatment will persuade the girl to talk, which is a great pity since she is undoubtedly a walking gold mine of information of important CI value.'

Carla still refused to talk even after a white handkerchief she carried had been heated over a candle to reveal the words 'ANHOERIGER DER ARMEE – LUFTFLOTTE ZU LEITEN' (Member of the Army – Lead to Air Force Headquarters), the identity document of an Abwehr Kommando 190 Agent. Not until 28 October, after some 60 hours of continuous interrogation, did Carla proudly admit that she was an enemy agent who had already completed two successful missions. But she still steadfastly refused, despite days of interrogation by Colonel Spingarn and a CIC colleague, as well as the Chief of Italian Intelligence, Major Cesare Faccio, to disclose any information about her employers, her contacts or other agents. Her only slip was to reveal that her home was in Rome. At once, a priority call was put through to the Air Force CIC in Rome, who responded with such extraordinary speed that within 80 hours they had investigated, collated, audited, typed and returned a 20-page report on Carla's background and that of members of her group, without which it would have been impossible to break Carla down.

Considering that she was only 17 years old, Carla's personal history was fantastic. She had joined the Abwehr group of a very active GIS officer known as Colonel David on 2 June 1944, just before the city fell to the Allies. Her reason for joining was her burning faith in the Fascist cause. Two days later she left Rome for Milan with the rest of the group and there met several German intelligence officers, including 'Dr Kora' of Abwehr Kommando 190. In August she went on two intelligence-gathering missions into Allied occupied territory – first to Florence and then to Rome. On her return she was summoned to Gardone on Lake Garda for a private audience with Mussolini, who told her he wished all Italian women could be like her, and then awarded her the Iron Cross (Second Class). Shortly afterwards she was recommended for the Italian Silver Star, the second highest Italian military award. On 14 October Carla crossed the lines a third time with Mario Martinelli and again made for Rome, where she collected information on Allied movements in that city and made contact with Nella David, the daughter-in-law of the GIS espionage chief. It was on her return from that final mission that she was apprehended.

When Carla Costa was finally broken the information she gave about herself and the group of women agents of Colonel David's Abwehr Kommando 190 was invaluable in helping the CIC to capture future line-crossers. But she never relinquished her political faith in Fascism. Because of her age and sex, Fifth Army took a special interest in her and tried very hard to make her see the error of her ways and the harm she had done to both herself and her family. The effort failed, though a poem she wrote while in prison awaiting trial showed that her conscience had been touched to some degree. Carla wrote:

> Fascist Carla Costa
> Was born and died a sinner,
> Betrayed God, her country, her family . . .
> O Pilgrim, you may dispense with your prayers!

On 18 December she was brought to trial, found guilty of espionage and sentenced to 20 years' imprisonment. Mario Martinelli was sentenced to death and executed by firing squad. Two days after the trial, Special Agent Gordon Messing of the Fifth Army CIC visited Carla in her cell, partly to clear up a few outstanding intelligence queries and partly to try one last time to make her renounce her views. He found Carla nearer to mirth than tears. It was, she said, the only response she was capable of in the situation in which she found herself. She could not understand why people were so interested in her, and made mock of the nuns who had come to console and comfort her. Messing rebuked her, telling her she was arguing like a little girl, to which Carla replied: 'Well, I am a little girl.' She was a hopeless case and after Messing left her he summed up his feelings in his report. Carla Costa, he wrote, 'was emotionally immature and incapable of appreciating the emotion of others. She is able to immune herself within the tight walls of her impervious fanaticism, caring nothing for other values and indeed despising them.'

Different in quality, both as a person and as an agent, but no less useful in the information he betrayed, was another apprehended GIS agent, Anthony Saponaro, who not only contributed considerable data of tactical intelligence value but became the prime factor in the capture of many of his GIS colleagues. Saponaro himself had appeared one day at CIC Headquarters claiming to be an American from Camden, New Jersey. He told an elaborate and wonderful story about how he had come to Italy before the war to study at art school and how he was sent to a forced labour factory in Germany when America entered the war and how he escaped and made his way to the German-occupied part of Italy where he contacted the SD in Verona and volunteered his services as a spy. He did this, he said, simply so that he could make use of the guise of this service to cross safely through the lines and then report to the US authorities for repatriation back to America.

The CIC listened patiently to this touching and patriotic tale and then twisted his arm and tweaked his ear, so to speak, and slapped his wrist and rapped his knuckles a bit, until he was forced to admit that he had really joined the GIS in the hope of a profitable career as a double agent. His present mission had been to gather information in Rome about the locations of the British Secret Service and American Military Intelligence, along with operating methods, communication systems and crossing points for Allied agents going through the lines into German territory. Thereafter Saponaro sang like a songbird. He sang names, places, dates, routes, methods. He warbled the entire plan of the major GIS assault for November.

Just as Saponaro had predicted, in November 1944 enemy agents of all shapes, sizes and descriptions began to pour across the front line into Allied territory. Some had been trained at the espionage school in Verona or at the sabotage school in Milan. German agents of Polish extraction were sent to obtain military intelligence about the Polish Army, and Russian agents working for the German side were sent to inflame Communist groups in the captured cities and towns. Some agents were ideologically motivated. Many were persuaded by the prospect of financial gain, and kept in line by threats of dire retribution. An enemy agent of the SD political espionage organization IDA, who was captured in Pistoia after crossing the lines during a heavy Allied artillery bombardment, told the CIC that his German case officer had warned him never to reveal his true mission to the Allies, for the punishment would be two-fold: his execution by the Allies and his family's internment in Germany. The same officer advised him to avoid all road-blocks and make friends with all Allied soldiers who stopped him by offering them a drink of cognac.

The CIC was ill prepared for the GIS onslaught. A major problem was the lack of qualified CIC personnel in the field, for tactically most of the Agents were in the wrong place. The Germans' main military thrust, as distinct from their espionage thrust, was through the II Corps sector, so this was where most of the CIC Agents – 45 in all – were positioned, since it was assumed that the CIC should be in the area with the most troops and the hardest fighting. By contrast IV Corps, whose sector covered an area five times greater than that of II Corps, had only 18 CIC Agents – and it was through their thinly-held sector that the GIS naturally chose to send their own spies. The lesson of this situation was that tactical counter intelligence interest was likely to be exactly the reverse of tactical military interest. But the army structure was too unwieldy to allow much to be done about it at short notice. So many agents poured through the II Corps lines that one road was nicknamed 'Spy Highway No. 1, Italy'. In vain Lieutenant Colonel Spingarn, commanding 305th CIC Detachment, sent a Secret Priority Wire to Major Ralph Powers, the CIC Chief at AFHQ, on 21 November 1944:

> URGENT SECURITY SITUATION HERE TEN SABOTAGE AGENTS CAPTURED WITHIN PAST FOUR DAYS THREE HUNDRED MORE REPORTED EN ROUTE OR TO COME SEVERAL CACHES OF ENEMY SABOTAGE EXPLOSIVES DISCOVERED ... SECURITY SITUATION MOST SERIOUS SINCE BEGINNING OF ITALIAN OPERATION ... ADDITIONAL AGENTS URGENTLY NEEDED.

At San Marcello the 204th CIC prepared for this deluge of spies by putting into operation one of the tightest controls on civilian movement of the entire Italian campaign. Road-blocks and roving patrols were set up all over the area and any civilian without an official pass in a forward area was to be arrested on the spot. All combat troops, military police, Civil Affairs officers and road patrols were asked to co-operate and the so-called 'Patterns Report' was implemented throughout the Fifth Army front. This Report involved the collation of all information obtained from captured enemy agents which might help identify other unknown agents by means of recognizable 'patterns' in their appearance and behaviour indicating that they were GIS trained and equipped. The information included details about clothes and shoes worn; pocket accessories, documents and food carried; personal, educational and military background; identification devices and conduct under interrogation. CIC experience of captured agents had revealed that German intelligence was an inflexible organization and undeviatingly systematic in recruiting, indoctrinating and equipping agents, who as a result tended to tell the same cover stories, wear the same make of shoes, the same clothes and the same weave of cloth for their suits, carry the same documents – and even the same torches, suitcases and leather briefcases, the same sandwiches wrapped in the same paper, and currency notes bearing continuous serial numbers!

There were other giveaways. Agents returning from missions needed to be able to identify themselves when reaching the enemy lines. The passes which identified them were found to be sewn into their clothing or the linings of their shoes. One suspect found to be mopping his brow more than the severity of his interrogation warranted had a handkerchief bearing a pass printed in an ink which dissolved when moistened. According to one Allied intelligence report, women agents could be identified in a particular way: 'Some of the enemy agents now carry as a means of identification a small piece of cloth about 3" × 1" which is reported to have identity particulars on it. The cloth is concealed by being sewn into either the elastic or the hem of the (Br) knickers (= US panties).' 'Be wary of anyone in your area,' a divisional memorandum exhorted American troops. 'Remember this is not Brooklyn, or Topeka, or Oakland, but a foreign country where espionage, intrigue and deception are ingrained in the people and is looked upon as another way of earning a living.'

The massive preparations the Allies made to contain the Abwehr assault turned the counter intelligence operation into a pheasant shoot. Everyone joined in the hunt – Italian Partisans and Carabinieri, American and British troops and, of course, the CIC, who masterminded the whole show. Before long Nazi spies and saboteurs were being hauled in at a fantastic rate. The 204th CIC caught 28 in November alone. By the end of the year 110 Abwehr or SD agents had been intercepted in Fifth Army areas and eight caches of explosives left behind by the Germans for use by saboteurs had been recovered as a result of information divulged by captured agents. Sometimes dummy explosives were substituted in the hope of catching the saboteurs for whom they were intended – not necessarily alive. As the commander of one CIC Detachment reported to Fifth Army regarding one such cache: 'The dummy is booby trapped with two sticks of dynamite and under surveillance. It is hoped that other enemy saboteurs will be so kind as to dig for the same box. If this happy event should occur, the remains will be shipped to you by wooden envelope. Attention is invited to the fact that the nearest military unit is a Fifth Army Graves Registration Service which has offered its services in any capacity.'

Inevitably mistakes were made. Two shepherds apprehended while behaving in a suspicious manner in the middle of a field near the front line were found on interrogation to have been engaged in nothing more sinister than the examination of a set of pornographic photographs which one of the shepherds was carrying in his wallet. Most suspects were *bona fide* secret agents, however, and usually confessed to being so after interrogation. Many of them gave extraordinarily elaborate accounts of how they came to enter the German Intelligence Service. The story of a certain Natale Racagni was one of the best.

Racagni had been caught by the partisans in an abandoned farm-house up in the mountains near Abetone, where he had found shelter from the bad weather in the company of a woman agent by the name of Anna Maria Dei Brenti. The partisans handed the pair over to a British artillery unit who in turn delivered them to the 204th CIC. Within a short time both confessed to being enemy agents from Abwehrtruppe 152 of the German Luftwaffe.

According to Racagni's story, he had owned a pharmacist supply warehouse in Bologna. One night in July 1944, the Germans smashed down the door of the warehouse and demanded to know why the hospital supplies were not being distributed. This angered Racagni so much that several nights later he was heard to utter several derogatory remarks about the Germans and was warned that it might be wise if he held his tongue. That same evening he was propositioned by an acquaintance called Carlo, who asked him if he was interested in making 'a lot of money'. He was then taken to Florence where he was further propositioned by a German in civilian clothes who offered him substantial rewards if he agreed to under-take certain work in the German interest but warned him that it was dangerous work and he might have to risk his life doing it. The German gave him 5000 lire as a *bona fide* downpayment and sent him back to Bologna for three days to think about it.

The more Racagni thought about it the less he liked it. He decided to turn down the proposition and stay in Bologna. Then one day a man came to his house and accused him of accepting money from the Germans without doing anything for it in return. He became threatening and abusive and ordered Racagni to accompany him to Milan to give an account of himself to the Germans. This was the point, Racagni explained to his CIC interrogators, when he was press-ganged into the service of the GIS. In Milan he was brought face to face with the notorious 'Dr Kora', the German officer in charge of Abwehr Kommando 190, and briefed about his role. At a special spy school he was trained in the identification of Allied units. Then he was sent on his mission.

The first part of the mission was to deliver 50,000 lire to an agent who was operating a clandestine radio in Florence. Racagni was to enter this man's shop and inquire of the owner, 'Have you got 17 tubes?' On receiving an affirmative answer, Racagni was to hand over the money. He was then to proceed to Rome for the second part of his mission. In Rome his task was to observe all Allied movements in the city. Between 1 and 2 o'clock every lunchtime he was to go to a small restaurant called the Trattoria Bolognese in the Piazza del Popolo and wait to be contacted. At some juncture two men would come up to him and say, 'Haven't we met in Milan?' Racagni would then divulge all his information in return for his pay.

On 8 November Racagni and his fellow agent Anna Maria set off for their intelligence mission in Rome. Little more than a week later they were arrested. The CIC did not believe Racagni had told them the whole truth and this was confirmed by Anna Maria, who declared that Racagni was a trusted and experienced agent who had already been through the lines on a previous mission. Both suspects were found to be pro-Nazi and pro-Fascist and were sent back down the line to the rear, where they were processed and tried and shortly afterwards shot by firing squad.

CIC success against the Abwehr assault was firmly based on sound and solid counter intelligence procedures: co-ordination between CIC teams, security indoctrination of front-line troops, co-operation of local native populace, thorough schooling in investigative techniques including interrogation. A textbook case illustrating first-class counter intelligence in action occurred in the 204th CIC area when four GIS agents were turned over to a US Army command post near Sagni di Lucca by a local peasant who, in accordance with well-publicized rules in the area, had led them there under the pretext of guiding them through the lines. The GIs immediately escorted the four men under guard to the 204th CIC HQ, located about five miles behind the front line. At 11 o'clock that morning the interrogation began and lasted until midday the next day.

The two CIC interrogators began by confiscating the suspects' personal effects and confining the men in separate rooms. They then checked the suspect lists in the CI Bulletins, which listed both true names and aliases currently in use. The next task was to obtain confessions from the men which could be used in their trial and also serve counter intelligence purposes.

The first man to be interrogated was Sergio Picchetti. He was allowed to tell his cover story without interruption and then to write it down, giving his previous occupations, routes of travel into Allied occupied territory, and destination. It soon became clear that he was well trained and would not confess readily, so the CIC interrogators turned their attention to another of the four, a 22-year-old ex-student from Milan by the name of Pedro Pedrotta, whom they considered the one most likely to break.

Pedrotta related his cover story, which the two CIC agents appeared to accept without question. He then wrote it down in his own hand in considerable detail. Before he signed it he was reminded that he was in an office of American counter intelligence and that if he wished to change any of his story now was the time. But Pedrotta replied that he had told the truth and without more ado he signed the document.

The CIC agents' manner now abruptly changed. In rapid succession they fired a stream of hostile and damaging questions at Pedrotta. They pressed him about discrepancies between his story and Picchetti's concerning their activities before arriving in Allied territory and their routes from enemy territory. They informed him that his identity card was false and the ink not more than three days old; that the 32,700 lire found in his possession were numbered in series; and that among his possessions they had found receipts from two bordellos which were places of entertainment reserved exclusively for German personnel or persons in the German service. They shook Pedrotta's confidence by addressing him by his various aliases and reminding him of the spy schools he had attended, the personalities he had met, the place he had been despatched from and the route he took. After an hour and a half of psychological bombardment, Pedrotta cracked. He blurted out that, yes, he *was* an espionage and sabotage agent in the employ of the GIS, and worked for secret organizations called Eins (c) and FIDE.

Eins (c) was a German organization interested primarily in Allied order of battle intelligence, while FIDE was an Abwehr sabotage section interested in military sabotage targets. Along with his three companions, Pedrotta had attended a GIS topography school at the Albergo Dolomite in Fai, then moved on to the GIS schools in Corredo, where they attended courses in order of battle intelligence, espionage and sabotage. The four men were then despatched to a GIS field post not far from Bagni di Lucca near the front, where they were briefed by their German despatching officer and assigned their targets. Pedrotto and Picchetti were given sabotage and espionage missions in the area south of San Marcello and told the location of an explosives cache near the town of Pontepetri. They were to select military targets of opportunity, and when the cache was empty they were to return to German territory, gathering political, economic and military intelligence on the way. The other two men had similar missions in the Piastre area. The whole operation was expected to last about seven weeks. Instead it lasted a single night and they were all arrested the next morning.

Armed with a full confession, the CIC agents soon broke down the third member of the group, Selmi Paradisi, an ill-educated 19-year-old from Bologna who had volunteered for the GIS after his father was injured in an American air raid on Bologna. Picchetti, too, confessed when he was confronted with the signed confessions of Pedrotto and Paradisi and other incriminating evidence. The fourth suspect, Lotario Billi, proved much harder to break down and for hours refused to deviate from his cover story or admit to any inconsistencies. But finally, after lengthy and intensive questioning, he gave way in the face of overwhelming evidence and confessed that he, too, was a secret agent on a mission for the GIS. In a model operation of its kind the CIC had thus disposed of a well-trained GIS group in little more than 24 hours.

It was, of course, rare to learn anything of what it was like to be on the receiving end of a CIC interrogation. But occasionally a glimpse was given. One of the defiant Fascist captives held in the cells of the 92nd CIC Detachment at Viareggio at the end of the winter was an unrepentant 23-year-old native of Messina named Francesco Mattei, who one dark night scrawled his bitter thoughts across a wooden panel in his cell:

> On this night I have written on six sheets of paper my statement concerning my confession, which was extorted from me by torture, lynching, hunger, lack of sleep: a true expression of 20th century civilization. These are the usual vicissitudes occurring to a defeated people. I too am a man defeated but not tamed. A lion that still roars until his last breath and I feel death still far, perhaps because I do not fear it . . .

The CIC dismissed Mattei's statement as 'unbridled lies and outright defamation' which they attributed to his emotional immaturity and ideological indoctrination. The man's defiance was indicative of the obstacles that lay in the way of CIC interrogators.

Most convicted spies were shot. This was the inexorable rule of the game. Only in especially extenuating circumstances was a lesser sentence passed down. From time to time Allied Headquarters made a great song and dance about death to spies and broadcast the facts about the toll of enemy agents who had paid the ultimate price for daring to wage a heinous and covert campaign against the Allied cause. Thus in September 1944 details were released of one particular trial in which one agent was sentenced to death and two others to 20-year terms of imprisonment. The execution of the condemned man was publicized in posters, with the facts of the case and a photograph, *pour encourager les autres*. Publicizing these dire tidings was among other things an inducement to other agents to co-operate once they had been captured, in the hope of receiving a penal rather than a capital sentence.

The last winter of the war in northern Italy was a dour time for friend and foe alike. As deep snow blanketed the Apennines and a still, icy silence settled over the mountainous countryside of Emilia, the great armies ground to a halt and remained huddled in their static positions along each side of the front line. This stalemate, with all its discomfort and frustration, spawned new problems for the CIC. The morale of the Italian civilians began to plunge. After the spectacular Allied advances of the autumn, the stalemate seemed to confirm Fascist rumours of impending Allied reverses and Mussolini's promise that Allied-occupied Italy's hour of liberation was near. Relations between troops and civilians deteriorated. The Italians now looked on the Allies as their providers rather than their protectors. Graffiti were scrawled in crayon and coal on the walls of the towns: *'Roosevelt, I tre etti di pane?'* (Roosevelt, where are the three hundred grams of bread?) and *'Basta cogli Americani!'* (Down with the Americans!) Resentment deepened when American soldiers began to succumb to the provocations of a certain kind of Italian girl. More graffiti were scrawled on more walls: 'Women, do not lend yourself to the game! Women, we repudiate you!' The problem of ferreting out Fascist elements and German agents in the face of these rumour and propaganda campaigns grew daily more complex.

Survival became an increasing preoccupation as the winter deepened – as much on account of the intense cold and snow as the risk of enemy action. CIC units took to taking over comfortable old abandoned farmhouses and winterizing them as a base of operations. One such was the CIC Detachment of the 91st Division. The Division was located high in the Apennine mountains outside the small town of Lioana, some 26 miles from the enemy-held town of Rimini. On the side of a mountain overlooking a broad valley CIC Agent Sampson W. Freestone and other members of the Detachment finally found what they had been looking for – an abandoned farmhouse where they could burrow down for the winter.

This venerable but dilapidated rural hideaway became the Detachment's pride and joy and the Agents spent many hours transforming it into a warm sanctuary for the icy months ahead. They boarded up the windows, braced the ceilings and replaced missing bricks with loving care, even pruned the trees in the garden outside. As far as they were concerned this was home, where they returned as often as they could after the daily rigours of the eternal struggle with the infernal agents of the GIS.

Then one day, when their labours were at last at an end and they were comfortably ensconced in their winter quarters, the CIC Agents spied a party of Allied soldiers enter the valley below. They were British artillerymen and they brought with them a single enormous gun – a huge brute of a cannon, with the longest barrel and the biggest calibre they had ever seen. Day by day they watched while the British soldiers, with infinite pains, poured the cement for the foundations, aligned the gun and rigged an iron railing round the catwalk. Freestone and the rest of the Agents felt proud that such good warriors and noble craftsmen were on their side. Finally they saw the supply lorries drive slowly away and they knew that the gun was ready.

In the early hours of the next morning, when the mountain was still plunged in the darkness of a midwinter night, and the snow lay frozen all about, and no living thing stirred for miles around, the CIC Agents, ever alert and vigilant, were wakened by the steady tread of a pair of boots crunching through the snow outside, and the firm knock of a fist on their farmhouse door. A British sergeant stood there, well wrapped and balaclava-ed against the intense cold.

'Beg pardon, gents,' said the British sergeant, 'for waking you up a bit on the early side, like. But I thought you'd like to know we're going to fire the gun.'

'What!' exclaimed Agent Freestone. 'At this time of night?'

'Catch Jerry napping in Rimini,' explained the sergeant. 'With his pants down, if you see what I mean.'

The CIC Agents thanked the British sergeant for his courtesy in letting them know what was happening, and were about to stumble back to their beds when the sergeant added: 'Beg pardon, gents, but I'll have to ask you to leave the house. For safety's sake, like, when the gun goes off.'

'But good grief, man,' shouted Sam Freestone, 'the damn thing's about two miles down the valley!'

'That may well be,' replied the sergeant, 'but I've seen a lot of funny things happen when that gun goes off. Better do what I say, there's a good lad.'

The sergeant remained adamant that they should leave the house, and more to humour him than for any other reason the CIC Agents trooped out into the icy snow and dark.

Within a minute or two they heard a mighty roar reverberate from the valley below and the eerie gobbling sound of a gigantic shell as it flew invisibly through the darkness towards the sleeping Germans of Rimini. Then the CIC Agents were battered by another stupendous roar, felt shock waves through the air and vibrations through the ground beneath their feet, and then heard a different kind of sound, nearer to hand and ominously structural in nature. They turned in time to see the boards drop off the windows of their beloved farmhouse one by one, and the chimney wobble and then fall, and the side of the building crack open. Before their very eyes, slowly at first but with increasing rapidity, their home disintegrated under the blast of the mighty British cannon. Transfixed with horror and dismay, the CIC Agents watched the door spring open and the tiles cascade from the roof. And as one man they turned to the British sergeant.

In the interests of inter-Allied harmony, Sam Freestone was to recall later, it was just as well that the sergeant was already on his way back to his unit and therefore unable to hear the endearments pointedly thrown in his direction. 'Rimini was 26 miles away,' Freestone recalled, 'and we had to pick a house directly in its path!'

So Christmas came to this frozen and torpid front, and then the New Year, and the Abwehr continued to fling its agents like kamikaze at the Allied lines, and the CIC continued to block and parry and pounce on them at a rate that must have struck fear and dismay into the heart of the German Intelligence Service. Portents of despair appeared when a new form of courier was caught making through the lines – a Nazi carrier pigeon from San Donino in German-occupied territory, one of a forward echelon that included eight other birds, apprehended *en route* to Modena in Allied-occupied territory with a pigeongram attached to one leg. 'Some concern was voiced at CIC Headquarters,' it was reported later, 'as to the designation of the solitary captive. Since he had crossed Allied lines, he was technically an enemy agent, but having wandered off course he seemed entitled to the rights and privileges of a prisoner-of-war. CIC agents were mindful of future attempts to transmit messages by these airborne carriers and all Fifth Army detachments were alerted to investigate cases of captured pigeons.'

By now the CIC were arresting and convicting an average of 15 to 20 German agents a week – a phenomenal record. By the time the spring offensive finally ended the static situation on the northern Italian front in April, more than 200 trained enemy espionage and sabotage agents had been captured in Fifth Army areas in the period between October 1944 and April 1945, a final average of more than one a day. The effectiveness of CIC work during this period became evident during the subsequent interrogation of 'Dr Kora', the German officer in charge of Abwehr Kommando 190, which ran large numbers of espionage agents into the Fifth Army area. According to Dr Kora, not a single one of his agents had returned between October 1944 and January 1945. Again, by the end of November 1944 all 15 trainees on an Abwehr course held near Como in October had been captured. The few successes achieved by the front agents of the GIS were thus purchased at a terrible price, for most agents captured by the Allies paid the traditional penalty meted out to spies.

The success of Allied counter intelligence on such a scale was the result of co-ordinated action and co-operation not only by Corps,

Division and Army CIC, but also by British and Dominion military security and Brazilian counter intelligence personnel from the Brazilian Expeditionary Force. Of the agents captured by US Detachments, however, the great majority were caught by either the 92nd Division CIC, IV Corps CIC or Fifth Army CIC. The 92nd CIC Detachment alone had been responsible for a total of 23,000 interrogations and the uncovering and convicting of 102 enemy agents – a remarkable record for a Detachment that had never been activated by the War Department and never found a place in official Army files. However, the CIC's impressive work with Fifth Army, which resulted in the apprehension of a total of some 500 enemy agents, did not pass unnoticed. When Lieutenant General Mark Clark finally left Fifth Army to command Fifteenth Army Group, he turned to Lieutenant Colonel Spingarn, the commanding officer of the Fifth Army CIC, and said: 'Spingarn, the CIC has done a grand job – outstanding. It has been a great help to the Fifth Army.'

But the 'job' was only part of the story. As the CIC recorded later: 'Etched deeply in the memory of each CIC agent were the little unimportant incidents which assumed such stature during the time between the Salerno landings and the spring victory in the foothills of the Alps. Histories could tell, but never recreate, the hell of Salerno and Anzio; the beauty of Rome; the bitterness of the Apennine winter; the sight of thousands of barefoot, dirt-encrusted children; the brief glints of comedy that sometimes spotted the tragic gloom of war. But in the minds of each agent were thoughts that no official records contain and no history can accurately relate.'

8

THE TROJAN HORSE

Along the Western Front the momentum of the Allied advance began to falter. German resistance had stiffened as the Allies drew near to the so-called West Wall that formed the Third Reich's outer line of defence beyond the Rhine; and the extraordinary speed of the advance through France had caused the Allies to outrun their supplies, so that one by one the lead formations came to a halt, gasping for shells, rations and gasoline. A brilliant attempt to turn the northern flank of the German lines came to a bloody end in late September with the bitter but heroic defeat of British paratroopers at Arnhem, and it became clear to the Allied commanders that there would be no easy end to this war in 1944.

Then the weather turned and the days began to shorten. Autumn brought rain and mud churned up by the tank tracks; at the first breath of winter, snow fell on the high ground in the Ardennes and the Eifel Hills, and the water froze in the radiators of the trucks, and the breath of the infantrymen panting along the roads that led eastward to the Rhine turned to vapour as thick as tobacco smoke in the icy air. This was the first North European winter the American soldiers had ever seen. It was not all that unlike winter in the northern States, but there were certain essential differences: there were no Panzers or Waffen SS in Vermont or Maine, and nowhere near so much sudden death, or even not-so-sudden death; and the people were different, of course, especially the girls, for never was a man more honoured or desired than a liberating soldier in a liberated town. 'I loved all the girls I met while living in those countries,' recalled CIC Agent Edward Koudelka. 'I could have made a proposal of marriage, but I had made a pact with myself that I would not do this, no matter how compelling the situation, because there was no assurance as to how long the war would last, or even if I would survive.' These doubts and reservations were very sensible and proper, especially in view of what was soon to happen in the centre of the Allied front as Christmas drew near.

The seizure of the port of Antwerp in late November greatly eased Eisenhower's problems of supply and the Allied drive to the Rhine was stepped up with renewed vigour. The First and Ninth US Armies had already resumed their eastward push in the region of Aachen, the first German city to be occupied by the Allies, and in bloody fighting American troops battled their way forward into the Hürtgen Forest and on 3 December reached the River Roer. Farther south the Third Army crossed the German frontier, reached the Siegfried Line near Saarlautern and captured Metz on 13 December; while in their advance through Alsace the Seventh Army had already taken Strasbourg on 23 November. Everywhere as the armies moved forward towards and into German territory the CIC clucked and fussed around and about them like mother hens in jeeps: academics, journalists, linguists whose careers had taken a peculiar turn on account of Hitler and the war and all these great historic events – one damned historic event after another. Thanks to their tireless vigil the great land armada remained intact and unsuborned; spies and saboteurs were intercepted, collaborators and subversives hunted down and rounded up, whole cities like Aachen and Strasbourg reduced with methodical, clinical precision by special 'T' Forces backed by the CIC.

Fortune indeed seemed to smile on the Americans and their Allies as the eventful year drew to its close. On 16 December Montgomery sent Eisenhower a letter reminding him of his bet that the war would be over by Christmas. Eisenhower replied that he would pay up on Christmas Day but not before. 'After all,' he wrote to the British general, 'I still have nine days left.' During those nine days the Allied armies were to be confronted with the greatest crisis they had faced since the black days of 1940, and the victory which had seemed so near was to recede into the fog and blizzards of winter in the Ardennes. During this period of grave military crisis the CIC were to grapple with the severest counter intelligence challenge in their history.

It was a challenge that took a most unusual – though perhaps not entirely unexpected – form. As early as August 1944 the CIC headquarter detachments had begun to issue warnings about the danger posed by German soldiers masquerading as American soldiers by dressing themselves in bits and pieces of American uniforms taken from dead or captured Americans and driving about the front in captured US Army jeeps. As far as the CIC could ascertain, such ruses were not part of any overall master plan, but simply the products of individual initiative carried out on a small scale, and since the incidents were scattered and few in number not much importance was attached to them. In November it was discovered that the Intelligence Officer of the 37th Panzer Grenadier Regiment had been sending English-speaking Germans on long-range reconnaissance patrols to gain US order of battle information; one such patrol admitted after capture that their mission had been to remain behind Allied lines for four days acquiring specific information by tapping military telephone lines. Later in the month, however, a report of a much more serious incident reached Sixth Army Group CIC. It seemed that a company of the 15th Engineers had been attacked by a force of some 70 German soldiers dressed in US Army raincoats and helmets and shouting 'GI!' In the middle of the month another report came through. A German prisoner-of-war stated under questioning that he had seen a secret order for all captured American uniforms and all English-speaking personnel to be sent to Osnabrück, where special training in reconnaissance, sabotage and espionage would be given. Something was happening – but what?

In the preceding month Obersturmbannführer Otto Skorzeny, Chief of the German sabotage arm of the SS Jagdverbände, was summoned to the Führer's Headquarters in Berlin to discuss a very important matter. Skorzeny was an outstanding expert in commando operations and irregular warfare, and a legendary figure in Germany since his boldly brilliant rescue of Mussolini from captivity in the Alps in September 1943. Hitler was himself one of the many admirers of Skorzeny's extraordinary special aptitudes, and with the help of General Jodl, Chief of the German Armed Forces Operations Staff, outlined to him his plans for a massive German offensive against American forces in the Ardennes with the object of driving a wedge through the Allied front to Antwerp and the North Sea. In this war-winning onslaught by a huge force of three German armies, two of them Panzers, Skorzeny learned that he was to play a critical part, the broad specifications of which were listed by Jodl at this initial meeting in Hitler's Berlin bunker.

The plan required a commando operation utilizing some 3000 German soldiers in a special Brigade designated the 150th Panzers (or so-called 'Trojan Horse'). The essential distinction of Skorzeny's special force was that some of its members should be able to pass themselves off as authentic US troops and make use of this deception in order to achieve certain vital objectives which could not easily be achieved in any other way. Some of these objectives were breathtaking by any standards. In a nutshell the overall mission of the Brigade was to infiltrate the American sector of the Ardennes battle front, create confusion in the path of the attacking German armies, and secure crucial bridges over the River Meuse along the line of the main thrust towards Antwerp and the North Sea. Confusion is perhaps a rather limp word for some of the operations Skorzeny's unusual organization planned to carry out. At a relatively elementary level they were to create confusion by occupying and obstructing roads and bridges, altering or removing road signs, using fake MPs to misdirect American military traffic, and infiltrate and ambush American units. One combat group was to latch itself to the rear of an American column and at a predetermined point branch off and move to stronghold targets which included not simply ammunition dumps and radio stations but higher US Army Headquarters as well. More than that, a few specialist groups were to travel all the way to Paris, where they were to penetrate SHAEF Headquarters and assassinate the Supreme Allied Commander, General Dwight D. Eisenhower himself – or so it was claimed.

Recruitment for Skorzeny's special American commando began at once. English-speaking officers and enlisted men who knew 'the American dialect' were culled from all corners of the shrinking Nazi Empire and told to report to Skorzeny's headquarters at Schloss Friedenthal, near Oranienburg, a suburb of Berlin. The men had to be physically fit, mentally alert, competent in close combat fighting, and suitable for special assignments. Some were volunteers, some were ordered to volunteer, all were rigorously tested for fluency in English by a board of three officers from the SS and German Navy. The most fluent were assigned to a segment of the commando known as the Einheit Stielau, so named after the group's commander, Lieutenant Stielau, and sent initially to the SS Interpreters' School in Oranienburg. Lesser linguists were despatched to American prisoner-of-war camps, where they associated with genuine American prisoners in order to familiarize themselves with current GI speech idioms and slang and with peculiarly American mannerisms, such as the American way of opening a packet of cigarettes, or using a knife and fork at mealtimes, or carrying a towel over one shoulder while washing. Subsequently all members of the Brigade were reunited at a special training camp at Grafenwoehr, where they were saturated in the American way of life. Cinema newsreels and Hollywood motion pictures like *Coney Island*, starring Betty Grable, were screened as training aids. A US Army manual was required study, and US military terminology, organization, identification, vehicle markings and close order drill were the staples of daily instruction. Specialized combat training was also part of the course, with emphasis on compass and orientation training, street and forest fighting (especially under night conditions), liaison and reconnaissance duties with tank units, use of close combat anti-tank weapons, firing of American weapons and practice with a plastic sabotage explosive called Nipolit.

Conditions for these men were sumptuous – just as they were for Japanese kamikaze pilots in another theatre of the war. The food was the best that could be provided in wartime Germany. The most efficacious medicines were lavishly prescribed to prevent winter colds and flus. But security arrangements were stringent. Once a man had entered the camp he could not leave it or communicate with anyone outside. The penalty for some of those who attempted to violate this decree was death or imprisonment. One soldier who was charged with a breach of security hanged himself. Three Dutch truck drivers who had delivered equipment to the camp were detained from leaving to prevent any leak of information.

In mid-November, when training was well advanced, the members of the special commando were briefed for the first time on the spectacular but near suicidal nature of their mission. Their morale plummeted when they learned what was expected of them. It plummeted even lower when, almost as a vote of no-confidence in the outcome, they were issued with hydrocyanic ampules with which to kill themselves when they were captured.

While the men were being prepared for their rôle in the forthcoming battle, the necessary American matériel was being collected together from dead, wounded or captured American soldiers, and from the litter of armed skirmishes and engagements along the front. Newly captured GIs arriving at prison camps in Germany were ordered to hand over their uniforms; some refused, preferring to desecrate them by burning or tearing them, so that in one case only 12 uniforms out of a batch of 800 were still serviceable. Red Cross contributions, including US Army clothing and new field boots intended for American POWs, were intercepted and confiscated. Adolescent fanatics of the Hitler Youth were recruited to scour the battlefields for US Army grenades, small-calibre ammunition, bayonets and other items of equipment. Even personal papers and army dog tags were taken from prisoners or dead American soldiers. Eventually almost every member of the commando was fully kitted out as an American soldier, from steel helmet down to stolen boots.

By December the commando also possessed a useful inventory of US Army machine-guns, carbines, jeeps, trucks and Sherman tanks. The white star of liberation, worn by all vehicles in the Allied armies, was prominent on those now pressed into the service of Skorzeny's force, as were counterfeit unit identification markings. Each vehicle carried army trip tickets, and watermarks on transport documents were faked with a wax stamp.

The Einheit Stielau teams were the most lavishly equipped. In addition to weapons, vehicles and documents, they were issued with $100 in various denominations of occupation currency and 100 counterfeit British one pound notes. Each team was also provided with ten energy-boosting tablets called 'Pervitin', various silent combat weapons like blackjacks, knuckle-dusters and coshes, a copy of the New Testament and American song books. As we have seen, vials of hydrocyanic acid were freely available and a chosen few were also provided with poison cartridges manufactured at Skorzeny's request by the Technical Criminal Institute of Berlin. The poison was aconite compound, encased in the head of a 7.65 mm pistol bullet. This had split sides, through which the poison could escape, thus ensuring the death of the victim.

Though Skorzeny was unquestionably the dominating spirit of the 150th Panzer Brigade, it was officially under the command of SS Lieutenant Colonel Hardieck. Its 3000 officers and men were divided into three Combat Groups containing various specialist combat elements, including tank, anti-tank, paratroop, mortar, machine-gun, engineer and other units. The first two Combat Groups contained the Einheit Stielau jeep teams, which were themselves divided according to their specialities – reconnaissance, sabotage, assassination and signals. In readiness for Hitler's great Ardennes offensive, the Brigade was now moved from Grafenwoehr to Cologne in a special train guarded by Gestapo and camouflaged to resemble a shipment of Christmas trees. Travelling only at night so as to evade detection by Allied reconnaissance planes, it took the Brigade two days to reach Cologne, where they detrained on the night of 14–15 December. On the following night, under strict black-out restrictions, a large part of the Brigade moved on to Munstereifel, while the rest bivouacked at Stadtkyll. Here the men of the special commando learned the fantastic plan for Operation Greif (meaning 'Grab'). Part of the operational orders read as follows:

Operation Greif will be made by our forces using American equipment, American weapons, American vehicles, and American insignia – in particular the five-pointed white or yellow star painted on the vehicles.

To avoid confusion with enemy troops, the forces employed in Operation Greif will identify themselves to our troops during the day by taking off their helmets, and by night by red-blue light signals from flashlights.

Forces of Operation Greif will also identify themselves to

friendly troops by painting white dots on houses, trees and roads used by them.

It was obvious that if such identification techniques became known to real Americans, the fate of many un-real ones would be swiftly sealed. Be that as it may, the start of the main German offensive in the Ardennes – soon to be known as the Battle of the Bulge – took the Allies completely off-balance. At dawn on 16 December – the very same day that Montgomery had reminded Eisenhower about his bet, and a day of exceptionally thick fog, both actual and metaphorical – Dietrich's Sixth SS Panzer Army, Manteuffel's Fifth Panzer Army and Brandenberger's Seventh Army suddenly struck in a hitherto dormant 100-mile sector of the front – the rugged, forested hills of eastern Belgium known as the Ardennes.

The Germans struck with tremendous weight and ferocity amid total surprise. The CIC were no more prepared for this bolt from the blue than the rest of the American Army. When the clenched fist of the German armies emerged from the mist and landed on the exposed chin of the US VIII Corps, the divisions that bore the brunt of the assault reeled under the impact, and several CIC detachments were overrun in the swift German advance along with everyone else. At St Vith eight agents of the 99th CIC were abruptly woken from their dreams on the morning of 17 December by the sound of burp guns and the sight of an endless column of German tanks rumbling past the house in which they were quartered. The CIC agents held their breaths when one of the lead tanks poked the muzzle of its 88 mm gun into a window, then made a dash for freedom through the back door under heavy German fire. Scampering from shell hole to gun emplacement hole some of them were able to escape to safety. But four of them – the CO, Howard Stephens, and agents Francis Cody, Vic Gordin and Charles Sloan, were pinned down by small arms fire in one of the shell holes and then hit by mortar bursts. Gordin was able to find medics to take care of Cody, who was badly wounded, but Stephens and Sloan were killed instantly.

Elsewhere other CIC detachments found themselves swept up in the bloody business of front-line fighting, trying to bear the double burden of counter intelligence duties while shooting it out shoulder to shoulder with their own combat infantry. In this way part of the 418th CIC under Kenneth Hardin found themselves fighting off an invading force of German parachutists that dropped on Bardenburg on the first night of the offensive and attacked installations in the town itself as daylight broke. Directing and participating in the skirmish that ensued, Hardin and his men were instrumental in rounding up 23 German paratroops and more than 30 German soldiers in civilian clothes. Under such circumstances, normal counter intelligence was a lesser priority. In Liège, at the very moment that German armour was pouring through the Ardennes in the direction of that city, CIC agents found 250 of the local Communists in the Cinéma Carrefour blindly hatching yet another plan to overthrow the provisional government of Belgium by means of yet another propaganda leaflet campaign. Because of the imminence of the impending battle there was little the CIC agents could do about it except make a note about 'this continuing Communist subversion', then duck out into the streets, where the sounds of advancing Nazi gunfire could be plainly heard in the distant hills.

By the afternoon of 17 December the Germans had committed 14 divisions to the battle. Realizing that he was faced not with a limited counter-attack but a full-blown counter-offensive, Eisenhower ordered the battle-hardened 101st Airborne Division to race to Bastogne, in the centre of the Ardennes front, and the Third Army to break off its attack in the Saar and carry out a highly complicated change of direction by wheeling left in support of the 101st at Bastogne. American units from Third Army and reserve areas manoeuvred to stem the enemy drive and stiffen the weakened American front-line forces. On the American northern flank First Army managed to block the main German thrust, but in the centre the 28th and 106th Infantry divisions sustained heavy losses and by the end of the second day of the onslaught were completely routed.

One of the Americans caught up in the rout was William F. Loebl, a prisoner-of-war interrogator well known to his CIC colleagues. After pulling back to Bastogne, Loebl's unit moved farther back to Sibret, where they holed up in the local police station with some of their prisoners.

Here events got really desperate [he remembers]. We had lost most of our infantry and we were defending Division HQ with 155mm howitzers and every able-bodied man we could find – cooks, postal clerks, bandsmen, everything. During the night of December 22, the police station was attacked by elements of the 5th German Parachute Division. I know, because I got into a hand-to-hand fight with one of them. That's when I got a grenade splinter in my arm. Two months later I got the Purple Heart through the mail. We lost the police station and we also lost our commanding officer, who was captured while trying to start the jeep in the yard of the police station. On Christmas Day we were taken to a school building in Neufchâteau, where we were to receive our first hot meal in some time. Shortly before noon, I was sitting on the can, and the next thing I knew I was sitting next to it. Then I heard the unfamiliar whine of a jet engine. An ME 262 had dropped a bomb in the schoolyard and the concussion had de-throned me. It also broke all the windows in the kitchen and our hot meal had to be thrown away because it was full of broken glass.

That last Christmas of the war, in the midst of that desperate and savage conflict in the Bulge, produced very different memories for one CIC agent who was there. Nelson Dungan recalls:

We were at Niederbronn les Bains, Alsace. The German army was a few miles away over the hill, engaged in a bitter battle with our army around Bastogne. At about 10.30 pm we all went to the local cathedral, a large and beautiful building. It was very dimly lighted because of the proximity of the German army. This seemed to give the church a magical glow. Soon our soldiers started to come in. They had their weapons with them and were ready for anything. Finally, the church was packed to the doors with combat-ready soldiers. What a sight! It was the most impressive service I have ever attended. Little did we think that less than two weeks later the German army would occupy the town and that German soldiers would be sitting in these same pews. The only thing that could have made that service more complete would have been the suspension of the war for the night and their presence at that service.

As early as possible on Christmas Day, Jim Elliott and I returned to our post at Seltz. Our hosts, who lived on the west bank of the Rhine in Alsace, prepared a wonderful Christmas dinner for themselves and us. It was not army food but all their own from their own meagre rations. They had a large flat bowl into which they poured some schnapps and put a few lumps of their precious sugar. After the sugar had absorbed the alcohol it was ignited. It burned with a soft flame that could barely be seen. Remember, this was in view of the German soldiers. There was nothing but a few trees between us. We each had a bit of the schnapps and after touching glasses we sang 'Silent Night', they in German and we in English. A moment of peace in the storm.

With Allied air cover grounded by continuous low cloud cover in the wintry weather of the Belgian hills, the Germans pushed forward in strength, and by 19 December an SS Panzer spearhead commanded by a brilliant and ruthless young colonel called Joachim Peiper, later to be branded a war criminal, had driven a wedge – the bulge from which the battle got its name – so deep into Bradley's Twelfth Army Group that they had split the American forces in two and threatened to break through to the plains and the sea beyond. As one CIC agent put it at the time: 'The Germans had burst through the lines and nothing but Red Cross girls and postal clerks stood between them and the Atlantic.' The Americans reeled back or valiantly stood their ground and took heavier casualties than at any time in the European campaign since the D-Day landings at Omaha beach. Their military commanders and the public at home held their breaths and crossed their hearts.

Skorzeny's so-called 'Trojan Horse' Brigade was scheduled to attack with the Sixth SS Panzer Army, racing through the American line at Stavelot to seize the Meuse bridges. It must be said that Skorzeny's activities were not entirely unexpected by CIC units in the Ardennes. More than a month previously two captured German documents had indicated that a special unit about two battalions strong had been formed for deployment on the Western Front using captured weapons and equipment. But, far more importantly, at the very beginning of the German assault secret orders outlining the plan for Operation Greif were found by troops of the 106th Infantry Division on the body of a German officer of the 116th Panzer Division, who had carried them into the front line in spite of a directive that below divisional level they were only to be transmitted verbally. Till now, higher echelons of US Intelligence had been sceptical of CIC reports about German deception operations. Now they were spelled out in clear; and as reports of the activities of the 150th Panzers came in it was plain that the Army was faced with a counter intelligence emergency of an importance and magnitude without precedent in any combat zone of the European war.

In the first two nights of the German counter-offensive some 40 of Skorzeny's jeep teams slipped through the disintegrating American lines, cutting telephone wires, shooting up radio stations, intercepting despatch riders and liaison officers, killing MPs, misdirecting army convoys, and blocking key roads with white tape to signify minefields ahead. One of the jeep teams actually reached the Meuse. A few of them managed to get back to their own lines. A number were captured. The psychological damage they inflicted was probably greater than the material damage. In the chaotic atmosphere of incredulity and near-panic that prevailed in some Allied quarters, the activities of Skorzeny's men gave rise to rumours of all kinds and greatly inflamed the uncertainty and confusion that prevailed. The aggressive intelligence and sabotage activities of Skorzeny's deception units called for the speediest possible mobilization of all available counter intelligence personnel to protect the security of the American front. Guards would have to be reinforced at all bridges and vital installations; counter intelligence control lines would have to be posted along all roads on the east side of the River Meuse; checking of identity documents and screening of refugees and displaced persons would have to be intensified; there could be no mistake, no chink in the security screen. Even General Patton's Third Army, which like its commander tended to do things its own way and never paid much attention to CIC warnings, began to tighten its own travel and security controls. And then, on the third day of the battle, the first Einheit Stielau Americans fell into the CIC net.

On the third day of the Battle of the Bulge, 18 December 1944, an American jeep containing three men in US Army uniforms was waved down by MPs in the First Army area and taken for questioning when they were unable to produce the necessary password. It was very soon apparent that there were a number of things wrong about these three soldiers. Though they were dressed in US Army uniforms, none of them wore field jackets and only one wore a regulation belt. Their military identification papers were reasonably complete, except that they had no personal papers. They carried US Army rations, two portable radios, .45 calibre pistols, British Sten guns and American ammunition. What damned them were the German Walther pistol and German Army grenades they had in the jeep, and above all the *Soldbuchs* (German Army pay and record books) which, unbelievably, they were carrying on their persons at the time of arrest. The *Soldbuchs* revealed the three men to be Officer Cadet Günther Billing, Corporal Wilhelm Schmidt and Private First Class Manfred Pernass. They had managed to operate for just 30 minutes behind American lines before their arrest. Five days later, after being tried as spies before a military court, all three were executed by firing squad.

The news of the capture of the first Einheit Stielau team was widely publicized and all Allied troops were alerted to any slight irregularities in dress, equipment, behaviour or attitude among soldiers held at road-blocks or check-points. MPs and CIC teams became experts in the most recherché nooks and niches of contemporary American culture. Skorzeny spies were found to be unfamiliar with jitterbug terms like 'rugcutter', 'jive' and 'corny'. Nor had many of them heard of current American comic strip characters such as Dagwood Bumstead, the name of Mickey Mouse's girlfriend or L'il

Abner's home town. One agent who spoke perfect American slang did not appear to know that the Browns and the Cardinals were the only big-league baseball clubs in St Louis. The problem was that neither did quite a few American officers, and for a while CIC offices were constantly cluttered with genuine colonels who had been arrested at road-blocks because of their deeply sinister ignorance of football, swing or boogie, or because they had not given a satisfactory or sufficiently courteous answer when asked by MPs whether Frank Sinatra 'sent' them. One Brigadier General was held prisoner for five hours because he told MPs that the Chicago Cubs were in the American League. The Commander of the Twelfth Army Group, General Omar Bradley, was stopped and questioned three times, finally admitting defeat when he was unable to identify Betty Grable's latest husband as bandleader Harry James.

But the extreme caution soon paid off. Only a day after the arrest of the first of Skorzeny's teams, a second team was captured in the First Army area. At a little before midnight on 19 December an MP stopped an American jeep at a control point near a large bridge over the Meuse. In the presence of agents of the 301st CIC the MP challenged the occupants of the jeep. Asked for the password, the men in the jeep replied 'Stamp', which was correct. But when the MP asked for the vehicle's trip ticket, he was handed a blank one. This aroused his suspicion. While he warily watched the passengers, the CIC agents searched the jeep. It was evident that the vehicle had been freshly painted and that the unit identification markings had been applied very crudely. Inside the jeep they found weapons and explosives. They also found that beneath their jackets the men were wearing swastika arm bands, which were evidently meant to identify the team when they returned to the German lines. The leader of this Einheit Stielau team was named as Lieutenant Guenther Schulz, and the other members as Lieutenant Karl Heinz Weisenfeld, Sergeant Manfred Browny and Lance-Corporal Hans Reich.

At First Army Interrogation Center CIC investigators and other specialists began a lengthy questioning of the four Germans. Lieutenant Schulz was highly communicative and readily outlined the objectives of the Skorzeny organization and the tactics used to achieve them. The main effort of the German drive, he said, was towards the River Meuse between Namur and Liège. A paratroop regiment was scheduled to drop in the vicinity of Liège in support of SS columns advancing on the city. A special force of the 150th Panzer Brigade, consisting of 70 tanks, some American and others camouflaged to resemble American armour, had the mission of exploiting the German breakthrough and seizing and holding three bridges over the Meuse till the arrival of two SS Panzer divisions. The tanks moved only at night; in the daytime they hid in the woods while teams of English-speaking soldiers reconnoitred American positions for an attack the following afternoon. Schulz's own team was on the way to reconnoitre various bridges over the Meuse when they were captured; the tanks would still be waiting for their report.

All this was reasonable enough. What really had the interrogators jumping out of their chairs was a casual statment made by Schulz concerning a separate mission Skorzeny had been given in December. According to Schulz, he had learnt from SS Lieutenant Colonel Hardieck that at an officer meeting early that month Skorzeny had been directed to form a special group of between 50 and 60 men – Schulz rattled off their names – most of them attired in American uniforms, but some of them pretending to be high-ranking captured German officers. This group was to make its way through France to Paris in jeeps, staff cars and civilian cars, and rendezvous at the Café de la Paix or the Café de l'Épée, where they would join forces with French collaborators and exchange information and instructions. They would then carry out the final part of their plan, which was to enter SHAEF Headquarters in the Palace of Versailles outside Paris and assassinate the Supreme Allied Commander, General Eisenhower, and all his high-ranking Staff, including General Montgomery and General Bradley.

To those who had heard the name of Skorzeny before – and by December 1944 very few people in Allied counter intelligence would not have heard it – this fantastic scheme would have seemed totally credible. This tall, scar-faced Austrian had not only engineered the spectacular rescue of Mussolini; he had also carried out the kidnapping of Admiral Horthy of Hungary; and, as reprisal for war plants destroyed by resistance groups in France and Denmark, masterminded the sabotage of countless factories producing consumer goods for civilians in those countries. Though his successes were relatively few, and his failures relatively many, everything he did he did with dash and panache, and he was believed capable of any undertaking, no matter how unorthodox or unethical, so that he quickly rose through the Nazi hierarchy until by December 1944 he was in sufficient esteem to report directly to SS Reichsführer Himmler himself.

In any event, few revelations in World War Two produced such instantaneous repercussions as this one. Forty-three road blocks were at once set up to obstruct mobile traffic and innumerable check-points were established to monitor the movements of the civilian population. In Paris the news was brought to Eisenhower by a very agitated American colonel who was certain he had 'complete and positive proof' of the murder plot. 'He outlined it in great detail,' Eisenhower was to write later, 'and his conclusions were supported by other members of the Security Staff. I was irritated at the insistence of the Security Corps that I circumscribe my freedom of movement, but I found that unless I conformed reasonably to their desires they merely used more men for protective measures.' Eisenhower had been living in von Rundstedt's former house in St Germain, but at the CIC's insistence he now moved his quarters closer to his office at Supreme Headquarters in Versailles. There-after Lieutenant Colonel Baldwin B. Smith, who bore a remarkable resemblance to General Eisenhower, went about as the Supreme Commander's double or stand-in, riding from the General's erst-while residence in St Germain to his office at SHAEF each morning and returning each evening. At the same time the proposed meeting places of the would-be assassins in the centre of Paris were kept under continuous surveillance by the CIC. Until the outcome of the Battle of the Bulge was decided there was never any reason to believe that the assassination was not an enemy intention or capability, and the CIC continued to gather information about it from captured agents in the Ardennes.

By 20 December there was evidence of increased activity by Einheit Stielau units. Near Stavelot two German jeep teams were spotted on the German side of the front line by troops of the 99th Infantry Division and shot to pieces. Further indications that Skorzeny's force was operating in forward areas came with the capture of three members, only one of whom – Alfred Franz, alias US Army Corporal Ted Darland – was wearing American uniform. Franz and his two companions were tried by the US Military Commission; Franz, as the only one in American uniform, was found guilty and sentenced to death; the others were acquitted and evacuated as prisoners-of-war.

On 21 December, the sixth day of the battle and the day General Patton committed his Third Army to attack the Bulge in the direction of Bastogne, the 150th Panzer Brigade undertook its first and last operation as an entity. The plan was for two of the Brigade's Combat Groups to strike in the Malmédy area with jeep teams at their head. Several of these teams were to overrun an important American road-block on the road to Malmédy by pretending to be part of an American army unit which had been cut off, thereby permitting the rest of the Combat Group to take the objective. Only three miles out from Lingueville, however, they entered a minefield, and as they halted they came under concentrated American small

arms and artillery fire which destroyed most of their precious
American vehicles, including all their tanks, and inflicted heavy
casualties on the Group's personnel. A number of Germans were
taken prisoner and handed over to the CIC for interrogation. Again
the CIC probed for further information about the Eisenhower
assassination plan. Lance Corporal Otto Struller, an ex-ballet dancer
who had danced on the New York stage before the war – his US Army
papers gave his name as Captain Cecil Dryer but idiotically his dog
tags had him labelled as Private Richard Bumbgardner – admitted he
had heard of Skorzeny's assassination mission and claimed that it was
already under way. Joseph Kania, a member of Einheit Stielau, also
claimed information on the Skorzeny mission. While most reports
suggested that Skorzeny was already *en route* to Paris, a later one
claimed that he had been detained in Lingueville and was recuperat-
ing in the Hôtel Moulin after being slightly wounded by shrapnel
near the right eye.

The plot thickened somewhat when seven soldiers of the Skorzeny force, captured on 23 December when they were prowling
about in American uniforms behind the American lines near
Geromont, divulged further details to interrogators of the 301st
CIC. According to them, an assassination squad equipped with
specially manufactured poisoned ammunition and a plastic explosive
called Nipolit was to be dropped by parachute near Paris. Some
credence was given to this twist in the plot, since unconfirmed
reports had already been received of parachutists landing near Paris
on 20 December, three days previously.

What was the truth about this bizarre, even preposterous plot? By
Christmas most counter intelligence specialists were growing increasingly sceptical of the assassination threat. Nevertheless counter
intelligence measures designed to protect key commanders remained
in effect. General Bradley, commanding Twelfth Army Group,
complained that he was hidden under 'an elaborate security wrap'
and his personal plane, a C-47, had been removed from Luxembourg
airport to a night fighter base. As for Eisenhower, the main target of
the supposed plot, he was even more restless under CIC security guard. In a diary entry for 23 December, Eisenhower's naval
aide, Commander Harry C. Butcher, described the Supreme
Commander's discomfiture:

> I went out to Versailles and saw Ike today. He is a prisoner of our
> security police and is thoroughly but helplessly irritated by the
> restriction on his moves. There are all sorts of guards, some with
> machine-guns around the house, and he has to travel to and from

his office led and at times followed by an armed guard in a jeep. He got some satisfaction yesterday in slipping out for a walk around the yard in deep snow, in the eyes of the security officers quite the most dangerous thing for him to do. I told him he now knows how it must feel to be President and be guarded day and night by ever-watchful secret service men. Our security officers are always supercautious, and with this alarming information [about the Skorzeny assassination mission] I can readily understand why they have thrown a cordon around the Supreme Commander, yet he is thoroughly disgusted at the whole procedure and seemed pleased to have someone to talk to like me, seemingly from the outside world. Ike's office was serene. Outside, through the high French windows, the snow was falling, and the setting seemed appropriate for the approaching Christmas.

Not even lesser mortals at Supreme Headquarters escaped the tight security net thrown round Paris at the CIC's insistence. On Christmas Eve T.J. (an unidentified staff officer) was being driven from Versailles to his quarters when the driver of his staff car, a Corporal Conrad, was stopped at a road block by MPs.

'Which state are you from?' an MP asked Conrad.

'Missouri.'

'What's the capital?'

'St Louis.'

'OK,' said the MP. 'Drive on.'

Otto Skorzeny, who survived the war, never formally admitted the existence of any plot to kill Eisenhower. To have carried it through, he later claimed in his memoirs, would have been a 'frightful crime'. Though such an operation might conceivably have been feasible, and certainly helpful from the German point of view, it is more likely that the entire business was simply another exercise in deception, and that the mere threat of an assassination attempt, spread about as rumours by the men of Einheit Stielau, was calculated to cause sufficient fear and confusion in the Allied high command to justify the negligible effort it required of Skorzeny's organization. However, it is interesting to note that some weeks after the scare had died down German intelligence *did* despatch agents to Paris – not, as had been expected, overland, but in a captured B-17 Flying Fortress. Flown by a German crew, the American bomber took off from Stuttgart on the night of 3–4 February with nine agents on board on whom German intelligence had spent considerable time and effort. Approaching Paris the agents baled out by parachute, but they were dropped too far from their objectives and eight of them were captured almost immediately.

One, a French wireless telegraph operator who was a member of the pro-Nazi Francist movement, was captured by the 307th CIC Detachment at a road block in Dalhain, Alsace, and interrogated by Special Agents Marion Porter and Origene Paquette Jr, who finally turned him over to Special Counter Intelligence. The one agent who did manage to get through to Paris was a certain Robert DuBois, alias Cabrol, who was one of three agents who came to earth near Maubeuge, south of Mons. However, in Paris he too was apprehended, with the result that the entire mission ended in failure. What exactly this mission consisted of has never been revealed; and though no claim is made that it entailed the assassination of General Eisenhower, this objective cannot be entirely excluded.

Whatever the truth of the matter, any real possibility of assassination vanished shortly after Christmas when the German forces suffered their first shattering reverse in the battle and their advance jolted to a halt. By 26 December German military resurgence on the Western Front had reached its high-water mark, with forward spearheads only 17 miles from Dinant. But by then the 2nd Panzer Division had been drubbed by the US 2nd Armored, and Patton's column had fought its way to Bastogne and linked up with the hard-pressed but defiant 101st Airborne. American resistance had been more resolute and resilient than the Germans had anticipated. German armour was running out of fuel. Worst of all, the cloud lifted over the Christmas weekend, allowing Allied planes to take to the air for virtually the first time since the battle began. In four days American and British air forces flew 15,000 sorties, ravaging German troop concentrations and transport bottlenecks in the Ardennes and ranging far and wide in their attacks on supply lines in the German rear. Hitler's last gamble in the west was facing disaster. By rushing out from their fixed defences the Germans had given the Allies the chance to turn their gamble into defeat. In atrocious weather the Germans slowly began to withdraw towards the Reich.

At first the collapse of the German offensive was only dimly perceptible, if at all, to the American soldiers in the field. CIC Special Agent Nelson Dungan, who was based in Seventh Army's patch of the fighting front in Alsace, recalled an alarmingly confusing experience in which all seemed lost when all was not:

It was dawn on New Year's Day 1945. This was to be the year of victory, but then victory seemed a dim and faraway hope. I was alone in an upper room of the Hotel Brill in Niederbronn. The US artillery had started on the stroke of midnight; the German artillery followed almost immediately. Then the Germans began to move their armour down the hill into Niederbronn. We heard the big guns first, then small arms fire in the distance, then small arms fire in the street in front of our hotel. We had no idea what was going on outside, so our group decided to stay in the hotel, and we each went to our respective rooms. At about 3 am all the firing stopped and there was absolute silence.

When I awoke it was dawn. I heard the sounds of hundreds of German boots in the streets below, seemingly marching in cadence. What a way to get awake! At first I thought it was a dream, but when I looked out I saw a long column of German troops. I thought: 'This is it!' Of all the dangers of war the one I feared most was to be captured. My mind raced. All I could think of was a back door and where to go from there. But before taking action I thought I ought to take another look and formulate an escape plan. I opened the blinds a fraction of an inch and suddenly I realized that the Germans had no guns. In spite of their disciplined marching, they were our prisoners. The Lord had been good to our troops again and we had won the day after all.

By 6 January 1945 Hitler had tacitly admitted that the Ardennes offensive had failed. He had lost 250,000 men, 600 tanks and 1600 planes, and by transferring the Sixth Panzer Army to the Eastern Front he effectively removed the last remaining threat to the Allied advance into Germany from the West. The American losses were almost equal to those sustained by both sides at Gettysburg; but they had won a brave and outstanding victory in what Churchill regarded as the greatest American battle of the war. In February the Allies resumed their march of conquest. This was the beginning of the second phase of the battle, the phase of the Allied breakthrough and final advance into Germany.

As far as Skorzeny's 'Trojan Horse' was concerned, the deception plans for the Ardennes offensive had failed largely because American soldiers, roving patrols and road-block personnel had assiduously applied the information which had been so rapidly collected and disseminated by the CIC. But this was by no means the last that the CIC were to hear of Skorzeny.

In an effort to retake Alsace and pin a stunning defeat on the US Seventh Army the Germans resorted to a wide variety of desperate moves. One of the commonest was to send teams consisting of three officers and a driver in American uniforms through the lines in jeeps painted olive-drab and bearing US unit markings. All the members of these jeep parties were equipped with vials of acid which could be thrown in the faces of inquisitive sentries or other alert soldiers.

American intelligence repeatedly advised sentries to allow no vehicles to pass without full identification of all its occupants, but laxity by sentries continued, sometimes to a foolhardy extent bordering on suicidal.

On 2 January 1945, for example, an officer travelling in a civilian car painted olive-green and bearing US markings was stopped at a road-block. The sentry peered into the vehicle, glanced at the driver, who was wearing no helmet liner and had no visible insignia, and waved the car on without a single question. However, before moving off, the officer – who happened to be a Third Army Detachment CIC agent – briefly questioned the sentry.

'Why did you stop this car?'

'This is a road-block, sir.'

'What are you looking for?'

'We are checking vehicles to see if there are any Germans in American uniforms.'

'Well, how do you know I'm not a German?'

'I know that you are an officer because I saw the bar on your collar.'

'Don't you ask for the password?'

'Yes, when we're not sure of the men.'

'What do you do if the passer-by doesn't know the password? I don't know it myself.'

'That's all right, sir. The password is BUZZBOMB. You'll need it at the next road-block down the way.'

It was easy-going sentries like these that made possible the extraordinary incident that follows.

During mopping-up operations after the American break-out in the Ardennes battle, there occurred one of the strangest cases ever to have involved the CIC in World War Two. The case involved a certain Master Sergeant Johannisberg, whose claim to fame was that he had been in charge of the lavatories at the Führer's Headquarters. A little before the Ardennes push the luckless Johannisberg had been overheard repeating what was described as 'an unfortunate political joke', presumably at the Führer's expense, and as a consequence had been transferred with dictatorial despatch to a low-grade, cannon-fodder front-line unit, the 62nd Volksgrenadier Division, which was then in the worst of the fighting at the sharp end of the Battle of the Bulge. Johannisberg's immediate response to this potential death sentence was to end his personal involvement in the war by making a separate peace with the Allies.

The news of the defection of Hitler's lavatory attendant was broadcast by Radio Luxembourg, now in Allied hands. When Hitler heard it he was said to have fallen into one of his periodic depressions.

As it was believed that Sergeant Johannisberg was in possession of information that could prove extremely embarrassing to the Führer, the order was given for the defector to be found and repatriated as soon as possible before he revealed all. The man put in charge of this delicate task of retrieval was, inevitably, SS Colonel Skorzeny. In the presence of none less than Heinrich Himmler and General Sepp Dietrich, Skorzeny briefed the man he had placed in charge of this mission – Captain Franz Erich von Frauenhofer, a resourceful young officer who spoke fluent English. Frauenhofer's unenviable task was to cross into the American lines, enter the prison camp where the defected sanitary sergeant was held captive, and return with him back to the German lines.

Wearing the uniform of a Major in the US Army, Frauenhofer set off for the American lines in a jeep driven by his driver, Friedrich Waldruch, who was dressed as a US Army Tech 5. Luck was with the Germans. After crossing the line into the 18th Airborne's sector on 15 January, they were stopped by a sentry who looked them over and permitted them to pass. Encouraged by this, Frauenhofer attempted to wheedle the password and countersign out of the sentry, but the sentry was sheepishly forced to admit that he did not actually know them, and waved them on. The German captain had better luck with the sentry at the next check-point, however, and armed with the current password was able to continue as far as Verviers with comparative ease.

After a good night's rest in the Belgian town, the intrepid German pair resumed their journey deep into American Army territory. Fairly soon they caught up with a truck full of German prisoners and fell in behind. The truck led them to the First Army prisoner-of-war enclosure, where they arrived shortly after 9 am. Getting into the enclosure presented no difficulty. Instructing his driver to wait for him in the jeep outside the main guard room, Frauenhofer simply produced a blue SHAEF pass and was waved through. At the POW camp office the German introduced himself as the head of a newly formed Prisoner and Prisoner of War Personalities Data Section and presented papers, described as 'unquestionable' and later found to be first-class forgeries, authorizing him to take Johannisberg into his personal custody and evacuate him from the camp. The sanitary sergeant was located, identified, processed and formally handed over to Frauenhofer, and the two departed immediately.

So far so good; indeed, quite brilliant. But when Frauenhofer got to the main gate of the POW cage he saw to his dismay that his driver, Waldruch, was no longer there. In his consternation the German asked the MP on duty if he had any idea where jeep and driver might have gone. The MP told him: the driver had waited at the gate for about eight minutes – just long enough to ask about the local houses of ill-repute – and had then driven off in their direction.

This put Frauenhofer in something of a quandary. Rather than stand about in an exposed position in the company of Hitler's head lavatory attendant, he decided, since it was nearing lunchtime, to accept an invitation to take lunch in the officers' mess, and so he returned to the POW cage. Given the circumstances – an SS hit man in a US Army holy of holies in the midst of a do-or-die battle – Frauenhofer found lunch with his American companions rather a jolly affair. By German standards the food (C-rations and left-over spam) was interesting, and the officers' liquor ration was a most acceptable bonus.

The paradox of the German captain's peculiar position was that, though in fact he could speak flawless English, his cover decreed that in American company he should speak English with a German accent. The rationale behind this apparent illogicality was this: in order to explain Frauenhofer's lack of general knowledge about the United States, Skorzeny's organization had cast him as a German expatriate, a refugee from the Nazi terror, or something of that order, who had attended the Military Intelligence Center at Camp Ritchie, Maryland, along with other persons of foreign extraction who were boning up on their English. This cover held good so long as Frauenhofer remembered to speak English with a good Teutonic accent, which at lunch in the First Army POW officers' mess he did do – until the third highball. Up to this point the Americans at table accepted his claim that he was a German refugee who had been a member of Class 6 at Camp Ritchie. But their eyebrows began to rise when, under the influence of the booze, his Teutonic accent began to melt away syllable by syllable, until even the most difficult words tripped off his tongue like quicksilver and his speech was finally transformed into loquacious, idiomatic and faultless English. The American officers began to pay closer attention to their unusual guest, and when he started to praise the meal of C-rations and spam he had just eaten their suspicions were confirmed. This was no American officer! Frauenhofer was arrested on the spot and a search party was sent out for his lecherous driver, Waldruch.

At the First Army Interrogation Center the penitent and crestfallen Captain Frauenhofer did his best to bluff his way out of his predicament, but he was no match for the seasoned interrogators who now confronted him. In vain he tried to strike a bargain, offering his services to the Americans in the future administration of conquered Germany. Frauenhofer's last words to a departing interrogator were: 'By the way, if you hear over the radio that my driver has been awarded the *Eichenlaub* (oak leaf cluster) to the Good Conduct Medal, please let me know.' And with that, more or less, he departed this life and entered history.

At least two other undercover sabotage and espionage organizations were formed under Skorzeny's auspices and sent into action against the Allies during the early part of 1945. Both were of special concern to the CIC. The first was the Brandenburg formation, a highly professional sabotage unit composed of politically trust-worthy officers and non-commissioned officers drawn from the Brandenburg Division, one of the Wehrmacht's crack Jaeger (or light infantry) Divisions which had been in the thick of the fighting on many critical fronts in Russia, Greece, Italy and the Balkans. Now under the control of the German Security Service, the new formation was of the highest possible calibre and stinted nothing; its members were given absolute independence and issued with the newest arms and equipment, special ID cards and travel permits. The first the Americans heard of this organization was in January, when two of its members were captured by US infantry in Alsace and brought to VI Corps CIC. Both men were dressed in what appeared to be crude counterfeit American uniforms – a camouflaged jacket with hood resembling standard American issue, and a pair of overalls similar in colour and shape to trousers worn by American tank crews. But under these curiously hybrid outer garments they wore the uniforms of SS troopers.

George Tostain and Jean Poignet proved to be implacable Nazis, but they eventually broke down under interrogation and admitted that they had been on a reconnaissance mission to locate American gasoline dumps and check whether a nearby airfield was in operation. The purpose of their reconnaissance was to establish routes for the raiding parties that would follow them as part of a major sabotage operation. Obviously intrigued by this redoubtable pair, the CIC interrogators pressed them for more information about their organization and soon a coherent picture of the Brandenburg formation began to emerge. The man in charge was Otto Skorzeny. The men under him were all hand-picked. Every member of a team was trained to be an expert, whether as a rifleman on reconnaissance or a demolition man on sabotage operations. The *esprit de corps* of the various teams was tremendous. Prime targets included obvious structures like bridges, railway lines and supply dumps, but also military and civilian post offices. Military garments were only worn by men on scouting missions. Saboteurs wore civilian clothes – dark overcoat or trench coat, ski trousers and jacket, and a beret. Weapons were usually foreign – a pistol of Czech or Belgian manufacture was the basic armament. American automobiles were the usual form of transport – a depot in Germany containing 35 American cars (Cadillacs, Buicks, Oldsmobiles and Packards) was at their disposal. In general the deception worked very well, as Poignet testified:

> The idea of our CO to have us wear camouflaged clothes and carry weapons resembling American equipment was very good. Even the Germans fell for it – and I was detained by the Volkssturm and Wehrmacht for two days! – and the civilian population took us for escaped Canadians. We could have carried out our mission with a good chance of success. Only one detail was overlooked – our German belts and buckles. The arms we had, particularly the new German sub-machine-gun, P144, extra flat, with short barrel and half-moon clip, didn't look like a German weapon. In my opinion, and according to all the German and Alsatian reactions I saw, the camouflage thought up by our CO was excellent.

When the existence of this professional sabotage formation became known it created a considerable stir. Sixth Army Group counter intelligence officials took the first defensive measures against the Brandenburg formation by issuing a list of 21 of its members who were on the point of crossing into Allied territory. Subsequently, to guard against airborne infiltration by airborne agents, Seventh Army CIC instituted a system of spot-location of parachute landings, using radar. A large-scale map of the vulnerable area was kept at CIC Headquarters, with an azimuth circle and a yardage range arm centred on the co-ordinates of the nearest radar unit. Range and azimuth figures on the course of the enemy plane were interpreted by the radar unit and then telephoned directly through to CIC Headquarters. When a parachute drop was suspected, CIC units in the area were immediately alerted, and they in turn alerted mobile squads consisting of ten soldiers and military police who were kept on five-minute stand-by especially for this emergency. CIC Headquarters served as the nerve centre for all anti-parachutist operations.

One January night in Alsace, enemy air activity was picked up on the radar screen and the patrols rushed out to the predicted drop-zone near Lunéville. They arrived in time to find parts of a shattered radio transmitter strewn over the ground and, realizing that this would not have been dropped at random on its own, they spread out to comb the area for the people it belonged to. Within a short time the search parties discovered nine German espionage agents dressed in standard-issue Wehrmacht jump-suits. Two of the agents tried to escape and in the shoot-out that ensued one of them was killed and the other wounded. The CIC soon determined that the parachutists were members of Skorzeny's Brandenburg Formation – an advance party for a major sabotage operation against the Allied forces.

Had German resistance held up longer than it did, there is little doubt that Skorzeny's Brandenburgers would have presented a formidable problem for Allied ground forces; but in the end they were destined, like everyone else, to be swept away in the Reich's final collapse.

Skorzeny played one last card while the Allied armies were still on the western banks of the Rhine. This was the deployment of German Flüsskämpfer units in a final desperate effort to sabotage the Allies' temporary pontoon bridges over the Rhine – initially those at Remagen. The Flüsskämpfer, or river fighters, were better known to the Americans as Gamma Swimmers – their original Italian name, from the Italian word *gamma*, meaning rubber, referring to the pioneer wet suits worn by the men involved. Fortunately the CIC in the 21st Army Group area had been forewarned about possible sabotage attempts by German river commandos and with the help of army engineers had taken steps to defend the installations at Remagen. They had placed searchlights at strategic points, fitted underwater nets, booms and barbed-wire entanglements, set up self-propelling guns to cover the river approaches, and warned all river guards to open fire on any floating objects. Then they waited.

On the night of 16–17 March six German frogmen plunged into the murky, swiftly-flowing waters of the Rhine and approached Remagen towing floats full of explosives with which to demolish the pontoon bridges. They never stood a chance. When the Americans opened fire from the river bank, one of the frogmen was fatally wounded; one was captured when he abandoned his mission to help his wounded comrade; one was swept away and never seen again; two others, after diving to avoid the gunfire, became so exhausted trying to retrieve their explosive charges that they had to swim to the bank and surrender;. and the sixth man was found hiding in some bushes two and a half days later. A week later American troops intercepted a similar sabotage mission by five of Skorzeny's Gamma swimmers who were aiming to demolish the Rhine bridges in the vicinity of Oppenheim. One of the saboteurs did actually manage to reach the pontoons but his explosive charges became so entangled in the nets that he punctured his float and lost the explosives before he could do any real damage. He was soon captured, along with another swimmer; all the rest vanished.

From interrogations of the survivors of the Rhine bridges sabotage missions at 12th Army Group Counter Intelligence Interrogation Center considerable detail was obtained concerning the training and equipment of German Gamma swimmers – still a novelty at this point in history. All combat swimmers who belonged to the SS were under the jurisdiction of the Sondereinzatzabteilung der Waffen SS directed by SS Lieutenant Colonel Otto Skorzeny. A number of schools were used to train both German and Italian swimmers – one at Valdagno in Italy, two near Vienna, one at Bad Tölz and another on Sylt in the Friesian Islands. The swimmers' rubber wetsuits, which had a swastika on the left breast, could be worn for 48 hours consecutively; but in cold water a standard Luftwaffe jacket chemically treated to generate warmth for a period of three hours was worn.

The Rhine was full of surprises. No sooner had Nazi bombers been fished out of it than a harbinger of spring emerged, a Rhine siren in search of a mate. Brought before agents of the 203rd CIC the young girl explained her motives for swimming across the river to the American bank from the Luftwaffe ground observer post where she served as a German WAC. 'Ten to one is a bad state of affairs,' she told her interrogators (according to the operations report). There were 200 girls in her camp and only 20 men, all middle aged and most of them married. 'They' had told her that she should fight to the last man but the girl had come home to fight *for* the last man. For the time being, the report concluded, she would have to take her pick at a Prisoner of War Enclosure somewhere in Europe, 'where on good authority we know that men prisoners of war are plentiful.'

Any hopes that German intelligence (GIS) might have had of rallying for the final struggle were shattered by a new American counter intelligence initiative implemented under the codename 'Operation Gisbomb' (short for German Intelligence Service bomb). Gisbomb was the brainchild of a CIC officer, Captain Ernest Sidney Baker, formerly commander of 219th CIC Detachment and currently serving with the Counter Intelligence Branch of the Twelfth Army Group. The rationale behind the operation was based on the thesis that prevention was better than cure. Enough information had been extracted from captured German agents for the Americans to form a fairly clear picture of the capabilities and potentialities of German intelligence. By aerial bombing of the training establishments from which German secret agents came it was hoped to demoralize future agents destined for Allied territory and inflict irreparable material damage to secret espionage installations within the Reich. The first targets chosen for the operation were the radio school and radio station at Hundsbach; the headquarters for Nazi sabotage units at

Leitstelle II West; the Waldburg radio school for agents on long-term missions; and Kloster Tiefenthal, the deceptive operations centre, sabotage training school for Werwolf guerrillas, and headquarters and training school of the Jagdverbände South West. On 13 February 1945 eleven P-38 fighter-bombers attacked the GIS installations at the Tiefenthal Convent with thousand-pound bombs which caused a gigantic explosion and fires that burned for two weeks. The following day twenty-five P-47s from XII Tactical Air Command completely destroyed the Waldburg Radio School, killing twenty-four agents and injuring all the members of the training cadre. In other raids the planes missed Leitstelle II West completely and in two separate sorties hit only one building at Hundsbach. But Gisbomb was judged an outstanding success. It hit the enemy hard, and not only inflicted serious casualties among trainee agents, who were difficult to replace at this stage of the war, but also destroyed irreplaceable equipment, which undermined the confidence of agents in the supportiveness of their own intelligence system.

With the Allied armies now pouring across the German frontiers, the CIC began for the first time to turn their attentions to counter intelligence operations within the enemy heartland – not only in the Rhineland and the Ruhr of western Germany, but in the south, where the Allies were at last rolling up the northern Italian peninsula in their final drive towards Austria and the underbelly of an enemy that had proved very far from soft.

9

OVERRUNNING THE REICH

Until they stepped across the German frontier the CIC had never set foot on real enemy soil in Europe. Guns had been turned against them when they came ashore in North Africa, it is true; but North Africa was French, an ambivalent thing to be in 1942, part Fascist, part not, certainly not a true enemy. In Sicily the populace had welcomed them. In Italy they had advanced through co-belligerent territory, in France and the Low Countries through liberated lands. But Germany was decidedly different. Germany was Jerry, Kraut, Nazi, Boche and Hun. Germany was an army for whom the Allied soldiery had formed a profound respect, and a form of régime and vision of society for which they had only loathing and contempt. Germany was something they all took very seriously, from Eisenhower down.

Every Allied soldier heading for the Third Reich carried inside his helmet liner a SHAEF homily which read: 'Don't get chummy with Jerry. In heart, body and spirit every German is Hitler.' Such instructions merely reflected the common feeling of the time. Even Roosevelt had declared: 'The only answer to total war is total defeat and occupation . . . I would keep Germany on the breadline for the next 25 years.' Entering Germany was seen as a giant leap in the dark. The fear of werewolves and other fanatical resistance organizations was universal. 'Do you know German women have been trained to seduce you?' an army pamphlet asked the Anglo-American troops. 'Is it worth a knife in the back?' Nazi inscriptions on walls and road blocks at the border confirmed their worst fears: 'See Germany and die!'

For the CIC, who were destined to be in the vanguard of the reduction and occupation of the Nazi Reich, the counter intelligence mission involved problems that were both unusual and unprecedented. Never would the security of the army be a more crucial business than in the homeland of one's foe. Never would the extirpation of Nazi spies, saboteurs, subversives, propagandists,

ideologues, party die-hards, officials and war criminals be more vital
for the future of the civilized world. The problems had to be worked
out meticulously in advance. A Twelfth Army Group Counter
Intelligence Directive for Germany ran to over 120 pages and left no
stone unturned. In its estimate of the situation at the beginning of the
invasion of Germany the Directive presented an almost apocalyptic
vision:

> With the advance of our forces into Germany, counter intelli-
> gence has become increasingly vital. The enemy secret intel-
> ligence services, aided by fanatical and sympathetic civilians, are
> intensifying their efforts. Our forces are opposed by an unscrupu-
> lous enemy nation desperately fighting its last stand on its own soil
> against unconditional surrender.
>
> The enemy secret intelligence services, security and secret
> police, and para-military organizations are believed to have
> made elaborate plans for progressively going underground as our
> forces advance. It is believed that the basic policy of the
> organized underground is of long-range character. In later stages,
> guerrilla warfare and sporadic resistance in the form of
> sabotage and subversive activity will probably be forthcoming to
> a much greater degree from resistance groups and fanatical
> individuals.
>
> Military collapse by the enemy may be accompanied by a
> general condition of internal chaos and disorder. Some eight
> million displaced persons will be seeking to return to their homes;
> many will seek revenge before departing from Germany. The
> belligerent attitude of the German population, a substantial per-
> centage of which is known to be armed, probably will not undergo
> any remarkable early change. The organized underground will
> take advantage of the confusion to strengthen its position for the
> future; plans for the destruction and secreting of documents,
> secret processes and equipment will have been implemented;
> plans for the penetration of all administrative offices, industrial
> programs and public enterprises to be established by Military
> Government will be set in motion. Many enemy intelligence and
> police agents, war criminals and NSDAP [Nazi party] officials,
> other than those individuals who have escaped, assumed new
> identities or gone underground, will seek to escape across neutral
> borders. *Others will surrender themselves into our control, hoping to
> obtain clemency in exchange for becoming informers.* [Authors' italics].
>
> Every native German and displaced person found within the
> Reich must be considered a SUSPECT INDIVIDUAL.

In setting about the daunting task which lay before it US counter intelligence was given specific directives on many points. The arrest of selected German scientists and industrial technologists was a high priority. As we have already seen, a basic principle of CIC operating procedures in the field, one of the cardinal tenets of American law, was to be reversed: suspects were to be considered guilty unless able to prove their innocence. Wanted Lists, Target Addresses and Black and White Lists of enemy intelligence agents, para-military personnel, SS and Nazi Party members, renegade Allied nationals and other counter intelligence subjects drawn up by MI5, MI6, MI9, MI14, OSS, PWE (Political Warfare Executive) and other sources were distributed to all CIC commanders. Confidential G-2 funds were allotted to certain headquarters for secret intelligence purposes; intelligence laboratory facilities were established in rear echelons and clandestine radio detection units set up.

Internment camps for arrested Nazis were also to be established with room for 5000 to 10,000 internees and accommodation for the solitary confinement of 50 CI arrestees. Strict guidelines were laid down for the treatment of the internees, and any change in the status of an internee (e.g. execution, escape) had to be reported to headquarters immediately. A rather sinister institution known as a CI Annex was attached to each US Army Interrogation Center for the special processing of 'those persons who are in possession of detailed information of value to our operations against the German Intelligence Service, Security Services, and subversive hostile elements.' Each Annex – torture chamber would perhaps be too strong an alternative label – was to provide 'secret solitary confinement' for up to 100 arrestees at one time; ten cells equipped for the secret monitoring and recording of any conversations which might take place among internees placed in those cells; ten private, soundproof interrogation rooms; 20 expert, full-time, German-speaking CI interrogators, and 20 stenographers. 'The ultimate disposal of captured members of the German intelligence services,' the Directive noted, 'will be decided by this or higher headquarters.'

The Directive extended little encouragement to democratic, anti-Nazi Germans or members of the anti-Hitler resistance movement, though provision was made for their employment – alongside ex-Nazis – as CIC informers among the civilian population, paid on a pro-rata or salary basis out of confidential funds. The whole of Germany was to be sealed off from the rest of the world like a leper colony and martial law imposed on all its inhabitants. There was to be blackout and curfew throughout the occupied areas. No German could move without an ID pass, and never more than six kilometres from his or her home. A Prohibited Frontier Zone was to be placed under armed guard and aircraft surveillance, and all forms of communication between Germans – mail, telephones, telegraphs and radio – were to be closed down, including the most arcane. 'Pigeon flights will be prohibited,' thundered the Directive. 'Pigeons will be confiscated or collected by Military Government. The birds, if not desired by the Signal Corps, will be killed or have their wings clipped.'

Like a cadaver at an autopsy, the anatomy of the Nazi State was laid bare and all the component organs, nerves and muscles that were to be cut out and destroyed were clearly identified and named, from organizations like the Führer's Chancellery and individuals such as the Reich Leader SS, down through the labyrinth of the Party machine, through the ranks of the heavies like the Gestapo, the Storm Troops and the Hitler Youth, the endless inventory of sinister initials, the NSKK, NSFK, RAD, SD.Rf.SS, to unique little cells of nastiness such as the Office for Racial Questions, the Committee for the Protection of German Blood, and the Beauftragter des Führers für die Überwachung der Gesamten Geistigen und Weltanschaulichen Schulung und Erziehung der NSDAP (which translates no less succinctly as the Office of the Führer's Commissioner for the Supervision of the Whole Intellectual and Ideological Training and Education of the Party), all the way down to the time servers and loyal and lowly mass of the National Socialist termite nest, the German Hunters' Association, the Party League of Student Old Boys, the rectors of universities, the mayors of cities of more than 100,000 inhabitants, the businessmen who boasted Nazi honours like the Order of Blood or Dagger of Honour. Root and branch the Nazi jungle was to be torn up. The list was endless; the targets ran into millions.

To cope with this mountainous mission during the occupation of Germany the CIC were to be reorganized into a single CIC detachment – the 'Occupation Detachment' – consisting of 323 officers and 1100 enlisted men divided into 83 teams composed of 3 officers and 11 enlisted men, the balance staffing various headquarters teams. Because of the precarious state of security during the initial combat phase inside Germany, the Directive issued explicit instructions designed to further the efficiency and protect the lives of CIC personnel operating in hostile territory. When undertaking missions in forward combat areas, CIC agents would have to deposit their badges and credentials in the Detachment safe, so that in the event of capture they could not be identified as intelligence agents and shot. For the same reason, they would have to try and destroy all notes and intelligence material obtained in the performance of their mission if capture looked likely. CIC armbands were not to be worn in Germany and Detachment Commanders were advised not to establish a publicly known CIC office in any locality where the most dangerous Nazi elements had not yet been arrested and security control measures established. Detachments were advised to work in isolated towns in daylight only, and to return at night to secure towns where they could billet with Military Government or MP units or the Command Post of the unit to which they were attached.

In addition to operations by standard CIC detachments, the Twelfth Army Group Directive for Germany outlined the mission and method of the Special Counter Intelligence (SCI) Detachment. The SCI Detachment's mission was to interrogate and 'make use of' captured German Intelligence Service agents and officers, introduce its own penetration agents into the GIS, and provide additional counter intelligence assistance of various sorts, including counter-sabotage operations and the handling of radio agents and double agents. The SCI was also to make available its own radio communication facilities to maintain direct contact with Armies, 'T' Force, Twenty-first Army Group and OSS headquarters in London and Paris, transmit information on the GIS collected in the field to London, Paris and Washington, and pass on from the British–US Counter Intelligence War Room in London special information about the GIS which was not suitable for transmission through ordinary intelligence channels because of its highly sensitive nature. Provision was also made for close co-operation between counter intelligence and psychological warfare personnel. The Psychological Warfare Division especially requested that counter intelligence personnel should keep on the look-out for documentary evidence from Nazi sources 'proving German guilt and the responsibility of the National Socialist Party for the moral degradation of the German people.'

A SHAEF Counter Intelligence Bulletin prepared at the time of the overrunning of Germany warned that since the SS had taken over German sabotage activities an increase could be expected in assassination and terrorist operations against the Allies and German nationals working for them. Terrorist tactics would include assassination attempts against important figures and the use of anti-personnel bombs such as the Buttermould Bomb (a booby trap device). German hit squads had been issued with poisoned aspirin tablets, chocolate bars and sugar. They had also developed a cigarette lighter that could kill any smoker who used it. A small round pellet of unknown chemical constitution, measuring only one millimetre in diameter, was fixed near the wick so that when the wick was lit the pellet became hot and vaporized to give off a deadly poisonous gas. The object of the Nazi terror campaign would be to foment trouble and general unrest as part of a long-term political subversion of Allied government.

SHAEF also reported on Abwehr plans for the post-hostilities phase of the Allied occupation of Germany. According to information developed from interrogation of captured Abwehr agents, special stay-behind sabotage tasks (R-Aufgaben) had already been assigned to Frontaufklärungskommando (front-line intelligence task-forces) on the Eastern Front, and it was believed blueprints had been drawn up for similar operations on the Western Front. Abwehr units had already undertaken these new duties on the Eastern Front. Weapons and explosives had been buried in Upper Silesia. Training in partisan warfare was being given at special 'Academies' in Koblenz, Linz, Innsbruck, Reichenburg, Spandau, Hagen and Dortmund, the courses being based on German experience of guerrilla warfare waged against them by Polish and Russian guerrillas, especially in Poland. Elsewhere local priests had been recruited as leaders of anti-Communist, anti-Russian resistance activities. The code name for the R-Aufgaben operations was a word that Allied officials were to encounter with increasing regularity in the coming months – 'Werwolf'.

A forecast of what CIC detachments could expect from German intelligence in the closing phase of the battle for Germany was prepared by CIC agents at First Army. Enemy activities included the installation of stay-behind radio agents in the larger towns; activation of long-range stay-behind saboteurs in the Allied rear; employment of increasing numbers of Hitler Youth agents for both sabotage and espionage missions; penetration of prisoner-of-war camps, foreign labour camps, Wehrmacht and Volkssturm units by German agents looking for somewhere to hide; penetration of Allied intelligence organizations; use of short-range line-crossing sabotage and espionage agents of German, Luxembourg, French, Belgian or Dutch nationality; use of mines, booby traps and delayed action bombs in large buildings likely to be taken over as headquarters or billets by Allied units; commencement of partisan warfare coinciding with a programme of black propaganda designed to arouse the German population against the occupying troops and discourage collaboration with military government.

As early as January 1945 Third Army Counter Intelligence had prepared a secret report, itself based on an OSS intelligence report from the field, which gave a detailed account of preparations for a

Nazi underground movement. The primary source of the information was a German who had been involved in the production of a top secret handbook prepared at the instigation of Heinrich Himmler, and printed under the rigid control of the SD. The book was entitled *Anweisungen für Klein – und Partisanenkrieg*, translated as *Handbook of Instructions for Nazi Underground*, and it was prefaced with an exhortation by Himmler which ended: 'We will fight them all and beat them on the Rhine, on the Elbe, on the Danube, on the Spree. Wherever we are we will be the eternal Third Reich. Victory is ours! The future is ours! Heil Hitler!' Although the OSS had not succeeded in laying their hands on a copy of this blueprint for a Nazi come-back in the post-war world, their source had committed much of it to memory – a compendium of the nuts and bolts of Hitlerite resistance.

Organization of the Nazi Underground was based on the cell, known as a Fünfergruppe, composed of five men who comprised an independent entity in their district, subject only to direct orders from Supreme Central Command of the SD. 'In every town and village,' the handbook directed, 'an Intelligence Section must be set up as a control nucleus.' Intelligence, sabotage and security functions were to be performed by specially trained personnel drawn from Waffen SS communication and engineer units and members of the SD itself. Those selected for these tasks were in the process of changing their names, passports and identity papers and assuming the identity of air raid victims, 'criminals' who had died in concentration camps or foreign workers who had been 'removed' to make room for their impersonators. Some of the SS and SD men had already been sent as prisoners to concentration camps to await liberation at the hands of the Allies. 'In the threatened western areas of Germany,' reported Third Army CIC, 'these men have already begun work and it is reported that their organization of resistance in these parts has already reached a high stage of preparedness, doubtless helped by the fact that these areas are thickly-populated regions in which concealment, particularly after the chaos wrought by Allied bombs, is a comparatively easy matter.' Women were also to be recruited for espionage and counter-espionage work, as they were less readily suspected and 'usually more fanatical than men in this kind of work'.

Each group would have access to secret arms depôts containing automatic pistols, machine-guns, tommy-guns, flamethrowers, high explosives, land-mines, corrosive acids, new sabotage weapons including pistols disguised as pens or pocket-knives and bombs resembling combs or cigarette lighters. A hospital would also be available, together with a forgery plant for making false identity papers, money and ration cards, a chemical laboratory, printing plants and telephone and radio stations.

The Gestapo had prepared two dossiers as a preliminary to underground operations. The first contained the names of totally reliable Nazis who could be counted on to lead the underground movement or organize cells for carrying out subversive activities against the Allies. All copies of this dossier would be burned as soon as the Allied breakthrough materialized. The second dossier contained the names of Party members who were considered unreliable and could be played into the Allies' hands. This dossier would be allowed to fall into Allied hands, causing them to arrest precisely those people the Nazi Party thought likely to co-operate with the Allies, thus diverting attention away from reliable Nazis. German-speaking foreign workers from countries bordering the Reich were being executed so that Nazis in Dossier No. 1 could take over their identity cards and pass as foreign workers in the event of their arrest by the Allies. Meanwhile the Frankfurt Police were in possession of a large number of Swiss passports for distribution to those Nazis who were to be saved for the formation of cells later on. The Gestapo had also issued a list of people who had been sent abroad by the Party as 'political refugees' and were administering Nazi funds in neutral countries.

Even as Germany was being overrun the CIC were giving special training courses for agents destined to handle counter intelligence affairs in the heartland of the Reich. The courses included background lectures on Hitlerite Germany, German psychology and the organization of German intelligence; together with practical instruction in handling informants ('How to get them, use them, get the most out of them'), carry out spot checks and screenings and interrogate suspects. Little was overlooked but not everything turned out as expected when the CIC plunged into the ruins of the civilization that had once been a nation called Germany.

Some counter intelligence predictions came true, others not. Reports came in that Skorzeny was broadcasting appeals to the German people to join the resistance and sabotage the Allied presence. Leaflets were intercepted, emanating from German Intelligence but purporting to be of Allied origin, which aimed to breed dissension among the victors by means of subversive propaganda. One handbill, alleged to have originated from American sources, denounced a supposed speech by Winston Churchill in which the British Prime Minister lamented the fact that the Americans had wiped out Britain's trade markets. Another emphasized the differences in pay, allowances and living conditions between British and

American troops. Other leaflets played on the theme of imminent conflict between the Western Allies and the Soviet Union. US Army jeeps were ambushed or pirated, spotter aircraft sabotaged, SS radio agents infiltrated through army lines. A number of former Luftwaffe pilots were captured when the seven Arado-type training planes they were flying were forced down in the First Army area and found to contain demolitions and secret documents. Subsequent interrogation revealed that the Luftwaffe men were part of a group of 50 planes and 100 airmen who had been recruited to fly special sabotage missions near their home towns.

But in the twilight of the war GIS agents were found to be operating with a lack of enthusiasm which was in inverse proportion to the expertise and determination of the CIC agents who opposed them. On 3 March 1945, for example, a female stay-behind radio agent turned herself in to the American authorities at München-Gladbach without having transmitted a single message. She also gave the names and localities of four other women radio agents who had been sent into the field with her to wait for the Americans to overrun their positions. She led the commander of the 29th CIC Detachment, Lieutenant Ellis Mayfield, to a second agent the same day. This agent said she had burned her codes and buried her radio set, and had not transmitted any tactical information. The next day Lieutenant Mayfield arrested a third agent in Suchteln. She had reported in to the GIS on 20 February and still held her codes, but her radio, too, had been buried in the garden and she denied having radio-ed any information to control. On 5 March Lieutenant Mayfield arrested a fourth woman in Krefeld who claimed she had destroyed both codes and radio and transmitted no information. Finding the fifth agent, however, turned out to be an instructive song and dance among the ruins and rubble of the streets that had once been Krefeld.

The name of the fifth woman was Anneliese Schmitz, a very common German name. Assigned to search for her was Special Agent Gordon Anderson, with Interpreter Serene Hepner and the first female German agent in support. On 5 March the party proceeded to the home of Anneliese Schmitz in Krefeld, only to find that it had been bombed out two weeks previously. Enquiries in a nearby bunker, where most of the neighbourhood were now living, failed to produce a lead, but in a second bunker a person who knew Anneliese Schmitz directed the searchers to a third bunker. There, in the dank dark and squalor of this concrete catacomb, a girl of that name did indeed dwell, but not the right one. However, she had heard of another Anneliese Schmitz who lived in a fourth bunker in the city. Here the party located yet another Anneliese Schmitz, again the wrong one, who said she too knew of a girl of that name. She promptly led the trio back to the first Anneliese Schmitz they had found.

To appreciate properly the extreme difficulty of this kind of search, one must picture the bizarreness of the environment in which it was conducted – the ravaged landscape of a bombed-out, shelled-out Rhineland city, where half the buildings had collapsed into the streets, all order and normality had long gone, and people lived troglodytic lives in cellars and holes in the ground, or seethed about in an inchoate mass of refugees and homeless persons; a shattered place where the arrival of an American soldier was still as startling to the native populace as that of a kilted Highlander in New York's Harlem, or a Papuan tribesman in London's Mayfair. To persist in the search for a Fräulein with a radio in these circumstances required a sense of duty and a spirit of the chase of high order, qualities which Special Agent Anderson evidently possessed in good measure.

The second Anneliese Schmitz now suggested that the wanted agent might be found through the records of the Deutsches Arbeits-front (German Labour Front), if they still existed. After a search of the ruins the office was found, mostly rubble but with its records intact, including a card file with the card of secret agent Anneliese Schmitz, complete with photograph and record of birth, but no address. Anderson's party now went to the agent's birthplace, and in a nearby bunker found someone who claimed to have seen her only a few days before and who directed the searchers to a house on the banks of the Rhine not very far distant. In this house a young woman by the name of Anneliese Schmitz, who bore a considerable physical likeness to the girl in the photograph, had indeed lived before she had crossed to the other side of the Rhine. Conversations with the woman's brother confirmed that this was not the wanted agent, however, but a third Anneliese Schmitz. The searchers retraced their steps to the last bunker. This time another informant came forward, a girl who had been at school with the wanted agent, who said she had seen the real Anneliese two days previously when she left the bunker. A further search in the area located a house where Anneliese had stayed with her mother only the day before.

The hunters were closing on their quarry. A man in the house had helped the girl and her mother move to a new address – Weierhof-strasse 101, Krefeld. He did not know her name but he identified Anneliese from the German Labour Front card. The party went immediately to number 101 and banged on the door; and so at last they confronted secret agent Anneliese Schmitz, the fourth woman of that name. The first radio agent formally identified the woman and her radio was found hidden in the basement. Along with the radio, Anneliese was taken away to the 29th CIC Detachment, and thence to Armor (XIX Corps) Interrogation Center, in the same manner as the four agents arrested before her.

This is not the end of the story, however. Because the CIC had preserved the secrecy of the investigation by using a high security classification, Special Counter Intelligence were able to turn Anneliese round and use her – and another of her fellow radio agents – to transmit false information back to control at GIS. Both girls were subsequently awarded the Iron Cross (Second Class) by the Germans 'for their bravery in furnishing much valuable information to the German Army and for their bravery in operations behind the American lines', while Special Agent Gordon Anderson was awarded a Bronze Star by the Americans for his part in the investigation, and Lieutenant Mayfield was promoted to Captain. Later 21st Army Group reported of the case: 'Our British associates at this Headquarters were greatly impressed by this display of efficiency, and unanimously acclaimed this work as a model job.' A highly satisfactory outcome for all concerned – on both sides.

One way or another, women played an increasingly important part in the human maelstrom of front-line Germany, and for a time during the period of the Allied occupation that followed military conquest they were the dominant sex in the civil populace. From the counter intelligence point of view, the problem with women secret agents, who were used in considerable numbers by the GIS, was that they *were* women. Female agents had instructions from the German Intelligence Service to use every means at their disposal to capture an American officer's attention and learn through him the intentions of the tactical forces. According to the 418th CIC Detachment's Monthly CIC Report, 'the seduction rate of American officers was, from the German Intelligence Service's point of view, still at an alarmingly low rate.'

Higher commands were not so reassured on this point, however – and with good reason. Though all Allied soldiers came under a strict non-fraternization order on crossing the German frontier, the order was widely flouted, especially by Americans, and particularly in relation to young children and attractive young German Fräulein. As Captain Saul Padover, an American intelligence officer with the Psychological Warfare Division, found in the cities across the Rhine: 'Everywhere women, some of them beautiful and most of them young, accosted us and whispered invitations. They would pass slowly, give us a long sideways look and murmur. "I live by myself;

would you like to come up and see me?"' In Padover's view, German women were the easiest white women in the world. American soldiers availing themselves of the boundless opportunities for female company in conquered Germany were subject to summary fines of $65 for violating the non-fraternization order – so inevitably the propositioning of German girls became known as 'the 65-dollar question'. Aware of the counter intelligence hazard posed by the alarming rapport between the Allied soldiery and the hordes of lonely young women who had lost their menfolk, First Army G-2 cited the 'thousands of young women behind our lines and through-out Germany' as 'a security menace that calls for more than passing consideration'. The report warned soldiers against trading military information for female companionship, but reassured them that 'not every woman is a Mata Hari.'

Some were, though. Perhaps the most remarkable in CIC experience was an extraordinary creature they called the Rhine Maiden, a German assassination agent who proved the most valuable catch ever made by the CIC on the banks of the Rhine. On the night of 12 March 1945 this woman was picked up on the west bank of the Rhine, quite fortuitously, by an American combat intelligence team on a routine patrol. She had obviously been in the water as her clothes – yellow sweater and slacks – were dripping wet when she was found, and she explained that she was a French slave labourer who had swum across the river from Mülheim in order to reach the American lines and from there make her way back to her family home in Brittany. Wrapped in an army blanket, and exhausted and cold, the woman was taken to VII Corps CIC headquarters on the Lütticherstrasse in Cologne, given hot coffee and a change of clothes, and asked a number of routine questions.

She proved a startling female. Among all the CIC agents who handled her case she provoked reactions of wonderment and suspicion. One of them, Joseph Rosen, remembered her as a woman with a photographic mind in a photogenic body. In the official report she was described as 'better-looking than average, with a rather appealing face, a pleasant and quiet manner, in her twenties, medium height, blond hair, and an interesting figure'. She gave her name as Héloise Bouconville and again described how she had swum across the Rhine to escape from Nazi Germany. She was not believed. In early March there was still much winter ice on the river – too much to make a swim advisable. A body search conducted with the assistance of a WAC lieutenant revealed that she had secreted a small pistol wrapped in oil-cloth next to her body, and a small red and white flashlight was found amongst her discarded garments.

'*Vielleicht haben Sie aber das flashlight gebraucht um den Nazis Signale zu geben?*' the interrogating officer, Captain Paul Halmark, snapped at her.

The woman understood well enough, for she was fluent in German as well as French, Flemish and Dutch, though she always insisted she knew no English. She denied that she had brought the flashlight in order to signal to the Germans across the river. As for the gun, it was for self-defence. She insisted she was not a spy, though she eventually admitted that she had come across the river in a boat which had capsized, drowning her companion.

The interrogators decided that the circumstances were sufficiently suspicious to justify referring the case to their superiors. Though it was two in the morning, and the woman was numb with fatigue, they bundled her into a jeep and drove her through the pitch-black streets of the ruined city to the quarters of one of their most expert agents, Fenton Moran, a former diplomat who spoke eight languages. Moran had some coffee brought for the woman, and a stiff slug of brandy, and then he began his interrogation. When the woman began to cry he had her locked up for the night, and after she had gone he began to look through his counter intelligence files. In a dossier marked 'Sybille Delcourt' he found what he had been looking for. In it was fully documented evidence against one of the Germans' most dangerous woman agents in the front-line areas of the Rhine, Alsace, Luxembourg and the Bulge. An old, not very satisfactory photograph indicated that the Héloise who had been brought before him in the middle of the night was this very same Sybille Delcourt, a Belgian Nazi sympathizer who worked for the SD with orders to kill.

Sybille, it seemed, was the mistress of a highly successful SD intelligence chief, Obersturmtruppführer Werner Krämer, who ran an SD kidnapping network and suicide squad of enemy agents. Krämer had been personally decorated by the Führer for his kidnapping operations and had been running agents across the Rhine and causing a nuisance by blowing up various Allied installations all over the American rear. It occurred to Moran and his CIC colleagues, Joseph Rosen, Daniel Badger and Henry Kent, that Krämer's name could be used to break Sybille, while Sybille herself could be used to entrap Krämer. And this is indeed what happened.

It was Special Agent Joseph Rosen, a reasonable German speaker, who finally broke the Rhine Maiden's resistance after two whole days of fruitless interrogation during which she had stuck coolly and steadfastly to her original cover story. Not even bribery had worked: food, clothes, cigarettes, chocolate, all sorts of extravagant promises

– none of them budged the woman from her set position. So Rosen tried Krämer.

'You don't know much anyway,' he told the woman. 'You're nothing but one of the cheap paid agents and stool pigeons of Werner Krämer.'

This was the first mention of the SD officer's name and it had the effect of a lash. Sybille Delcourt leapt up and angrily yelled: '*Das ist eine gemeine Lüge!* That is an outrageous lie. Werner Krämer loves me.'

She had taken the bait. The CIC agents showed her the dossier they had on her, disclosing all the essential details of her compromised past – how she came in fact from Belgium not Brittany; how she and her mother ran a profitable little bar-café in Bruges, much frequented by the local Gestapo, who came there for the obliging young girls they found waiting for them; how Werner Krämer met Sybille at the café, and took her on first as his translator, and then as a courier, and then as an espionage agent, and finally as his mistress. Many Belgian resistance workers and Allied agents had fallen into the hands of the Gestapo on account of the information Sybille had whispered in the attentive ear of her SS lover over the last four years.

Since Sybille loyally refused to utter a word against Werner Krämer, Fenton Moran called for Krämer's file and began to peruse it. At length he turned to the woman and asked her: 'Isn't it true that Krämer chose you for this dangerous mission in order to get you out of the way because he has met another woman? We know her name – they call her Marie.'

And so they began to turn this attractive and dedicated professional killer. Drop by vitriolic drop, the interrogators poisoned the girl's mind against her lover, and so manipulated her raw emotional response on this subject that before long they had her agreeing, out of revenge, to work on their behalf against both Krämer and his network. She admitted that her mission in Cologne was to have included the assassination of a former Gestapo interpreter and the chief of the *V-Männer* (petty informer) network of the Cologne Gestapo; the release of Cologne Gestapo personnel who had been rounded up as prisoners-of-war by American troops after changing into ordinary police uniforms; and the establishment of operational sites for radio agents who were to come in after her. And she revealed that she could lead them to the hideouts of a whole spy network of stay-behind agents now in place in Cologne with false identity cards and passports, waiting for Krämer's orders. A secret cache of arms, ammunition and explosives was stored at an address in Limburgerstrasse, she said, under the care of a German agent by the name of

Franz Matthias, a storm troop leader. Matthias was expecting her and would lead her to Engelhard, the Cologne Gestapo's Dutch interpreter who was now trying to save his skin by collaborating with the CIC. Her orders, she told her interrogators, were to shoot Engelhard before he could betray any more members of the Gestapo. Before killing him, however, she was to obtain from him the address of the CIC headquarters. This would then be blown up using the explosives from the secret cache. As soon as she had the address and had disposed of the Dutch collaborator she was supposed to use her flashlamp to signal the news to her people on the other side of the Rhine. It seems the signals were also meant to activate the radio agents waiting to cross the river to Cologne.

The next night the CIC agents took Sybille down to the river in order to try and establish signal contact with the GIS people on the opposite bank and if possible give the start signal for the radio agents to come across the river. For an hour Sybille flashed a red beam – two long flashes, followed by two short – over the darkened, empty Rhine, while the CIC agents lay in ambush, waiting for the agents to arrive. A light flashed from the other side in acknowledgement of her signals, but no agents turned up and after two nights the CIC abandoned this ploy and turned their attention to the Gestapo agents still under cover on their own side of the river.

Already the CIC personnel who were handling this woman were profoundly impressed by the extraordinary coolness and calm, amounting almost to complacency, with which she went about her lethally dangerous task as a double agent under operational conditions. Soon she was to confront Gestapo personnel who would have killed her on the spot if they had the slightest suspicion she was working for the Americans. But only rarely did she lose her collected, blasé composure. One occasion was when a soldier assigned to guard her left his loaded .45 pistol on a table in her room as she slept. In the early hours he left the room to get a coffee and she woke up and found the gun beside her. She was shocked. She interpreted the loaded weapon as an invitation to kill herself because she was no longer any use to the Americans. 'She got hysterical,' Special Agent Joseph Rosen recalled, 'and it must have taken three or four days to get her calmed down.' But by and large she was a paragon of whom VII Corps CIC were to report later: 'Beyond her physical attributes, no resemblance to ordinary womanhood existed . . . a gangster's moll is a haloed angel in comparison.'

The next day a German-speaking member of the CIC team put on civilian clothes and accompanied Sybille Delcourt to the address she had given in Limburgerstrasse. A tall German answered the door.

Sybille gave him the agreed password, '*Nacht und Nebel*' (night and fog), and the German led them to Engelhard, the Dutchman she had been sent to liquidate. Confronted with Sybille he almost passed out, then asked the Americans for protection. Four hours later, while in CIC custody, he tried to kill himself by slashing his wrists with a knife; but he was unsuccessful and after treatment was taken away to the First Army Interrogation Center.

The CIC now began to hope that Sybille would set about rolling up the whole of the Gestapo network known to her in Cologne. With a squad of CIC men under Special Agent Henry Kent travelling through the ruined streets in a convoy of three black limousines, she pointed out one German face after another, all of whom were arrested on the spot. But they were all small fry – policemen, bartenders, railway workers. The next day Sybille and Henry Kent, shabbily dressed in tattered clothing, arrived at the Cologne Displaced Persons camp posing as a poor Dutch DP couple, Mr and Mrs Henk Kemp, who were trying to make their way back to Holland. After being deloused and processed, the couple – the American agent and the Nazi agent – settled into camp life together and Sybille began to identify Nazi agents sheltering there. Six arrests were made but they were still small-time operators of no great consequence, and Fenton Moran, the CIC chief, had Sybille hauled out of the camp and brought to his headquarters. He told her bluntly: what she had accomplished so far would not earn her a reprieve from the firing squad.

'We will not tolerate double-crossers,' he warned her. 'Either you produce Werner Krämer or we will try you as a spy.'

Sybille confessed that she really did not know where Krämer was any longer – not since he left with the woman called Marie. But she did know where all the secret Gestapo files were hidden. The CIC then dressed her in an American nurse's uniform and followed her directions to an abandoned factory near the Rhine. Here they dug up the official Gestapo files, with the names of every Gestapo agent in the Rhineland. As a result of this information provided by Sybille the CIC were able to arrest nearly 150 wanted enemy agents, and though Krämer was not among them the immense value of her contribution to the Allied cause could no longer be denied.

Under pressure from a fresh interrogator on the case, from Special Counter Intelligence, Sybille Delcourt was eventually persuaded to lead investigators to a house in Cologne which she remembered belatedly was a safe house where Krämer and his new girlfriend might have holed up while hiding in the city. The house was in an advanced state of dilapidation, with smashed windows and doors and not a soul in sight. But in one of the rooms the searchers found a pair of old shoes and a discarded red dress, which Sybille identified as Marie's. Sybille became hysterical at the sight of it, and sobbing bitterly turned to her interrogator and said: 'I should never have given a false flashlight signal to save his life when he was living here with that French bitch.'

'What false signal?'

'"I am in enemy hands."'

Sybille Delcourt was returned to the prison at Reichenbach. She did not emerge again until after the Americans had occupied the other bank of the Rhine. There, in a house in the woods near Mülheim, the CIC had tracked down a woman and a tall, blond, Teutonic-looking man with a Hitler moustache who answered to the description of Obersturmtruppführer Werner Krämer. The man of course denied that he was any such person and Sybille Delcourt was brought from prison to help identify him. Pale and trembling she was led into the room where the man was held.

'Who is this man?' Special Agent Harry Kent demanded.

Sybille took a step forward, looked straight at the man, and smiled. 'I don't know,' she said. 'I've never seen him in my life before.'

Within the next twenty-four hours six witnesses were found who were able to identify the man as Werner Krämer. Sybille Delcourt – the Rhine Maiden, and a legendary figure in the annals of the CIC – had thus sacrificed herself to save the man she had once loved and loved still – the very man who had deceived her. The CIC had no alternative but to hand her over to the Belgian authorities, who eventually tried her and duly sentenced her to death. At the end of the war the CIC wrote a letter to the Belgian authorities testifying to the fact that she had helped in the arrest of a number of Gestapo agents, and asking for mercy to be shown to her. At her appeal the court commuted the death sentence and shortly afterwards released her into the anonymity of post-war civilian life, in which she successfully buried herself in complete obscurity until the present day.

Few cases were as important or as involved as that of the Rhine Maiden. During the period when the GIS in its last paroxysm before the German collapse was throwing every man or woman they could muster into the sabotage and intelligence war, German agents fell into the Allied counter intelligence net in droves. In an analysis of CIC arrestees for the month of March 1945, Twelfth Army Group CI revealed that 45 per cent of the arrestees were interrogated and cleared as displaced persons or refugees; 30 per cent were German Army deserters in civilian clothes; 15 per cent were Nazi officials or pro-Nazi civilians liable to internment; and 10 per cent were

Gestapo informers and *V-Männer* informers. At the same time, more than ten different GIS despatching units had been identified as operating against the Twelfth Army Group. The failure of these units to achieve any notable successes must be attributed in part to the efficiency with which the Allied counter intelligence system organized its defences and in part to inherent deficiencies in the GIS itself.

Commenting on the failure of German Intelligence during the final battle for Germany, one CIC agent who served throughout the North West Europe campaign, wrote:

> All this grandiose scheming by the RHSA ignored an enormous lack in their planning. There was no manpower, no special equipment in quantity, no time to mount an effective underground resistance. The Germans were nearing the end of a mad two-front war. The Bulge was their last gasp. The crossing of the Rhine was a parade. What good were left-behind spies when no one could exploit their information – if it got through? They had done worse than simply run out of manpower, for *any* German man behind our lines was an automatic suspect. This is why they turned to women for their secret work, hopelessly unprepared and ill equipped though they were, with frantic last-minute instructions from men fleeing backwards. The Rhine Maiden certainly had glamour, but think for a moment. She never committed even the most petty act of espionage. She was picked up on landing. Even if she had managed to communicate back across the Rhine, there was nothing she could say except that the Americans were planning to cross by the hundreds of thousands. And no one knew when! The CIC neutralized most line-crossers at the front. Even rear-echelon CIC, such as Army-level detachments, were operating under such tight and austere conditions that enemy spies would have had the devil of a job obtaining anything really vital and getting it back across the lines via radio or whatever. Real espionage could only take place far in the rear. Only in some place like Paris was there any chance for a Mata Hari to circulate.

Some successes were achieved by the Germans, however. The most sensational of these was the murder, on the night of 25 March, of the Burgermeister of Aachen, who had been appointed to the post by the Allies. According to eye witnesses, three German soldiers dressed in jump-suits had done the killing. They claimed they had been forced down during a return flight from Brussels and asked for his help. When he refused, they shot him and vanished into the night. CIC agents of the 203rd Detachment in Aachen were sceptical about

this version of events. The killing had every appearance of a deliberate assassination operation carried out as part of a Nazi plan to create
disorder and confusion among the civilians in Allied occupied territory. An organization known as *Vehme* (Revenge) was rumoured to
exist in the locality with the aim of killing officials appointed by the
Allies, along with any other Germans who chose to co-operate with
the Allied forces. In the eyes of III Corps CIC the assassination in
Aachen had all the hallmarks of a Skorzeny-directed mission, though
no evidence was ever found to prove or disprove it.

At about the same time as the Nazis eliminated the mayor of one
major town in Germany, the Americans appointed the mayor of
another. This was Konrad Adenauer, destined to be West Germany's
first post-war Chancellor and the man who was to pull his nation out
of the ruins and degradation of World War Two to a place of honour
and power among free nations. Special Agent Joseph Rosen, who was
involved in the Rhine Maiden case, was one of a group of American
army officers who were responsible for Adenauer's return to public
life. In late March 1945 Rosen moved into the devastated Rhineland
city of Cologne, where his job was to work with American Military
Government officials in finding qualified Germans to take over the
city's government. Rosen recalled:

One day some Germans came in and said they had found Konrad
Adenauer.
    'Who's he?' we asked. 'He's not on our "good guy" list or any
other list.'
    They told us Adenauer had been Mayor of Cologne before the
Nazis took over and had been under house arrest since then. I went
out with several companions and we finally located the former
Mayor in the basement of a bombed-out house. We started
knocking on the door but there was no answer. So then we had to
kick on the door a number of times before a man's voice spoke in
German.
    'Go away,' he said, 'or I'll call the police.'
    'As far as you're concerned,' I replied, 'we are the police!'
    It took us quite a while to get the old gentleman – he was 69 then
– to open the door. When he finally opened the door, there was
this emaciated little man, who didn't speak any English and didn't
want to know us at all.
    When we finally got inside we talked to him about becoming the
first post-war German Mayor of Cologne. But Mr Adenauer said
he wasn't interested in politics or any job in government. He told
us he wanted no part of the American army or government because

his son was a captain in the German army and still fighting right across the Rhine river from Cologne. He was worried the Nazis would kill his son if they found out that the father was co-operating with the Americans.

At length I just said: 'Get in the jeep. Whether you like it or not, we're appointing you Mayor again.'

So we took him to Military Government and returned him to history.

After talking to him a number of times in our office we finally got him to agree to become an advisor to the civilian mayor of the city – a sort of unofficial Mayor of Cologne. It was a sort of sub-rosa deal but of course he finally took over as full-time mayor and did a real fine job.

When I knew him, Mr Adenauer was very co-operative but never condescending. No one could push him around.

Even while the CIC were helping to establish the Allies' new order in the conquered territories, they continued to run grave risks in those wild regions of Germany where the Nazis still held sway. But though GIS agents were scooped up like tadpoles by Allied counter intelligence, few CIC agents ever ended up in enemy hands. In the main this was due to the differences in rôles between the two sides. Positive intelligence agents worked behind enemy lines and took all the risks. Counter intelligence personnel normally stayed within their own lines and were thus less exposed to the danger of capture. However, it did happen, most notably to three agents of the 104th CIC Detachment, who were caught in a town in the Ruhr pocket in early April and treated to a rare glimpse of the German Army in a state of advanced disintegration, then sentenced to death.

Lieutenant Allan Fial and Agents Robert Robertson and Paul Schurf, who were fluent German speakers, had the task of covering a group of Ruhr towns for intelligence targets in the immediate wake of the American advance. The morning of 11 April found them driving their jeep along the empty road to the town of Scharzfeld. Their information was that the place had been cleared of enemy troops during the night, and certainly they could see nothing to suggest otherwise – there was not a soul in the streets, no activity of any kind. A Polish girl in the town hall told them that, in fact, a few German soldiers were still scattered about the town, though she was not sure exactly where; but since American tanks were due to arrive at any moment the three agents decided to stay, and Robertson left the building and went across the road to where the jeep was parked to get their remaining weapons – a sub-machine gun and a German rifle.

Casting a glance over his shoulder, he was aghast to see that his two companions were no longer alone – four German paratroopers had emerged from a room in the building and were busy disarming Fial and Schurf, while a gun was aimed at himself. In vain the CIC men tried to persuade the Germans that it was they that ought to surrender – the whole darned American Army would be trundling along in a couple of minutes, they said, and the war was as near as damn over, so why make life difficult? The Americans were ordered back into the jeep at gunpoint and the paras piled in behind them. Then they drove to the first of many destinations on a bewildering tour of the bewildered German lines, where their presence proved either a puzzle, an embarrassment or an object of intense curiosity to German soldiers and camp followers alike.

Their first port of call was an army hideout in the mountains. Here they were hauled in front of the commanding officer of a German unit, a young, ardent Nazi, who looked them up and down and decided he wanted nothing to do with them. He ordered a guard detail to take them to the battalion command post, and from there they were shunted farther down the line to the regimental command post. Here they were thoroughly searched and their CIC credentials and investigative notes and papers taken from them. But their interrogation was interrupted by a runner who arrived with a message that the Americans were to be brought immediately to divisional headquarters, and they were bundled into a German Army vehicle and driven along the country lanes into deepest, darkest Germany.

At length they came to a large country house where they were ordered to get out and led indoors. A drinks party was in full swing inside; the schnapps and the hock were flowing, and pretty women circulated among straight-backed officers in shiny riding boots. The unexpected arrival of three American gate-crashers wearing no unit insignia or badges of rank served only to redouble the jollity and babble of noise at the party. Fial, Robertson and Schurf were taken into the kitchen. Almost immediately the kitchen was filled with German women, who crowded around the Americans, took them by the sleeve, asked them question after question. So had it been in England, and so had it been in France, and now so it was in the Fatherland. Only here there was a greater urgency to the questions, which harped on one basic theme: 'What will the Americans do with us when they come?'

Evening had fallen at the end of a very long day. A colonel came into the kitchen and put an end to the impromptu gathering. Apologizing for the makeshift quarters in which they would have to spend the night, he despatched them under guard to a barn, where they made themselves as comfortable as they could in the straw. Their guard offered a glimmer of hope. He had been on the Russian Front but deserted and made his way back to Germany by way of Norway. He seemed disaffected and not averse to the idea of defecting to the American lines with his three prisoners. But he could not make up his mind. Endlessly he debated the pros and cons with the CIC men. Perhaps, he said, he could put off a decision till the morning.

The morning proved too late. Soon after daybreak the CIC agents were moved even farther back down the line, from division to corps. Corps headquarters was located in a hotel in a resort town. Here the serious questioning began. The German intelligence officer had all the agents' credentials and investigative documents on the table in front of him. What he was basically interested in learning was what sort of organization the CIC was – he had not heard of it before. The agents managed to parry most of his questions and the interrogation came to an inconclusive end. The CIC men were moved on once again, this time to the headquarters of a Waffen-SS battalion, where they were engulfed by a crowd of rough young soldiers and their girlfriends, all of whom clamoured to know one thing: 'What are the Americans going to do with us when they come?' An officer arrived on the scene and dispersed the crowd. Taking the agents confidentially on one side, he too had a question to put to them: 'When the Americans come, will I be able to get a job with Military Government?' Later that day the agents were taken upstairs to the council room of the local town hall, where the entire German officer hierarchy were seated round a large table. On the entry of Lieutenant Fial and his fellow counter intelligence colleagues into the room the assembled officers rose as one body. They too had many questions to ask, and one above all: 'When the Americans come, what will they do with us?'

Next day the 1st US Division entered the outskirts of the town. The SS refused to permit evacuation of the town, even though there were many wounded soldiers in the hotels, which had been taken over as emergency hospitals, so the Americans turned their artillery on the place and began to shell it to bits. The three CIC men sat out the bombardment playing Black Jack in the gaol in the town hall basement. From time to time various German soldiers in various stages of disenchantment and dismay burst into their cell. One officer, whose wife and children had been killed in an Allied air raid on Paderborn, came near to shooting them on the spot. Then the gaoler came and said he was very sorry but the order had been given to execute the prisoners, as the town was being evacuated and no prisoners could be taken along, especially ones from American intelligence. Another officer came in. He had come to carry out the execution, he said – terribly sorry but it couldn't be helped. The Americans had to talk very fast and very persuasively. Eventually the officer agreed to lock them up instead of shooting them, and left to join the retreating forces.

Up at street level American troops were moving into the town. The gaoler unlocked the cell but it was too dangerous for the agents to go out into the streets, for the soldiers were firing at anything that moved. Civilians began to crowd into the cell, hoping to find greater security in American company, and all asking the same old question: 'What are the Americans going to do with us when they come?' The agents were worried that the soldiers might resort to their occasional practice of tossing grenades into basement windows first and looking later. Robertson decided it was time to move. Knowing GI psychology, he selected the prettiest girl in the cell and persuaded her to go upstairs and walk down the middle of the street till she found some American soldiers she could guide back to the gaol. 'Whatever else they might do they won't shoot you,' Robertson told the girl. And he was right. So CIC agents Fial, Robertson and Schurf escaped with their lives and regained their liberty, and the Germans at last found out what the Americans did with them when they came.

Another serious loss involving the CIC occurred in Sixth Army Group area at a somewhat earlier date. This was an incident of a quite different sort, potentially catastrophic and totally embarrassing, though fortunately it turned out not to be the work of the German Intelligence Service. In February 1945 a GMC 6×6 truck belonging to a US Army signal unit was stolen after being left without a guard. Since the truck contained a top secret US diplomatic code and decoding devices of the highest importance, the theft was a matter of the utmost gravity. The secret material could be in the hands of the enemy or of a foreign power – for even at the time of the Grand Alliance the British and French were still foreign powers when it came to global diplomacy. A squad of sixteen agents, six from CIC, two from the FBI flown over from the United States, six CI agents from the French Army and two French civilian Secret Police, was put on the case by Colonel David Erskine, the Chief of Counter Intelligence at Sixth Army Group, and the strictest security was placed on the investigation. The G-2s of all units in the entire European Theatre were alerted, and in distant Washington DC code clerks were dragged out of bed to set up new codes when news of the loss reached the Capitol at 11 that night.

The missing code and decoding material were contained in a field safe and two combination chests which had been on the back of the truck when it was stolen. At the start of the search the only source of information was rumour. According to one rumour, the truck had been on the Rhine bridge when it was blown up. CIC agents walked along the west bank of the Rhine looking for clues, the Germans sniping at them the while from the other bank. Other agents flew in Piper Cub spotter planes all over the canals and rivers in the vicinity of Colmar in the hope that they could sight something on the river bed from the air. In vain. Then the truck was found. A French warrant finally located the thief, a French truck driver, and extracted a confession from him. He had stolen the truck, he said, because someone else had stolen his. He had been allowed through an army roadblock and had then stopped in the middle of a bridge over the River Geissen and got rid of the cargo, which was no use to him, by manhandling the three heavy steel containers over the side into the river below – no mean feat on his own, because each container weighed 550 pounds (about a quarter of a ton).

Deep sea divers were now brought over from Cherbourg to search the river bottom in the area below the bridge, a task hampered by the high level of the river after heavy rains. On 9 March the water began to subside a little and the two combination chests were found a hundred yards downstream. But there was still no sign of the field safe with the diplomatic code inside. Day after day CIC agents tramped up and down the sodden banks of the Geissen – 'with such frequency,' CIC records reported, 'that unknowing travelers might have surmised that the whole US Army was lonesome for the Mississippi.' So seriously was the matter taken that Colonel Erskine drew up plans for a Herculean solution – the diversion of the river. Then on 20 March, just before these plans were due to be implemented, an unknown CIC agent making one last search detected something gleaming deep in the waters of the river all of 600 yards from the bridge. The gleam came from the missing safe, whose coat of army paint had been scoured away as the safe was tumbled over and over along the river bed by the headlong rush of the water. The safe was quickly recovered and trucked rearward over the Vosges Mountains to Paris, with Colonel Erskine riding in escort. As a result of this incident Colonel Erskine was awarded the Bronze Star, the negligent parties were court-martialled, and orders were issued that diplomatic codes were no longer allowed to be taken forward of Army headquarters.

In theory, at least, the CIC's main task during the conquest of Germany was the security of the Army. But given the virtual disappearance of the German Intelligence Service, the failure of the Werwolf resistance, the collapse of the German armed forces, the disintegration of the Nazi state, above all the Allies' overwhelming supremacy in men, matériel and morale, significant threats to the Army's security were actually minimal, and in practice the CIC was mostly preoccupied with a secondary task which had been given it by the Joint Chiefs of Staff – the round-up of the functionaries of the Nazi state. One Special Agent recalled:

> The round-up didn't get under way until we jumped the Roer River and then it was continuous on through the post-war occupation. We were given orders to arrest all Nazis from Ortsgruppenleiter on up, all Gestapo, all SD, all SS from Gefreiter up. It became routine, like the endless succession of spy and security suspects. All officials – Burgermeisters and the like – were automatic suspects. In thousands of cases they were told to report to the CIC office with toothbrush and change of underwear and they could often be discerned peering round a nearby corner, waiting until the precise reporting time before they came to the office. Some, of course, fled. Many couldn't conceive of themselves as criminals and in many cases eased our job – unlike espionage suspects. But with more than 11 million Nazi Party members in a population of 66 million or so, we didn't bother with the rank and file, except for war crimes.

The main counter intelligence emphasis became the hunting down and arrest of known Nazi leaders and Black List personalities – a process which continued long after the war was over. Among the many Nazis apprehended by the CIC during the wartime period were several who boasted high rank, deep wickedness or both. One of them was the Chief of the Amt Ausland of the RSHA, SS Brigadeführer Heinz Jost, the head of all Gestapo activities outside the territorial limits of Germany, who was discovered hiding in civilian clothes in a secluded house in the Letzlingen Forest by Agents Darrel Drolsum and Alfred Ronleder of the 35th CIC Detachment. Another was the Nazi publisher Max Amann, whose Nazi Party membership number was 3. Yet another was the notorious ex-Governor General of Poland, Dr Hans Frank, the No. 1 on the Russian Black List, who was captured by agents of the 36th CIC Detachment at Eischhausen am Schliersee.

Several no less repulsive individuals fell into the CIC net, including two concentration camp doctors whose corrupted medical ethics led them to conduct horrendous medical experiments on live inmates of the camps as a result of which most of the victims died. Two agents of the Seventh Army CIC were the first investigators to arrive at Dachau concentration camp, scene of the Nazis' most brutal and wanton outrages against their prisoners. Their immediate mission was to ferret out SS guards who had gone into hiding, using committees of prisoners drawn from every nationality present in the camp. The CIC agents soon discovered that the cruellest guards made the most cringing prisoners. Indeed, few Nazis failed to earn the direst opprobrium from their American captors, not simply on account of their past records, but also because of their conduct when in custody. For one thing, they were consummate pathological liars – in the view of one Special Agent 'the greatest alibi-makers in the world'. For another, they were men totally devoid of all sense of honour. Reporting on the mass arrest in an underground hideout near Mülheim of a number of Nazi and Gestapo officials and agents, some of whose names ranked high on the SHAEF list of wanted persons, the CIC noted a typical Nazi characteristic:

> The once-proud Nazis proved to be very willing to co-operate with their CIC interrogators, to the point of informing on each other and members of the group who had not yet been apprehended. The men had been in the service of Nazidom since the early days, and their high ranks indicated the esteem with which the Reich considered them. As captives, deprived of their death grip on the German people, these Nazis were ready to sell out anyone or anything. They were so despised by the German people that none had given them food or water in their travels, and CIC had received three phone calls from German civilians that they were in the area.

Paradoxically, some CIC detachments made use of the past reputation of the now despised Gestapo to achieve their own ends. Captain Ellis Mayfield's 29th CIC, for example, took to introducing themselves to Burgermeisters and Chiefs of Police as 'The American Gestapo', and warned these officials that they would be held responsible for the compliance of German civilians with all CIC and Military Government decrees. 'Under such an understanding,' Captain Mayfield reported, 'there has been complete deference to the CIC by all officials.'

The documentary records of the Third Reich were no less valuable. One of the most important document discoveries of the entire European Theatre of Operations was made by Special Agent George Novak of the 9th CIC Detachment operating from the town of Pansfelds in the Harz Mountains. On 17 April Novak was instructed to make a search of a castle, or château, buried deep in the heart of a fir forest in the surrounding countryside, where the German Foreign Minister von Ribbentrop was believed to be hiding. Novak arrived at the castle at the head of a column of jeeps and was met at the main door by the castle's owner, Baron Witilo von Griesheim, who had a large board from which hung the keys of every room in the place. Though there was no sign of the Foreign Minister, there was abundant evidence that he had been there, and it soon became clear why. As the Baron led the American round the castle, he unlocked room after room to reveal carefully stacked piles of neat packages containing hundreds of thousands of documents representing the entire archives of the German Foreign Ministry throughout virtually the entire period of the German state's existence (that is, from 1871 to 1944). Among the papers were the official exchanges between Berlin and London during the run-up to the war, the documents relating to the notorious Ribbentrop Pact with the Soviet Union in 1939, and a letter sent to Hitler by General Pétain in August 1944, three weeks before the liberation of Paris, in which the old Marshal begged the Führer to save the city from destruction by declaring it an open city. The Baron showed Novak a telegram that had been sent to him from Berlin a few days previously ordering him to destroy the entire archives immediately. Instead, the wily old Baron burned a few old newspapers, just to make it look as though he had complied with the directive; for, as he explained to Novak, he was determined that the documents should be saved so that historians in the future would be able to determine the facts and responsibility for the war.

Fully aware of the importance of his discovery, Special Agent Novak posted Military Police around the castle and put up a CIC notice warning that the castle was off-limits to all military personnel. He then took the Baron under arrest to higher headquarters and reported his find. When the report reached SHAEF they at once sent a two-man team representing the State Department and the British Foreign Office to authenticate the documents in the castle, and soon afterwards a long column of 200 trucks wound its way through the mountains and took the archive back to Army headquarters. After hostilities had ended the documents were transferred to Berlin and their contents examined and eventually produced as evidence against von Ribbentrop and other officials of the German Foreign Ministry in the Nuremberg trials.

Other important caches of Nazi records were uncovered by CIC detachments during the Allied race from the Rhine to the Ruhr. In a salt mine 1300 feet beneath the ground near Grasleben agents of the 35th Detachment found the complete records of Goebbels's Propaganda Ministry. In the Kyffhäuser Hotel at Sangerhausen, CIC agents with the 3rd Armored Division, spearheading VII Corps' advance on Dessau on the Elbe, came across one of the Nazis' more than usually insane record collections – that of the SS Marriage Bureau, which had been responsible for investigating the ancestry of all SS personnel and their brides-to-be to ensure that their pedigrees were nothing less than 100 per cent pure Aryan.

Sometimes the caches were composed of more solid stuff. To Victor de Guinzbourg, the larger-than-life CIC special agent whom we last encountered enlisting the help of the French Foreign Legion to break a Communist strike in Marseilles, fell the singular adventure of unearthing several tons (nearly 8 tons in Western Austria according to Guinzbourg, 4 tons in Southern Bavaria according to US records) of Nazi gold bars and coins from various hiding places including a farmer's house and the home of a Protestant pastor. Later agents of the 36th CIC Detachment of Seventh Army located another cache of hidden treasure, believed to be Himmler's personal fortune, concealed in sacks under the floorboards of a small barn in the grounds of the residence of the Chief Forester of St Johann, a village near Salzburg. The sacks were sealed with Himmler's stamp and contained some 2 million dollars in US and other currencies, together with a miscellaneous collection of bullion, coins and jewellery which had been taken from Berlin by SS General Gottlob Berger on Himmler's instructions towards the end of the previous month. Still in pursuit of Nazi treasure a CIC team resorted to dynamite to blow up the vaults of the bombed-out Reichsbank in Plauen and recover 35 bags of gold coins (including a million Swiss francs and a quarter million US dollars) which had been deposited there in April – again on Himmler's instructions.

Scientific and technological knowhow was also a prime CIC target. One of the big catches of April was Dr Albin Sawatski, one of Nazi Germany's leading scientists, the designer of the Royal Tiger super-tank and of the V-1 and V-2 rockets, who was apprehended by agents of the 104th CIC Detachment in the vicinity of Halle and described by his captors as 'the typical MGM character to play the part' – slightly stooped, round shouldered, apologetic, with thick-lensed glasses. Because of his valuable scientific knowledge, Sawatski was sent for special interrogation by Army technical intelligence.

Another weapon specialist who fell into CIC hands was Werner Piel, described as a special air courier of secret technical devices for the Luftwaffe. During his interrogation Piel claimed that the same laboratories that had devised the V-1 and V-2 had also devised an array of other diabolic weapons, including a so-called 'secret ray' produced from a device known as an Adlergerät, or Eagle Apparatus. This device, according to Piel, was capable of knocking out the engine of a tank, truck or plane by firing a ray at it, and it was reckoned to be of particular importance to Luftwaffe night fighters. At Detachment level it was often impossible for CIC agents, who were usually without specialist knowledge in secret ray technology and the like, to authenticate the claims of people such as Herr Piel. If he was genuine then it was fortunate the war was almost over. But was he a poseur, or a crank, or a con man trying to peddle bogus intelligence in return for favours from the occupation powers? The only safe thing with a man like that was to ship him back down the line for the technical experts to puzzle over. Sometimes, however, puzzling cases that were difficult to assess could be sorted out with the help of common sense and a knowledge of human nature – attributes which most CIC agents, with their prolonged exposure to the woes and wiles of humanity at war, had developed to a high degree.

One such puzzling case involved the self-styled Chief of the American Secret Service – in fact, he was an American-born German who had spent five years in German prisons for his opposition to National Socialism and had somehow achieved his liberty shortly before the final German collapse. Once at large he had begun forging American credentials for himself and for three former Wehrmacht soldiers he had pressed into his service, and with the help of a home-made pass identifying him as the Chief of the American Secret Service had set about removing Nazi officials from public office and disarming Wehrmacht deserters and issuing them with travel passes so that they could return home. This one-man crusade against Hitlerism came to an end with the German surrender and his own arrest by XX Corps CIC Detachment. Since he could give no coherent reason for his actions, the man was sent to an Army Interrogation Centre, and his 'aides' were evacuated as POWs.

Lamentably, all forms of German opposition to Nazism – before, during and after the war – received the same short shrift from the Allies. A somewhat similar case occurred in Salzwedel, where an agent of the 84th CIC was approached by a German civilian policeman volunteering to serve as an interpreter for a CIC officer who appeared to speak no English. This rival CIC agent was eventually located a few doors from the American Military Government headquarters, and was found to be a German Parachute Regiment veteran who had set himself in office as the local CIC and was conducting investigations at full blast. This enterprising enemy subject was swiftly put under arrest and his name added to the list of cases to be tried at the Military Government court next door but one.

Such cases sometimes enlivened the routine of the hard-pressed CIC day in Germany, but few provided a more enduring topic of banter than the case of the Burgermeister of Bomengion. This gentleman came to American attention when the commanding officer of a combat battalion located near the town noticed that the civilian populace seemed to have been furnished with an unprecedented number of official passes. The American officer decided to have a word with the local Burgermeister and eventually tracked him down to the Rathaus where he found him in what he described as 'a rather unprofessional situation' with a pretty young stenographer. Hastily backing out of the office door, the American on reflection concluded that such behaviour did not fall in the category of official business conducive to the restoration of order and good government in occupied Germany and reported the matter to agents of the 84th CIC Detachment.

Like a Congressional Committee, CIC descended on the hapless Burgermeister [ran the official account of the investigation]. The latter, of Napoleonic height, 35–40 years of age, with popping blue eyes, was again enjoying the delights of feminine companionship. Thus encouraged, CIC took to their task with unbounded zeal. Six more women were discovered in connecting offices. Further search revealed five policemen and a jail in which was lodged an irate individual who claimed that he was the real Burgermeister and that the incumbent Don Juan was a usurper.

Presented with these allegations, the incumbent was indignant and with kindly gestures waved his accusers away. Much against his wishes, the pseudo-Burgermeister was searched and papers found proving him to be a slightly cracked nut only recently released from an insane asylum.

Back at the asylum, the usurper was heard to remark, 'It was a lot of fun while it lasted,' to which we can only echo our agreement.

Such comic cameos tend to stick in the minds of men who have been at war. Special Agent Vince Cleary recalled a similarly bizarre encounter when he entered Krefeld with his CIC detachment in a convoy of eight jeeps and five trailers:

We sort of got lost and stopped along the street. There was rifle fire here and there and several middle-aged men huddled in a sort of entrance. One man came over to Ken Hardin, who was in charge, and said: 'I think you have made a mistake.' Hardin asked:

'Why?' The man said: 'This part of Krefeld hasn't been taken by the Americans yet. There are still German soldiers here.' So we drove around the block, saw a hotel, and Hardin said: 'We will stay here until we know what's going on.' So we each went in, put our barracks bag on a bed, and began searching the hotel for German soldiers.

Hardin told me to check out the basement. The basement consisted of a large storage area *and* a small corner saloon. I checked this out carefully. It had a well-equipped bar and out of sheer curiosity I pulled on a handle and beer came out. So I laid my grease gun down and poured myself a beer. And as I was sipping it slowly, in came a man in civilian clothes and spoke excitedly to me in German. We were at stand-off; I didn't understand German and he didn't understand American. So as a good CIC agent, I improvised. I poured him a beer and said: 'Drink.' He looked at me kinda funny and I said: 'Drink.' So we drank a bit and every time he tried to talk I said: 'Drink.' And he did.

Then my friend Winkler, who could speak German, came down the stairs, and I said to him: 'Winkler, this guy is all excited, find out what his problem is.' So Winkler talked to him in German and then turned to me and said: 'He's a German soldier and he wants to surrender.' How about that? So we let him drink his beer and then took him upstairs for processing.

It turned out this soldier lived in Krefeld and when the German Army retreated to it he silently sneaked away and went home. He took off his uniform and burned it in the furnace. Then he put on his old civilian suit and walked out into the street to see the show, a free man. And then it suddenly dawned on him that here he was, a German soldier in civilian clothes. Hell, he might be shot as a spy! So as I was the first American soldier he saw, he came to me to surrender and I poured him a beer. But it was fortunate, for his sake, that he never knew he had surrendered to the CIC, the spy catchers!

The most daunting targets in Germany were the great cities, swarming with shattered populations of enemy subjects running into hundreds of thousands, where the bewildering maze of bunkers, basements and holes in the rubble provided a labyrinthine *terra incognita* in which Nazi fugitives and subversives could hide out almost with impunity. The Rhineland cities of Cologne, Bonn and Koblenz were the first German cities the CIC entered in which the civilian population was still largely in place. A 'T' Force consisting of 973 persons and 175 motor vehicles, together with 214 investigators from 24 different intelligence agencies, including the CIC, reduced all listed targets in Cologne by the end of March. Smaller 'T' Forces dealt with Bonn and Koblenz, where CIC personnel travelled over the same ground that agents of the Corps of Intelligence Police had worked 27 years before.

As they fanned out into the German interior from the east bank of the Rhine the CIC detachments found themselves responsible for vast swathes of enemy territory and a plethora of German towns of all sizes and states of ruin and disaffection. The 1st Division CIC Detachment, for example, had to look after the counter intelligence security of 60 towns in addition to the city of Bonn. The 87th CIC Detachment worked in more than 70 German towns including Koblenz in the first 25 days in March, while the 89th covered 71 towns, interrogated 17,000 Germans, screened 5000 foreign displaced persons, and made 700 arrests, four of the arrestees committing suicide, including Hitler's brother-in-law, Martin Hammitzch, who fired a pistol into his temple as CIC agents came to pick him up. In terms of sheer space these areas were more than the detachments had the capability to cope with, and many German towns had to be by-passed in the general advance. Captain Mayfield, commanding the 29th CIC Detachment, complained that his detachment was not physically capable of carrying out its counter intelligence mission in an area 200 by 50 kilometres if they were also forced to do much of the work of 14 Military Government detachments as well. Half their time, Mayfield complained, was spent establishing civilian government and investigating war crimes, which were not part of the CIC's role. At the extreme end of the American advance, the 3rd Armored CIC Detachment was to find itself responsible for counter intelligence security in an even vaster area measuring 3500 square kilometres around Dessau on the banks of the Elbe.

Time, too, became a commodity beyond the CIC's power to control. As the Allied advance into Germany turned into a headlong pursuit, it was all the forward CIC teams could do to keep up with the lead tanks and spearhead infantry, and they could no longer find time to process the mountains of records they had collected, or maintain their vehicles and equipment, or even collect their wits. So swift was the German rout that the CIC found Party records intact, and tea and toast half finished on the desks of recently decamped Nazi officials, and the bodies of officials who preferred suicide still warm. In the race to the Elbe the CIC detachments rarely spent more than a day in any one place before galloping on. On 18 April a CIC 'T' Force with engineer and artillery battalions as guards entered the Nazis' holy city of Nuremberg and in a period of 100 hours reduced in rapid sequence a series of targets which included the Party headquarters, the SS headquarters and scientific and industrial establishments. At the end of the month Munich was similarly reduced – the last big city in Germany to see CIC operations in wartime.

Special Agent Richard W. Beebe was to write of this hectic period of the war:

> After leaving the Ruhr area, our 2nd Armored Division continued its dash across Central Germany toward the Elbe and Berlin. Some of us travelled at times with the 82nd Reconnaissance Battalion, which was far out in front of the main division. We were living on adrenalin, working 18 to 20 hours a day. Many times while *en route* to the Elbe we entered completely unoccupied areas or villages. The Germans were in a state of shock and we figured that if we got into a town with the leading elements of our division, we could locate Gestapo, Nazis and German Intelligence person-nel before they could hide out. Our 14 men, in fact, arrested more than 1000 of these persons as we crossed Germany. The kind of operation we were in was probably without precedent and we constantly improvised.
>
> I have the satisfaction that along a fairly wide swathe across Germany, our little detachment went a long way in extirpating the Nazis and setting up local governments which had a chance to flourish as democratic institutions. A military government unit of the army was supposed to do this work, but we never saw them and drifted into it as a by-line of our major function.

In this final, chaotic phase of the European war, with the German state disintegrating by the hour as the Russians and the Western Allies poured in from east and west, little was seen of the German Intelligence Service, which vanished like a will-o'-the-wisp, de-stroying its files in key cities like Karlsruhe, Stuttgart and Baden-Baden (but keeping certain intelligence records relating to the Soviet front which could be traded with the Allies after the war). The Werwolf resistance organizations proved equally chimerical. Or-ganizing piecemeal and too late, the Werwolf never became prop-erly operational, and though the CIC uncovered numerous caches of arms and explosives intended for sabotage and resistance activities against the occupation powers, and rounded up groups of Hitler Youth and other fanatics who had been detailed to wage guerrilla war behind the front line, Werwolf actions against Allied forces were few and ineffective. Seven artillery spotter aircraft belonging to VIII Corps were damaged by saboteurs, and on 17 April the commanding officer of the 44th CIC Detachment, Captain Peter Cummins, was found dead in the forest near Eherbach, along with a fellow officer from Division, both men minus their credentials, papers and boots. At first it was thought the two Americans had been tortured and then murdered, presumably by the Werwolf, but it was later revealed that they had been ambushed by a small stay-behind battalion of German infantry after losing their bearings in the woods. The divisional officer was killed outright in the gunfire, but though Captain Cummins was only wounded he was led away and shot on the German commander's orders.

Such incidents were rare, however. During its victorious drive across southern Germany Seventh Army encountered no serious acts of sabotage and their arrival was greeted with a profound sense of relief by the civil populace, who willingly co-operated with the CIC and readily volunteered their services as informants. The situation was somewhat different in central Germany. Unlike the Rhinelanders, who had welcomed the Americans with garlands and wine, the population of this section of Germany eyed the conquering Americans coldly. Here Goebbels' propaganda has taken a firmer grip and old attitudes died hard. As late as 25 April a Nazi Kreisleiter from the Nuremberg region believed that the war would be decided in Germany's favour, but if by some remote possibility the Americans should win the war, Hitler would take up arms and join his troops in the field, where he would fight until he was killed. In this way, he contended, the Führer, like Christ, would be martyred at the hands of his enemies, and his ideas would live on eternally. A twelve-year-old Hitler Youth *Jugendschaftführer* by the name of Dieter Klemm put the whole Nazi ethos even more bluntly to bemused agents of the 103rd CIC:

'I hate you Americans. I wish I had a pistol to kill all of you. I shall never betray my Führer as long as I live. I realize that you are going to put me away in some camp or prison, but some day I shall be released and then I shall continue my fight for Hitler and Nazi Germany. Do not hope ever to eradicate our National Socialist ideals or ideas. There are enough of us left to continue the fight as long as we live. That is all I have to say. Now you can do with me whatever you please.'

From the first crossing of the Rhine on 7 March it had taken barely two months for the Western Allies to overrun Nazi Germany. By the time Hitler killed himself in Berlin on 30 April it was clear the end of the European war was an imminent formality. The litany of German defeat was monotonous and unvarying. On 1 May a million Germans laid down their arms in Italy; on 2 May Berlin fell to the Russians; on

3 May Hamburg was taken by the British; on 4 May, the day Hitler's house at Berchtesgaden was occupied by the Americans, American units pushing down through Austria met up with American units coming up from Italy; on 5 May two and a half million German soldiers on the northern flank of the Allied battlefront surrendered to Field Marshal Montgomery at Lüneberg Heath; on 7 May, VE-Day in the West, the Germans signed the unconditional surrender of all their remaining forces on all fronts. The war which had left 40 million dead and a whole continent in ruins was over. For many Americans, CIC included, VE-Day was not a day of unrestrained joy alone; for many combat troops their first emotion was to mourn their fallen comrades who would not see this day. Nor was VE-Day the sudden end of all military activity. The CIC mission in Germany, where the problem now was to win the peace, continued unabated for months and even years to come; and in the Pacific the fighting carried on undiminished. But for many veterans a strange new future beckoned as demobilization or redeployment of the Armies in the European Theatre got under way.

Before embarking on the homeward bound troopship at Le Havre, CIC Special Agent Edward R. Koudelka handed in his weapons, including his .38-calibre revolver issued only to CIC personnel, and in return was issued a parting document purporting to come from US Army headquarters entitled 'Indoctrination for Return to US'. This tongue-in-cheek document not only served to advise departing soldiers about the half-forgotten way of life in the Zone of the Interior to which they were now returning, but to remind them of the bizarrely rough and ready soldiers' life they had led on their long march from the shell-pocked beaches of Africa to the rubble-blocked streets of Munich and Nuremberg. Among the document's many words of advice were the following:

1. A typical American breakfast consists of such strange foods as fresh eggs, milk and butter made from cream. If you wish some butter, you turn to the person nearest to it and say quietly, 'Please pass the butter.' You do not say, 'Throw the goddam grease.'

2. In the event the helmet is retained by the individual, he will refrain from using it as a chair, wash bowl, foot bath or bathtub. All these devices are furnished in the average American home. It is not considered good practice to squat Indian fashion in a corner. When it is desired to take a bath, it is not considered good form to find the nearest stream.

3. In travelling in the US it is often necessary to spend the night. Hotels are provided for this purpose. The present practice

of entering the nearest house, throwing the occupants into the yard and taking over the premises will cease.

4. In motion picture theaters it is not considered good form to whistle every time a female over eight and under eighty crosses the screen. If vision is impaired by the person in front of you, do not hit him across the back of the head and say, 'Move your head, jerk.'

5. It is not considered proper to go around hitting everyone of draft age not in uniform. Ask for his credentials, and if he can't show them THEN slug him.

6. Air raids and enemy patrols are not encountered in America. Therefore, it is not necessary to wear a helmet in church or hold a weapon at the ready, loaded and cocked, when talking to civilians in the street.

All individuals returning to the US will make every effort to conform to the customs and habits of the regions visited. Any actions which reflect upon the honor of the uniform will be promptly dealt with.

Standing on the ship's fan-tail as he sailed away from the shattered continent of Europe towards the red ball of the westering sun and his distant homeland on the other side of the ocean, Special Agent Edward Koudelka was lost in thought. 'I turned and faced forward,' he was to remember long afterwards, 'and dared to think of the future that lay somewhere beyond that calm and solemn sea. Would it be a long future of fulfilment, or would that future be brief and possibly violent in some Pacific adventure?'

For he knew, as every veteran who had survived Hitler's war also knew, that the defeat of the Third Reich did not mark the end of America's war.

10
THE MARCH TO JAPAN

Japan had entered World War Two with an offensive plan which called for the occupation of what was variously known as the New Order in East Asia or the Sphere of Co-Prosperity in Greater East Asia, euphemisms for a new and greatly expanded Japanese Empire which the Japanese government had been in the process of building since the end of the previous century. The region included Korea, Manchuria and much of northern and eastern China, which had been seized before the Japanese attack on the United States fleet in Pearl Harbor; and British, Dutch, French and US possessions, including French Indochina, Malaya, Burma, the Philippines and the Dutch East Indies, which were to be taken in a lightning offensive following Pearl Harbor.

In a very short time Japanese forces largely achieved their initial aims. The Americans under General MacArthur were driven from the Philippines. Hong Kong, Siam, Malaya, Singapore, Burma, Sarawak, Borneo, Sumatra, Timor, Bali, Java all fell. When the Allies established bases in Australia for future counter-offensives, the Japanese embarked on a further offensive designed to expand their perimeter and cut the American line of communications to Australia. They invaded New Guinea and the Solomon Islands, seized the US Aleutians and menaced Midway Island, off Hawaii. But Midway ended in defeat for the Japanese and marked a major turning in the war in the Pacific. For the Allies it was a great strategic victory. For the Japanese it represented the loss of their strategic initiative and the end of their plans to invade Fiji, Samoa and New Caledonia.

The war in the Pacific had thus undergone a decisive change by the time CIC agents began arriving in some number in those Pacific and Far Eastern theatres in which the US Army bore the brunt of operations. By then the entire area had been placed under the strategic direction of the US joint chiefs of staff, who divided the Pacific into two major theatres. Admiral Nimitz, commander of the US Pacific fleet, was appointed C-in-C of the Pacific Ocean areas, and since this was an essentially navy affair, few, if any, CIC agents ever saw service there. At about the same time General MacArthur was appointed Supreme Commander, South West Pacific area, which included the Dutch East Indies, the Philippines, Australia and part of the Solomon Islands. It was from this area, from Australia in the south, that the greatest mass of Allied forces under MacArthur would fight its way into Japan itself; and it was among these forces that the greatest number of CIC personnel would be deployed in the Japanese war. In the meantime, ever-mounting pressure would be applied against the enemy from the Central Pacific to the east and the China-Burma-India Theatre to the west, where CIC agents were also deeply involved in safeguarding the security of the American front.

For half a century Burma – a country of rugged mountains, dense jungles and disease-laden swamps – had been known to most Americans only through the stories of Rudyard Kipling and Somerset Maugham. But by the early summer of 1943 Burma had assumed a strategic importance probably unsurpassed by any other area in the world. For Burma offered the *only* lifeline to China; and the free Chinese forces under General Chiang Kai-shek could not hold out against the Japanese much longer unless the United States could find a way of supplying them with their immediate needs – trucks, artillery, tanks and other heavy equipment.

American planes were desperately trying to ferry in 10,000 tons of supplies a month from Assam, India, to the Yunnan plateau in China via the 'Hump' of the Himalayan mountains. But it was not possible for them to fly the badly needed heavy equipment. And if China fell, Japan would then be able to exploit her tremendous resources without harassment, and even find a refuge there for her government and warlords to hold out almost indefinitely if the Americans ever came to threaten her home islands.

Appreciating the immense importance of the Chinese struggle within the big picture of the war in Asia, the Americans had established a China command only a few months after joining the war. Known as the USAF CBI, or United States Forces China-Burma-India, its headquarters were activated in Chungking, China, in March 1942 with the mission of increasing the effectiveness of US assistance to the Chinese war effort. This effectiveness depended in large measure on the development of overland communications to China, and early in 1943 plans were made to construct a road through northern Burma, together with a parallel oil pipeline which would connect with a similar pipeline to come in from Calcutta. The road and pipeline to China would make it possible to achieve a dramatic jump in the monthly supplies to 85,000 tons of general war matériel and 54,000 tons of petroleum products. This would not only help relieve Chiang's hard-pressed forces, but would also enable B-29 bomber bases to operate inside China, from which a devastating air assault could be launched against the Japanese islands.

This, then, was the plan. It was a plan that posed such tremendous security problems for the military that in May 1943 the CBI Theatre requested the War Department to provide it with a field grade counter intelligence officer and a CIC detachment of one officer and five Special Agents. Such was the Army's general lack of knowledge of, and hesitancy in using, this little known branch of the service, that the CIC role was envisaged as being purely experimental. The CIC, however, knew better. Six CIC men were sent out almost immediately, and the Chief of the CIC ordered a search of the files for more men with special qualifications for this far-off Theatre of Operations. Several were found with years of valuable experience in the Orient. They included Ali Mohammed, a former resident of Lahore, India, in civilian life a professor at the University of Southern California; Leroy Newland, who had spent his first 18 years in Korea as the son of a missionary; Edwin Simpson, also the son of a missionary, who had lived in Bombay for 17 years and spoke several dialects fluently; Thomas Kendall, a longtime resident in China, whose mother was a prisoner of the Japanese; George Mah, whose uncle turned out to be the Mayor of Nanking; and William Tyng, who had spent eight years in China and spoke a number of the local dialects. Such were the arcane qualifications and not inconsiderable calibre of the outrageously lowly ranked personnel on whom the CIC could call for service in some of the remotest and most alien nooks and crannies of the warring globe.

By September 1943, when the CIC agents began filtering into the Theatre, the situation in Burma had grown graver still. The Japanese had by now conquered the whole of the country except for the fringes of mountain, jungle and swamp on the north and west, and they threatened to seize the British base at Imphal and sever the Bengal –Assam railroad to the south. On these important points the air transport over the 'Hump' and the projected new Burma Road – the whole China strategy, in fact – depended. Overwhelming Japanese presence in Burma also greatly increased the likely danger from enemy agents and it was this that initially preoccupied George L. Wilson and his advance party of five CIC agents when they began their first security survey in December. Behind them came a large group of over a hundred officers and agents who had received special instruction in CBI conditions in the US and North Africa, and were given further special training on arrival in India, either at the British Intelligence school in Karachi or at the British Jungle Warfare School in Budni. The new arrivals were then deployed in 12 detachments located as far apart as New Delhi, Calcutta, Assam, Chabua, China and the XX Bomber Force at Kharagpur, India.

From the outset it seemed clear that the problems which beset them in other Theatres around the world would not be entirely absent in the CBI. In vain the CIC pleaded that their role in CBI was overwhelmingly a logistical and advisory one; that their agents should not be utilized in a tactical situation, and have to operate in the field with divisions, corps and armies as they did elsewhere, even though CBI was considered a Combat Theatre. Intelligence officers on headquarters staffs seemed as blind as ever to the CIC's proper role and completely unaware of the meaning of counter intelligence and security. Their attitude seemed strange when it was remembered that eight months previously numerous reports had stated that the Japanese were sending not only espionage agents but also trained saboteurs in large numbers to operate in the vicinity of Kweilin and Kunming and had organized an assassination squad of some 200 men, their targets being British and American officers in CBI, with rewards of from 500,000 to 700,000 Chinese dollars per target. In addition there had been numerous reports of sabotage to telephone lines, including occasions when lines in the air warning net had been cut before Japanese air raids on Hengyang and Yunnanyi.

The CIC received a more sympathetic understanding from the British, with whom they soon established a close liaison. The British had perceived the need for security and counter intelligence during centuries of imperial administration – never more so than during these troubled war years when political unrest, nurtured by the hatred of Hindu and Burmese nationalists and played upon by communist agitation, provided fertile ground for Japanese propagandists. This explosive combination of circumstances made protection against sabotage CIC's most important mission – a danger hard to control in that it could come from any direction. When it was found that the telephone line between Calcutta and the US bomber base at Kharagpur was being cut as part of a systematic sabotage programme, Agent Richard Klise travelled the whole length of the line, visiting local police chiefs and village elders along the way, and cautiously reminding them that each village was subject to a fine whenever an accident 'happened' to the line in their locality.

CIC agents likewise travelled the length of the vital gasoline pipeline between Calcutta and the new Burma Road from Ledo, a major target for saboteurs, issuing similar instructions to establish the local responsibility of each village. Investigating breaks in the gasoline pipeline between Myitkyiana and Bhamo, Agent William Adams found containers of gasoline in three small villages along the route and discovered that villagers had been using the gasoline to ferment a rough kind of Burmese moonshine rice liquor. Adams warned the village elders that any future incident would incur a stiff fine, but the local police, less inhibited by diplomatic niceties, issued a blunter threat – next time there was a break in the pipeline their villages would be razed by fire. Meanwhile, as the famed Ledo-Burma Road (later known as the Stilwell Road) pushed ever deeper into Burma, Agent Edwin W. Simpson set out to travel its entire 1120 miles, from Doom Dooma in Assam to Kunming in China, in order to check the security planning along this vital doorway into the Burma combat zone and collect counter intelligence information.

Wherever they went in the CBI, CIC agents plotted their own missions and soon so demonstrated their value to the military mission of the Theatre that before long they had earned warm commendations from the Commanding General down. As the CIC detachment attached to the 10th Air Force prepared to leave for China, the 10th Air Force Commander commended them for their devotion to duty and described them as a major asset in the maintenance of the security of the Air Force. Endorsing this, the Commander of the Theatre Army Air Forces, Major General George Stratemeyer, added: 'You have justifiably won the respect and pride of the Services.'

In late October 1944 CIC agents were sent into Burma. Viewed initially with suspicion by the Northern Area Combat Command (NACC), they soon proved their worth when their assistance was requested for a legendary special combat group known as Merrill's Marauders, commanded by Brigadier General Frank D. Merrill. A Marauders Task Force, code-named Galahad, had cut off the Japanese ahead of General Stilwell's Chinese Division and laid siege to Myitkyina. Several CIC detachments operating as a single unit under officer-in-charge John H. Thorne were brought into Myit-kyina Port, where they were briefed by the NACC G-2, Colonel Joseph W. Stilwell, Jr. Their specific mission was to apprehend enemy agents, collaborators and saboteurs, maintain security at the front as well as rear areas, effect close liaison with British Civil Affairs, and install a rapid system for classifying native inhabitants into 'Black' (*watch them!*) and 'White' (*friendly?*) categories. When John Thorne, with Leroy Newland, Carl Manwell, Jean Curran and James Carr, entered Myitkyina with the first assault troops of the

Galahad Task Force, they found two-and-a-half tons of documents in enemy headquarters and 'Black' collaborators scattered so far and wide that it took CIC Agent Edmund Fong, who was suffering from malaria and jaundice, two weeks of jungle travel by boat, plane, jeep and his own two sore feet to reach the remote village of Kansi in North Burma, where the headman, one Sinwa Nawng, was arrested for seizing, disarming and handing over to the Japanese 15 Burmese soldiers and an American pilot.

Increasingly these jungle safaris were what most CIC work in Burma was about. In October 1944 most CIC detachment agents were reorganized into Combat Interrogation Teams (CITs) consisting of two or three agents each, plus native interpreters from OSS Detachment 101. Each team was equipped with necessary camping equipment and food, in order to travel unhampered throughout their assigned territories, and their mission was, as before, to apprehend enemy agents and collaborators, obtain names of Black List suspects, and secure all possible information about the enemy, including enemy documents. For many of the agents involved in these CIT missions there now ensued adventurous weeks and months of arduous bush whacking through the forested interior of primeval Burma.

CIT No. 1 began operating out of Mohnyin, south of the Stilwell Road, and took their first scalps when they trapped the leaders of a Japanese-operated gang that had captured and tortured many Allied soldiers. The leader of the gang, Saung Swe, and his second-in-command were later tried and executed, along with others rounded up in the same area. The team then moved over to Katha near the Chinese border, an area seething with intrigue, where they arrested a gang which had tied an American soldier to a tree and burned out his eyes, and at Tigyaing they rounded up a group of collaborators who had ferried a party of Wingate's force of British Chindits to an island in the river and then betrayed the location to the Japanese. CIT No. 1 was then ordered to join the 36th Chinese Division that was operating midway between Katha and Mandalay. The team accompanied the forward troops of the division in the occupation of captured villages, but progress was impeded by the ruggedness of the terrain, and on occasion the CIC men had to stop and hire natives to build rafts to get them across the rivers that lay in their way.

Meanwhile in November 1944 CIT No. 2 moved to Schwegu on the Irrawaddy River, working in wild, heavily forested country where there were no roads. The team had been given a boat with an outboard motor for use along the river and neighbouring streams, and where the boat couldn't go they went on foot. For 12 days agents

Robert Edriss, James Carr and Sick Foon Woo, with their interpreters and radio men, slogged over 120 miles of barely discernible
trails through a rough land of steep mountains and deep valleys
drowned in jungle, visiting 15 villages in the course of their arduous
trek in order to learn the extent of their food problems, check reports
of Chinese guerrilla raids, secure intelligence about the Japanese and
discover the names of collaborators. This was a remote and complex
world of guerrillas and bandits, secret societies and feuding tribes,
pro- and anti-Japanese and pro- and anti-British factions. The
Americans trod warily in this ethnic and political cauldron and in
their monthly report noted the one sure fact in an insecure world –
'that the physical condition of CIC personnel continued to be
stressed.'

Other CIT teams had similar tales to tell. Team No. 3, moving
into Namhkam with the Chinese First Army hard on the heels of the
retreating Japanese, found the native Shan tribesmen so happy to
get rid of their Japanese oppressors that they forgot their petty
grievances against the British, and even dropped their feud with the
Kachins of the hills in appreciation for their help in driving out the
Japanese. The team reluctantly left Namhkam to move on to Muse,
near the border between the northern Shan state and Yunnan, where
they found the counter intelligence situation greatly confused by the
activities of gangs of Chinese bandits who were operating across the
border into Burma in the guise of intelligence agents, ostensibly to
hunt down Japanese spies but in reality to ambush rich wayfarers for
their ransom money. Team No. 4, meanwhile, entered the city of
Katha only days after its fall. As the only American unit in the area,
the team was called upon for a variety of tasks, from the handling of
Japanese collaborators to the disposition of a squad of 18 military
elephants and their drivers trying to make contact with their unit, the
Kachin Levies. The CIC quickly won the respect of the local
population in Katha. 'If one was picked up by the CIC jeep,' went the
saying, 'one did not come back.'

To CIT No. 5 fell the dubious distinction of being the first team to
come under enemy fire and to have the first agents to be awarded
Purple Hearts in the CBI Theatre. In February 1945, learning that
two Americans had been caught in a Japanese trap six miles south of
Kutkai, agents James Lucas and Seymour Abeles volunteered to go
to their rescue. The Americans had been killed before their arrival,
however, and as the team began digging up their bodies they came
under withering Japanese machine-gun fire, and Abeles was
wounded before the team managed to escape the ambush. A few days
later Lucas and Agent Edmund Fong joined up with Agent Joe

Breechen and the 50th Chinese Division and marched with it into Penghai while the city was still under Japanese artillery fire and snipers were still riddling the streets. Here Breechen became the second agent to gain the Purple Heart when he was wounded by a splinter from an enemy shellburst.

By July 1945 the CIC had completed its tactical mission in India–Burma and the bulk of the China-bound detachments had already crossed over the Hump. All CIC detachments in Assam and Burma were combined operationally, and Major George L. Wilson became Theatre Chief of CIC. Though there still remained the tremendous task of protecting the supply line – the Life Line – to the forces fighting in China proper, the brunt of CIC work on the war front of the mainland of Asia now fell on the detachments operating in the vastness of war-torn China.

It is one of the subtler ironies of CIC history that it was in the China Theatre, perhaps the most remote and ineffable region in which American forces ever operated in World War Two, that CIC agents at last found their true niche – an operational environment in which they enjoyed greater authority and freedom of movement than any other Theatre. All this was due to the foresight of the Commanding General of the newly created China Theatre, Major General Albert Wedemeyer, who in December 1944, only a few days after the CIC advance party reached Chungking, put teeth into the CIC's status in China with a directive which read: 'CIC personnel are authorized to call on all military and civilian personnel of this command for any assistance they may require in the performance of their duties. Personnel of this command will extend to CIC personnel such administrative assistance and other facilities as may be necessary to protect the identity of CIC personnel and expedite the accomplishment of their assigned missions.'

These missions Wedemeyer saw as the neutralization of the activities of enemy agents – a task which in the peculiar context of China was easier said than done. The task was enormous. Danger to security came not only from the Japanese but from dissidents within the Chinese forces on the Allies' side of the front. Among these dissident elements, the Communists in particular seemed less interested in defeating the ostensible common enemy than in preparing the foundations of their own future assumption of power. CIC agents knew instinctively that the utmost tact and diplomacy was called for. Diplomacy was also needed in coping with the Chinese Army's complete disregard for security, and in dealing with all the competing local law enforcement agencies. China was a hotbed of jealousy, red tape and jockeying for power. It was also perilously poised between victory and defeat, for at the time of CIC's arrival the Japanese had made their deepest penetration westward towards Kweiying, and if they could take Kweiying they would succeed in cutting the main overland supply route to Chungking.

China was also vast. CIC personnel found themselves scattered to the winds as Resident Agents at a multitude of Army and Air Force headquarters across the length and breadth of the land: James Brook and George Reynold at Chengtu; Lawrence Ballou and Eugene Tilley at Hsian; William Boggs at Paoshan; Lawrence Hughes at Yunnanyi; William Hoffman at Chanyi; Robert Scott at Kweiyang; and Kong Louie at Peisheii. Great responsibility fell on the shoulders of these isolated young men, and much was left to their own individual judgement and ability. As one area commander was advised about a resident agent assigned to him: 'His mission is of vital importance, for it is essential that effective measures be taken to prevent the enemy from obtaining information on our projects and installations.'

From the beginning, US personnel were keenly conscious of the vulnerability of information given to Chinese unit commanders. This was due to the weakness, or even non-existence, of Chinese military counter intelligence. In April 1945 agents Edward White and George Mah set out on a 30-day trip to survey the situation in the Kwangsi command, visiting Poseh headquarters and all the subordinate units except guerrilla battalions, interviewing most of the Chinese generals and ranking members of their staffs, American liaison officers, members of the French military mission in Tingsi, and representatives of OSS.

Throughout the command the two agents found a happy relationship between the Chinese and their teams of American advisors, but they also found an equally serene disregard of the importance of security. They found that the telephone was the principal means of communication, with telephone wires running in plain view over mountain trails rarely patrolled by repairmen. The line was often shared by civilians, and daily intelligence reports from divisions and regiments to higher echelons, along with directives for tactical operations, all went over these lines in the clear. Often directives to troops *en route* were delivered to the only householder in the village who had a phone, to be relayed to the unit commander when he arrived. They also found that in all the subordinate command headquarters the intelligence and situation maps showing Chinese and enemy troop dispositions, routes and direction of movement hung unprotected and clearly visible on the office or bedroom wall of the commanding general or chief of operations staff. Unit moves were usually preceded by drinking parties to which the townspeople were invited to help swell the festivities.

The one security danger which the Chinese recognized – but considered insoluble – was the problem posed by the penetration of the area by thousands of Japanese troops disguised as Chinese coolies or Chinese soldiers. These Japanese performed combat and reconnaissance missions, ambushing Chinese patrols and attacking Chinese units on the flanks. Often they would seize villages in advance of Japanese troops by infiltrating the villages and mingling with genuine refugees until at a signal they would turn on the defending troops and 'subdue' them. The thousands of infiltrating 'refugees' were natural barriers, virtually impossible to identify as enemy troops since they were so similar in appearance to the local Chinese. As Colonel Harwood Bowman, commander of US forces in Quansi, explained: 'The Japanese have a genius for infiltration. God Almighty might have identified them, but no one else could.'

At the same time, Agent James Hunter, a Chinese linguist with long experience in China, was studying how the Chinese Services of Supply HQ protected highly classified information. He soon discovered that they didn't, and cited a typical example of Chinese handling of a top secret document. Knowing the US Army's rigid control system, the Chinese made only one translation of the document in question, and appended to it a distribution list of the Americans who should have access to it. But at the same time they made an unlimited number of copies in Chinese and distributed them around headquarters with absolutely no record of their distribution.

As a result of these surveys by CIC, a seven-man detachment was assigned in early June 1945 to work with the Chinese Combat Command on an experimental basis, and CIC agents were the first Americans to enter Kweilin on 29 July, hard on the heels of the front-line Chinese combat troops. But the Japanese surrender brought an abrupt end to Chinese–American unity in the face of a common enemy. The intensification of Soviet and Chinese Communist activities to bring about a radical shift of power and undermine the prestige and interests of the United States in China during the post-war period was soon to lead to a radical change in CIC's mission from military counter intelligence to positive political intelligence gathering. This is an episode to which we will return later. For the moment it is time to turn to the decisive Theatre of the war against Japan and move the scene to General MacArthur's mighty military empire in the South West Pacific.

*   *   *

CIC operations in the South West Pacific Theatre (SWPA) varied widely from those of other theatres. The enormous geographical distances kept detachments widely separated. Manpower was scarce because of the priority given to the war in Europe. Changes in structure and personnel within the command took place with bewildering frequency and confusion. During the first few months of 1942, for example, the Theatre G-2, responsible for counter intelligence activities, was changed no less than seven times, and there were nine changes in Commanding Generals during the same period. SWPA Headquarters shuttled back and forth between Sydney, Brisbane and Melbourne, the principal cities of Australia, as General Douglas MacArthur began the steady process of build-up in preparation for the great northward push against the Japanese tide that had swept south across the Pacific: first back to his beloved Philippines from which he had been so brutally ejected in 1942, then – somehow, some day – on to the home islands of the Japanese heartland itself in a final drive to victory.

The story of the CIC's participation in the war fought in this vast amphitheatre of seas and islands is no less bewildering. The confusion is compounded by the fact that Headquarters either destroyed or secreted in some forgotten hideaway most of the wartime documentation relating to CIC operations in this area of World War Two. For example, only one roster of CIC personnel now exists, dated 28 February 1945, and even this is demonstrably erroneous. Otherwise it is unclear from the records which agents were serving with which combat units in which island or battle front of the South West Pacific war. From such documents as have survived, however, and with the help of eye-witness recollections, it is possible to build up a picture of the main course of CIC operations in the South West Pacific.

Counter intelligence operations got off to a slow start. It was not until United States Forces surrendered on Bataan that the first trained CIC officers arrived in Australia to join the troops preparing for the long island-hopping drive to Tokyo. Working under Colonel (later General) Elliot E. Thorpe, G-2 of US Army Forces in Australia, the pioneer nucleus of the CIC presence in the Theatre numbered a mere 14 officers and agents, at a time when the Japanese were advancing in leaps and bounds from island to island and an actual Japanese foothold on the mainland of Australia seemed imminent. Colonel Thorpe rightly perceived that Headquarters G-2 would have to operate primarily as a counter intelligence agency but realized that the acute shortage of personnel made adequate coverage of the base sections impossible. When his request to the War

Department for a further 40 agents from America was ignored, he set about recruiting them locally from American military personnel already in Australia. He set the same high standards required by the CIC in the United States and refused to consider anyone who scored less than the minimum requirement for Officer Candidate in the Army General Classification Test. He preferred men with backgrounds as lawyers, investigators or newspapermen, and of the 1500 men who were screened for CIC only 14 survived the selection process. By February 1943 there were still only 23 CIC officers for the whole of the South West Pacific war.

But by then the Japanese war had taken a decisive turn. For in September 1942 the Allies had halted the Japanese in the Owen Stanley mountains of New Guinea, a mere 20 airline miles from Port Moresby, which itself seemed a mere step away from the shores of northern Australia. A month later the first CIC agents were assigned to New Guinea, first to Port Moresby and then to the easternmost tip of the island, where an advance base had been created after Japanese troops had been expelled in a decisive action of the war. From then on, agents were assigned as quickly as they could be trained to the various bases where the proximity of the enemy posed a threat of espionage and subversion.

The year 1943 saw the CIC finally come into its own as an integral part of South West Pacific operations. A reinforcement of 20 special agents made possible the physical separation of the G-2 and CIC offices, and the arrival of more than 40 CIC officers and agents attached to General Krueger's Sixth US Army provided the first infusion of genuine combat-trained CIC agents into the South West Pacific Threatre. All through 1943 the huge build-up of American troops in the Theatre continued. A CIC training school was started in Brisbane, where students studied field problems simulating jungle battle conditions and from a study of Japanese administration of conquered territories learned that a straight, intelligent, sympathetic approach would win the allegiance of the natives, who detested the crude, cruel methods of their Japanese overlords. CIC agents were now ready to begin the long march to Tokyo in close step with American frontline troops.

By the middle of 1943 the Allies had not only checked the Japanese onslaught but even assumed a tactical offensive. Allied units had inflicted heavy losses on the Japanese in the battles of the Coral Sea and Midway. The Allies had begun a two-year campaign to drive the Japanese from New Guinea and American soldiers and marines were firmly entrenched on Guadalcanal. On 22 July 1943, in their first combat test in the South West Pacific, CIC detachments landed with elements of the Sixth Army Task Force on the tiny islands of Kiriwina and Woodlark, midway between New Guinea and the Solomons. From then on island-hopping became a way of life. In November CIC agents waded ashore on Bougainville in the Solomon Islands and in early 1944 began landing in the Admiralty Islands with advance reconnaissance elements of the 1st Cavalry Division. In April Allied forces began a major drive to Aitape in British New Guinea and Hollandia in Dutch New Guinea. The operation was a great strategic success. More than 50,000 Japanese troops were cut off in the east, and for months to come stragglers from these lost units attempted to make their way westward along the coast, around the strongpoints thrown up by the American forces. They were too disorganized to constitute a serious threat, but every trail had to be guarded continuously against their intrusion. Most of these waifs of war were killed but a few were captured. the first prisoner taken by the CIC was an enemy soldier so starved and emaciated that an agent had to put him in a wheelbarrow and wheel him back to a first-aid tent. Medics gave him an injection in an attempt to save his life, but he died shortly afterwards, to the chagrin of his CIC captor.

A huge bonanza of enemy documents was found in the Hollandia post office by Special Agent Duval A. Edwards, yielding a great number of highly valuable military documents which he carted box after box, on a liberated bicycle with flat tyres, over mountain trails too narrow for jeeps, and dumped in front of the Nisei translators in the ATIS (Allied Translator and Interpreter Section) teams up with the forward elements of the troops. Every day the Nisei translators would bring documents of intelligence importance to the CIC tent, where Duval Edwards would place them in a specially prepared envelope to ensure it made the daily special delivery plane back to Theatre HQ in Australia for detailed translation.

Captured documents were valuable not only from a strictly military viewpoint; they also divulged clues to the identities of native collaborators and formed the basis of a comprehensive Black List. The Japanese seemed reluctant to destroy sensitive documents, even to prevent them falling into Allied hands, and the CIC often had to collect them from the macerated remains of enemy corpses or stinking billets full of the dead. They collected so many of them – 350,000 all told – that they had to be counted by the ton rather than individually. So fast was the flow that the ATIS were unable to keep up with translating the volume of paper – hardly surprising in view of the complexity of the Japanese written characters, which demanded three document translators to one interpreter on language teams in SWPA (the exact reverse of the European Theatre). Many of the documents were prize discoveries, revealing the strength, disposition and fortification of enemy units on Japanese-held islands, as well as army and navy code books, orders of battle, casualty reports and maps showing enemy unit locations.

High officials were elated by these document finds, which enabled American troops to bypass revealed Japanese strongpoints in an island-skipping manoeuvre that greatly shortened the war. Since loyal Nisei soldiers in American uniforms happened to look like Japanese soldiers in American uniforms, it was an unwritten mission of the CIC, adopted in the New Guinea jungles, always to accompany ATIS Nisei when they were required to move up to frontline positions to question a dying Japanese soldier or translate a tactically valuable captured document. It was a mission that CIC agents were proud to perform.

To help ensure that American GIs turned in any souvenirs of intelligence interest, the CIC established a souvenir 'grab bag'. This contained items of no intelligence value, such as Japanese postcards, stationery, pictures and clothing, and any GI who handed over a souvenir needed for intelligence analysis was allowed to take an item from the 'grab bag' in exchange. The CIC also found that the Christian missions were especially useful. When native Christian converts were summoned to church service by the beating of drums from village to village, they came to a central location, bringing with them pigs, goats and other domestic animals – and found the CIC there in attendance. After the service, agents would mingle with the congregation and cultivate their friendship, so that at times they would be rewarded with intelligence information or led to the hideouts of Japanese stragglers. Interrogation of natives proved valuable in revealing Japanese combat techniques and movements of Japanese units and their prisoners-of-war, as well as providing information about atrocities committed by Japanese troops. The co-operation of the local populace was enhanced by the offer of a reward of a half guilder (26 cents) for every Japanese soldier turned over to the CIC, and double that if the soldier was an officer. During the month of May more than 100 Japanese were turned in for this reward money.

The natives used ingenious methods to capture these enemy soldiers. One native patrol promised 13 isolated Japanese soldiers that it would lead them to food. Instead, it took them into an American encampment. Realizing that they had been betrayed, one of the Japanese hurled a grenade, but succeeded only in killing himself and one of his comrades. On another occasion, a native patrol out of Jefase learned that seven Japanese soldiers armed with swords were *en route* to the village. The patrol scurried back to tell the village chief. The chief set out to meet the Japanese and, finding that they were lost from their units, promised to escort them back to their lines the next morning. He urged them to board a large canoe and covered them with a sail, explaining that it would hide them from scouting American planes. Unknown to the Japanese, however, the leader of the native patrol had been recruited by the CIC, and when the canoe set sail he covered his Japanese passengers with his US-supplied carbine and held them until they reached Depapre, where American MPs, summoned by despatch rider, were waiting to receive them.

Hollandia was now the location of the forward HQs of the American advance. General Krueger had moved his Sixth Army HQ there in July. General MacArthur brought his headquarters up from Brisbane in September. At the same time, General Eichelberger took over the Command of the newly activated Eighth Army with its HQ also at Hollandia. With the 441st CIC also moving forward to Hollandia, CIC took a major part in the security planning before each invasion of Japanese-held islands by American forces, and in collating intelligence of all kinds, operational as well as counter intelligence. One over-age CIC agent, rejoicing in the rank of master sergeant, headed an intelligence analysis unit composed entirely of officers. In MacArthur's kingdom the question of age, like that of rank, was significant. In the European Theatre the army had eventually learnt that it was a waste to send CIC agents into combat with the front-line troops. Not so in the South West Pacific. Here agents were as often as not at the sharp end of the battle. Going ashore as a CIC agent was a little different from the normal GI doing so. At Biak Island, for example, to the east of Hollandia, the Special Agent in charge of the team attached to the 41st Division, Duval Edwards, went over the side of the landing ship and down the rope into the waiting landing craft, carrying not only his back pack and his .38 revolver and tommy gun, but his commanding offficer's .45 and carbine as well, together with the detachment's official briefcase containing all the team's paperwork and written data. And this was with the third wave of the 41st's assault troops, against stiffening Japanese opposition from small arms fire and strafing runs by Japanese Zeros from Biak airfield.

When the Sixth Army's Task Force landed on Insoemoar Island in the Wakda-Sarmi sector of Dutch New Guinea, CIC took their first combat casualty in the SWPA when Agent Woodrow G. Hunter, a lawyer from Cincinnati, was killed in action on the morning of D+1, 18 May 1944; he was struck down by a sniper's bullet. When the Task Force was relieved by the 6th Infantry Division early in June, CIC teams with the three regiments of the division advanced with their respective command posts through an area made hazardous by enemy small arms, mortar and artillery fire. When the Japanese took refuge in a complex of caves with interconnecting passages, CIC agents searched the caves for intelligence materials before they were sealed and dynamited by US army engineers. In the Maffin Bay sector of the Wakde-Sarmi front, agents took to the air in spotter planes, looking for abandoned enemy command posts; on the ground they ran into sniper fire and booby traps.

The vexed question of rank was potentially just as fraught. Only in MacArthur's Theatre was the CIC required openly to carry its agents' actual ranks on all records. In the European Theatre, and in China-Burma-India, agents wore shoulder patches of the sort worn by war correspondents to indicate that they were civilians even though they wore uniform. As pseudo civilians CIC agents in Europe associated with army officers on equal terms, which made their job easier in more ways than one. When an agent needed to identify himself and his mission, he presented a gold-plated badge carrying the words 'MILITARY INTELLIGENCE – WAR DEPART-MENT' and if necessary supplemented this with credentials which stated that he was a Special Agent of the War Department. Neither the badge nor the credentials ever revealed the rank of the agent. Not so in SWPA. This led to many problems, especially in dealing with officers in other branches of the service in the course of couter intelligence work.

CIC agents, being resourceful men of at least officer rank IQ, resorted to many ruses and stratagems to get round this handicap. Some would hint that they were really FBI temporarily attached to the Army. Others would carry their official agent's badge in the same place a major, captain or lieutenant would pin his – not, as in non-combat situations, on his shoulders, but on the underside of his fatigues lapel, where a Japanese sniper, on the look-out for enemy officers' insignia, could not see them. In this way it was easy for a canny agent when the occasion demanded to casually flip his lapel just sufficiently to provide a quick glimpse of a flash of gold – a major's leaf!

Such ruses did not always work, of course. Special Agent Duval A. Edwards, attached to XIV Corps, recalled that for months he had been known to the G-2 and his staff around Corps HQ by his enlisted rank. One day, during the chaos following the liberation of Manila, a G-2 officer, a full colonel, visited the CIC team, which was then housed in a former residence of the Kempei Tai (their Japanese equivalent), one of the best mansions in the small city of Santa Rosa, just to the south of the Philippine capital. The G-2 colonel was stopped by a local guerrilla guarding the entrance and had to be announced to the CIC team headed by Master Sergeant Duval Edwards before he was allowed to enter. He found three agents, each attended by a male amanuensis, interviewing suspects, including a couple of high-ranking Filipino guerrillas. The G-2 was invited to stay for lunch and was fed sumptuously on freshly caught trout, while a servant in attendance fanned the ever-present flies away. Sumptuously regaled in a style to which he was not accustomed in his own senior officers' mess, the G-2 officer finally got up to leave, and as he did so made a solemn promise. 'Mr Edwards,' he said, addressing the CIC agent, 'I will *never* call you sergeant again!' And he didn't.

CIC teams went in with every invasion as MacArthur's forces continued their island-hopping progress towards the Philippines. When 'G' Detachment went ashore with Cyclone Task Force at Noemfoor Island, just north of Dutch New Guinea, on 2 July 1944, it was their fourth beach assault in four months. Special Agent George Charon deserves a mention for his unique accomplishment on Noemfoor. This small island was so remote from the outside world that its inhabitants spoke their own unique language as yet unknown to any foreigner. A descendant of French and North American Indian stock, Charon had taught Spanish in Oklahoma before the war and was endowed with a remarkable gift for picking up languages. When he joined the CIC, a capability in at least one foreign language was essential. But Charon's ability to assimilate new tongues proved to be phenomenal. He was on Noemfoor for three days. By the end of the third day he had mastered enough of the local language to be able to converse freely with the inhabitants. They idolized him, the one white skin they had ever been able to talk to, and when he went to the airfield to fly away the entire population flocked to the field to wish him a sorrowful farewell.

By midsummer of 1944 the Japanese had been driven from most of New Guinea and in August ten agents of the 31st CIC began a vigorous security programme for the 31st Division's combat troops in preparation for the assault on Morotai, the last major stepping-stone to the Philippines. The following month an advance party consisting of Malay-speaking Agent William R. Morris, two native guides, a representative of the Netherland East Indian Civil Service and a small force of infantry engineers and radar technicians, landed on the north-west section of Cape Sopi to set up and guard a radar station there, while four agents of the 31st CIC began a three-week patrol of the island and neighbouring Naoe to check the security of the radar stations and question the native inhabitants about

Kempei Tai agents who had established controls in the island villages.

When the bitter battle for New Guinea and its offshore islands was finally over, all the islands of any consequence between Australia and the Philippines were under Allied control. Like their SWPA combat units, the CIC now turned their sights towards the return to the Philippines. Rear echelon regional CIC teams moved up to take over the counter intelligence coverage of liberated areas, while CIC combat teams began the intensive security training of the troops to which they were attached. For the first time in the Japanese war, the CIC became officially airborne when a CIC parachute detachment under George B. Spencer arrived with the 11th Airborne Division in March 1944; it was rapidly augmented by agents who volunteered for assignment as paratrooper agents and qualified for their paratrooper wings in New Guinea. By the early autumn of 1944 the increase in CIC strength began to parallel the growth of combat reinforcements in the Theatre. New arrivals were attached to corps and divisions coming in from America, or were hauled in from scattered outposts in the Solomons and other islands. By the end of September CIC rosters listed 73 officers and 381 agents in nearly 40 detachments under Colonel Vreeland's SWPA Theatre Detachment, the 441st CIC, which for the rest of the war and during the occupation of Japan was to direct CIC operations in the Far East.

With the big push to the Philippines now imminent, the CIC became obsessive about pre-invasion security indoctrination of troops. Rightly so, it seemed, for evidence was emerging that serious leaks of information were seeping out of Australia. On several occasions documents taken from the enemy showed that the Japanese had learnt the strength of American units and their plans. Security somewhere, Australian or American, had stumbled. An intensive CIC indoctrination campaign began. Ten teams used every means – radio, motion pictures, posters, lectures – to get the message across to the tens of thousands of troops now moving up to their invasion jump-off centres. Any means that could dramatize the urgency of the matter was employed. In Rockhampton, Australia, for example, troops mingling in a crowd at a railway station were brought to attention when a loudspeaker blared:

'Attention all troops! This is Military Intelligence speaking. Enemy agents are operating in this area. There's only one way to avoid giving aid and information to the enemy, and that is: DON'T TALK! No matter who starts discussing military information, from motherly welfare workers to cute little country girls. Be smart!

Dummy up! Change the subject. Don't be ashamed to say "Don't know."'

Eventually the campaign was stepped up to include the US Navy, the Australian Army and Navy, even GHQ. At the last minute before embarkation for the Philippines, CIC agents directed inspections of American troops to make certain they were not carrying personal items that would disclose their unit identity in the event of capture. As troops evacuated their quarters, other agents combed them carefully for any classified materials that might have been left behind. In some small part due to the CIC's intensive security campaign, the American landing on the Philippine island of Leyte on 20 October 1944 produced one of the most sensational tactical surprises of the war. It was chosen because of its potential airfield sites, good anchorages and extensive harbour facilities, free and undefended coast from the east and good access to the other islands; and on the day of landing the startled Japanese occupation forces buckled under the sheer weight of MacArthur's men and matériel.

It was a day in which many CIC combat agents first won their spurs. As in the island campaigns to the south, plans called for a CIC combat detachment with each army, corps, division and task force, consisting of two officers and ten special agents, plus five qualified Filipino soldiers trained in counter intelligence measures. These Filipinos were for the most part Filipino-Americans from the American west coast, not well educated, nor fully measuring up to the high standards required for the specialized work of CIC agents, but useful as interpreters and in performing the less glamorous but necessary daily duties of a CIC team in the field. Eight CIC teams, headed by the 306th, plus the attached Filipino CIC 'agents', participated in the original action with the Sixth Army Task Force which smashed into the Leyte beach-head, and six other CIC combat detachments also took part, while behind them the occupation detachments waited for the opportunity to move into the liberated territories.

The CIC did not emerge unscathed from the fighting on Leyte. During an air raid a Japanese bomb scored a hit on a landing ship in which agents of the 306th CIC were waiting to disembark; Agent Elvin C. Jensen was killed and Agent Daniel J. Coakley seriously wounded. On the same day, all but one of the 24th CIC agents were trapped inside their headquarters at Palo by 80 fanatical Japanese soldiers who had infiltrated American lines and tried to storm the CIC office in a *banzai* suicide attack. Although caught off guard, CIC agents hastily set up a makeshift defence and repulsed the Japanese, inflicting heavy losses. Enemy infiltration continued to plague the 24th team as Japanese soldiers often stayed behind in little towns and villages in the guise of natives, while others passed through the American lines dressed in women's clothing. Special CIC patrols were set up to guard against such infiltration.

In one of the most dramatic episodes of the war, General MacArthur had waded ashore on Leyte on 22 October, with President Osmena beside him, thus fulfilling his promise to the Filipinos that he would one day return. On the following day CIC agents witnessed a colourful ceremony in the capital when General MacArthur turned over control of the Philippine Government to President Osmena. In the same ceremony MacArthur presented the Distinguished Service Cross to Colonel Ruperto Kangleon, an outstanding guerrilla leader who had already given CIC an extensive suspect list compiled by his forces. Then President Osmena immediately appointed Kangleon the Governor of Leyte. Two CIC agents were detailed as personal guards for Osmena, though General MacArthur declined to be mollycoddled in this way.

Shortly after the appointment of the new Philippine President, CIC chiefs conferred with him on crucial aspects of the CIC's role in the liberation of the country. It was agreed that CIC would investigate all appointees to office, including all constabulary and municipal officials, to clear them of any taint of disloyalty. Agents were assigned far-reaching responsibilities with regard to Philippine civilians. Chief among them was the arrest and interrogation of all known enemy agents and collaborators – including Pastor Salazar, the puppet Governor of Leyte, who admitted he had secretly conferred with Japanese military commanders even after US troops had landed.

Since the Army had not entered large population centres in SWPA before, new duties had to be added to the CIC burden, including civil affairs and the maintenance of order, civilian movement control and newspaper censorship. Throughout Leyte, CIC agents faced hosts of problems not previously encountered. They had to cope with some million and a half civilized inhabitants, representing an unbelievable mixture of races and nationalities from every country in Asia and Europe, and influenced by several years of Japanese propaganda and culture. Sorting out those who had been active Japanese agents and party members was a complex task. One agent (Arthur Hurlburt, whom we last met in New Guinea in Chapter 2) recalled:

> We put out a shingle board in front of the house: 'CIC'. It needed no explanation. Word got around like wildfire and we had people coming to visit us from all directions. One of the biggest jobs was to sort out the false accusations, the spite cases. We took all this as

a tremendous responsibility – to pick up an individual and without habeas corpus, no lawyers, no judges, just take him to the prison and throw him behind barbed wire for the duration of the war, plus. It was not pleasant work, and it was dangerous. It involved locating our man, sometimes out in the barrios (or suburbs), 3 or 4 miles out in the jungle, across the river, through the woods for a couple of hours, finally arriving at a collection of grass huts. We would locate the Barrio Teniente and have him find our man, whom we would place under arrest and march back to town. I never put handcuffs on them. I felt two armed men behind them should be sufficient. CIC agents carried a .38 revolver in a hip holster, constantly. I mean 24 hours a day. We slept with them beside our head at night.

Another tricky business was the matter of the guerrillas. Some were *bona fide*, others were self-styled, motivated by private vendettas and personal ambitions rather than ideals of freedom and justice. All too often the guerrillas resorted to the unofficial justice of the kangaroo court and the summary execution of those deemed to have collaborated with the Japanese. The slow process of American military legal procedures was tiresome to men who had lived hard and fought long against their oppressors up in the hills. On one occasion several armed guerrillas reported to a CIC office with a letter which began: 'You are hereby ordered to liquidate the following traitors.' On another occasion a lone CIC agent had to resort to several bottles of *tuba*, the native firewater, as well as miracles of casuistry and diplomacy, before he could persuade a guerrilla cut-throat to deliver his trembling captives to the nearest police stockade rather than whisk them off to the hills for a kangaroo trial and instantaneous extinction.

For Special Agent Arthur Hurlburt the peculiar conditions led to some ghoulish situations. He wrote later:

> The first thing that called my attention was the number of funeral processions. There was apparently a great deal of dysentery, due to the privation attendant upon the hostilities. Pushcarts carrying home-made coffins were passing our house hourly or oftener. And they were stopping in front of the CIC house, waiting. I asked my local boys why they stopped and they replied that the 11th Airborne CIC had ordered it. It seems that a pushcart carrying a coffin had fallen over and, instead of a body, out sprawled a tommy-gun, ammunition and hand grenades. At that point all funeral processions were required to pass the CIC house and open the coffin for inspection.

Then there was the business of the heads. Right up until the time we left the island our local farmers were catching Japanese stragglers, one by one. The poor fellows would come down out of the mountains, looking for chickens or vegetables or anything to eat. The farmers had armed themselves with home-made guns made out of pipes. They used match heads for powder and fired old bolts, rocks, anything. This was enough to knock a man off his feet, then they would rush him with bolos. The first head they brought to me while I was out at supper. Coming back down the street I noticed this huge throng round the house. Going in, I saw several of the neighbours in the living room, with a head on the floor. I hit the ceiling, made them bury it immediately, and lectured them with arms waving about the Geneva Convention, the rules of land warfare, human decency, and all. I couldn't understand why they were bringing in the heads.

Later I learned that, while the 11th Airborne CIC was there, they brought in ears. The 11th boys chewed them out for desecrating the dead and they misunderstood. They thought they were being chewed out because it was thought they were bringing in Filipino ears. Aha! The answer to that was to bring the whole head. I tried my damnedest to work up some sympathy for those poor Jap wretches, who were finding both living and dying so difficult. But I had little success. To a man, they had mistreated the entire population of the islands. Any Japanese soldier could rape, torture and murder any civilian with impunity. Prisoners were beheaded on a whim, routinely.

In December 1944 the last pockets of Japanese resistance on Leyte were quelled. Before moving on to Luzon, American troops next invaded Mindoro, the most densely populated of the islands, with eight million inhabitants. Here for the first time in the South West Pacific Theatre the CIC began to discharge its mission on a tremendous scale, employing 29 CIC detachments – 16 of them combat ones – in the fighting phase and the days that followed. As combat troops passed through villages and towns, a dozen area CIC teams moved in to relieve the CIC combat teams. When elements of the Sixth Army launched the invasion of Luzon, the main Philippine island, on 9 January 1945, three CIC detachments were on Luzon soil within an hour of the first assault troops hitting the beach. Many more followed in amphibious landings up and down the coast. CIC agents followed their host units closely in the rapid push across the Luzon plain towards Manila, the capital. At each town on the way CIC agents placed prominent and reliable citizens in key municipal offices, while search and seizure teams located documents and counter intelligence matériel in the public buildings and former Japanese garrisons – especially the offices of the Kempei Tai.

Fighting raged in Manila City for another month as the enemy clung tenaciously to its well-fortified position. The Japanese defenders had dug in behind the enormous ancient walls of old Manila, on the banks of the Pasig River. While gunfire was exchanged across this natural barrier, CIC agents were making their arrests of collaborators and enemy saboteurs within a block and a half of the front line. So long as the Japanese held their safe positions in strength, Manila remained a nightmare, and day by day was piecemeal reduced to rubble by bitter house-to-house fighting and Japanese fire-and-dynamite brigades. CIC agents, ducking through the fire storm, were preoccupied first and foremost with sabotage, for the Japanese were using Filipinos of all ages and both sexes to wreak destruction upon the city in every possible way. One seven-year-old boy questioned by agents admitted to being one of a gang of infantile fire bugs whom the Japanese paid 350 pesos for tossing grenades into buildings. To implement any kind of adequate counter intelligence control in the midst of this mayhem was an almost impossible task. It was scarcely more possible even after the fighting in Manila came to an end in the first week of March 1945.

Nearly one and a half million people swarmed amidst the rubble of the ruined streets of the capital – the greatest number ever known in the city. This human flood was composed of the tongues and races of Babel. The Chinese colony alone numbered 18,000, and there were teeming groups from India, the East Indies, Formosa, the Soviet Union and virtually every country in Europe, including German, Italian and Spanish nationals. CIC interned more than 200 Germans in special compounds at the Holy Ghost College and Bilibid Prison. Japanese agents were more difficult to dispose of, however, for many of them were disguised as Filipino or Chinese citizens. Mixed up in this tumultuous mêlée were some 8500 American civilians who had somehow survived the Japanese occupation. Many of these became bitterly critical of the CIC when (on the orders of the newly arrived American Consul) they found they had to be screened before they could be issued with visas and allowed to be sent home.

It was a relief to turn from unbearable scenes of human chaos to more bearable incidents of human greed. The guns had no sooner grown quiet in Manila when the 801st CIC were sent out on a treasure hunt. Apparently an 801st agent had overheard a conversation between a group of GIs in a Manila bar who were planning to recover a large quantity of silver Philippine pesos from the bottom of

Manila Bay. This money, representing the US paymaster's funds for the payment of US troops in the Philippines before the Japanese invasion, had been placed in bags and sunk on the orders of General MacArthur. The soldiers in the bar knew the approximate location of the sunken treasure and had secured the help of some Navy divers to retrieve it. The agent managed to talk his way into joining the group and was present when the divers recovered the money, which filled a box six feet long, two feet high and four feet wide. But before the treasure could be shared out amongst the members of the group, the agent took off his shirt – a pre-arranged signal to other agents waiting nearby – and the group found themselves surrounded and their haul confiscated as rightful US property.

Week after week the fighting for the islands of the archipelago went on. On beach after beach and in town after town the CIC agents followed hard on the heels of the fighting troops. On 18 March 1945 they splashed ashore in the initial assault on Panay Island; in early April they splashed ashore on Cebu and Bohol; a few days later they splashed ashore with the first assault elements at Mindanao, the second largest island in the Philippines and the most rugged. Agents in the European Theatre, having learnt the hard way at Oran, Salerno and Anzio, would have been aghast that so many agents had splashed ashore on so many beaches in the thick of so many battles in the Pacific war. But it was how MacArthur's army saw the CIC; and at least it got the agents where they were needed by the shortest possible route in the shortest possible time; and in any case the war was almost over. By the summer of 1945 combat operations in the Philippines had ended except for skirmishes with isolated pockets of fanatical Japanese soldiers hiding in mountain caves. As in France after the liberation, the problem confronting the CIC – and indeed the whole Allied military and political apparatus – in the immediate post-hostilities phase in the Philippines was not the erstwhile enemy, who were as good as dead and buried, but those former old pals of the Communist-led resistance, who were very much alive and kicking. These, the Hukbalahap, were to preoccupy the CIC throughout the remainder of their time in the Philippines.

In general, the guerrillas in Luzon divided into two principal camps. On one side were those known as the USAFFE guerrillas – that is, the guerrillas supported by General MacArthur and the US Far East Command. Sharing these groups' hatred of the Japanese, but diametrically opposed to them politically, was a rival camp known as the Hukbalahap, more commonly known as the Huks. Led by the Moscow-trained Communist Luis Taruc, with Luis Alejandrino, this group was determined to achieve a Communist

Korea—the CIC's last war:

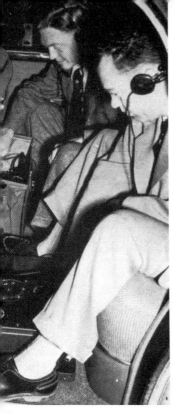

Left: Locked in a dire struggle with Soviet agents at the sharp end of the Cold War in Vienna, 430th CIC Detachment personnel in civilian clothes carry out radio surveillance from the back of an unmarked sedan. *(National Archives)*

Below left: Agents of the 2nd CIC Detachment interrogate a captured enemy agent who had infiltrated Allied positions through the UN lines from North Korea. *(US Army Intelligence and Security Command)*

Below right: In the Korean War the CIC operated at both the front and the rear of the US Army. The HQ of the 45th CIC Detachment in a sandbagged bunker in the front line. *(US Army Intelligence and Security Command)*

Left: Arthur Komori. He and Richard Sakakida were the first Japanese Americans to be recruited into CIC and almost the only agents of the Philippines detachment to survive the Japanese invasion. *(Duval A. Edwards)*

Below: Mrs Roosevelt with Trude Pratt and Joseph Lash at the White House. When the CIC got the two women muddled up during a routine bugging of Lash's bedroom, the resulting presidential uproar nearly spelled the end of the CIC in America. *(Harris & Ewing)*

The Thin Blue Line — CIC agents in their counter-intelligence outposts around the world:

Below: Winter quarters in remote Iceland, circa 1943. Back row — Special Agents Piekarski, Stopelli, Schaub, Meyers, Reeves. Front row — Edgar and Young. *(Edward Koudelka)*

Left: The future author of *The Catcher in the Rye,* J. D. Salinger, a CIC special agent who served with the 207th CIC detachment in Europe.

Below: Section 'R' at Avranches, Normandy, 1944. Back row — Earl Browning, Bill King, Frank MacCleer, Jon Young, Andy Swantek. Front Row — Herman Goldbeck, Del Reeves, Bill Rakow, Frank Loftus. *(Edward Koudelka)*

Foot: Have jeep, will travel. Special Agent Eugene Green, 704th CIC Group, in Tague, Korea, 1953. *(Eugene Green)*

Left: One of CIC's most legendary stars — Russian-born Special Agent Victor de Guinzbourg, dressed for secret mission in the North African desert. 'He was truly a giant among us.' *(Robert R. Richards)*

Below: At a big parade of French and American forces in Casablanca, Special Agent John Schwarzwalder was responsible for the personal security of General Mark Clark and the unpopular French Resident General in Morocco, General Auguste Noguès. 'I have never been so frightened in my life,' quipped Schwarzwalder afterwards. 'Thirty thousand people were shouting for Noguès' death!' *(Keystone)*

Rare wartime publicity for CIC — *Look* magazine photographer Bob Hansen's picture story shows a CIC detachment in action in the Sicilian campaign in 1943:

Left: Lieutenant Rupert W. Guenther (in helmet) looks over orders from Divisional Intelligence with fellow agents. He will enter the town of Castelverde, cleared of Nazi troops the night before, to collect intelligence material and sort out takeover from local Fascist rule.

Left: The hard way to tell if a road is mined is to drive your jeep down it. Here a peasant describes German forces he has seen in the vicinity — three pieces of artillery and a dozen troop-carrying trucks.

Left: Speaking fluent Sicilian, Special Agent Messina lays down the law to the people of Castelverde: there will be no rioting, no lynching or hanging of Fascist officials. *(Look magazine)*

Above: Captured German radio agents display their wares and contemplate their imminent deaths at a US interrogation centre in Epinal, France *(Defense Audiovisual Agency)*

Left: A German secret agent caught by the CIC after parachuting into France with radio transmitters. *(Robert R. Richards)*

Below: Manfred Pernass (right) and his two commando companions, with blindfolds bound over their eyes and targets pinned over their hearts, await the firing squad's order to shoot. *(Süddeutscher Verlag, Bilderdienst, Munich)*

Above: CIC Agent William Bomer
with captured German radio
equipment dropped by parachutist.
(Robert R. Richards)

Right: One of the commandos of
Otto Skorzeny's 'Trojan Horse'
Brigade, Manfred Pernass, caught in
American uniform behind American
lines during the Battle of the Bulge,
is tied to a stake by MPs before his
execution as a saboteur and spy.
*(Süddeutscher Verlag, Bilderdienst,
Munich)*

Above: The CIC intercepted hundreds of German Intelligence Service spies and saboteurs in Italy France and North-West Europe. Most of them ended up like this man — tied to a stake and shot. *(Defense Audiovisual Agency)*

Left and below: Scenes from the major 'flap' at Colmar, where a sa with top secret US codes and decoding devices disappeared. CIC Agent Jim Elliott by the river wher divers searched in vain. *(Nelson V. N. Dungan)*

society by armed revolution if necessary. Adding to the general aura
of confusion was the difficulty CIC agents experienced in dif-
ferentiating between *bona fide* members of legitimate guerrilla groups
and bands of opportunists who found it expedient to pose as guerrillas. In Manila the guerrilla situation approached the level of farce. 'It
appeared that anyone who could scrape up an army shirt was, *ipso
facto*, a guerrilla captain,' wrote Marvin Goff, 214th CIC commander, in a report at the time. 'If he also had shoes he became a
major.' Even gangs of common pickpockets were organizing themselves into 'guerrilla' units because it proved a more lucrative
business than their own.

With power as their aim, the Huks were a grave security threat to
both American and Philippine interests, often forcing legitimate
appointees out of office – at gun point if necessary, pulling the trigger
if it came to it. Law, order and justice were of no meaning to them
except in so far as they helped secure their political goal. Atrocities,
kidnapping, even rape were acknowledged instruments of political
terror. Agents Leslie R. Harrison and Charles D. Lindsay of the 40th
CIC, sent to San Fernando in Pampanga Province to assist in
working out some sort of solution to the immediate Huk situation,
found themselves at a dinner meeting attended by the Huk leaders,
Taruc and Alejandrino. The Huks bitterly criticized the US Army
for recognizing the USAFFE guerrillas instead of the Huks. Taruc
boasted that he had over 7000 followers and insisted that the United
States should commission him as a General. As the evening progressed the atmosphere deteriorated sharply. The CIC agents
objected to the increasingly vehement anti-American comments of
the two Huk leaders. They were fully aware that Luis Taruc was on
the directorate of the Communist Party and that he had at his
disposal a private army of up to 100,000 armed Huks, which made
them a force to be reckoned with. But they could not sit idly by
without some corrective action. At last, Agent Harrison stood up and
warned the Huk leaders that as a representative of the United States
liberating forces in these islands he was empowered to arrest both
Taruc and Alejandrino if they continued to make further inflammatory and subversive remarks about the United States and the legitimate political leadership of the Philippine Commonwealth. At which
point both Taruc and Alejandrino stalked out.

But this was not the end of the affair. Later that night the CIC
agents, accompanied by 40 American soldiers, raided the Huk
headquarters. The raid was resisted and in the gunfight that ensued
two Huk guerrillas were shot dead. The agents ransacked the Huk
files and came up with some interesting documents. One of these

revealed that the CIC's main Filipino contact, a judge by the name of Pable Angeles David, was actually a Huk informant. Another, of even greater interest to agents Lindsay and Harrison, was that both of them were on the Huk hit list as 'wanted persons No. 2 and No. 3'. As a result of mounting evidence against Taruc and Alejandrino, both were interned by the CIC.

No episode in the annals of CIC's tortured dealing with the Huk can rival that of William Owens, a former university professor in Texas and one of the authentic CIC heroes of the war. The biggest coup pulled off by a CIC agent may well have been his. In the fighting on Luzon, when the Americans had cleared Clark Field and pushed on to Manila, most of their supplies were reaching them from the landing site in the Lingayen Gulf. This meant that food, fuel, ammuniton had to be trucked right through the heart of the stronghold of the local Hukbalahap, who were intent on staking out a claim in Central Luzon, at the very least. The Huk were causing difficulties, of that there was no doubt. Trucks were being ambushed, overturned, pilfered and robbed, and drivers murdered; bridges were being dynamited, thereby bringing the replenishment of supplies for the American offensive to a halt. All fingers of suspicion pointed directly at the Huks. But troops from the fighting front could not be spared to deal with the problem. In any case, Bill Owens had a better idea. He made friends with the commander of a Huk regiment. For some reason, the Huk commander and his staff called him 'Cap'n Bilowens', or it may actually have come out as 'Blowens'. Being an astute agent, he did not correct them, and Captain Blowens he became. His triumph was to persuade the Huk regiment to come over to the Americans, for the specific purpose of guarding the vital bridges and control points against the recurring sabotage which was proving so harmful to the war effort. A deal was made, and the Huks were brought in as Filipino Scouts, an auxiliary force of the Sixth US Army, at whose HQ (where Bill Owens was stationed with the 306th CIC) they were formally received at a grand official ceremony.

But a sad thing had occurred. Someone in the War Department finally woke up to the fact that the CIC was composed of men of talent performing miracles – and nearly all of them enlisted men. Something would have to be done. So, six months before VJ-Day, it was. Large numbers of longterm CIC agents were promoted by direct commissioning to the giddy rank of Second Lieutenant. And as a consequence Captain Blowens, a university professor with three degrees, an author of scholarly books, a man with an extra high IQ, suddenly found himself required to fasten a little gold bar under each lapel, to signify his ennoblement to Second Lieutenant.

Feeling a little trepidation, Cap'n Blowens went on to the parade ground in his second looey rank and took the salute alongside General Krueger as the entire Hukbalahap regiment passed by, dipping its colours to him. But he had nothing to fear. Even if they did glimpse that little flash of gold under each lapel, the Huks remained staunch to their friend and ally, and continued to address him as 'Cap'n Blowens'.

But CIC's powers in these matters were soon to be strictly limited. In the first weeks following the liberation of the Philippines, no less than 74 CIC units were operating in the islands. But in August the CIC was instructed to cease its investigation of wartime collaborators in the Philippines and turn over some 5000 interned Filipinos charged with treason, collaboration and subversion to the Department of Justice of the Philippine Commonwealth Government. From that time on, with their power to arrest Filipinos gone, all CIC agents could do to influence the civil affairs of the islands was to observe and report. Almost immediately the General Secretary of the Communist Party, Pedro Castro, sent a letter to the US High Commissioner in which he demanded the Americans get out of the Philippines. To the Huks this was tantamount to a signal for revolution. A rebellion broke out in the Huk stronghold in Central Luzon, and effective control of the government in the region was seized. But the responsibility for quelling the Huk rebellion was now the Philippine Army's. CIC agents were despatched to observe and report this latest effort to subdue the rebels. But in the context of the Pacific Theatre there were now greater priorities to attend to – Japan.

Even while the last Japanese stragglers were being mopped up in their Philippine strongholds, CIC combat teams had pushed on to Okinawa, almost in the shadow of the Japanese mainland, while CIC teams that remained in the Philippines were training for Operation Olympic, the planned invasion of Japan itself.

Before the guns were silenced in the Philippines, CIC agents were aboard ships steaming north towards the Ryukyu Islands, the main one of which was Okinawa. What lay ahead they could only guess. There were no loyal guerrilla armies sending vital information or harassing the enemy's rear, as there had been in the Philippines. But of one thing the CIC was very certain: the remaining Japanese would fight savagely. The big question was the attitude of the Okinawan populace towards the Japanese, who had occupied these islands since 1916.

Four CIC detachments landed in the initial assault by Tenth Army on 1 April 1945. They had landed fearing the worst from the native Okinawans. But from their earliest contacts it was clear that the islanders, who had been treated as inferiors by the Japanese, were happy to co-operate with the new arrivals. Word was soon passed from village to village that it was a 'good thing' to work for the Americans. Often after that CIC agents found the natives eagerly awaiting their arrival when they entered a town or village for the first time. The use of natives as 'CIC aides' proved remarkably successful on Okinawa. Never before in the Pacific war had CIC relied so heavily on the assistance of the local populace – the severe shortage of loyal and competent linguists demanded it, if nothing else.

One of the greatest problems CIC faced in Okinawa was apprehending Japanese military and labour battalion personnel who had donned civilian apparel and were wandering about behind the American lines. Some of these were deserters, some were members of army units that had been by-passed, but others were commando raiders, suicide squads who had been detailed to slip through the American positions in civilian garb and cause as much death and destruction as they could. These ground-based Kamikaze were not unsuccessful. Reports came in of fuel dumps and bridges being blown up and on 13 June two CIC officers, Raymond L. Cobean and Glenn S. Dunbar, were killed in an ambush while driving across the Motobu peninsula in northern Okinawa for a meeting with native Okinawans. Investigation revealed that enemy infiltrators were most likely responsible, as bullet holes in their jeep were made by Japanese 7.6mm ammunition.

During the last three weeks of the Okinawa campaign, the Japanese frantically increased their attempts to infiltrate the American lines; and to cope with the problem CIC agents operated down to battalion, regiment and even company level. Another problem was caused by small bands of enemy troops who continued to fight as guerrillas and terrorized the Okinawans in an effort to turn them against the Americans. Okinawans who had been impressed into service with the Japanese labour battalions were warned by the Japanese that if they ever fell into American hands the Americans would cut off their ears and gouge out their eyes and commit all manner of horrors against the Okinawan people, so many of the Okinawans who had deserted from the labour battalions carried grenades or bamboo spears with which to kill themselves rather than be captured alive. The Japanese were punitive against all Okinawans they believed had co-operated with the CIC. In a night raid on one village, Japanese guerrillas beheaded the Hancho, or headman, for just such a misdemeanour. The Japanese leader then ordered the remaining villagers to flee to the south, and when the villagers told him they preferred to stay he lined fifty of them up against a wall and ordered his men to throw their grenades at them. Thirty-five of the villagers were killed outright in this atrocity and the rest were severely wounded.

CIC captured a total of 900 prisoners during the campaign on Okinawa, including many on espionage-sabotage missions. By the end, one detachment had taken more prisoners than any single infantry regiment on the island. But some high-ranking Japanese eluded them. When CIC agents arrested ten Kempei Tai agents making their way across the island in civilian clothing, one of them led the CIC to a cave where the Kempei Tai commander was hiding. But as the CIC moved in to arrest him, he committed suicide moments before they could reach him. CIC organized an informant network of volunteer Japanese prisoners to help locate many of their comrades who in their desperation had taken to hiding out in caves. In this way agents located the cave housing the Japanese head-quarters, but when they raided the cave they found that both General Ushijima, the Japanese Commander, and General Cho, his Chief of Staff, had sought the traditional solution for Japanese soldiers of their rank, and committed *seppuku*, more commonly known to foreigners as *harakiri* – that is, an honourable ritual of suicide.

Such intense levels of fanaticism and resistance were what MacArthur's forces feared above all when they contemplated the imminent invasion of Japan. The prospect of fighting their way ashore on the home islands of Kyushu and Honshu filled every American soldier with dread, CIC included. The Japanese were bereft of fuel, food, ammunition, almost all the matériel required to fight a prolonged defence, but they would have sold their lives dearly, wielding clubs and swords if necessary, so long as their Emperor demanded it. In such a bloodbath American leaders predicted appal-ling losses among their own men and an incalculable slaughter amongst Japanese soldiers and civilians.

Practically all the combat CIC teams in the Pacific area were now gearing up for the final onslaught of World War Two. As part of a pre-invasion campaign aimed at the destruction of the remaining units of the Japanese Navy and of Japanese industrial sites, the American and British Pacific Fleets carried out the first bombard-ment of the Japanese home islands on 17 July, while carrier planes launched massive bombing raids on Tokyo and other vital targets. Two vast amphibious landings were in preparation, one on southern Kyushu, to be followed later in 1945 by another in the area of the Tokyo plain. But in August two events electrified the world and marked a new watershed in human history. On 6 August an American B-29 bomber destroyed the Japanese city of Hiroshima with a single atomic bomb; three days later the city of Nagasaki was razed by a second atomic bomb. On 14 August Japan agreed to the absolute surrender of all her military forces and on 2 September signed the formal surrender before General MacArthur on board the American battleship *Missouri* in Tokyo Bay.

Among the first CIC agents to go ashore in Japan two days later was Arthur Hurlburt, who was then attached to the Americal Division. Of that profoundly momentous occasion he was to write many years later to his granddaughter Julie:

Early on the morning of September 4 we entered Yokohama Bay. On the right side the land is low; on the left, high hills command the channel. These were seasoned troops in this convoy and they all felt the presence of hostile artillery in those hills. We understood that MacArthur had every confidence that the Japanese would obey the order of their Emperor to lay down their arms. We also understood that they had been propagandized for four years about what devils we were. We all fervently hoped against hope that among the people looking down on us from up there was not some kook who would say the hell with the orders and open up. You could cut the tension with a knife. Breakfast was ignored completely. All of a sudden, from somewhere on that ship, someone blew up a white balloon, tied it and tossed it over into the breeze. The idea caught like wildfire and within 30 seconds a great cloud of white balloons drifted off over the convoy. A roar of relief went up. The tension dissolved in an instant.

Yokohama, sitting next to Tokyo, made one big metropolis. You could not tell when you left one city and entered the other. Only there wasn't any city left. There had been a raid of a thousand B-29s in April, dropping incendiaries. In one night they had caused this destruction to Yokohama and Tokyo. This was a city comparable in size to New York. Complete devastation. There were no vehicles moving, hardly any people at all on the streets. The one building that we could see still standing was a tin shack someone had thrown together out of the rubble. A long line of American sailors stood patiently in front of it. Sailors do have a reputation to uphold, they will have you know. The rubble made a uniform pile from four to six feet high and it still contained the stench of death. The ruin here was the absolute equal of Hiroshima and Nagasaki, except that they were about one mile in diameter, where this was more like five miles, with the ruins of

Tokyo beyond that. Julie, believe me, there is nothing glamorous about war. It is as close to hell on earth as man has yet devised. But dead is dead. The destruction to life and property that we had seen at Yokohama far surpassed that wreaked by the atomic bomb.

And so, amid the stink and litter of total defeat, Hurlburt and his fellow agents of the CIC began their post-war duties in the American occupation of Japan – and a short while later of the former Japanese dependency of Korea as well. These duties were many and onerous. They dismantled the Japanese intelligence framework, including the Tokko Ka, or Thought Police, and the Kempei Tai. They screened Japanese political and military organizations, including former members of the Black Dragon Society and the Great Japan Political Society. They hunted down war criminals like General Tojo, former Prime Minister and number one war lord of the Japanese Empire, and American traitors like the American radio propagandist popularly known as Tokyo Rose. They searched out caches of weapons and ammunition and hoards of money and precious metals, including 13 tons of silver in Osaka and 11 crates of platinum uncovered in a chicken coop on a mountain top. And gradually their attention wandered away from the ultra-nationalists and the old guard who had supported the Japanese war of imperial expansion, and were now found to be generally harmless, to the activities of the Japanese Communists, who posed a new and far more serious threat.

In this respect the work of the CIC in Japan mirrored that of the CIC in Germany, where the occupation had already got into swing several months earlier. The difference was that in Germany the crisis brought about by the shifts in the post-war power struggle seemed considerably more urgent and menacing, and for the first time the CIC was brought into the forefront of the international intelligence war. It is therefore to the Germany of that victorious summer of 1945 that we now return.

11

IN THE RUINS OF THE REICH

There had never, in the whole history of the world, been a place quite like Germany in the first eerie, havoc months and years of peace after the war. Not even Russia, for all its vast waste of material damage and the wholesale slaughter of a tenth of its population, could equal Germany in the widespread levelling of its cities, the almost total dismantling of the political and economic fabric of society, and the moral unhinging of the lives of its citizens. Germany after 1945 was a nation at the end of its tether, and the statistics of destruction and deprivation read like a litany of awfulness, of absolute negation.

Six per cent of the pre-war population of Germany, totalling nearly 7 million human beings, had either died in the war or were about to die in the post-war expulsions from the east, and another 2 million were crippled in one way or another. Of all male Germans born in 1924, 25 per cent had been killed and more than 30 per cent had been wounded by the end of hostilities – a casualty rate of more than one in two. Many of the towns and cities of the former Greater Reich were no more. In Austria the town of Wiener Neustadt emerged from the air raids and the street fighting with only 18 houses intact and its population reduced from 45,000 to 860. In Düsseldorf 93 per cent of the houses were uninhabitable. In Hanover only 1 per cent of the buildings were undamaged. It was calculated that the devastated areas of Germany lay under 400 million cubic feet of rubble – equivalent to an area of 100 square miles completely covered in rubble to a height of several feet. 'More than 20 million Germans are homeless or without adequate shelter,' SHAEF reported. 'The average basic ration is less than 1000 calories. The ability to wage war in this generation has been destroyed.'

An Allied fact-finding mission predicted an acute coal famine which would destroy all semblance of law and order in Europe. To prevent this, coal would have to be taken from Germany without any regard for the consequence to the Germans. 'Should it become necessary to preserve order by shooting,' the report concluded, 'it

would surely be better for this to occur in Germany than elsewhere.'
The Germans called it *die Stunde Null*, hour zero, the moment of
hiatus when the nation touched rock bottom. Germany had sunk to a
level unknown in the western world for a hundred years. Its people
were treated as barbarians whether they had been Nazis or not. The
Allies had power of life and death over them. They could shoot to kill
or imprison at will. The Germans had no rights or authority of any
kind. They were subject to curfew and liable to compulsory labour.
Their bank accounts were frozen and they could be searched or
seized and their property requisitioned at a moment's notice. In the
early days they could not travel or even use the telephone. Their
country was like a gigantic concentration camp in which they lived in
enforced isolation from the rest of the world.

The death rate of the very young and the very old reached a level
not seen since the Thirty Years War nearly three hundred years
before. Nineteen out of twenty babies died in the American sector of
Berlin in the first July after the war. Germany, it seemed, was on the
brink of the worst scourge of pestilence and famine since the Middle
Ages. In some places the daily ration level had sunk to 400 calories –
or less than that in the notorious Belsen concentration camp. For the
330,000 inhabitants of Stuttgart it was reported there were only 70
overcoats to go round. There was no fuel for heating and during the
first peacetime winter in Berlin over 50,000 people succumbed to
hypothermia and frostbite. The prospect of famine and insurrection
overshadowed all else. By the beginning of 1946 Berlin had become
the crime capital of the world and the Germans were forced to submit
a petition to the Allies begging for assistance in 'breaking up the
bands of deserters, criminals and degenerates of every European
nation which infested the countryside and bombed cities and towns,
stealing and murdering.'

The war had caused a displacement of peoples without precedent.
Sixty million Europeans from a multitude of nations had become
displaced persons. Eleven million German soldiers rotted behind
barbed wire. Ten million German city dwellers had migrated to the
countryside. Seven million *Volksdeutsch* German expellees from Eastern Europe added to the chaos and deprivation inside the redrawn
German boundaries. Ten million foreign forced labourers swarmed
over the land like locusts in an historic ebb and flow of human masses,
whole armies of tramps, homeward bound along the road and railway
networks of the continent.

To survive in such a ravaged land required special skills. Hungry,
homeless, lonely German women, outnumbering their own dead or
imprisoned menfolk by three to one, took to the streets and dives in

droves and sold themselves with alacrity to the Allied soldiery for a pack of cigarettes or a chocolate bar, a can of bully beef or a pair of silk stockings. In December 1945 a German police official reported: 'It is impossible to distinguish between good girls and bad girls in Germany. Even nice girls of good families, good education and fine background have discovered that their bodies afford the only real living.' By December 1946 the number of girls selling love for goods was getting on for half a million, or one-sixth of the total population of the city. Syphilis spread like a medieval plague and illegitimate births rose by ten per cent.

In a land where the native currency was next to worthless the people reverted to a more primitive form of exchange-barter. Germans no longer bought and sold, they swapped. No article of barter was so highly prized as the cigarette. Indeed, before long the cigarette had replaced the mark as the basic unit of exchange, the universal currency of the people. Anything and anyone, from diamonds to love, could be traded for an English or American cigarette. The butt ends of the Allied soldiers were pennies from heaven to the starving Germans, for it was calculated that seven butt ends made one cigarette and for one cigarette a man could buy his next meal. In time the German black market developed into a well-organized alternative economy. What most Germans sought on the black market was food and the essentials of existence, but there were many who made a killing. Big-time gangsters, the *Grosschieber*, ran large illegal organizations which dealt in priceless commodities like penicillin, insulin, cocaine, industrial chemicals, furs, old masters, precious stones, silver and gold.

But in general it was the Allied soldiery that profited most easily from the German black market. Every week an American soldier could buy 10 packets of cigarettes for 50 cents and sell them for $100. From the proceeds of black market deals in PX liquor, candy bars and gift parcels from home he could make as much as $200,000 a year over and above his pay. In this way GIs in Berlin were able to buy up apartments in the city's West End and even afford to own cinemas and restaurants. In the first five months of the Occupation American military personnel sent home over $16,000,000 more than they were paid. By the summer of 1946 they were buying an average of one million marks' worth of antiques each month. A few turned to crime for a greater profit. Three US Army officers made off with the Hesse crown jewels, worth nearly $10 million today, and one general was known to have sent home in a single shipment 166 crates of silver, tapestries, paintings and ceramics acquired from various German castles and estates.

'Germany will become the cesspool of Europe!' thundered the Assistant Chaplain-General to the British Occupation forces. 'These conditions,' reported two American economic advisers on a visit to Berlin from the States, 'created an atmosphere so unreal, so night-marish, so demoralizing, that official work was almost impossible. The whole situation – the aftermath of the war – was such that it gnawed at all men's character like maggots. The destruction all about, the demoralized state of the German people and the demoral-izing influence of the black market – the entire environment made life profoundly depressing.' Such was life in the ruins of the Thousand Year Reich in the first few piping years of peace. 'Give me five years,' Hitler had told his people before the outbreak of the war, 'and you will not recognize Germany again.' Now the survivors chalked their derision on the walls of the ruined cities: *'Das verdanken wir Hitler.'* For this we thank Hitler.

Into these ruined cities, this surrealist tableau of disaster, this land of rubble peopled by ghosts, without government, order or purpose, without industry, communications or the proper means of existence, came the CIC. They came as part of an experiment unique in the history of man. Never before had four civilized industrial nations tried to work together to govern a country inhabited by a fifth – for such was the Quadripartite Occupation of Germany. In the division of Germany into four zones shared out between the armies of the victorious Allies, it was said the Russians in the east got the corn, the French in the west got the wine, the British in the north got the ruins (and the industry), and the Americans in the south got the scenery. But the Americans also got a part of Berlin, an island in the middle of the red sea of the Russian Zone, and it was here that CIC agents began to encounter the most urgent and complex problems thrown up by a human society in shreds.

The CIC in Berlin were confronted with a strange and multifarious task. CIC responsibility was not clearly defined, and there were times when it seemed to know no bounds. Every agent in charge of one or other of the six CIC field areas in the American sector of the city became in effect a city manager, responsible for an unknown number of 'residents' of unknown origin within his area. Every day he was faced with administering the problem of survival for those living, hiding or just existing among the bombed-out ruins, the huge pile of rubble that was Berlin. Colonel Theodor J. Girouard, who was a young CIC lieutenant in Berlin in 1945, recalled the abnormal and complex circumstances of everyday life in that razed metropolis:

Each day, starting at daybreak, a steady stream of administrators flowed through each agent's office. Those administrators that the Chief Agent had been lucky enough to locate in the DP camps or in the rubble reported with their daily problems. The police chief reported: the number of men he had for duty that day, how many were not present and why – no uniforms, no shoes, no food stamps, sickness, death. The medical administrator reported: the hospitals that had been set up, the doctors available, the medical supplies to be had on the black market, the number of people who had died, and why. Then the Mayor reported. His job was to help establish order out of the chaos that was the American Sector of Berlin: potato and fat rations to issue, charcoal briquettes for fuel, ex-Nazis to be assigned to the rubble gangs for cleaning and stacking old bricks.

Housing problems were many. People were digging holes in the rubble to find a place to sleep away from the bitter winter, or sharing usable rooms in shifts. Every night through the long, bitterly cold hours of darkness, teams of CIC agents with US infantrymen and German police with dogs combed the ruins for illegal residents. It was during these searches that we discovered the Germans had built a secret city under Tempelhof Airport. The subterranean city consisted of seven levels, the uppermost of which led from Berlin into the Russian Zone. Many Russian soldiers who had slipped across the border to spend the night with their German girlfriends were found during these nocturnal raids. One of them was tracked down to a bedroom on the third floor of a bombed-out building with only two walls. In this precarious open-air love-nest was a bed and on the bed just about everything possible to protect the occupants from the biting cold was piled so high that it was impossible for them even to turn over. When the 'covers' were finally removed by the CIC agent and German police they discovered the Russian and his girl. Both turned out to be illegal. The CIC agent maintained that he did not know what the girl looked like nor what she wore. All he could remember seeing was the dirtiest pair of longjohns and the biggest and dirtiest feet he had ever set eyes on in his life. Russian discipline was brutal for border-crossing lotharios, so the CIC had the local infantry escort him to the border and turn him loose.

When the CIC first crossed the German frontier the detachments had been organized on a war footing, with agents attached to the main fighting formations of the US Army at division, corps and army level. All this changed once the Americans had settled down to the long haul of occupation government. All CIC personnel serving in Germany – some 300 officers and over 1000 agents in 1945 – were regrouped in a single detachment serving the whole of the American Zone. This was the 970th CIC Detachment (later renamed 7970th CIC Group and later still the 66th Detachment), which for the first few years had its operational and administrative headquarters in Frankfurt, and subsequently in Stuttgart. As well as directing CIC efforts throughout the US Zone, headquarters also operated the extensive Central Registry, which contained dossiers on all persons who had come to CIC attention in Germany, and was one of the CIC's greatest assets in Germany.

Out in the Zone lay a number of subordinate headquarters, a network of Regional and Sub-Regional offices in the larger cities and towns, together with their own subordinate field offices and resident agents in the smaller country towns and villages. By means of this network the CIC hoped to cover not only the three Länder (the equivalent of American states) of Bavaria, Württemberg-Baden and Hesse which comprised the US Zone, but Berlin and the American enclave around the northern port of Bremen in the British Zone as well. In 1949 the network was re-organized so that CIC headquarters also served as headquarters for 12 CIC Regions, while investigative personnel at Regional level were reorganized into four teams which served as the primary working tools of the Regional commander. The Political (or Counter Subversion) Team was assigned targets dealing with right- and left-wing political activities in all the Zones of Germany. The Counter Espionage Team was responsible for exploiting positive intelligence from sources in territory under US control, suspected espionage, foreign missions and non-German national groups in the US Zone. To the General Investigative Team fell a variety of targets, including security of installations and suspected sabotage, surveillance of scientists, subversion, screenings and arrests. The Visa Screening Team was charged with investigating the backgrounds of foreigners, especially displaced persons from East European countries desiring to emigrate to the United States – a task that turned out to be infinitely less straightforward than expected.

Ostensibly CIC operations in Germany were masterminded by a staff section at Theatre G-2 (Intelligence) known as the Counter Intelligence Branch or Operations Branch. However, Theatre G-2 seemed to have no uniform or purposeful concept as to how it should employ the capabilities of the CIC and gave little clear-cut guidance as to intelligence-gathering requirements and targets. In practice, therefore, CIC's intelligence-gathering was largely directed by the

Operations Officer at the headquarters of the 970th Detachment, located in the European Command (EUCOM) Headquarters building in Frankfurt. This raised some problems, for the CIC was in no position to evaluate the overall intelligence requirements of the American Zone of Germany, and sometimes found itself groping in the dark in highly sensitive areas of intelligence work, or competing with foreign agencies or rival American ones, simply because the big picture was missing. This did not affect the CIC's basic mission, which entailed the receiving, recording, co-ordination and dissemination of all counter intelligence information that was channelled up to the 970th CIC from the Regional offices. To carry out its functions, the operations section was divided into two sub-sections during the early years: the Central Registry and Case Direction.

The Central Registry catalogued all counter intelligence information of value and kept elaborately cross-indexed files from which case details could be compiled. The Central Registry was also responsible for Top Secret Control and a network of teletypes that linked all echelons of the 970th CIC. Eventually the Central Registry contained 1,350,000 personality cards, 275,000 dossiers and 42,000 titles.

The Case Direction Section evaluated all the counter intelligence information coming in from subordinate echelons, checked it against information already on file, and passed it on to other interested agencies. To expedite the processing of this information, the Section was divided into two sub-sections known as the internal and external desks.

The internal desk was concerned with counter intelligence activities as they related to the German population, and included such areas as subversion, security control, war crimes and automatic arrestees, Operation Mesa or Paperclip (the exploitation and protection of German scientists), as well as an historical section which collected information on former high-ranking Nazi officials and the German Intelligence Service, and screened German repatriates for counter intelligence information.

The external desk was mainly responsible for monitoring the Russians and their satellites and was divided into separate divisions which covered Soviet, Czech, Hungarian, Yugoslavian, Bulgarian, Romanian, Polish, Ukrainian and White Russian activities, and also Jewish. The activities of each group were broken down into specific categories – for example, the Soviet Activities Section gathered information on the operations of agents of the MGB (Ministry of State Security) and the MVD (Ministry of Internal Affairs) – both the immediate predecessors of the KGB – as well as Courier Liaison with the German Communist Party, the Soviet Reparations Mission, the Soviet Repatriations Mission, Soviet DP Propaganda, Soviet Army Intelligence, Soviet Illegal Wireless Transmissions and Soviet Mass Briefing of Returning POWs.

As a result of the reorganizational changes of 1949, when the CIC Detachment in Germany was redesignated the 66th, CIC's operations section underwent considerable changes. Headed by the 66th CIC Operations Officer and his assistant, this section was now divided into seven sub-sections: the Case Section (with four desks handling counter-subversion, counter-espionage, security and positive intelligence); a Technical Specialist Section (for running informants); a Screening Section, a Training Section, a Reports Section (which produced the CIC Top Secret Target Survey and Bi-Weekly Orientation and Guidance Report, listing all operational missions in detail), the Central Registry and the Services Section (including Top Secret Control).

In Austria a somewhat similar set-up prevailed. Though Austria was officially regarded as a liberated rather than an occupied nation, it was still a hotbed of Nazi, Soviet and Jewish activity of urgent counter intelligence interest to the CIC, and the 430th CIC Detachment maintained a substantial presence in that country, with a headquarters in Vienna and three Sub-Detachments in Salzburg, Linz and the American sector of Vienna. Eventually these Sub-Detachments were organized into two main branches: Positive Intelligence and Counter Intelligence. While the Positive Intelligence was sub-divided into External and Internal Affairs, the Counter Intelligence Branch consisted of six sections: General Investigations, Security, Research, Denazification, Police and Visa.

The CIC's biggest headache, in Austria as in Germany, was its own people. The end of the war brought about a crisis in the CIC. With the end of hostilities, the longest-serving and most experienced agents seized the first opportunity they could to return to the States and civilian life. All through the second half of 1945 the CIC in occupied Germany was steadily drained of many of its best and brightest men; in Austria the 430th Detachment was reduced from 235 agents to 65 (less than half of whom had been with the CIC more than eight months) as a result of the demobilization of their most experienced men.

To make up for these losses the CIC sought replacement agents from among the American troops already in the European Threatre, but these were for the most part half-trained and half-baked and as often as not more of a hindrance than a help. According to a 1947 army survey, some 20 per cent of agents were unqualified for counter intelligence duties. New CIC agents specially trained in the United States began to arrive in the spring of 1946, but their 5-week course in FBI-style detective work ill equipped them for occupation duties and the extraordinary situation in post-war Germany and Austria with which they were rudely confronted. These new agents were very young and very green. Their lack of German background indoctrination was remedied to some extent by a 10-day blitz course (later extended to 7 weeks) at the European Command Intelligence School at Oberammergau in Bavaria. But few could handle wisely or maturely the exceptional power and privileges bestowed upon them by membership of an American intelligence organization operating amongst a subject population in an ambience of widespread material chaos and moral ambivalence.

A CIC officer from CIC Headquarters in Fort Holabird, Baltimore, on a liaison trip round the US Zone of Germany, put on record that a CIC agent had to be of more than just average intelligence: 'He must be of sufficient intellect to thoroughly comprehend the complex political and economic situation which exists in the European Theater during the present quad-powered, partitioned occupation of Germany.' In many localities the CIC agent was the sole representative of the United States Army. Maturity and judgement were therefore prime requisites. In dealing with informants, for example, without whom much of the CIC effort in Germany would be impossible, an agent simply had to inspire confidence, otherwise the informants might fear that their information could be compromised. Tact and diplomacy were also essential traits in a good CIC agent.

But the right character and personality alone were not sufficient qualifications to turn an individual into an effective field agent. In addition to training in such investigative techniques as interrogation, use of informants, report writing and basic principles of conducting an investigation, an agent in Germany or Austria had to have at least a basic familiarity with the German language. 'There was no adequate substitute for an agent who could speak German fluently and, in highly sensitive assignments, for qualified agents who could speak local accents in order to maintain their covers.'

A few of the newer CIC men did manage to bring linguistic ability and a familiarity with the German background to their job. Mostly these were German refugees, generally of Jewish origin, who had sought sanctuary in the USA during Hitler's rise to power before the war. One such was 22-year-old Henry A. Kissinger, later President Nixon's Secretary of State, but in 1945 a CIC Staff Sergeant in Hesse, where he was the absolute ruler of Bensheim and lived like a lord in a luxurious villa whose German owner he had evicted.

Sergeant Kissinger's speciality was identifying Gestapo and SS officers hiding out amongst the German populace. He coupled his expertise at Nazi hunting with a ready adaptability to the German ambience in which he operated. After a visit to the Kissinger ménage an old friend from Washington wrote in his diary for 21 October 1945: 'What a set-up! Like a castle. Had dinner with him. What an intelligent girlfriend.' The girlfriend was German. So were the cook, the maid, the housekeeper and the secretary – and the white 1938 Mercedes-Benz he had confiscated from a Nazi baby powder manufacturer. Kissinger, his friend recalled, 'really enjoyed the trappings of authority.'

Not many of the young, inexperienced boys sent over from post-war America could measure up to the exacting standards demanded of them; and in any case their tours of duty in Germany were so short that by the time they had gained adequate experience it was time for them to be sent home. As one senior CIC officer explained: 'While CIC still had the pick of the available personnel, the best we could hope for was bright young college graduates and mature Army veterans whose military experience was mostly unrelated to intelligence work.' But it was not just the new boys that were the problem. Some of the old hands were a major cause of concern too. A few of those who had served through the rigours of the war years shared the same tendency to relax and let up as the rest of the military in post-hostilities Germany. A CIC officer or plain-clothes agent could have a good time in war-torn Germany, just like all the rest of the Allied occupation forces. As a former member of American Military Government reported:

> We became an 'India Service' – poobah Sahibs – masters of a conquered people, rulers of an occupied colonial State. Like India Service personnel, in the midst of ruins and near starvation, we lived well. We requisitioned the best houses. We wined and dined as we had never done at home. The most beautiful women we had at our price. There were servants to minister to our every need. For a few packs of cigarettes we even had music with our meals. And on the streets, before the opera, groups of Germans gathered to fight each other for our cigarette butts.

Some of the old hands, using their familiarity with the German people and the local conditions, grew lazy and sybaritic, and allowed informants – mostly Poles and other East Europeans, but also Germans and even former Nazis – to carry out investigations, write reports, conduct operations and run their offices for them. A classic instance was that of Captain George Spiller, a veteran of the Italian campaign, who had won two silver stars for bravery and twice been severely wounded. Spiller was the commander of a small CIC detachment at Memmigen in Bavaria and after his wartime sacrifice he evidently felt he was entitled to enjoy an easier life. Every Thursday he left his office and picked up his German girlfriend for a long, four-day weekend of hunting, wining, dining and bucolic romance. Every Tuesday he would return to his office to sign the weekly reports. Such conduct by some of CIC's low-fliers in Germany earned the scorn of their colleagues in other American investigative agencies and of the rather more tight-laced British agents with whom they came in contact. Antony Terry, a German-speaking British commando who had been taken prisoner in the ill-fated St Nazaire raid and after the war worked as a leading interrogator of high-ranking Nazis at the London Cage (an interrogation centre for special Nazi targets) and was later the correspondent of the London *Sunday Times* in Bonn, took a dim view of the *modus operandi* of some of the CIC agents he came across:

> I never felt very happy when I was dealing with the CIC in Germany. They had a marvellous time and behaved like nabobs but they seemed very haphazard in their job and they didn't keep their files very secure. They may have been effective in the combat situation during the war, but they were running to seed a bit by the time I met them afterwards. They ran around with a lot of fancy ideas and wrote vast memos full of sound and fury and signifying not very much. They were for ever posturing, glamorizing themselves as spy catchers, but in my estimation the American OSS and British Intelligence were more professional and the US Army CID did a better job in Germany. What worried me most about them were all those gorgeous blonde German girls who worked for them as secretaries. Those girls ran rings round them and put them in a potentially corruptible situation. I mean, the Nazis could get to them via the girls.

A CIC veteran of the campaign in north-west Europe, who was persuaded to return to help out CIC in Germany in 1946, was appalled at the deterioration in the proficiency of the Corps since the late war years. He found chaos in the filing system, a standard of security so leaky that German civilians were handling Top Secret documents which no American civilian could have handled without having been screened for months, and secret instructions being imparted to informants over the open German telephone system. He found commanding officers who 'knew as much about intelligence as your grandmother' or were rejects from their own arms of the military, uninterested in any form of activity except the pursuit of Fräuleins. 'The army system was taking over,' he wrote. 'The army was relentlessly sending over higher-ranked men for CIC jobs – men who came from the artillery, infantry, Air Corps, etc. These officers were about as prepared to take over a counter intelligence outfit as they would be to suddenly move into a hospital and start to do surgical operations.'

The raw new agents being sent over from America seemed to have no skills or aptitudes to bring to the job. Major William Larned, the Operations Officer at Region VI Bamberg, was totally dismayed by them:

> These guys did a few weeks' course at Holabird, got on the boat, landed at Bremerhaven, and then would arrive on the train at Bamberg as replacements. We usually sent three-quarters of them back on the next train as being totally unusable. They didn't speak German, they didn't know the political history of the country, they didn't know the people, they didn't know anything. They were college graduates, they were fairly smart young guys, but my gosh – are you going to send them out in the field on espionage investigations? No. We were struggling with a terrific handicap. The CIC got into an awful lot of trouble and difficulty simply because of this immature fumbling-around by inexperienced, untrained agents who really didn't know what they were doing. Those of us at headquarters level had to spend an awful lot of time and trouble putting out brush fires before they did some real damage.

Some of the tyro agents brought such an alarmingly fanciful and trigger-happy gung-ho attitude to the delicate business of catching spies that the hard-boiled Executive Officer fired them on the spot, with the words: 'I don't care what the army thinks in America. We want to catch Martin Bormann alive. We don't want him to die laughing when he sees what we send after him.'

The situation was gravest in CIC Region IV (Munich). Operations in this region were described by an inspection team as 'bewildered, inept and chaotic'. A member of this swoop team wrote to us:

> The entire region was a charade of intelligence. For instance, well known to Region IV HQ was a German character called 'CIC Huber', who roamed in a big car all over the area from Munich to Garmisch, bullying his way into blackmarket deals and intimidating people in a way that scared the Germans and brought shame on CIC. But what did this matter to an HQ whose key 'safe house' in

Munich was a bordello which was raided by MPs and German police who forced half-clad girls and so-called 'agents' into the street? I do not condemn everyone in Region IV. There must have been those good agents who, sickened by abuses, carried on. It was capped by the final tragedy of transferring an ex-OSS clown to command it. He used to 'run' a secret agent he called 'The Shadow' to whom he gave secret instructions over the German telephone system. What a joke he was to Region IV! Does it come as a surprise to you that Region IV was spawned by General Patton's Third Army, the closest thing to an SS general we had, who had no time for anything as off-beat as a CIC?

Entire CIC offices were controlled by Germans with access to Top Secret American files. Solitary field agents, buried deep in the German countryside and long forgotten by headquarters, existed in incommunicado isolation from the German populace amongst whom they worked because they could not speak a word of the language, and turned in no work for months. SS fugitives were taken on the payroll and black market business boomed. Sub-standard agents were ignorant of even the most basic terminology – like the Top Secret code word, 'Project Happiness', used all over the occupation zones for Communism. As one inspecting officer remarked: 'I am beginning to lose my faith in human nature.' As an expression of their disconsolate lot experienced agents took to naming their jeeps with permutations of the wartime army slogan SNAFU such as TARFU (Things Are Really Fouled Up) and FUBAR (Fouled Up Beyond All Recognition).

Fortunately there was still a sizeable nucleus of hardworking, competent and experienced agents on whom Headquarters and the Regional commanders could rely to carry out the many complex assignments that cropped up in Germany. As one agent wrote at the time: 'The headquarters men and a few good agents are still on the firing line of the cold war. The endless hours of loyal work by the tiny residue of good agents in the field is still accomplishing some excellent results amid the welter of confusion. They have succeeded admirably in maintaining the illusion that there is an intelligence organization in Germany.' Such men included the likes of Lieutenant Colonel Earl S. Browning (Headquarters Operations Officer and CO of Regional headquarters at Bamberg and the Bremen enclave), Captain James H. Ratliff (like Browning a veteran of the campaign in North West Europe, and Browning's deputy at headquarters in Frankfurt), Major George Sheldon (another veteran and former journalist, commander of Region VI at Bamberg), Major George Wilson (head of the case section), Lieutenant Colonel Anthony W. Lobb (a World War Two veteran, commanding the Third Army CIC, and then Chief of Operations for the 430th CIC at Linz, Austria), Major William Larned (one of a handful of highly-prized West Point graduates in Germany, Operations officer at Region VI Bamberg and then CIC Headquarters) and Lieutenant Richard B. Snyder (CIC Bamberg, then head of the headquarters training section). Such men, in the words of one who knew them, 'shone like stars' among the duds.

Many of the best agents were former enlisted men who had been civilianized – otherwise they would not have stayed in Germany. Many of the best CIC men in Germany were sent to Berlin, where counter intelligence work (and eventually positive intelligence work too) often proved the most difficult and involved, requiring the expertise of men with considerable intelligence background. But though there were just enough good men to take on the toughest jobs, there were not enough to cover the whole field of counter intelligence operations in Germany, and the deficiencies of the less satisfactory personnel took their toll on CIC operations. As William Larned commented later:

> In those years we also had a positive intelligence-gathering mission. We were the CIA, FBI and military security all in one, because those agencies weren't functioning in Germany at that time. Considering the resources that were placed at our disposal in those immediate post-war years 1947 to 1950, and all the multitude of missions we were required to perform – espionage, black market, security, political activities – we were achieving a minor miracle every day in getting as much information as we did. Now what the value of it all was back in Frankfurt and over in Washington at high intelligence levels we never knew. It was a steady stream of information of which about 5 per cent was quite valuable.

The impression amongst the German populace of the CIC, with its almost unlimited powers of search and arrest, was as the 'American Gestapo', and it was one that the wilder elements of the Corps did little to change. James McGovern, a former American intelligence officer in Germany with an intimate insight into the working methods of some CIC outfits, has written an unflattering description of the treatment meted out to Nazi suspects in a CIC headquarters in Berlin. Though the account is dressed up as fiction, it conveys an all too raw authenticity. In McGovern's account, the fictional German protagonists, eight young women and an old man, are arrested by GIs and taken to a former Gestapo jail now used by the CIC, where they are confronted by a hostile captain called Uhl and a long-haired corporal called Baldy.

'The women,' wrote McGovern, 'were somewhat of a nuisance to CIC, whose main job was picking up would-be spies and any Nazi war criminals who might still be at large. Some of them had been caught by the MPs in American billets after curfew; others were suspected of spying for the Russians, or past leadership in Nazi women's organizations. They were a varied crew ... hordes of unfortunate trollops recruited by the NKVD.'

The old man, however, was a former leading industrial engineer and believed (wrongly) by the CIC to be a big Nazi catch. The captain fixed the old man with a stern look and said:

'So. We finally caught up with you.'

The old man began to recover from his astonishment. 'What is all this? What are you arresting me for?'

'You ought to know.'

'I want to see your search warrant.'

'We don't need one. Not with Germans.'

'I want to get in touch with my lawyers.'

'You have no right to counsel.'

'But a writ of Habeas Corpus is basic to Anglo-Saxon justice.'

'Nazis have no right to Anglo-Saxon justice.'

'I would like to see someone from Military Government.'

'Military Government has no authority over CIC.'

'These are Gestapo tactics!'

'Oh, what you said,' laughed the hulking corporal, in mock horror. He rapped the back of the old man's skull with the flattened palm of his hand, and said, 'What now, Captain Uhl?'

'Throw him in the Pen, Baldy. No, wait a minute. He's a big one. Put him in Alcatraz.'

'Alcatraz', according to McGovern's account, was the cell block in the CIC Building where important internees were detained in individual cells under 24-hour surveillance. By contrast the 'Pen' was a single large room where up to 50 small-fry male suspects were herded together to await processing. Other sections of the CIC Building included the 'Tank' for women detainees, which was the same as the 'Pen' except that it was furnished with cots; the 'Chapel', a seldom-occupied, dank, windowless cubicle in the cellar, used for solitary confinement or violent internees; and the 'Ball Room', the former Gestapo interrogation room, still equipped with Nazi instruments of persuasion, including a battered old phonograph in the corner, upon which Uhl would play *Wiener Blut* and *Die Fledermaus* at high volume whenever the internees' cries became too loud.

It was seldom necessary to bring a suspect into the Ball Room [McGovern noted], because the Army had captured the Nazi Party records and it was impossible in most cases to lie about one's role in the thousand-year Reich. There were occasionally more complicated cases, however, for which the Ball Room seemed to Uhl to provide the only answer. [It was here that the elderly suspect was taken.]

Uhl liked the internees to cringe, display the proper amount of respect, confess quickly to their crimes, and beg forgiveness. He only used force as a last resort, but now he decided that he would have to put this old man in the correct frame of mind before the serious business of interrogation began.

'Jump up in the air!' he shouted.

The old man jumped up with surprising spryness. As his feet landed on the floor, Uhl rapped him over the back with his cane.

'Who told you to come down?' he shouted. 'You do what you're told here, nothing else. You keep coming down after you jumped up. Nobody ordered you to come down. Germans are supposed to be good at following orders.'

Uhl cranked up the battered phonograph and soon a jaunty song from the *White Horse Inn* resounded through the Ball Room. '*Aufstehen!*' Uhl shouted. 'Get up and dance.'

And so, as the old man waltzed round the former Gestapo torture chamber holding an imaginary partner, the CIC interrogation proceeded.

The CIC's deficiencies were startlingly highlighted by one of its more outspoken agents. Guenther Reinhardt could hardly be described as one of the best agents the CIC had ever had, but he was certainly one of the most critical and vociferous. A 43-year-old German-born Jew, Reinhardt rated high in intelligence and integrity but low in emotional stability and the common-sense and discretion which are *sine qua non* for any successful intelligence agent. Bill Larned remembers him as a highly amusing and entertaining man but a first-class rogue. 'I didn't have much respect for him. He was very charming but not very ethical or creditable. He was a fabricator of amazing stories which contained no more than 10 per cent of the truth.' Reinhardt was hysterical, paranoiac and suicidal. He was also boastful and prone to monumental exaggeration, so that sometimes he would go about posing as the Chief of the CIC, and on holiday in Czechoslovakia (not long before the Communist coup of February 1948) described himself everywhere as the 'Chief of American Intelligence in Germany'.

Reinhardt was no fool. As Case Officer on the Communist Desk of CIC Region IV (Munich), he was acknowledged as one of the CIC's top Communist investigators. But his persistent breaches of security and his increasingly irrational behaviour led his superiors to repatriate him to the States in November 1947. In his shock and fury at his dismissal, Reinhardt decided to get his own back by revealing all. 'When I got back to the States I was so damn mad I wanted to blow my top,' he wrote to a friend. 'You know that I can't keep my mouth shut when I see something wrong or crooked.' He was going to bend the government's ears about 'the incredible extent of irregularities' in the US Zone of Germany. It was not simply the CIC he was gunning for – 'all the irregularities and the faking of intelligence reports in the Munich Region' – but the whole of the American occupation as well, what he called 'the rotten mess of graft, stealing, smuggling, incompetence – and the danger to our entire intelligence system'.

In the course of two reports sent at the beginning of 1948 to the Military Governor and Commander-in-Chief of the American Zone of Germany, General Lucius D. Clay, Reinhardt accused the CIC of corruption, incompetence and idleness, all of which he diagnosed as being due to the rivalry and lack of co-ordination of five overlapping army intelligence agencies. The United States, he claimed, was 'facing another Pearl Harbor in Germany' because of the conditions prevailing in the CIC. After citing nearly 50 specific charges against the CIC in Germany, Reinhardt listed five recommendations for improving the situation, including the replacement of dud commanders, a general tightening of discipline, an improvement in the system of selection and training of personnel, and the institution of a special inspection service.

The Secretary of the Army took Reinhardt's allegations very seriously and sent his Special Assistant, Orville J. Taylor, to conduct a fact-finding tour in the US Zone. In a subsequent report, which some have described as a whitewash, Taylor found Reinhardt's charges had only limited foundations and in the main was 'a mass of glittering generalizations emanating from the fantastic imagination of which the reporter must be possessed'. However, Taylor admitted the presence in CIC of 'some individuals with ulterior motives and questionable ethics' and urged continual scrutiny of all intelligence personnel 'because of the tremendous temptations for wrongdoing and because of the possibilities of damage to the security, interest, prestige or operational effort'.

In fact, the CIC had begun to put its house in order some months before Reinhardt blew the gaff. Earlier in 1947, on the order of General Clay, CIC agents were ordered back into uniform and back into military barracks. Gone were the good old days when agents lived independent of military control, resided in private houses and ran their own messes in sumptuous style. Agents were once again reminded that they were basically soldiers and members of the American military occupation. At the same time unannounced 'swoop inspections' by officer teams from headquarters put even the remotest CIC backwater back on its toes and commanders were empowered to dismiss personnel for inefficiency, character deficiency, undesirable attitude and failure to perform CIC duties properly. The hurt inflicted on agents' morale at this sudden shattering of their privileged status was thought to be outweighed by the double gains achieved in standardizing operations and improving agents' behaviour. This was not the view of some of the most responsible CIC men in the field. Not long after the event, one of them wrote:

> In vain were the protests of CIC officials who pointed out that these men were not lining up each day for duty in an infantry company, but might go out at any time in disguise to work against the underground. Useless were the protests that secret contacts of intelligence agents could not seek out an American agent by asking for him from a sentry at the barracks. These men might even forfeit their lives if seen by their clandestine enemies while boldly approaching army installations. It was useless. The army said that everyone would go into barracks and an order is an order. Perhaps if someone close to Clay had had some idea what intelligence was all about, the situation could have been better explained. So indifferent to intelligence in Berlin were some of the brass that last summer a Top Secret officer intelligence courier was kicked off a plane leaving Berlin in order to make room for a Colonel's German maids.

In Berlin, then the hottest intelligence spot on the globe, agents complained bitterly that the regulations had made a farce out of their service. Some were subjected to a humiliating régime as a result of the new orders, and were required to make as many as six changes of clothing a day as they changed into civilian clothes to conduct their undercover work and back into uniform when they entered barracks to eat and sleep. (In Austria all CIC personnel wore uniforms until the summer of 1947; after that, they all wore civilian clothes.)

Relatively few investigations were undertaken personally by CIC agents, apart from those involving American military or civilian personnel. This was because in the majority of CIC operations direct investigation by American agents was ruled out by barriers of language, customs and appearance. Instead, the CIC made use of widespread informant networks which covered the whole of the US Zone and beyond and reached every level of German society. Thus the role of individual American agents was usually confined to directing the informants' activities and checking and evaluating the information which they produced. In addition, the recruiting and handling of informants was one of the most important things an agent new to Germany was taught: the proper approach to a likely prospect, testing for dependability, the preparation of a cover story, means of preventing the burning-out of an informant, methods of using an informant to assist in a mission without divulging the primary nature of the mission, and so on. Standard operating procedures for the use of German informants were outlined in a CIC directive of 1946: 'In certain circumstances German civilian personnel may be used under the control of a CIC agent as an informant or undercover agent. Extreme caution will be exercised to insure that such personnel have the appropriate security clearances and do not have access to any classified information other than what those individuals may have produced themselves.' A number of Poles who could speak several languages and had had previous wartime experience in the OSS or British intelligence were also employed by the CIC as intelligence leg-men on special investigations. The Poles were warned that in the event that any of them got into trouble on an intelligence assignment, the CIC would disclaim all knowledge of him or her.

During the early days of the Occupation, when the CIC's main preoccupation was rounding up Nazis, the average CIC informant was a denouncer, a malcontent who had suffered under the Nazi régime and jumped at the chance of helping the organization which was believed to be the 'American Gestapo'. But later, from about 1947 onwards, when American forces in Germany settled into a long-term role, and a more or less covert battle against Soviet espionage became one of the CIC's most persistent and time-consuming missions, it became apparent that the CIC would have to maintain informants in every sphere of activity which remotely affected the security of the Occupation – not only German groups and organizations but the teeming DP camps which had become a breeding ground of Soviet espionage.

Among the new breed of informants there were some who were

genuine idealists, anxious to help the Americans in any way they could in the hope of building a new and better Germany. Other informants were motivated less by any particular fondness towards the American Occupation than by an intense hatred of Communism and the Soviet Union. But most run-of-the-mill informants worked for the CIC because of the compensations they could get out of it – the food, coffee, cigarettes, soap and other precious commodities which were almost unobtainable in devastated Germany during the early years of total deprivation. Very occasionally the special requirements necessary for a particular job led to terrible compromises being made, and former Gestapo agents and other Nazis – some of them guilty of the most appalling crimes – were employed as informants where no one else could fulfil the task. For such informants, and for others who found themselves in jeopardy because they had given valuable service to US Intelligence, the Americans made every effort to facilitate their emigration to South America or the United States, usually under the guise of a new identity.

Eventually some system was injected into the informant nets in a scheme devised by James Ratliff at headquarters in Frankfurt. Thenceforth all CIC informants were systematically listed in code. As Ratliff explained:

> First, the capital letter 'A' was to identify an Automatic Informant, one that anybody would systematically contact on a visit to any town. Thus the mayor and chief of police, who knew everything that was going on in their towns, were Automatic Informants. Next, the letter 'O' was an Ordinary Informant, any citizen who had volunteered information already, or was in a good position to do so. Then came 'P' for Penetration Informant, who was used to penetrate any conspiracy, such as the Communist Party. You have to 'plant' a 'P' informant, in fact more than one, to check on the other. Finally came the 'X' Informant, who was a full-time, salaried, undercover agent that the CIC 'ran'. These 'X' informants greatly facilitated and extended our operations because as German nationals they enjoyed perfect cover, and were picked for their counter espionage attributes. Thus a former Kripo (Kriminalpolizei) detective was a perfect 'X' prospect, though no one was permitted to use a former SD or Gestapo agent. Each informant also bore a personal three-digit number and the Roman numeral of the CIC Region for which he worked.

There were many advantages to being a CIC informant in Germany but even more advantages to being an actual CIC agent. Occasionally more unscrupulous individuals were known to set themselves up as bogus agents in order to claim the privileges that went with the job, or for even more devious reasons. One of the more notorious cases was that of a 22-year-old Fräulein by the name of Ingeborg Petersen, an exceptionally good-looking brunette with an unusually attractive personality who spoke English with hardly a trace of accent and formed many friendships in US Army circles. Crossing into the American Zone from Russian-occupied Germany in December 1945, Petersen 'transformed' herself into a US Army investigator by donning WAC uniform with CIC insignia and for nearly a year travelled through the American Zone on forged papers, usually representing herself as an undercover intelligence agent and receiving food and lodging from the US authorities wherever she went, together with luxury items such as jewellery, nylons, expensive souvenirs and dresses from fashionable New York stores given to her by her American admirers. Petersen's nemesis came when she was emboldened to arrest two Germans on spurious security charges. Two days later real Army investigators nabbed her in an army hotel in Kassel – still in full Army uniform. Tried before a Military Government court for posing as an American intelligence agent and wearing US Army uniform, the young impostor was sentenced to a 10-year term in the penitentiary.

A much more serious case was that of the notorious British traitor, Harold Cole, a British Army deserter and habitual criminal, who was hired by British intelligence (MI9) as one of its key agents running escape routes in occupied France, only to go over to the Germans and betray scores of Allied agents to the Gestapo. According to Scotland Yard, Cole was without doubt 'the worst traitor of the war'. After the war, one jump ahead of the retribution that was his due, Cole passed himself off as Captain Robert Mason, a British secret agent captured in France by the German Security Service, and quickly ingratiated himself with the American Army in Bavaria. In Garmisch-Partenkirchen he was advised by 206th CIC Detachment attached to VI Corps Headquarters to 'stick around for a while' and provided with an American lieutenant's uniform and an official CIC identity card. Thus disguised, Cole set about pursuing a private vendetta against former Nazis, culminating in the cold-blooded execution of one of them. Eventually, however, British investigators caught up with Cole, now operating as a CIC officer in a safe, obscure little haven in the French Zone, and imprisoned him in the SHAEF detention barracks in Paris to await trial. Here Cole, a much practised escaper, made a last bid for liberty but in January 1946 finally met his justly deserved end in a shoot-out with the French police in a room above a bar near St Germain-des-Prés.

By contrast, a CIC agent might occasionally strike pure gold as he strove to put together an informant net. One of the most remarkable of such cases involved a veteran CIC Special Agent in Germany who, while investigating the details of the 20 July bomb plot against Adolf Hitler, was able to gain the confidence of one of the plotters, a leading member of the German aristocracy, Baron Gottfried von Cramm, through a common interest in tennis. Von Cramm was the pre-war world Number Two tennis ace, and the CIC agent had himself been a talented tournament player in the States, with friends who included world-class players such as Tony Trabert. The day the American agent first arrived at von Cramm's magnificent ancient castle at Bodenburg, south of Hanover, it was just about to be taken over as an HQ by a US combat group and the Baron was diffident about talking against his country.

'But you are a well-known anti-Nazi,' the CIC agent told him. 'We are trying to find people we can trust.'

The Baron was finally won over when the American was able to persuade the combat group that the castle was a vital intelligence source and safe house and should be left alone. Immediately the American became the darling not just of the Cramms but of dozens of counts and dukes and princes who had zeroed in for refuge at the castle after their flight from the Russians in Germany's eastern territories. Among those who were there was another anti-Hitler plotter, Countess Marion von Doenhof, once one of the richest women in Germany, who had left her estates in East Prussia and galloped away from the Red Army on horseback; and a beautiful 18-year-old brunette aristocrat who had fled from Berlin with nothing but the clothes she was wearing and had swum the Elbe to get there; and, perhaps more usefully, a former Abwehr captain by the name of Otto Kurrer, who had worked as a spy in Lisbon and was a fountainhead of information.

Von Cramm's role in the anti-Hitler plot, the CIC agent learned, had been to go to neutral Sweden under the cover of being an SD agent, and there make approaches to the King of England and the British Foreign Secretary, Anthony Eden – both of them pre-war tennis friends – to see if they would agree to peace terms with the plotters once Hitler had been disposed of. But London told him that 'unconditional surrender' were the terms and they would deal with no Germans, though they acknowledged trust in von Cramm personally.

All that was history. What really fascinated the CIC agent was the link between von Cramm's ménage and the East German Communist hierarchy. The American continued to cement his friendship with the Baron by playing exhibition tennis matches with him before large crowds in Berlin, Heidelberg and Bad Nauheim, and by acting as a go-between between von Cramm and his true love, the Wool-worth heiress, Barbara Hutton. Though von Cramm had always been her 'Number One', she had married the film star, Cary Grant, on the grounds that at the time it was impossible for her, a loyal American, to marry a German, even if he was a Baron of rich and ancient lineage. But von Cramm was desperate to get word to his Barbara, if only to let her know he was alive and well. Under the laws of the Occupation, Germans could neither send nor receive mail, so the CIC agent hit on a stratagem to get round the rules in von Cramm's case. He, the American, would write her a letter as if it were from von Cramm, and she was to reply only to the American.

> From then on [the Special Agent recalled], I had a fabulous correspondence with one of the richest gals in the world, who wrote to me as 'Darling Jimmy'. Then early in 1947 Barbara went to Stockholm and von Cramm called me in excitement to report he was going to get to see her. 'You must join us,' he said. So in late spring we had two days of wonderful restaurants, noble country homes and castles, and a whole day cruise out through the rocky channels of Stockholm as guests of a Swedish industrial millionaire. It's great to live like the nobility, isn't it? But it didn't spoil me. When they finally married in Mexico in the 50s, they sent me a telegram of triumph.

More importantly, from the CIC point of view, the exhibition tennis matches that von Cramm and the American played together led to an astonishing intelligence coup. As the American related:

> One of his tennis friends – can't name him, even today – had a lead to a person with inside access to the office of Wilhelm Pieck, the future President of Communist East Germany. I met this contact at von Cramm's castle and then flew to Berlin. At that time we were being begged to do much of the espionage in Berlin, and we did indeed do a lot of espionage in Berlin, even after the CIA was trying to get started. In Berlin I got Serge Wallach, one of the crack remaining CIC veterans, to 'run' our spy in East Germany, using the tennis friend as a cut-out, and it worked out great.

'Making friends with important people,' the CIC agent concluded, 'can lead to important breaks.'

If one of the main uses of informants was to sniff out suspects, the interrogation of such suspects was strictly a matter for the CIC agents themselves. As we have seen, experience showed that when interrogating German civilians it was usually more effective to adopt a friendly rather than an aggressive approach. As one CIC officer in Frankfurt reported to CIC Center, Baltimore, in May 1947:

> Use of psychology in interrogating Germans is enormously important because of their generally uniform behaviour. They all tend to feel very sorry for themselves, thus paving the way for disarming them by clever sympathy; they love to be flattered with their success in obtaining positions of importance; and their characteristic of dog-like obedience makes it possible for the interrogator to shift from them to someone higher, thus eliciting from them (in their innocence) the true story of their past. Their obedience also invariably makes them succumb to any order to tell their story, and once they are started talking one of the important battles of interrogation is won. Rare indeed are the Germans of the 'I-ain't-sayin'-nothing-see-my-lawyer' school. Once they have become confused, the injection of firm orders will often start the obedient German on the way to 'breaking'. Thus the militant approach may be held for certain types of Germans and for occasional psychological opportunities which present themselves during an interrogation.

Time has not softened this former officer's views of German psychology. In a letter to the authors, written more than 40 years on, he commented:

> I don't trust the Germans even today. An American psychiatrist once said: 'The German is a guy who wants to be killed while he's crossing the street on a green light. This satisfies his need to sacrifice all while doing his duty.' They are the greatest responders to authority the world has even seen. All the independent-minded ones emigrated to America in the nineteenth century. Of those that were left, the aristocracy were above politics, and the common man proved to be the most loyal and hard-working follower of orders in history. Germans stiffened to attention in front of us as if we were noted Nazi officials. Our German auto mechanic at CIC would zoom across the garage and quiver to attention whenever I called out 'Hans!' And of course 'they were never Nazis' and of course 'they knew nothing about the concentration camps.' But there are many good things to say about Germans, and you can balance their authoritarian weaknesses against their extreme loyalty to anyone they accepted as a master or friend, their intense camaraderie, their bravery as soldiers, their resourcefulness, their

ingenuity. I hope to God they are on our side if we ever have to fight another war.

Given the nature of the German nation at the end of the war, we had the motive and the opportunity to have turned the CIC into a real Gestapo outfit. Yet we never, as far as I know, swerved from an unwritten code – we didn't abuse anyone physically to get results. Our task was made easier for us because the Germans bowed down to us as the ultimate authority and because all the Nazis and all the Gestapo and SS always considered that they had just been doing their duty for Germany and obeying orders, no matter how immoral and inhumane – so it was no problem to get them to talk. Some of them described unbelievable events *outside* concentration camps. For example, the Gestapo chief of Hildesheim calmly told us that he shot every prisoner in the town jail three days before the Americans arrived. Diabolically, he said he had gone down the line of prisoners, all with their faces to the prison wall, and executed them with a pistol shot in the back of the head, brutally reloading after every six shots while the next victims in line stood there trembling. 'You'll hang for this,' we told him. 'You can't hang me,' he wailed in self-pity, 'the Gauleiter ordered me to leave none alive.' That was Germany.

Some 11 million Germans, out of a total population of over 60 million, had espoused the Nazi cause during the course of the Hitler régime. A number of these, no doubt, were among the 7 million Germans who had perished in the war; a substantial proportion could be counted among those who had been forced to join the Nazi Party or lose their job, or worse; many others, the so-called 'small Nazis', were humble folk from the *petite bourgeoisie* who had voted for Hitler in the hope of better fortune for themselves and their country, never foreseeing the horror they helped to introduce into the world. There remained, however, a hard core of dedicated ex-Nazis – self-seeking opportunists on the make, ideologically committed National Social- ists who had served the New Order well – and these were the Germans (and Austrians too) who were of the greatest interest and gravest concern to the Allied occupying powers in the months immediately following the end of the war.

The extirpation of Nazism and Nazis was something to which the Allies seemed totally committed in the hot-blooded days of approaching victory. 'Nazi tyranny and Prussian militarism are the two main elements in German life which must be absolutely de- stroyed,' Churchill had declared at the Yalta Conference in 1944. 'They must be absolutely rooted out if Europe and the world are to be spared a third and still more frightful conflict.' His words were echoed by the Supreme Commander, General Eisenhower, in his Proclamation to the German People in the summer of 1945: 'We shall obliterate Nazism and German Militarism.'

During the first ten months of the American occupation of Germany, therefore, the CIC found themselves preoccupied with one major task above all – denazification. The idea of excluding former Nazis from positions of influence in post-war Germany was theoretically feasible and desirable, but in practice the sheer magnitude of the task was daunting, for virtually the whole adult population had to be screened. In the American Zone every German over the age of 18 had to answer a questionnaire, or *Fragebogen*, containing over 130 questions about their past career and affiliations. The purpose of this process was to determine whether the person concerned had been associated with the Nazi Party or its supporters, and if so, to what degree. The penalties for not telling the truth were severe, and in any case the Allies were able to check the answers against a complete card index of Nazi Party members which had been found waiting to be pulped in a paper mill in Munich in the summer of 1945. After the *Fragebogen* had been filled in, it was assessed by a denazification court and classified in one of five categories: major offender, offender, lesser offender, follower and exonerated person. A variety of penalties, from imprisonment to fines, forfeiture of all property, forced labour and exclusion from every job except manual labourer, were decreed for the first four categories.

The Americans were by far the most zealous of the four occupation powers. By the time they had finished, sentences had been handed out to nearly a million German nationals, and of those arrested for more serious Nazi or military crimes the Americans had tried just under 170,000, while the British, French and Russians had tried only some 20,000 apiece. But denazification tended to be very rough and ready justice. Not many of the Allied officials spoke German or understood the nuances of the Nazi background to each case. They were easily misled by informers who denounced individuals in order to settle old scores or gain personal advantages. They did not appreciate that some of the most culpable and Nazi-minded servants of the Third Reich may not have been members of the Party at all, or that membership alone did not necessarily make a person a real Nazi. Many of the Nazis penalized by the denazification courts were small fry, the so-called *Muss-Nazis*. When the Germans began to see how many big Nazis escaped retribution, denazification became a joke. 'Did you play with toy soldiers as a child?' they quipped, parodying the *Fragebogen* questionnaire. 'If so, what regiment?'

A special group of Germans fell into the automatic arrest category and could be apprehended on sight. This group included top Nazis, members of the SS and Gestapo, high-ranking officers of the armed forces and suspected war criminals. This was the group that loomed large among the CIC's prime activities in the first ten months of the occupation, and by the end they would have apprehended a total of 120,000 Germans who fell into this category – the greatest round-up of human beings in American history. The normal protocols of Anglo-Saxon law were ignored in occupied Germany. No warrant was needed to break into a house or tap a telephone or haul a person out of a house or off the street, and no habeas corpus was required to keep behind bars or barbed wire the many thousands of individuals who ended up in the Allied prisons and internment camps to await interrogation and trial (sometimes in former Nazi concentration camps, like the one at Dachau, which was run on distinctly Nazi lines by its American guards). It would have been easy, given the suspension of legal democratic procedures, to have cut fast and loose amongst the subject German population, and perpetrated all kinds of abuses of power and privilege on guilty and innocent alike. Such abuses undoubtedly did occur, in all four zones of occupation, but by and large the best CIC men, the chief Nazi hunters in the American Zone, seem to have refrained from indulging in revanchist brutality or gratuitous violence against the many contemptible Nazi criminals who fell into their hands. One CIC agent wrote of a colleague in those Nazi-hunting days:

> At the end of the war we were given a brilliant former Czech, now an American, Frank Eisenstein, who learned at the time that his family had perished in the gas chambers. In spite of this, he carried out his job of arresting Nazis with a superb impartiality and without so much as 'liberating' even a camera. We were dealing with people who in many cases were evil beyond belief, but we also had our own conscience to satisfy. We could not strike the most evil, lest we sink to their level. It infuriated us that we were known as the 'Amerikanische Gestapo', for we indulged in none of the brutality, torture and beatings that have made the word Gestapo a criminal insult in virtually every language of the world.

In the early days of occupation the CIC found the round-up of Nazis and SS personnel – all Gestapo carried an SS rank – an endless task. A CIC officer then based at Hersfeld in Hesse recalls:

> We were aided in this stage of the Nazi round-up by the curfew the Army established at 8 pm, which left lots of daylight to carry on

our investigations at suspected Nazi homes. With Germans under orders to be indoors, we could corner them more readily. Germans were fascinated by our deliberate trips from house to house and the 'window-leaners', usually women, followed our every move. It was during this period that we were called the 'American Gestapo'. You might enter an ordinary German home to follow leads and be greeted by a Nazi salute and a 'Heil Hitler', at which point the nervous citizen would collapse as he realized his standard greeting was now being given to an American uniform. Party members were more sophisticated and rarely made such a mistake. We generally started with the Burgermeister, or mayor, who was almost always a Nazi of Ortsgruppenleiter rank – the lowest Party level we were ordered to pick up – and from him it was generally simple to coax the names of all his staff, also automatically arrestible. Party officials at that level were easy to 'break' in questioning, because they held known public jobs and did not think they were incriminating themselves if they admitted it. They were unbelievably subservient to our authority, and extraordinarily co-operative. 'Always at your throat, or at your feet,' as Churchill once said. And they had no compunction about ratting on their associates. Only bestial concentration camp guards tended to lie and deny everything.

Germans in general proved amazingly emotional, not at all the stoics we arrogant Anglo-Saxons always thought them to be. Witness the hulking Gestapo agent we interrogated at Hersfeld, who admitted his membership but burst into enraged tears when we brought up his alleged brutalities, so that he was pitiful to see. Then there was the SS Brigadeführer I interrogated in the jail wearing only his socks, for some reason – every time I got close to the truth he would twist one foot over the other and vice versa, over and over again. Then there was the young Waffen-SS private. Only 17, we believed his story that he had been muscled into the 'all-volunteer' SS late in the war. I went back into my civvies and he and I rode bicycles around to the haunts of suspects he could personally identify. The SS boy was astonished when I shared lunch with him – me, an *Offizier* of sinister origin! – and I got him talking. Of seemingly modest background, he was far more intellectually curious than our spoiled brats of his age.

Eventually arrest procedures became standardized, at least in the case of petty Nazis. Instead of going out to look for the wanted person, the CIC would simply send a note stating that he should report to the CIC office at a specified time. Sometimes a wider net was cast, involving large-scale unannounced search-and-seizure operations by troops and screening teams of CIC and Military Government personnel, and planned with as much secrecy as important military attacks. Really large-scale operations of this sort were zone-wide manoeuvres; on a smaller scale were the 'swoop' operations, raids which had specific aims and covered a limited area.

The first big sweep, in July 1945, was Operation Tally Ho, a huge undertaking designed to speed up the apprehension of war criminals and involving as many as 160,000 American troops in the Seventh Army area alone. Ambitiously designed to check the credentials of every single human being in the American Zone, this huge razzia by the might of the US Army (the CIC among them) took the German populace completely by surprise and had an electrifying effect, so that they were both bewildered and frightened. Rumours circulated wildly that the operation had been mounted because there had been a mass SS jail break or because an American had been murdered or the Americans were getting their own back for the losses they had suffered in the war. Eighty-five thousand German suspects were detected in the course of Tally Ho, along with a whole arsenal of weapons and equipment uncovered in German homes, including pistols, bazookas, grenades, tear gas, bayonets, radio transmitters and wire cutters.

These large-scale security sweeps often had completely different aims. Operation Lifebuoy, for example, was intended to remove Nazis from all positions of responsibility in Germany and was carried through so thoroughly that in the zone as a whole more than a third of all office holders had to be removed as a result of CIC screening, and in some areas more than a half, including some of the most efficient and best suited people for the job. In the town of Geislingen it was found that screening out all Nazis from the schools meant the removal of virtually every teacher in the town, since during the Hitler period every teacher had been compelled to join the Nazi teacher's organization, the *Lehrverband*. In deciding which individuals should be dismissed, the CIC had to establish a date before which Nazi Party membership would be considered automatic grounds for dismissal. The date selected, after much discussion, was 1 May 1937. This upset many anti-Nazi Germans, who claimed that often more recent recruits into the Party had been the most vehement Nazis. As a school teacher remarked to a CIC team in Giessen:

It is a pity for the Americans to discharge thousands of people, many of whom are old and have worked all their lives in one position. They will have no money, and where can they find work?

Most are loyal to the Allies. Much suffering will ensue next winter, and it may encourage underground activity, for which the Americans will be partly responsible. It could be avoided by a more common-sense policy. Most Germans approve of the general idea, but the Americans are making a mistake in its application. Too much emphasis is placed on nominal membership in the Nazi Party. Military Government should have an advisory anti-Nazi commission to assist in weeding out the real Nazis and thus avoid injustice.

Targets for more limited swoop operations were not always geographical areas. For Operation Choo Choo the target was a train – specifically, the Bamberg to Nuremberg passenger train leaving Bamberg at 12.45 on 2 February 1946. An estimated 1200 persons had jammed into the ten dilapidated passenger cars at Bamberg – a representative cross-section of the post-war population shuttling about the American Zone of Occupation. An army engineer officer rode on the footplate as the train pulled out and a little way out of the city ordered the driver to bring the locomotive to a halt. While armed troops deployed either side of the track, a team of ten CIC agents, ten MPs and 15 infantry soldiers began to search the train. One by one all the passengers were taken off, questioned, searched and then taken to a field by the railroad track where they were kept under armed guard, with the suspects segregated and guarded separately. When the train was completely empty every compartment was searched for weapons or other prohibited items. Seventy minutes after the train had been halted, the passengers were allowed to continue their journey, while the suspects were led away for interrogation at CIC headquarters in Bamberg. Whatever else Operation Choo Choo may have achieved, it undoubtedly impressed upon the German public the thoroughness and efficiency of the Americans' grip on its zone of Germany, and their determination to root out Nazis and all subversive and illegal activities.

The CIC had a liking for stopping trains, though not always for the same reasons. Major Bill Larned, Operations Officer of Bamberg CIC, recalled:

One of the most exciting things we ever did was to stop the Orient Express in Nuremberg because we thought a high-level Soviet agent was a passenger on board. It was the middle of the night and the dead of winter and we stopped the train at gunpoint and turned everyone out in their nightgowns and pyjamas in the snow, which was two feet deep at this point. And they stood there shivering and cold as hell while our agents went up and down the line with flashlights trying to identify the Russian. I thought that was pretty damn exciting – except the Russian wasn't on the train!

Trains were not the only things the CIC boarded. Ships and fleets of ships were also attractive targets – though again not necessarily in the pursuit of Nazis. One of the most dramatic actions in which the CIC were involved in 1946 was an operation code-named Grab Bag. Intelligence information in the early months of the year had indicated that a mothball fleet of the Hungarian Navy, totalling some 375 vessels anchored along the Danube between Passau and Deggendorf, might be the nexus of a widespread smuggling ring and an important link in an underground escape route that was being used by former SS troops escaping from Germany. The ships were inhabited by several hundred members of the Hungarian Navy and their families, who had fled from the Black Sea towards the end of the war and sought safety behind the American lines. Since this raggle-taggle fleet represented a serious security hazard, the Americans decided that the ships would have to be seized and impounded and their crews sent back to Hungary as prisoners of war. For the CIC it was a massive exercise, involving possibly the largest operational congregation of Secret Agents in any one place at any one time in the Corps' history.

At dawn on 21 May 1946 the boarding force struck – 120 CIC agents, 20 CID agents, troopers of the US Constabulary and 1st Infantry Division, and 90 members of the German water police specially brought in from the Rhine. Sealing off the 25-mile stretch between Passau and Deggendorf, the CIC and CID men climbed on board to search the ships and screen the crews, numbering almost 2000 all told. In all 232 of this motley crew were arrested and held for interrogation, including Admiral Trunkwalter, the flotilla's erstwhile commander, and a number of machine-guns, small arms, land mines and an anti-aircraft gun were confiscated, along with a counterfeiting set for forging documents. The security of the entire operation had been well kept from the start and a potential source of counter intelligence trouble neutralized. A few months later the 430th CIC in Austria carried out a similar raid on 160 Yugoslav vessels moored along the same stretch of the Danube, and after four days spent interrogating some of the 500 Yugoslavs on board uncovered an active Communist intelligence organization run by the Tito regime.

By contrast with most large CIC operations, which were overt raids and searches, Operation Nursery was a covert, long-range penetration of those subversive organizations that aimed to keep alive the National Socialist ideal. Following penetration of the Nazi underground organizations, a wave of arrests formed the start of a mass clean-up in the south. One by one, figures on the underground lists were trapped by the CIC agents. So skilfully had the agents covered their moves that not one person on the primary arrest list managed to escape. In a final phase of this secret operation a master target sheet was issued to all field units, together with details of a co-ordinated swoop operation that would be taking place simultaneously in the British as well as the US Zones of both Germany and Austria. April 1 1946 was the swoop date; 0200 was 'H' Hour. When the CIC struck the core of the underground movement was destroyed and most of the funds which had been hoarded for long-range subversion were impounded. Bereft of both its key personnel and its financial support, what was left of the Nazi underground was judged to be helpless and moribund.

Inevitably Nazis liable to automatic arrest – the war criminals, the SS – took such evasive action as they could; and a few of the more fanatical and less well balanced of the old Nazi fraternity fought back. So-called *Persilscheine*, or Persil certificates, were greatly in demand and fetched high prices. These were in effect whitewash documents, genuine Allied-issue papers, generally falsely filled out, which cleared the bearer of complicity in Nazism in the Hitler era. Given their high value, it was not altogether surprising that Persil certificates gave rise to some lucrative rackets among Allied occupation personnel. In one case, the US Army commandant of an internment camp for suspected Nazis near Garmisch-Partenkirchen in Bavaria peddled official discharge papers to the inmates at extortionate prices, and when he had run out of bidders he recruited more by the simple expediency of having more Germans arrested in the streets 'on suspicion'.

Another popular method of escaping the nemesis of automatic arrest for SS personnel was the illicit removal of the blood type tattoos that were inscribed under every SS man's arm. Former German army medics were known to carry out the simple excision which removed the tattoo and some CIC agents were much taxed for a while in putting an end to the practice – though the number of SS men who were able to take advantage of it was never very great.

As late as mid-1946, a year after the end of the war, the prime CIC mission remained the apprehension of former Nazis who were on automatic arrest lists. Many Nazis had slipped through the original CIC screening operations. There were many reasons – the vastness of the undertaking, the shortage of experienced CIC agents, the shattered state of the country, which made it much easier for a fugitive to hide and much harder for a hunter to find him. Names of former Nazis were supplied to the German police but many leads came from denouncers such as neighbours who did not hesitate to inform on suspicious strangers in their locality – often in the hope of a reward in the form of food, cigarettes or soap. Once a suspect had been targeted, the arrest was carried out by CIC agents accompanied by German police. Usually suspects were arrested at their homes, generally at three in the morning, a time when most people were likely to be in bed and unprepared to offer resistance or attempt escape.

The sheer statistics of the denazification programme in the American Zone make extraordinary reading today. By late 1946 there were still 3,000,000 German civilians chargeable under the Law for the Liberation from National Socialism and Militarism. Two hundred thousand cases had been tried, 370,000 Nazis had been removed from their jobs, but 1,300,000 cases remained to be heard; 72,000 persons were in prison awaiting trial and the internment camps were stuffed to bursting with desperate SS men – many of whom had been drafted into the Waffen-SS whether they liked it or not – who at the prevailing rate of processing would have five more years behind barbed wire before their cases could be heard. And this was just the American Zone, remember, and with everybody born after 1918 exempt from prosecution as a result of the so-called 'youth amnesty'. For a foreign power to purge the native society of a modern state was clearly a task verging on the impossible. This quickly became evident when the western Allies finally relinquished control over the young democracy of West Germany. By 1950, 85 per cent of Party officials removed in Bavaria had been reinstated, and 60 per cent of the civil servants of Württemberg-Baden were ex-Nazis. Both these Länder were in the former US Zone where the Americans, with the CIC in the vanguard, had bustled so busily to cauterize the canker in the German body politic.

Not surprisingly former CIC agents, recalling those days when scores of thousands of Nazi suspects passed through their hands, can conjure up only a blur of dismal faces, an endless processional of sullen and downcast functionaries of the Hitlerian empire. CIC records of the time constitute a kind of roll of dishonour in which are inscribed the now long-forgotten names of endless suspected Nazis seized in streets and beds and small back rooms, on bridges and buses and station platforms, at border crossings and in all the holes and hideouts that the city rubble and darkened countryside provided for a ragged ex-official or fugitive Gestapo agent or extermination camp guard in the ravaged Germany of the occupation years. But a few incidents and a few names stand out in the midst of that scuttling rat pack.

Among the first big names to be delivered into the hands of the CIC was one of Allied intelligence's prime adversaries during the war, Otto Skorzeny, Chief of the Sabotage Section of Himmler's RSHA, who voluntarily presented himself to the Americans on 16 May 1945 and was interrogated the next day by Special Agents Victor de Guinzbourg, Alan Dinehart, George Perper and William Bower before being passed up the line to higher headquarters. Another was a fanatical Nazi by the name of Joseph Spacil, head of Amt 11 of the RSHA, whose last act before fleeing Hitler's burning capital was to snatch at gunpoint nearly 10 million dollars' worth of gold and jewels from the vaults of the Reichsbank headquarters, and whose first act on being confronted by a CIC screening team at a POW detention cage at Fürstenfeldbrück was to barter his safety in return for information that could lead (in his fanciful view) to the discovery of Hitler's body and diary, together with the whereabouts of the gold crown and sceptre of Charlemagne and other riches. Yet another was the head of the RSHA itself, Ernst Kaltenbrunner, who had been responsible for the Gestapo and all German intelligence, and one of the worst war criminals still at large in Europe. Seized by CIC Special Agent Robert Matteson in a remote Alpine cabin high on the Austrian Alps above Alt Aussee after a long five-hour climb in the dead of night, the scarfaced No. 2 in the SS, a terrifying giant of a man, was not finally identified until his mistress, Countess Gisela von Westrop, ran up and impulsively kissed him as he was led away into custody.

Obscurer top Nazis held out longer: the former leader of the Reichsfrauenschaft, or Nazi Women's League, for example, whose name was Gertrud Scholtz-Klink, and August Heissmeyer, director of the Nazi Party special schools under Heinrich Himmler. Not names to conjure with now, perhaps, but in their time formidable embodiments of the Nazi machine. Originally thought to have been killed in the bomb-proof shelter of Hitler's Chancellery in Berlin near the end of the war, these uncongenial National Socialists were tracked down by the CIC when persistent rumours that they had been seen alive began to swell. CIC agents instituted a widespread dragnet in the US Zone and combed the cities of Southern Germany for clues. Finally, acting on a tip-off from an informant in an internment camp, agents closed in on a small house in the grounds of a castle near Tübingen, in the French Zone of Occupation.

One wintry midnight in 1948 they arrived at the house and beat on the door. After prolonged rapping the door swung open, revealing a woman garbed in dishevelled peasant's night attire. Her face was haggard and lined; her hair spread in disorderly fashion over her shoulders. Though she looked like a woman in her 60s, the agents perceived that this was indeed the Frau Scholtz-Klink they had been seeking, once a haughty high official of the Nazi state, and still only in her mid-40s. A man was still asleep in an inside room. When he was roused from his slumber, the CIC agents were surprised to discover that this was another suspect on their wanted list, August Heissmeyer, and even more surprised that he had been married to the prematurely aged crone beside him since 1940. Himmler's former minion still carried a brass cartridge containing a glass ampoule of potassium-cyanide poison in the lining of his waistcoat. A further search of the house revealed two knapsacks packed with heavy clothing and other necessities, evidently kept in readiness for hasty departure. Only the CIC's prompt apprehension of the Nazi couple prevented their burying themselves even deeper in the German countryside.

Some arrests were more exciting than others. One evening in September 1945, for example, four Special Agents were summoned before their Detachment chief in Linz, Austria, to formulate a plan for a particularly dramatic arrest – that of a notorious wanted war criminal, SS-Obergruppenführer August Eigruber. Eigruber had been the Gauleiter and Reich Governor of Upper Austria, the location of the infamous Mauthausen concentration camp outside Linz where 35,000 prisoners of all nationalities had been murdered by the Nazis. The CIC had received word that Eigruber, accompanied by his SS Colonel bodyguard and a chauffeur, was planning a break for Vienna. Apparently he was armed and desperate and quite prepared to shoot his way out. The problem facing the CIC agents, therefore, was how to capture Eigruber and his companions without losing any of their own men. One of the CIC agents who took part in this episode, Special Agent Michael Suszan, later described how the plan they worked out was put into effect:

> Bright and early the next day several agents, including the Chief, left and took up positions in a wooded section at the designated spot alongside the narrow road winding thru the mountains. This was the route which Eigruber was to take. A little later, Jack MacDonald and I dressed as plain GIs started off in a jeep to the designated area and took up our positions. We arrived at the spot and pulled off the road to await the signal.
>
> Our two torpedo men (Czech nationals) had already arrived and taken up their position. They were dressed as civilians in a civilian

car and were about 50 feet in front of us, positioned just ahead of the bend in the road and facing in our direction – just off the road also waiting for the signal.

The plan was to simulate a wreck, locking bumpers and blocking the road so Eigruber's car couldn't get thru. One of the agents was positioned at a strategic spot where he commanded a complete view of the road and its approach. He was to wave a handkerchief at the approach of Eigruber's car.

Everything was set and everyone at his station. The farmers working in the nearby fields weren't aware that a drama was soon to unfold. Cows were grazing in the meadows and the lazy late summer sun was high in the blue sky . . . As we waited I fingered the soiled handkerchief I promised Loren my room-mate I would stuff in Eigruber's mouth. This was a precaution to keep him from committing suicide. Several of the top Germans had provided themselves with small poison capsules which could be concealed in their mouths.

At long last the spotter trained his binoculars on the car we were all awaiting. The signal was given and I turned the ignition key and started up the jeep. The civilian car with our two torpedo men did likewise and just as we tangled bumpers Eigruber's car rounded the bend and witnessed the simulated wreck.

We got out of our jeep to inspect the extent of damage and the 'civilians' did likewise, all four of us milling around. Adding to the confusion was the fact that we as GIs spoke in English and the 'civilians' in German. This apparently irritated the Eigruber party, because the chauffeur soon started blowing his horn madly. We immediately chided them to stop leaning on the horn and get out and help us untangle the cars. Apparently Eigruber saw this confusion was hopeless and all three got out of their car to help clear this mess so they could proceed without additional delay, remarking something about the 'dumb Americans' in German.

It was our purpose to be as near the Eigruber car as possible, two men to each side of the car, so that when Eigruber and the SS Colonel alighted – we tackled and pinned them down to the ground. The chauffeur was also roughed-up but only as a token, because he was working on our side too!

The handkerchief I carried expressly for this mission went into Eigruber's mouth, but only after he bit the Chief's finger in searching for the capsule. The agents who covered us from the roadside came out of the wooded section heavily armed and moved in fast to help if needed. All three of our prisoners were handcuffed and herded into separate cars and whisked to jail, Eigruber and the SS Colonel arrogant and defiant to the end.

Our plan was successful – we had got our men and not a single shot had been fired. A twenty-four-hour guard was posted on our prisoners, who were held to be tried by the Allied Commission as war criminals.

Eigruber was later sentenced to death by an American military court in Landsberg and hanged on 28 May 1946.

All but the topmost figures in the Nazi hierarchy soon fell like fruit shaken from the trees. Goering, Ribbentrop, Speer and the rest were carted off to a converted hotel in Luxembourg called 'Camp Ashcan', the processing centre for Hitler's most senior surviving ministers, state secretaries and generals on their long road to trial and retribution. Of the remaining top four, Himmler blundered into a British security checkpoint and took cyanide while undergoing a physical inspection. But of Goebbels, Bormann and Hitler himself there was no sign, and the CIC were called in – along with many others – to try and pick up such spoors and clues of them as might be found across the ravaged land that had once been the Greater Reich. Bormann proved the most elusive, and decades were to pass before the remains of his corpse, with the fragments of a glass cyanide capsule still clenched between the teeth in the skull, were discovered on a building site outside the Berlin railway station where he had taken poison rather than fall captive to the Russians during his final desperate flight from Hitler's bunker.

The fate of Hitler's missing Party Secretary was unknown, however, in the first months after the war's end, and the CIC continued to follow up all possible leads. Tipped off that the missing Nazi leader was hiding up among the high peaks above Garmisch-Partenkirchen in Southern Bavaria, a team of CIC agents spent days scrambling across the ridges and peaks of the mountain range and staking out remote mountain lodges in the Alpine valleys, sometimes under the pretence of looking for mountain goats, sometimes under cover of night. But they found no one. Meanwhile, on 12 October 1945 Special Agent John H. W. White, of the CIC Munich Detachment 303, had reported a poignant twist in the Bormann mystery:

Approximately three weeks ago a Herr Hans König came to this Office, stating that he was in search of his five-year-old son and had come from Berlin for that purpose. Further questioning of König revealed that he had left the child in the NSV [National Socialist Public Welfare Organization] Kindergarten in Garmisch in the spring of this year, and that the child was kidnapped from there by Martin Bormann.

The reasons for the kidnapping were the following: Martin Bormann had nine children of his own. He kidnapped five more children from the NSV institution in order that his wife, travelling with a total of 14 children, could pose as the director of a bombed-out children's home. Then Bormann had arranged for his wife, two nurses and the children to travel toward Tyrol, where they were believed to be hiding. The whole movement was done with such cleverness and exacting co-ordination that it appears to have been Martin Bormann's, not his wife's, plan. Since Bormann was known to be unusually fond of his children, it appeared probable that Bormann himself would be near the hiding place of the children, or at least, if alive, would attempt to maintain contact with his wife. This Agent then suggested to König that he pool their interests and that the CIC assist König on his search.

Special Agent Alex Raskin was assigned to accompany König in civilian clothes on a strictly undercover basis. On 1 October, König received word from a friend that Mrs Bormann was at Grödnerthal (Val Groedeno), Wolkenstein, High Tyrol, living under the false name of Bedmann. Mrs Bormann was located at the given address, 20 miles NE of Bolzano, together with the 14 children and two nurses, one of whom is Mrs Bormann's sister-in-law, widow of a fallen SS officer.

Mrs Bormann, who has a cancer, was operated on in Bolzano Civil Hospital, and according to the surgeon has only four to five months left to live. She could not be removed from her villa.

Interrogation regarding the whereabouts of her husband, Martin Bormann, revealed the following:

On 21 April 1945 she received a telephone call from her husband in Berlin, telling her that he had found a wonderful hiding place for her and the children in Wolkenstein. He then arranged for the kidnapping and the trip.

On 29 April 1945 she received a radiogram from her husband from Berlin, telling her that all was lost, that there was no hope for him to escape from Berlin.

MRS BORMANN IS CONVINCED THAT HER HUSBAND IS DEAD. According to Special Agent Raskin, Mrs Bormann is in such poor physical shape that it would be practically impossible for her to lie under pressure of interrogation.

Regarding the kidnapped children, König's son Reginald was well and healthy, and König took letters to the parents of the other four children with him.

It is recommended that the case be considered closed.

The CIC were nearer to the truth about Bormann than the world would allow for many a year. The case of Adolf Hitler was rather different – and a great deal more urgent. All the world now knows that Hitler committed suicide in his bunker on 30 April 1945 by shooting himself in the head, possibly biting on a cyanide capsule as he did so. But in 1945 this fact was known to only the handful of Germans who were on hand at the time, and most of these were soon to die or fall captive to the Russians. In a very short while, Stalin and a small circle of top Soviet army and intelligence officers also knew the circumstances of the Führer's demise. It was the Russians who had found Hitler's half-incinerated body and carried out an autopsy on it. It was the Russians who interrogated the eye-witnesses who could provide a coherent account of Hitler's death. But for highly devious reasons of their own the Russians chose not to divulge the knowledge in their possession to their former allies in the West. At a time of mounting distrust between the Russians and their former Anglo-American allies, it suited Stalin to encourage uncertainty about Hitler's fate, and even concoct deliberate disinformation to add to the belief, widely held for a while in Europe and America, that Hitler might still be alive – a belief fuelled at intervals by the highly speculative stories that appeared in many newspapers, some of them of Soviet origin. Thus it was reported that Hitler had been seen living as a hermit in a cave near La Garda, as a shepherd in the Swiss Alps, as a croupier in a casino at Evian, as a monk in the monastery at St Gallen, as a head waiter in a restaurant in Grenoble, as a fisherman on the Aran Islands off the Irish coast, and a denizen of a moated castle in Westphalia in the British Zone of Germany. So the situation developed which the Allies had wanted most to avoid – an aura of mystery and speculation, a Hitler myth which was to last for two decades.

This, then, was the environment in which the CIC were obliged to follow up, in the interests of national security, any leads which even hinted at the possibility that Adolf Hitler was alive and well and living in wherever he had last been sighted. As early as 1 May 1945, only a few hours after Hitler's death, the American Chief of Staff, General Marshall, had realized it might be necessary to counter the Hitler martyr myth being put about by Hitler's successor, Admiral Dönitz, to the effect that the Führer had died at the head of his troops while heroically defending Berlin. It was a matter so urgent and grave that it transcended political considerations and required clearance by the Head of State.

The man chosen to spearhead an enquiry – a British MI5 initiative – which would establish Hitler's fate was an academic historian and Oxford don-cum-intelligence officer, Major Hugh Trevor-Roper (later the Emeritus Professor of History at Oxford and now Lord Dacre), to whom the 4-volume CIC dossier on Hitler makes a number of references. This dossier was a cornucopia of everything that could be gleaned about the former Führer – his medical condition, the organs of his body, the state of his mind, his various inclinations and proclivities. Expecting to piece together a mosaic of a monster, the CIC analysts found to their embarrassment that the scourge of the human race gave presents to children, hated blood sports, disliked excessively fanatical people and was conservative and fastidious in his habits. 'Every day at the same hour,' testified one informant, 'he would go with the same dog to the same corner of the same field and pick up the same piece of wood and throw it in the same direction.'

On 1 October 1945 it was noted that Trevor-Roper, in the course of his fact-finding tour on behalf of British intelligence, would be making enquiries at a couple of places in the American Zone, including Innsbrück. A further reference was made to the investigation on 9 October, when the Chief of the Operations Branch sent a two-page message to the Chief of the Counter Intelligence Branch outlining the salient points which had thus far been revealed. Already some facts were beginning to emerge about the fate of Hitler and his wife, for the penultimate paragraph read: 'The disposal of the bodies after burning has not yet been indicated by any [complete] evidence and the bodies themselves have not, of course, been identified.' Shortly after this, on 2 November, the Director of Intelligence for OMGUS (Office of Military Government, United States) wrote to the Assistant Intelligence Chief of Staff at USFET (United States Forces, European Theater) to say that the Russians were reported to have found a body believed to have been identified by the teeth as Hitler's. Could the Russians be persuaded to state the extent of their observations? 'It might be,' concluded the Director of Intelligence, 'that you have now, or might acquire within the next few days, the one piece of information which might fill out the jigsaw puzzle.' It seems the Assistant Intelligence Chief of Staff was unable to oblige. But on 1 November Hugh Trevor-Roper gave a press conference in Berlin at which he outlined the basic facts of Hitler's demise based on his reconstruction from eye-witness accounts. The salient features of the story were there, though there were still many gaps, and many eye-witnesses still to be found.

But exciting things were to happen in the course of Trevor-

Roper's delving down in wintry Bavaria. Word came that a gardener by the name of Paustin living in the village of Tegernsee was in reality former SS Standartenführer Wilhelm Zander, the adjutant to Hitler's Party Secretary, Martin Bormann, during the final days in the Berlin bunker. This was a catch not to be missed. For three weeks British Secret Service agents and CIC Special Agents Weiss and Rosener trailed and hunted the fugitive. Then on the day after Christmas Major Trevor-Roper and the CIC agents raided the suspected house, only to find that Zander had left the area to visit his fiancée near Passau. Meanwhile, on 28 December an informant reported to the 303rd CIC that a suitcase belonging to Zander could be found in the home of a Frau Irmgard Unterholzener in Tegernsee. The suitcase was immediately picked up and thoroughly searched and a hidden packet was found in it containing several historic documents which Zander had brought out of the bunker 48 hours before Berlin fell. They turned out to consist of Hitler's personal will and political testament, together with Goebbels's appendix to the latter and the marriage contract of Adolf Hitler and Eva Braun.

The documents were turned over to Major Anthony W. Lobb, Chief of the Third US Army CIC, who gave them to the Assistant Chief of Staff G-2, who in turn shipped them to the United States where a laboratory test by the FBI confirmed their authenticity. The documents were then sent for storage in the National Archives. According to a report by CIC Special Agent Arnold Weiss dated 12 January 1946, Colonel Zander was cornered by Trevor-Roper and Weiss in a small village called Vilshofen, near the Czech border, and after a short gunfight overpowered and taken prisoner. After 10 hours of interrogation in Munich, Zander finally broke and revealed corroboratory details of the extraordinary story of the last days in Berlin. For his action in the case Major Trevor-Roper received the Order of the British Empire and Special Agent Weiss received the Army Commendation Medal and a citation from the Commanding General of the Intelligence Services, along with a recommendation for the Bronze Star.

However, in spite of the considerable progress made in unravelling Hitler's final disposition, reports of sightings of the missing Führer continued to come in from all over the world, and most of them are contained in Hitler's CIC dossier. They make beguiling reading today. The first sighting had occurred back in July 1945, when the US Office of Censorship intercepted a letter addressed to a Chicago newspaper by an American citizen living in Washington DC to the effect that Hitler could be found in a subterranean hideout at a

German-owned hacienda 450 miles from Buenos Aires. A search request sent to the US Embassy in Argentina added: 'Source states that there is a western entrance to the underground hideout which consists of a stone wall operated by photo-electric cells, activated by code signals from ordinary flashlights. Entrance thus uncovered supposedly provides admittance for automobiles.' Hitler, it seems, had thoughtfully provided himself with two doubles and was busy with plans for the manufacture of long-range robot bombs and other secret weapons. The matter was taken sufficiently seriously for J. Edgar Hoover, the head of the FBI, to intervene. 'To date,' he wrote to the War Department, 'no serious indication has been received that Adolf Hitler is in Argentina.' This is hardly surprising, for the source of the information turned out to be the 97-year-old leader of an arcane spiritist cult with a gift for clairvoyance.

Hitler now began to pop up thick and fast. In August an American lawyer wrote to Hoover to announce that Hitler was now living under the alias of Gerhardt Weithaupt in the house of a Frau Frieda Haaf in Innsbrück, Germany (sic). With him was his personal physician, one Dr Jodl. The author of this hallucination added that he wished to make it known that he was not under the influence of either drugs or alcohol. There is no record what action the FBI took to corroborate this statement or check out the real Herr Weithaupt. But it was curious that many of these sightings came from professional people who were trained observers or investigators in their own right. The next sighting, for example, was by a German doctor and deserved to be taken a great deal more seriously, as the Military Government officer who heard his story reported to Berlin in September: 'This man came to my attention casually and I considered it of sufficient importance to take this deposition. A copy of these statements has been given to the local CIC.'

According to the German medic, a Dr Karl-Heinz Spaeth, he had treated Hitler on 1 May 1945 at his Berlin casualty clearing station in the cellar of the Landwehrkasino 'right across from the bunker at the Zoo'. Hitler had been wounded at a tank barricade in the fighting around the Küstrin area of the city. 'I was called shortly thereafter,' Spaeth recounted in a sworn deposition. 'Hitler was lowered to the floor. A shell fragment had pierced the uniform, went through his chest and entered the lungs on both sides. It was no use to do anything. I took a few first-aid bandages and bandaged him. During this time Hitler groaned continuously. He was not fully conscious. To relieve his pain I went back to the collecting station to get some morphine and gave him a double strength injection. The general opinion was that Hitler would die. I examined his pulse and respiration and found that after about three minutes he had stopped breathing. Heartbeats continued for about three minutes and then ceased. After I had pronounced the Führer dead and had informed the SS leaders of this fact I was released and went back to my work.' Shortly afterwards the surviving SS leaders blew the body into the air with two 3-kilo charges of high explosive. Thus perished this convincing Hitler look-alike, one of Germany's myriad unknown soldiers who had fallen for the Fatherland.

Hitler fell to earth again in Spain, where he was reported at the end of September as lurking in a wolf pack of U-Boats somewhere off the coast, suffering from sea sickness. The Führer was next reported to be living on a farm at La Falda in Argentina, but just to confuse everybody he had had his facial features remoulded by a famous plastic surgeon during the U-Boat voyage to the New World. By January 1946 he was back in Germany again, however, with CIC Region II (Mannheim) hot on his trail. CIC reported: 'Allegedly reliable informants of the French intelligence services advised high French authorities that the ex-Führer was in hiding in the vicinity of Heidelberg and was in communication with the resistance leader in Weinheim, and had visited Weinheim disguised as a US soldier or as an old bearded hunchback.'

A raid on Weinheim by five CIC Special Agents and 25 men of the US Constabulary failed to find any trace of Hitler or the elusive hunchback. Nor did a number of other CIC paperchases. An American soldier reported that he had seen Hitler, Eva Braun and her sister, Gretl, in the house where he collected his laundry in Bensheim, and noticed that Hitler flew into a rage at the mention of the V-1 weapon and 'exhibited great sentiment over the photograph of a dog' which seems to have closely resembled Hitler's own canine friend. Again it was the CIC who were required to check out this implausible tale – with totally plausible results.

Having succeeded in giving the CIC the slip yet again, the Führer surfaced three months later in Munich, having lost an arm in the meantime, then in Zurich, where he was reported to be living with a woman called Hilda. Not surprisingly, the poor devil had changed for the worse during his surreptitious peregrinations around the globe. 'Today he looks like an old man; features wasted, hair turned nearly white, takes short steps with his body bent forward and is believed to have a lung infection since he coughs persistently. He dresses himself very carelessly, not modern, and prefers dark suits and overcoats as well as hats.' His appearance was, it seems, 'similar to that of a pensioned official.' The Deputy Director of Intelligence at EUCOM had no choice: he had to see it through. 'I feel that we would be remiss in our duty if we failed to follow up any report of this nature,' he wrote forlornly in his request for help to the Chief of the Swiss Federal Police in Berne.

It was not surprising that the Führer was looking rough these days, for according to a letter addressed to the 'Chief of the American Zone' and received by the US Embassy in Stockholm just before Christmas 1946, he had undergone one of his most picturesque metamorphoses and was now living rough as well, this time as a troglodyte in a remote Shangri-La called Bauerska (=Bauern=Bayern=Bavaria?), as Nordic and mythical as any fastness in the *Nibelungenlied*. The anonymous informant reported:

> If you look in the Bauerska mountains you will find a long cave about 466 metres or maybe even longer, with about 92 doors, well camouflaged. Hitler has here a room 30 by 30 metres, with electrical stoves, one big, one small. There is food there, cans of all kinds for several years ahead and lots of money of all kinds of currencies. There is also a pipe from the top of the mountain in which food can be dropped down. Those who bring food there are called 'ravens'. Those who built this in the mountains have been killed long ago so it would not be discovered. When you have found it I demand 1/6 of what there is there and a jeep and a tractor. You will know my name when you have found him. *You see, he is there.*
>
> PS Be careful for there are probably capsules there.
>
> [On the reverse:] They have stolen horses and cows, hay and so on. They have plenty of ammunition and guns. A Swede who has a sixth sense is with them. He tells them all. Find these gentlemen. What will be done will be done soon.

But Hitler had given them all the slip. In a letter to 'His Excellency General Feldmarshall Dwight D. Eisenhower' an anonymous Dutchman reported that the scar-faced owner of a coffee room in Amsterdam was none other than the elusive dictator. The man had a long torso in relation to his body and his hands nearly touched his knees. When he noticed the informant staring at him, he made a telephone call to a former Gestapo agent, requesting him to hurry over to the coffee shop and kill the informant: 'The man is here now, please come immediately and shoot him, for he already knows too much.' The War Department sent the report to the Director of Intelligence at EUCOM, with the usual predictable result.

Ironically in 1948 the CIC had within their grasp the means of verifying one of the most crucial details concerning Hitler's fate. In September of that year CIC agents tracked down a certain Dr

Michael Arnaudow, a medical practitioner then living in the British sector of Berlin. As a dental expert specializing in jawbone surgery at a leading Berlin hospital Arnaudow had, in May 1945 and at the Russians' behest, aided two German dental technicians familiar with Hitler's dentistry positively to identify Hitler's teeth in a jawbone taken from a corpse found at the Führerbunker a few days after Hitler's suicide. Afterwards Arnaudow had been made to swear an oath of secrecy concerning his part in the identification of Hitler's jawbone in front of a number of senior Soviet officers at their headquarters in Eberswalde. Although he lived in the British sector, he was still terrified at the possible implications of talking about his experiences to the CIC. At a time when all the dental technicians who had connection with Hitler's teeth were imprisoned (for that very reason) in the Soviet Union, Arnaudow promised to verify his story and furnish charts and drawings of the jawbones he had identified for the Russians – provided the Americans guarantee him and his family safe passage and allow him to continue to practise his profession. His ambition was to emigrate to the United States and he had already submitted an application for an immigration visa to the US Consul in Berlin.

The Operations Officer of CIC Region VIII (Berlin) obviously took both Arnaudow and his offer seriously. 'Dr Arnaudow makes a very good impression,' wrote Special Agent Venters, 'and is a perfect type of European intellectual. He was involved in the case of Hitler's death against his will (the CIC was able to trace him through an undercover informant) and his reputation as a scientist, University teacher and dental expert is well established in Germany. He is definitely pro-Western orientated, unpolitical, and very much concerned with his personal security and the personal security of his wife.' Venters recommended that Arnaudow's offer be accepted, since 'it is expected that the contribution of Dr Arnaudow will clarify the question of Hitler's and Eva Braun's death.' The CIC headquarters deputy commander, Lieutenant-Colonel George R. Eckman, took up the refrain: 'It appears that Arnaudow's statements are definitely worth further investigation,' he wrote on 17 September 1948.

A few weeks later Eckman received his answer. 'The referenced procedure outlined,' wrote the Operations Branch at EUCOM, 'is disapproved and no consideration should be given to Dr Arnaudow's offer.' So that was that: case closed. The CIC narrowly missed what might perhaps have been their biggest post-war coup and the answer to a question which was to keep the world wondering for another 20 years.

Meanwhile the spurious sightings of the missing dictator continued. According to CIC records Hitler was last seen in September 1949 by Mr Leslie Graham Fraser, of 14 Efed Avenue, Rhyd Felan, Pontypridd, Wales. Hitler was in a café in Cologne when Mr Fraser spotted him, smoking a cigar and wearing a ginger moustache, with a fierce expression and 'a good set of white teeth'. And that was that. Adolf Hitler was never seen again. Preposterous though these reports may sound now – and some are clearly the demented concoctions of crackpots – they simply had to be taken seriously by Allied intelligence in the early postwar years. The CIC dossier highlights the diligence and concern of the Allied intelligence agencies in ensuring that, however far-fetched, these stories were properly and thoroughly checked out.

The ghost of Adolf Hitler should have been finally laid to rest when the results of Hugh Trevor-Roper's investigation were published in 1947 in a book entitled *The Last Days of Hitler*, a classic piece of investigative research intended to allay all rumour and hypothesis concerning the Führer's ultimate destiny. But it was not until August 1968 that the Russians released their autopsy report, in which the identification of Hitler's teeth and jawbone was the most important evidence, through the unofficial medium of a book by a former Soviet intelligence officer, entitled *The Death of Adolf Hitler*. We now know that Hitler's body was retrieved by intelligence officers of SMERSH, the Red Army counter intelligence organization, shortly after the surrender of Berlin, and was eventually disposed of in an unknown hiding place in the USSR, so that the Germans might be permanently deprived of a martyr's relics. 'Like Alaric, buried secretly under the river-bed of Busento,' wrote Trevor-Roper in a recent edition of his book, 'the modern destroyer of mankind is now immune from discovery.'

Though Austria had been every bit as fervent as Germany in its enthusiasm for Nazism at the height of the Hitler régime, it was not so much the Nazis as their victims that became the overriding concern of the 430th CIC in Austria during the early years of the American presence in that country. By July 1946 investigations involving DPs – liberated concentration camp inmates and forced labourers from almost every nation of Europe – represented some 73 per cent of the workload of the 430th Detachment. Traumatized, alienated and riotous, the DPs milled about Austria in their hundreds of thousands, posing serious problems for the native populace and the forces of occupation alike. Screening DPs for eventual repatriation to their homelands or emigration to the United States was one major task for the CIC. Another was the Jewish problem, which soon became a painful headache.

Plans for the creation of a national state for the Jewish people in Palestine had got under way soon after the end of the war but had rapidly become bogged down in the thorny problems of defining the bounds of the projected state and of separating Arab from Jewish land. In the meantime only a small monthly quota of Jewish immigrants were legally allowed into Palestine, with the result that many rootless and footloose Jews, shattered survivors of the Holocaust, soon lost patience and began to move in a steady stream from all over Europe on an illegal exodus to Palestine via underground routes to Italy and thence by secret shipments on leaky freighters across the Mediterranean. Once at their chosen destination most of these refugees were drafted into the several illegal armies which had formed to fight for the rights of Jewish people.

The DP camps in Germany and Austria served both as gathering points for the prospective illegal emigrants to Palestine and as headquarters for the leaders of the Jewish underground. The Jewish DP camp at Bad Gastein, for example, contained some 1500 Jews from Eastern Europe who were in the process of moving westward with Palestine as their ultimate destination. Among them was a hard core of fanatical Palestinian nationalists, some of them uniformed members of the organization's militant honour guard, which organized agitation and civil disorder at the slightest provocation and was constantly engaged in underground political and para-military training in preparation for the major changes they planned for the status of Palestine. At Camp Haid in Upper Austria, Jewish DPs rioted in November 1946 after an inspection of the camp by the military commander of Upper Austria. Protesting about conditions, groups of demonstrators began smashing property at the camp. Six MPs were rushed in and arrested 11 riot leaders. But as the 11 were being loaded on to a truck to be taken off to jail, a mob of a thousand DPs stormed the MPs. In the resulting mêlée a DP seized a carbine which accidentally went off and struck one of the crowd. The mob then turned on the MPs and beat them and stoned them ferociously, and all efforts to remove the injured men to hospital were obstructed. MP riot squads soon arrived, however, dispersed the mob and arrested the ringleaders.

Illegal crossing of Austrian borders by groups of Jewish refugees travelling by night without semblance of travel authority posed one of CIC's greatest problems – especially as it was feared that enemy agents might infiltrate themselves among the ranks of the refugees. Extensive underground activity had developed in Austria through the work of the Brycha, the overall Jewish organization guiding the mass of Jewish emigration out of Europe towards Palestine. As a cover for their activities, many Brycha leaders obtained key positions in the Jewish Agency for Palestine and in the Jewish DP camps created by the Allies. These camps soon became important stopover points for refugees being smuggled from behind the Iron Curtain. Because Brycha functioned underground, its escape routes were not generally known, with the result that espionage agents bound for the Allied occupation zones began to utilize the Brycha network for their covert activities. The Brycha were also reported to have connections with Jews in intelligence networks in every Central and East European nation. The CIC therefore had every reason to maintain a keen interest in Brycha, and its leaders and activities.

The Jewish problem intensified in 1947 when a Zionist terrorist group blew up a British leave train *en route* to Klagenfurt, narrowly failing to hurl its 200 passengers into a deep abyss to the side of the track. Sections of the Austrian populace now began to show open hostility towards the Jewish DPs, and in January the Salzburg CIC reported an alarming increase in incidents between Austrians and Jews in the streets. At Bad Ischl a Communist-led demonstration spilled over into violent agitation against the Jews. 'The Jews are growing fat!' yelled the mob. 'Down with the Jews! Out with the Jewish pigs!' And they threw rocks through the windows of the Jewish refugee camp and manhandled and clawed the camp's director until the police, at the instigation of CIC agents, dispersed the mob and arrested the principal agitators.

In Germany the CIC's mission was to keep track of the illegal Jewish movements by means of a surveillance and penetration operation code-named Rummage. When it was discovered that the Jews were purchasing German weapon stocks in order to smuggle them out to the embryonic Jewish armies in Palestine, surveillance had to be extended to the shipment of arms as well. But the CIC only observed and reported these activities in Germany. The agents made no attempt to break them up.

The birth of the state of Israel in May 1948 brought an end to the covert activities of both the European Jews and the CIC, and by 1949 the majority of the Jews had found a new home in *Eretz Israel*, their Promised Land. No such straightforward solution was to hand in the intelligence confrontation between the east and west which characterized the mounting tension of the Cold War – a confrontation that by 1948 had become an all-out struggle. In this war it was the CIC who were now to occupy the American front line.

12

THE CIC'S COLD WAR

One of the more tragic outcomes of World War Two was that it failed to lead to a World Peace. The fighting war between Germany and the Allies had barely died down, when a Cold War between the Soviets and the Western Powers broke out. Such an outcome had long been feared and predicted by Churchill but had been fatally ignored by Roosevelt. The Red Army had no sooner overrun Eastern Europe and Eastern Germany than an Iron Curtain shut off the Sovietized nations from the rest of the world. Though as yet there was no bloodshed, fear once again seized a large part of the population of the northern hemisphere.

Stalin's intentions were still unclear in 1945. But by 1947–48 they were all too evidently hostile. With half the continent in Russian hands, Allied intelligence gathered wind of alleged Soviet plans to destabilize and then occupy Western Europe. Berlin was blockaded by the Russians and General Clay gave warning of the danger of imminent conflict. At the same time, the entire American intelligence community was put on a war footing.

In this escalation of mutual hostility between Russia and the Western Powers, Germany was in the front line, and it was inevitable that in the ensuing intelligence war between east and west there should be a considerable shift in the priorities of the intelligence services – away from the Nazis and past hostilities and towards the Soviets and potential future ones. This shift of emphasis was to have a considerable impact on the actions of the CIC in Germany and lead to much soul-searching and confusion. For in the drawing up of the battle lines of the intelligence war, both sides were to resort to the services of the CIC's most despised foe – the erstwhile Nazis of the recently defunct Third Reich. But by the time that happened the whole picture of American intelligence had changed, and the role of the CIC with it.

The initial failure of the early Truman government to perceive the change in the relationship between the Soviet Union and the

Western Allies at the end of the war led to the dissolution in October 1945 of America's only centrally co-ordinating intelligence agency, the wartime OSS (Office of Strategic Services). Elements in this defunct organization were shared out among the surviving intelligence agencies. Thus the counter intelligence section went to the War Department, where it was renamed the SSU (Strategic Services Unit), while the political intelligence section was taken over by the State Department. The return to a fragmentized intelligence effort of the sort America had laboured under before the war had two effects. In the first place, it meant that the ultimate recipient of American intelligence – the President – suffered from all the drawbacks of an unco-ordinated intelligence apparatus, so that the information he received tended to be confusing and contradictory and failed overall to reveal a clear picture of Russian intentions. In the second place, a greater burden of responsibility for overseas intelligence activities fell on the principal surviving overt and 'legitimate' intelligence agency in the field, the CIC.

In order to fill this intelligence vacuum, the CIC's role was gradually widened until eventually it included activities that had previously been excluded from its brief. At the same time, newly created covert agencies battened on to the CIC as a convenient cover and source of practical assistance, even to the extent of creating dummy CIC detachments behind which to hide in the furtherance of their *sub rosa* activities.

This was especially, if not exclusively, the case in occupied Germany, the front line of the Cold War in the period 1945 to 1950. There the CIC was required to carry out an increasingly delicate, complex and ambivalent mission in a politically and ethically muddied arena in which all the occupying powers spied on one another, all the American intelligence agencies spied on the other American intelligence agencies, and all competed for the services of their erstwhile enemies, the former Nazi intelligence operatives.

To chronicle events of this nature, many of which still fall into the category of 'sensitive', is not an easy task. The intelligence personnel involved are under no obligation to speak; documents in intelligence archives are often unavailable, or have been removed by other agencies or mislaid or destroyed by various interested parties. Thus in understanding such episodes as have surfaced from the murky days of the shadow war in occupied Germany, it may be helpful to have a bird's eye view of the quagmire in which the various agencies fought the not-so-good fight in the course of their bitter clandestine struggle.

All four occupation powers fielded their full range of intelligence outfits in Germany. The British had their MI5 and MI6, and though they maintained a high level of co-operation with their American allies, even in the most desperate and controversial fields of endeavour, this did not preclude them from competing with the Americans for informants and spy networks and attempting to maintain their perceived (if not actual) position at the top of the intelligence heap in the western zones of Germany. The French were something else again. Ostensibly they were the allies of the Anglo-Americans, though none actually believed them to be so. The French intelligence services in Germany – particularly the positive arm, the Deuxième Bureau – was considered to be so riddled by pro-Soviet Communists that it was viewed as a virtually hostile organization second only to the intelligence organizations of the USSR. A secret shared with the French, it was argued, was a secret imparted to the Reds.

At least one knew where one stood with the Soviets themselves, whose various intelligence agencies were for convenience collectively known to the CIC as the Russian Intelligence System (or RIS). Russian intelligence was implacably persistent, intransigent and crude. The MVD (successor to the NKVD and predecessor of the KGB) waged the intelligence war much as the Red Army had waged the fighting war – by committing cannon fodder *en masse* and accepting high casualty rates in the knowledge that a few of their men (and women) would get through. While SMERSH, the counter intelligence division of Russian military intelligence – the Soviet equivalent of the CIC – roamed the Soviet Zone of Germany in a restless hunt for western penetration agents, the personnel of the offensive sections of the MVD established themselves in western Germany under a variety of covers, notably and notoriously that of the Soviet Reparations Mission and the much hated Soviet Repatriations Mission operating in the DP camps.

The American intelligence service in Germany, of which the CIC was one of the most down-to-earth and ill-used components, was perhaps the most Byzantine and fantastical of all. Deeply riven by internecine jealousies between rival organizations, and often diametrically opposed to one another's aims and methods, the US agencies in Germany had little awareness of what their compatriot competitors were up to, and often this was far outside the laws of the United States or international practice.

Post-war US intelligence developed along two complementary and ultimately unified lines – that of intelligence gathering and that of covert (and essentially offensive) operations. The first had its origins in early 1946 when President Truman, tiring of a mass of inchoate information cluttering his desk, set in motion the formation of what was eventually to become (in September 1947) the Central Intelligence Agency or CIA. The first step was the formation of the Central Intelligence Group (CIG) to co-ordinate information from the State Department, Army, FBI and a multitude of other sources. The CIG took over the SSU from the Army and renamed it the Office of Strategic Operations (OSO). It also received a share of information coming from another intelligence-gathering agency which began operating in Germany under American sponsorship from July 1946. This was the Gehlen Organization, composed largely of former wartime Nazi intelligence officers under the ex-chief of the eastern section of German military intelligence, Reinhard Gehlen, who was responsible for directing espionage activities against the Soviet Union and its satellites and of whom we shall hear more later.

Towards the end of 1949, when the CIC Detachment in Germany was redesignated the 66th CIC, the headquarters underwent considerable reorganization, and the Case Section was split into four desks to handle counter-subversion, counter-espionage, security and positive intelligence. The latter was something quite new in CIC history, as a report summarizing the mission of the 430th CIC in Austria indicated:

Early in 1947 there was a change in emphasis from the denazification mission to the collection of positive intelligence ... The collection of positive intelligence is a departure from the usual mission of CIC. Normally a mission of Military Intelligence Section, the Director of Intelligence of the US Forces in Austria charged CIC with the collection of information from which positive intelligence can be produced. This includes the collection of information on economic, political, psychological, scientific, military (order of battle), topographical, sociological and who's who intelligence (foreign intelligence personalities). Strategic intelligence is of primary interest to the Department of Army, Intelligence Division.

The location of Austria is advantageous for the collection of information on Russia and the Russian satellite nations [notably Czechoslovakia, Hungary and Rumania], the Balkans and the Baltic states. From a modest beginning with a small section, the positive intelligence branch has expanded to a point where up until October of 1948 about 70 per cent of the effort entailed the collection of positive intelligence. The sources of such information are: political refugees from satellite countries, deserters from the Russian Army, displaced persons, travellers into the satellite countries, anti-Communist groups, religious organizations and network operations. Personalities arriving in Vienna are given a preliminary interrogation in Vienna and then transported via a 'Rat Line' to the US Zone, where exploitation is continued in Linz, Salzburg or one of the sub-offices in the US Zone.

During the year many high governmental officials have been given refuge and assistance by CIC, and valuable information has been obtained for the Department of Army. The networks are operated on a business basis. They must produce results or they are discontinued. Operating on the principle of a military patrol in combat, the nets are given specific EEIs (Essential Elements of Information) and definite objectives; consequently information is obtained in a systematic and efficient manner and at a cost commensurate with the results obtained. Although security measures are enforced in the handling of political refugees and the operation of networks, a calculated risk must be taken in the possibility of penetration of CIC [by foreign agents].

As an example of the typical positive intelligence activities carried out at sub-detachment level in Austria, the City of Vienna Sub-Detachment listed as its priorities the operation of underground routes of escape and communication, the operation of penetration nets in satellite countries, the screening of political refugees, the handling and preparing of false documents, and close liaison with Allied counter intelligence units.

During the war the CIC had been tightly controlled in the conduct of its duties by a set of meticulous, unambiguous orders which amounted to its own private laws of engagement and closely circumscribed the bounds beyond which it could not go. In Occupied Germany all this changed. It was as though someone had secretly changed the rules of the game – and even shifted the goalposts as well. The ethics were no longer the same. Indeed, it was not clear that there were any ethics at all. This was especially true of the CIC's rival intelligence agencies in Germany. As a special committee appointed by General Eisenhower to enquire into the débâcle of OPC's clandestine operations behind the Iron Curtain (of which more later) reported:

It is now clear we are facing an implacable enemy whose avowed objective is world domination by whatever means and at whatever cost. There are no rules in such a game. Hitherto acceptable norms of conduct do not apply. If the United States is to survive, longstanding American concepts of 'fair play' must be reconsidered. We must develop effective espionage and counter-espionage services and must learn to subvert, sabotage and destroy our enemies by more clever, more sophisticated and more effective methods than those used against us. It may become necessary that the American people be made acquainted with this fundamentally repugnant philosophy.

Under the pressure of this new Machiavellian outlook, the CIC seems to have undergone some sort of sea change. In addition to its normal counter intelligence activities against Nazis and Soviet agents in the American Zones of Germany and Austria, it embarked on a positive intelligence gathering mission of its own, not only in the American Zones but in foreign territories like East Germany and possibly Czechoslovakia as well. In March 1949 the Soviet Desk at CIC Headquarters in Frankfurt received orders from EUCOM's Director of Intelligence to break new ground and embark upon a positive intelligence mission codenamed Operation Devotion. Personnel at the Soviet Desk were advised that 12 miles from the border separating the US Zone from the Soviet Zone of Germany lay the most extensive Red Army manoeuvre area in East Germany. It was vital for American military interests that a watching brief should be kept on the number and disposition of Soviet forces operating in this area, and it was logical that the CIC, with its vast network of informants and its years of experience in covert intelligence work in Occupied Germany, should be the agency detailed to carry out this task.

So began a six-year espionage mission of extreme importance and immense sensitivity in which CIC operatives repeatedly risked their lives to enter Soviet-controlled territory and monitor the Russian order of battle along the front line of the Iron Curtain. A Positive Intelligence Desk was established with Lieutenant Colonel LeRoy C. Pierson as its Chief, and Positive Intelligence Teams were set up in Berlin and CIC Regions VI (Bamberg), VII (Bayreuth), X (Bad Wildungen) and XI (Wurzburg), with agents being sent into East Germany from all these areas. No extra funds or personnel were available for Operation Devotion, so key CIC informants were taken off their normal counter intelligence assignments and transferred to positive intelligence duties.

The most favoured practice was the so-called 'pyramid coverage' in which agents from two Regions and from Berlin were sent to the same point. Their three separate reports were then compared so that the accuracy of the information could be verified. However, as Communist border controls were tightened under the mounting stress of the Cold War, it became increasingly difficult, not to say dangerous, to infiltrate agents into East Germany from anywhere in the west except Berlin, and in place of forays by individuals based in West Germany the CIC established informant nets permanently *in situ* in the east, the contacts in the Soviet Zone relaying information back to the US Zone. This was a slow process, however, and when information was needed urgently an informant was immediately despatched from the city to make a rapid spot check of a given area in the Soviet Zone, which lay like a sea all around the four-power island of Berlin. The secret information compiled on the Soviet order of battle was given a limited distribution to other intelligence agencies until June 1954, when the mission was transferred, as the CIC put it, 'to another agency' – meaning the CIA.

Meanwhile, elements of other non-military American intelligence agencies, notably the CIA and OPC, were grafted on to the CIC, and their agents were at times required to don CIC uniform, which further added to the confusion. The CIC thus found itself acting as cover and providing leg men for all sorts of clandestine activities which were not normally regarded as part of CIC's regular mission. The CIC was the agency called upon to run the errands of the Department of the Army Detachment (or DAD for short), which was the highly secret umbrella organization for all non-military intelligence agencies operating in Germany under US military cover after the disbandment of the OSS. In 1948 most DAD personnel joined the newly formed CIA, but until then they utilized CIC outfits of their own devising. One such outfit was the Special Squad, a small group of some 20 or so very experienced CIC agents selected for their linguistic ability and discretion. Originally the group had been formed to investigate such delicate matters as the liaisons between senior officers and girlfriends of dubious loyalties suspected of being threats to American security in Germany. Later, under cover of the 7881st CIC Detachment, it took part in Operation Rusty, the CIC's original codename for General Gehlen's secret American-run intelligence headquarters at Pullach. The Special Squad was disbanded in 1947 and then re-formed in 1948 as the Central Squad under Lieutenant Colonel George Eckmann, ostensibly the deputy head of the CIC in Germany, but also the representative of DAD, for which the Central Squad provided field agents. According to John Loftus, a former officer of the Office of Special Investigation at the US Department of Justice in Washington DC:

> While the rest of the CIC was hunting Nazis and working on counter intelligence, Eckmann's group was performing foreign or

positive intelligence for DAD. Eckmann's men had contacts with communist East German politicians who passed information to DAD. Central Squad acted as a secret arm of the non-military intelligence services and sometimes received directives from the Office of the Secretary of Defense, by-passing the normal Army chain of command. 'It was all very hush-hush,' one man told me. 'Some of the stuff they were involved in would make your hair curl.'

Some of the 'stuff' in which CIC was involved was the case of the former Gestapo torturer, Klaus Barbie. The story of the ex-SD-Hauptsturmführer and chief of the Gestapo in Lyons is now well known. How he tortured to death the head of the French Resistance, Jean Moulin, and other French patriots; how he sent Jewish children to their deaths in Auschwitz; how he was recruited by Allied intelligence in Germany after the war; how the Americans arranged for him to find sanctuary in South America; and how he was tracked down by two private West German Nazi-hunters and extradited from Bolivia to France; how, in 1987, at the age of 74, he was tried for crimes against humanity and sentenced to life imprisonment by a court in Lyons – all this has been the focus of world-wide publicity. What is less clear are certain aspects of the role of the CIC, which first came to popular attention with the Klaus Barbie case.

At first sight it would seem that Barbie, who during the war had specialized in tracking British and American intelligence agents parachuted into France, Belgium and Holland and in penetrating the French Resistance in the Lyons region, was recruited as a CIC informant in 1947 and employed as such until 1951, when the Americans engineered his escape to Bolivia. At the end of the war Barbie's name had been included on two Allied lists of wanted war criminals, yet he led a charmed life. In August 1946 he was arrested by the CIC at Marburg in the American Zone, where he had set up a home under the pseudonym of Klaus Becker, but almost immediately escaped. He next turned up in Hamburg in the British Zone but again escaped after his arrest by British intelligence in November 1946. In February 1947 a combined British and American swoop team carried out a series of raids to round up members of an illegal association of former SS officers – described as the 'last large organized group of Nazis to be formed in the Western zones of Germany' – of which Barbie was a leading light, but just missed catching Barbie himself, who escaped yet again.

In April 1947 Robert S. Taylor, a CIC operations officer at Memmingen, near Munich, was advised by an ex-Abwehr informant called Kurt Merk of the availability for intelligence assignments of an old wartime colleague of his by the name of Barbie. Taylor informed Lieutenant Colonel Dale M. Garvey, the commander of CIC Region IV (Munich-Augsburg), and both agreed that in spite of Barbie's 'wanted' status he could prove a valuable tool in the intelligence war against the Soviets in Germany – specifically against Soviet-sponsored organizations and intelligence operations in the US Zone, France and Eastern Europe. In a report Taylor sent to CIC headquarters in Frankfurt at the end of May 1947 he stated his argument for employing Barbie:

> Barbie impressed this agent as an honest man, both intellectually and personally, absolutely without nerves or fear. He is strongly anti-Communist and a Nazi idealist who believes that he and his beliefs were betrayed by the Nazis in power. Since Barbie started to work for this agent he has provided extensive connections to French intelligence agencies, to German circles, to high-ranking Rumanian circles and to high Russian circles in the US Zone.

At this time Klaus Barbie was only known to the 970th CIC as a former SS captain who had served with the Gestapo in France. He had none of the notoriety which was later attached to him, and the expression 'Butcher of Lyons' had not yet been coined. Nevertheless, the hiring of an ex-Gestapo officer did not go unchallenged within the CIC, where even in 1947 there were still a number of officers and agents who, for every good reason, carried on their struggle for retribution against the Nazis. The operations officer at CIC Headquarters in Frankfurt, Lieutenant Colonel Earl S. Browning Jr (whom we last met in wintry Iceland in the mid-war years), was aghast when his deputy operations officer, Captain James H. Ratliff, came to his office in October 1947 in a highly emotional state – 'as mad as I've ever seen him' – and exclaimed: 'Garvey's double-crossed us. After having us chase after Barbie, he is sitting in Munich using him as an agent.' The central registry of informants (known in the trade as 'tech spec', short for technical specialists, the cover name for informants), which had been set up by Browning at CIC head-quarters in Frankfurt, had revealed that Barbie had been listed as an informant of Region IV under Garvey since the spring. Though Browning and Ratliff had the highest regard for Colonel Garvey, they were amazed that he had been able to order the hunt for Barbie when he was Operations Officer at CIC Headquarters in Frankfurt and then at the drop of a hat hide him away as a special informant once he had become Regional Commander in Munich.

Recently Ratliff has stated his view that the recruitment came

about because of 'the naivety and stupidity' of post-war CIC operatives who filled key posts after more experienced wartime agents had
returned to the States.

These new guys didn't know Nazism from rheumatism [claimed
Ratliff]. They were a wide-eyed group wandering around
Germany, utterly naive, some real eight-balls. I'd give them
briefings when they arrived, ask them if they had any questions and
they'd say, 'What time is the PX open?'

I blew up at this unbelievable nonsense. In 1947 we were still
rounding up members of the 'automatic arrest' list. Any Gestapo
agent was automatically on our arrest list. Barbie should have been
picked up immediately and put in a stockade. The use of him as an
informant violated the highest orders of the highest authorities in
the United States and Allied cause, and the direct orders of the
chiefs of staff. Nobody at headquarters in Frankfurt had known he
was even in Germany. Nobody knew where he was until we saw his
name on our own list of informants.

Disgusted, I demanded to go home. They said no, all officers
were frozen in the Theatre because of the Berlin Airlift. I
threatened to take it to my Senator, the famous Robert Taft – and
they put me and my wife on a boat to the US. When I got there I
resigned all connection with the military and wrote a scorching
letter to Secretary of the Army, Kenneth Royall, in Washington
DC. I told him there would be disasters in intelligence unless
changes were made. The Army immediately put a case on me and
sent it to Frankfurt for investigation. They laughed at it, cleared
me, and the Army apologized. It had gone to Browning, my good
friend, who also came home before Barbie was smuggled out to
South America. Who was ultimately responsible? The Chief of
CIC was. He was a timid West Pointer, the only one I ever saw,
who whimpered, 'You paint a bad picture,' every time I told him
how rotten things were. He was your World War One Colonel
Blimp without the belly.

Browning at once ordered the Munich CIC to arrest Barbie
and have him sent for intensive interrogation to the 7907 ECIC
(European Command Intelligence Centre) at Oberursel, near
Frankfurt. So began a see-saw struggle for Barbie's scalp between the
forces of light and the forces of darkness. The Munich CIC resisted
the order to hand Barbie over, and even went so far as to claim that
Barbie had already escaped, whereas in fact he was being held in a
DAD safe house in Augsburg. Barbie was kept in a cell at Oberursel
and interrogated at length until May 1948, when the 7907 ECIC

expressed the fear that 'Barbie's knowledge as to the mission of CIC, its agents, sub-agents, funds, etc, is too great. If Barbie was interned, it is the opinion of the interrogator that upon his release or escape he would contact either the French or British Intelligence and work for them.'

On Barbie's release, the ECIC recommended that he cease to be a CIC informant as 'he was of no further counter intelligence interest.' However, the new CIC commander, Colonel David G. Erskine, decided to allow Barbie to stay on at Region IV under controlled conditions. Earl Browning has commented on this decision as follows: 'Colonel Erskine was normally an extremely cautious man whose habitual response to any new proposal was "Will it hurt us?" In this case, however, he seemed to feel that the ECIC had cleansed Barbie of any former sins and that he should not arbitrarily deprive a subordinate commander of an important resource for carrying out his mission. This is a normal attitude for any US commander on almost any occasion.' So Barbie was removed to the Augsburg safe house with an American guarantee of immunity from prosecution and resumed his work as a CIC informant.

By now the Cold War was approaching a period of acute crisis. Allied intelligence needed all the help it could muster – and in the crucial area of informant networks ex-Nazis were often the only effective people available. At any rate, by the summer of 1948 Barbie was again at liberty. When Browning continued to press Region IV to drop him, his continuing employment was once more defended on the grounds that he knew too much.

From his safe house in Augsburg Barbie continued to carry out his duties as a paid informant, a major figure in a network which operated against Soviet agents and the German Communist Party in Bavaria and head of the network's operations against French intelligence in both the French and American Zones. Barbie was also deemed to be an expert on secret communist cells throughout Europe, with scores of sub-agents in Czechoslovakia, Romania and Yugoslavia. His first handler, Erhard Dabringhaus, grew to dislike Barbie for his arrogance and boastfulness; but his successors, Herbert Bechtold and Eugene Kolb, found the ex-Nazi an outstanding pro and a personable companion. Kolb especially admired Barbie's skilful methods of interrogation of CIC suspects – 'how to milk a source', as he put it. 'He was shrewd,' reported Kolb, 'extremely intelligent, good in manipulating human beings.' But it was Barbie's connection with the *Kameradschaft*, the underground association of ex-SS officers, many of whom had now worked their way back to key positions in post-war German society, that proved his greatest asset and source of information. By and large, the CIC agents who ostensibly controlled Barbie in Region IV, most of them German-born, entertained a personal and professional respect for Barbie, and glossed over whatever they knew of his wartime activities in Lyons. With Berlin under Soviet blockade, and Czechoslovakia a new recruit to the Soviet bloc, differences between victors and vanquished rapidly vanished to a point where the Americans and the old Nazis came to share a common cause as equals in the intelligence war.

In vain Earl Browning continued to urge Barbie's dismissal from CIC employ. In Munich Barbie had long been considered indispensable. The commander of Region IV defended Barbie as 'the most reliable informant this headquarters has.' In June 1949 Browning issued a directive on CIC policy towards former Gestapo personnel. 'It is the policy of this Headquarters,' the directive stated, 'to discourage the use of Gestapo personnel as further sources of this organization except in unusual circumstances.' These unusual circumstances entailed: (1) the use of the Gestapo man to introduce a CIC agent to other Gestapo personnel, or (2) to effect a meeting with former sources of the Gestapo man, or (3) to control a former source of the Gestapo man if it was impractical for the CIC agent to control that source himself. 'There is no objection to the use of the Gestapo man for the purposes of 1 and 2 provided the amount of time involved is short. A major project involving a long period of time [as in the case of Barbie] is to be discouraged. All requests for the use of Gestapo personnel to accomplish 3 will be cleared . . . by this Headquarters. An extremely strong case must be presented . . . before the request will be approved.' That said, Browning left Germany for America, as Garvey had done before him, never to return.

However, the need to dump Barbie grew even greater through 1949 when first the French press and then the French government began to reveal the unsavoury details of Barbie's nefarious activities with the Gestapo in Lyons and claimed that Barbie was being shielded by American intelligence. By March 1950 the French government's demands for Barbie's extradition had grown strident. But still the CIC held on to their man. In May Colonel Erskine, the CIC commander in Germany, decided that he would under no circumstances hand Barbie over to the French. The Americans still considered him too valuable and were mostly ignorant of the atrocities he had committed in France; moreover, they totally distrusted the French. 'If the French had got Barbie,' Kolb explained, 'I have no doubt that he would have been in Moscow within a few days.' This time there was no Earl Browning to protest. He had been replaced as operations officer by a new boy who knew nothing of the case. As Eugene Kolb wrote in a report:

'Due to his long association with CIC, Subject knows more about CIC targets, modus operandi, etc, than most CIC agents. Subject also knows identity of most KPD [German Communist Party] penetration sources used by this office, due to the fact that he either handled those sources or because he recruited or turned such sources.'

If Barbie were turned over to French intelligence, which was widely infiltrated by pro-Soviet Communists, the CIC in Germany would itself be at risk. Moreover, the fact that Barbie had actually been used to spy on America's French allies could provoke a major scandal. So the CIC blocked three French extradition moves by claiming they no longer knew where Barbie could be found, and even told the US High Commissioner in Germany that Barbie had left the CIC payroll in May 1949. In fact, until the autumn of 1950 Barbie remained in Augsburg interrogating suspects and recruiting Communist agents, first with Herbert Bechtold as his CIC handler, and finally Leo Hecht. But it seems that the US High Commission, for reasons of its own, felt no desperate urgency to see Barbie turned over to the French. The Director of Intelligence at the High Commission noted that the policy question was 'whether US-French relations would be more damaged by delivery of Barbie, assuming we could find him, than by non-delivery.' In the end it seems that the CIC, the Intelligence Division of the European Command and the US High Commission were in agreement on one thing – Barbie should not go to the French. But it is the view of Earl Browning that the full responsibility for withholding Barbie from the French and his ultimate escape should be borne by the Intelligence Division of EUCOM rather than the CIC. The CIC did not exist in a vacuum in Germany, but received from the Intelligence Division its guidance, missions and assignments in a relationship of close and constant liaison. (For Browning's full account of the Barbie affair, see Appendix I.)

There had always been something very special and strange about Barbie's terms of employment. Though it was common practice for Allied intelligence to employ Nazis, it was rare for them to take on out-and-out war criminals. It has also been suggested that Barbie was paid in dollars instead of the more normal blackmarket commodities like coffee and cigarettes. Nor was Barbie involved in the counter intelligence activities which were the CIC's proper brief. His sphere was positive (or offensive) intelligence against foreign states. Moreover, according to the OSI investigator John Loftus, the CIC sub-detachment which employed him was not really a CIC unit at all. Erhard Dabringhaus is quoted as saying that his own CIC sub-detachment in Augsburg was renamed the 7247 CIC – indicating that the unit was actually controlled by the CIA or OPC, which used four-digit numbers beginning with 7 for non-military intelligence operating under army (and specifically CIC) cover. Other agents confirmed, however, that at no time did Barbie ever work for the CIA, and neither the CIA nor the CIC ran safe houses in the Augsburg area.

According to one of Loftus' non-American informants, Barbie was 'first and foremost an agent of the British Secret Service' – even though Barbie always claimed to have an undying hatred for the British because they once roughed him up in Hamburg. He had been recommended to British intelligence and employed by them to recruit agents for a new, British-initiated intelligence organization in Germany run by his former wartime chief in the SD, Walter Schellenberg. The British, it was alleged, always headed the pecking order when it came to intelligence matters in occupied Germany. Many of the masterminds of the Nazi intelligence war against the USSR – Gehlen apart – had been taken to Britain after the war, Schellenberg among them. For Schellenberg's new British-style SD, which rivalled Gehlen's, Barbie found SS intelligence officers in hiding and organized safe houses and courier systems for them. When his usefulness was over he was passed on to DAD, then to the CIC. When the French demanded his extradition, it was the British, fearful that their own involvement would be exposed, who insisted the Americans should get rid of him.

By the end of 1950 it was clear even to the CIC that Barbie would have to go. Various methods of disengagement were tentatively considered. The least troublesome was simply to dump him in the streets of Augsburg and let him find his own way home. Another was to pay him off, then shove him into a refugee camp as an illegal border crosser. Yet another was to shoot him. In the end the Americans decided to ship him out of Germany down the 'Rat Line', the underground escape route devised by the 430th CIC in Vienna in 1947 to smuggle American agents and Russian and East European defectors out of Soviet-occupied Europe when their position behind the Iron Curtain became untenable. The 'Rat Line' led from Austria to Italy and thence to South America, and in 1949 over 1000 persons had used it to effect their escape from Europe. For Barbie's vanishing trick the 66th CIC (new designation for the 7970th) would obtain travel documents in the false name of Altmann, together with fictitious references. So in March 1951 the 'Butcher of Lyons', disguised in an American uniform, left Augsburg with his family and a CIC escort *en route* for Salzburg and Genoa, then set sail for South America. When he had gone the CIC congratulated all the agents involved for the efficiency in which 'the final disposal of an extremely sensitive subject had been handled'. The CIC added: 'This case is considered closed by the Intelligence Division, European Command, and this detachment.'

Looking back, the man who first warned CIC of Barbie's presence in their midst, James Ratliff, remains highly contemptuous of those who continued to employ him:

> After we got Barbie arrested, how was it possible that he was tolerated back in Augsburg, which happened to be the worst CIC office in all Germany – and that's saying a lot. All this baloney about him 'knowing too much about CIC and our new efforts against Communism' is so much pap. Apparently these idiots had grown to like their Gestapo captain. I practically retch over the 'danger' of turning him over to the French. Barbie went his merry way, sheltered by his friends. They apparently never understood what the war had been all about. But there is no blame at Augsburg. They never had the slightest idea what they were supposed to be doing. Innocent by insanity.

All this had taken place in Bavaria, in what was then CIC's Region IV (Munich-Augsburg), which Ratliff rightly decried as 'a shambles'. But even so, Ratliff claims that Barbie was a truly unique case. 'That's not an alibi; I'm just explaining what happened. Barbie was an exceptional case, the only case of a Gestapo agent being allowed to run free. It was even worse that we used him only because of these boobs' naivety and ignorance. But we, much more than our allies, were locking up war criminals. They were allowing Germans to run wild.'

In his report on the 1983 investigation into the Barbie case for the US Department of Justice – the Ryan Report – US Special Investigator Allan Ryan came to the following conclusions:

> Those who made the decision to employ Klaus Barbie were, on the whole, conscientious and patriotic men faced with a difficult assignment. Under the circumstances, their choice to enlist Barbie's assistance was neither cynical nor corrupt.
>
> They were acting within the scope of their official duties. Their actions were not taken for personal gain, or to shield them personally from liability or discipline, but to protect what they believed to be the best interests of the United States Army and the United States government.

No other nation in occupied Germany – France, Great Britain or the Soviet Union – is in any position to criticize the decision to use Klaus Barbie now that the United States government has revealed the facts behind that use. Each of these governments made essentially the same decision at the time: to invoke the available resources of the former German régime to protect and advance what each government perceived to be its national interest. The very nature of intelligence gathering abroad required the use of informants and it would be grossly unrealistic to require that they be subject to the same standards of character, uprightness and conduct that are required for, say, civil or military service with the United States government.

Sadly, records indicate that the Barbie case was not as unique as had been supposed. At least one other fugitive Gestapo agent also found sanctuary on the informants list of CIC Region IV. This was the former chief for the Munich Gestapo's Communist section, Eugene Fischer, who like Barbie was employed to help penetrate the KPD in Bavaria. In return for his fund of information on concealed Communists in Bavaria, the CIC agreed to provide Fischer with a comfortable house, reunite him with his wife and children, and support him modestly and adequately. At the same time it was agreed he should be protected from prosecution, since just for being a recipient of Hitler's personal decoration, the Blood Order, Fischer was liable to eight years' hard labour if he ever came before a denazification court. According to one CIC Special Agent, Guenther Reinhardt, Fischer proved 'an enormously valuable adjunct to American security in Europe.' Fischer recruited doyens of his former Gestapo informant net to help the work along. But unlike Barbie, Fischer did not have the good fortune to be smuggled out of Germany by his American employers when the going got rough. During his CIC service he was arraigned for trial at the Denazification Court in Munich on charges of mistreatment and torture of prisoners whilst in his custody at the Munich Gestapo headquarters; and after being carelessly exposed as an American informant, he was abandoned by his protectors.

Other notable Region IV employees included such Nazi gallants as Anton Mahler, a former Gestapo officer and confederate of Fischer in Munich, who was the special prosecutor responsible for the interrogation of two young Munich University students, Hans and Sophie Scholl, the leaders of the White Rose anti-Hitler resistance, who were executed in Munich in 1943. It seems that Mahler may also have been employed by the Americans, and reports still being checked out at the time of going to press suggest that he acted as secretary for Barbie and his CIC control, and may possibly even have worked as administrative assistant at the CIC office in Augsburg. Another CIC employee (*and* Gehlen man) was Dr Emil Augsburg, formerly the leading SS authority on the Soviet Union, who as an adviser with Eichmann's S-4 department had been responsible for the deaths of thousands of Jews in Eastern Europe, and had acted as an important informant for Barbie's CIC network in Augsburg.

Meanwhile the 430th CIC tangled with the sinister figure of Wilhelm Höttl, former deputy chief of the SD foreign intelligence department, another wanted war criminal who worked as an informant in Austria. In fact, the 430th in Austria boasted a number of skeletons rattling about its cupboards. In June 1988 the Office of Special Investigations at the US Department of Justice produced a report which revealed that at least 13 Nazi war criminals – a number of them guilty of the murder of Jews in occupied Europe – had been employed as US intelligence informants in post-war Austria. The main text of the report concerned the case of Robert Jan Verbelen, a Belgian Nazi and wanted war criminal, who worked for the CIC in Vienna for ten years after the end of the war. But other war criminals who worked for the 430th Detachment were also listed in the document. One of them was a former Gestapo officer who was involved in the murder of the pre-war Austrian Chancellor, Dr Engelbert Dolfuss. Jailed for his complicity in the murder, the officer escaped from prison, then ran a Gestapo sabotage training centre. After brief imprisonment by the British at the end of the war, the ex-Gestapo man then enrolled himself as a double agent in the CIC with the code name of 'Informant M'. His employment terminated when the CIC discovered that he was performing the same work for the British and probably the French as well, though he probably owed his primary loyalty to the Soviets.

Another CIC informant in Austria was a former Gestapo official from an *Einsatzkommando*, a mobile detachment of the SD responsible for apprehending and executing Jews, Communists and other 'undesirable elements' in Eastern Europe. Yet another was a general in the notorious Yugoslav Chetnik guerrilla organization 'who committed atrocious crimes which merited his extradition to Yugoslavia.' Yet another was a leading member of a pre-war Fascist movement in a Balkan country who became a Gestapo agent during the war and served as deputy commander of a German-sponsored military organization whose tactics included burning villages and murdering unarmed civilians.

It was the 430th Detachment in Vienna which 'cleared' Dr Kurt Waldheim, the present President of Austria, before he was allowed to begin his diplomatic career in the Austrian Foreign Ministry. Dr Waldheim belonged to a Wehrmacht unit which committed atrocities in Yugoslavia during World War Two, though no evidence has yet emerged that he was himself personally involved in war crimes. The OSI report concluded that the CIC 'was not averse to using individuals with tainted pasts. In pursuing its mission of ensuring the security of the United States, the CIC, like most intelligence organizations, followed the policy that the end justifies the means.'

An even more controversial case came to our attention during the course of our researches in this murky area. This was the case of General Heinrich Müller, the overall chief of the Gestapo, who as Adolf Eichmann's immediate superior was responsible for implementing the 'Final Solution', the extermination of European Jewry, and was thus by far the most important Nazi war criminal still to be accounted for. Müller was last seen in Berlin shortly before the Russians captured the city, and then vanished totally. Though nobody can be sure what happened to him after the end of the war, informed opinion has hitherto favoured the view that he was spirited away to the USSR, where his special expertise in secret police work still had its uses.

We were therefore somewhat surprised when in July 1988 we received a telephone call from an anonymous caller in the United States informing us that a large CIC file on the Müller case had accidentally been released to him from the US archives. The file consisted of 427 pages of documents which indicated that the Gestapo chief had survived the war and that both he and another wanted war criminal, SS-Obergruppenführer Odilo Globocnik, former SS and Police Leader in Lublin, head of Operation Reinhard, founder of the notorious extermination camps of Belzec, Sobibor, Majdanek and Treblinka, and the man selected by Himmler to play the key role in the liquidation of the Polish Jews, had been retained by the CIC as intelligence advisers. This was, of course, a sensational revelation, if it was true. Heinrich Müller and Odilo Globocnik were far more important Nazi war criminals than Klaus Barbie had ever been. To say that Müller had been employed by American intelligence was like saying Himmler had become an agent of MI6. Our informant continued by saying that he felt it was important that these documents should be published and that he had got in touch with us as acknowledged experts in the field of CIC history to discuss this possibility. He also informed us that the US Army Intelligence and Security Command archives at Fort Meade, Maryland, did not appear to have a copy of the file in its possession.

We explained to our caller that although we did have a CIC file on

Müller, it amounted to no more than a few pages of inconsequential information, and we would therefore be extremely interested to receive from him at least a summary of the contents of the documents he had acquired. Shortly before this arrived, we discovered that a leading British quality newspaper was also working on the case. Also involved was one of America's top news magazines. The British paper had been approached by the same individual some months previously. Subsequently we were approached by a US government investigative agency, who sought our assistance in verifying certain aspects of the file, a copy of which they had recently acquired.

An examination of the file revealed that it consisted of documents apparently signed by two genuine CIC agents in Region VIII (Berlin) towards the end of 1948 in connection with the employment of Müller and Globocnik as CIC advisers. One of these agents was Andrew Venters, who was Dr Michael Arnaudow's case officer during the investigation into the whereabouts of Hitler's body; the other was Severin Wallach, who once ran a secret agent inside the office of the man who was to be the President of East Germany, Wilhelm Pieck (see preceding chapter). Headed 'Soviet Investigations – Project UEBERSEE/3', a preliminary Agent Report dated 30 November 1948 read:

> Recent investigations by special teams of Soviet agents in the Western Zones seeking definitive [sic] information about the possible whereabouts of former SS Generals Heinrich MUELLER and Odlio [sic] GLOBOCNIK have apparently uncovered sufficient information to justify increased activity.
>
> Allegedly the Soviets have uncovered leads which cause them to suspect that the two above-named subjects were not killed at the end of the war. This is part of their ongoing probings in re [sic] the possible possession by the West of high level Nazi leaders wanted by the Soviets either for trial or possible intelligence use by their agencies . . .
>
> MUELLER's value to Western intelligence is beyond doubt but continued protection of GLOBOCNIK might prove to be an extreme embarassment [sic]. British intelligence . . . has become increasingly insistant [sic] that GLOBOCNIK either be terminated at once or relocated in such a manner as to totally remove him from Soviet investigators area of search . . .
>
> Original appraisals of former SS personnel with unsavory backgrounds such as GLOBOCNIK . . . should certainly be reconsidered, whereas the obvious value of MUELLER and

SKORZENY are self-evident and are clearly in line with the policy recently set.

The documents were sufficiently convincing to encourage the British paper to commit some £30,000 to research on the story, a sum perhaps more appropriate to an advance payment on a substantial book. However, though the agents' signatures and the typeface of the typewriter used to prepare the documents seemed authentic, the language was not typical, the spelling was bad, and the 'SECRET' security classification was not sufficiently high and not printed in the normal typeface. It was not possible for the agents involved to authenticate the material, as both were now dead. Nor could forensic experts offer verification, as the documents were all photocopies.

It was our considered judgement that, on various grounds, the alleged CIC Müller file was a forgery counterfeited by a skilful but rather confused person, and that the signatures were simply photocopies taken from other, rather more innocuous documents signed by the two agents. Our view was corroborated by Colonel Earl Browning, who was Operations Chief at CIC Headquarters in Frankfurt at the time the documents were supposed to have been produced. Colonel Browning made it clear to us that as head of CIC operations all special activities in Germany would have come to his attention – certainly something as sensitive as the employment of Heinrich Müller and Odilo Globocnik as CIC advisers. Nothing of the sort ever took place, however, and the whole idea was in any case ludicrous.

Regretfully, therefore, we have to conclude that the fate of the Chief of the Gestapo in the Third Reich remains shrouded in mystery and speculation, as it has always been, and probably always will be. Globocnik, meanwhile, rests in the grave into which he was thrown after his suicide in 1945.

The damage that could have been inflicted by this ingenious hoax was so internationally inflammatory that the US government took an exceptional interest in the case and enlisted our assistance (as did the British paper). The revelations, had they been true, would have created a world-wide sensation, with implications to match, and generating more ramifications than even the Barbie Trial, with all its manifest international political aspects.

A significant development, a raising of the stakes to truly fantastical heights, occurred in May 1948 with the formation by the State Department of a permanent agency dedicated to covert operations against the Soviet Union, indeed nothing less than a crusade to roll back the Iron Curtain. This was the Office of Policy Co-ordination, or OPC. Under the direction of a former OSS agent by the name of Frank Winser, the OPC enjoyed a virtually limitless charter from the National Security Council – the supreme intelligence body of the United States – and was seen as the front line vanguard of the secret war against the Soviet Union. The mission of the OPC was ambitious – to help overthrow the Soviet Empire from within by building a secret army and supporting guerrilla warfare and armed rebellion inside the USSR and the countries of the Eastern Bloc.

To implement this impractical dream the OPC turned for assistance to the wartime members of the Nazi puppet governments of Eastern Europe and their Waffen-SS auxiliaries, whose names were conveniently supplied by the Gehlen Organization. Most of these men had sought sanctuary from Soviet retribution by hiding in the DP camps, and many of them were on the Allies' wanted lists for the heinous crimes they had committed during the Nazi occupation of their countries. They included veterans of the Vlasov Army of Russian soldiers who had fought on the German side and SS collaborators from Byelorussia, the Ukraine, the Baltic states and several nations of Eastern Europe who had espoused the Nazi cause during the war.

Though the Americans had conducted clandestine operations inside Communist Romania in 1947 – an obscure undertaking which met with little success – the National Security Council's authorization of a significant expansion of US covert warfare operations marked a turning point in the history of American intelligence and of the Cold War. From now on the CIA and other intelligence agencies were no longer confined to intelligence gathering alone but were free to carry the war to the enemy in a far more physical (and frightening) form.

One of the State Department's most important covert projects for the period 1948–1950, for example, was Operation Bloodstone, whose special operations programme formed part of a covert warfare, sabotage and assassination operation which went far beyond anything that had yet been attempted in Europe up to that time. Under the Bloodstone programme, former Nazis and Nazi collaborators, many of them war criminals of the worst kind, were smuggled into the United States to assist in intelligence gathering operations, to train American intelligence and covert warfare specialists, and to prepare for large-scale covert warfare, sabotage and assassination missions. These unsavoury Nazi émigré groups, where double, triple and quadruple agents were the norm and political murders and

arrange immunity from prosecution for war crimes by his American backers.

One of Gehlen's first operational moves was to use his network of Byelorussian informants to help the CIC flush Soviet agents out of the DP camps in a sweep known as Operation Tobacco. The teeming DP camps of Occupation Germany, populated by hundreds of thousands of displaced survivors of Nazi mayhem, were recruiting grounds for the intelligence agencies of all four of the occupation powers. The Communists were particularly active in these camps and had established extensive intelligence networks controlled by MVD agents posing as liaison officers with the Soviet Repatriations Committee.

Operation Tobacco was just one of a number of sweeps in which CIC investigators fingered Soviet spies identified by Gehlen's new organization. The German hoped that in this way he could ingratiate himself with the CIC, but the plan backfired. The CIC had already come to the shrewd conclusion that Gehlen's embryo spy apparatus could have been infiltrated by the MVD and that much of his information could be spurious intelligence deriving from MVD plants. During parallel CIC sweeps designed to round up Nazis hiding out under the cover of the DP camps, CIC agents found that many Nazis would claim immunity from arrest by producing a special card with the phone number of Gehlen's organization on it and that higher authority would then order the CIC to release these men. When the CIC complained that Gehlen's men were former Nazis who were believed to be peddling the same information to the Russians, higher authority ignored them.

When the CIC picked up one of the Byelorussian leaders, Stanislaw Stankievich, for 'aggressive questioning' as a Nazi collaborator and war criminal on the Soviet wanted list, the staff of General Lucius D. Clay, the Military Governor of the US Zone of Germany, persuaded the CIC not to prosecute him, even though he had confessed, on the grounds that he was working for British intelligence. When the CIC agreed, Clay's intelligence staff then informed Washington that Stankievich was an anti-communist victim of Soviet vilification.

The formation of the CIA in September 1947 and the OPC in the following summer only served to exacerbate the relationship between the CIC and other American intelligence agencies. The OPC under Frank G. Wisner was in the front line of the covert war against the Soviet Union, bent on an undercover programme of destabilization, subversion and outright guerrilla war intended to roll back Soviet power in Eastern Europe and the Soviet republics of

Byelorussia and the Ukraine. Its director enjoyed virtually unlimited powers to pursue whatever means he thought fit to achieve policy ends – including, of course, the employment of ex-Nazis, war criminals, former SS intelligence networks. Anything justified the OPC's dream of overthrowing the Soviet empire, operating (as a future Director of the CIA was to put it) 'in the atmosphere of an order of Knights Templar, to save Western freedom from Communist darkness'. Even General Clay, the American supremo in Germany, was in Frank Wisner's confidence, cognizant of his plan to reconstruct the wartime SS underground networks in Eastern Europe, Byelorussia and the Ukraine and use them to set up caches of arms for OPC's Special Forces. Before long, Wisner argued, the USSR would begin to disintegrate as a result of internal rebellions which the OPC would assist and even instigate.

In this masterplan the Byelorussians seemed to perform an ideal function. They had run a network of secret informants who were in place behind the Soviet border. They had already given proof of their allegiance by collaborating with the Americans in the anti-Communist sweeps that were part of Operation Tobacco. Given the OPC's formidable support from the all-supreme National Security Council, the State Department, the CIA and the ruler of American Germany, it was clear that any objections the CIC might have over the moral perfidy of re-employing the monstrous lackeys of Nazism in the name of freedom and democracy could be easily by-passed or brushed aside.

Wisner's plan required that ex-Nazi exiles such as the Byelorussians should be protected from the attentions of Nazi hunters like the CIC. General Clay concurred. When CIC agents investigating the death of Adolf Hitler entered the Byelorussian DP camps looking for any of Hitler's former employees who might have gone to ground there, Clay's intelligence staff ordered them out. The scrupulous CIC got their own back in their Top Secret *Consolidated Orientation and Guidance Manual for 1948*, which not only listed most of the former Nazi Byelorussian leaders who lurked in the DP camps but cross-filed them by the atrocities for which they were responsible as well. John Loftus, a former trial attorney for the US Office of Special Investigations, who undertook an exhaustive investigation of the Byelorussian Nazis to which we are indebted, has written of the CIC's part in this affair:

The CIC was proud of its role in helping to ensure that Nazis were barred from entering the United States. As early as 1945 the agency had assigned a special denazification section to each major district in the American Zone in Germany to apprehend Nazi war criminals and prosecute them before special tribunals that supplemented the Nuremberg trials. The CIC record of prosecutions was an admirable one, and on the whole it carried out the will of Congress with integrity and efficiency. To be sure, the CIC recruited its share of Nazis to help track down other Nazis, but for the most part these informants were rewarded only with cigarettes or scarce rations. Only a handful of extremely valuable agents were helped to emigrate – and they were sent to the United Kingdom rather than the United States. Unfortunately, a few zealots in the CIC knowingly permitted Nazi informants to process through for immigration to the United States. Such instances were rare, however, and must be considered in the context of hundreds of thousands of German denazification and refugee investigation cases that the CIC conducted.

Nevertheless, many Byelorussian Nazis, and their Ukrainian counterparts, were successfully smuggled into America as part of OPC's plan to bring over the leaders of the future independent eastern states along with the recruits for the special forces who were to be trained at OPC's secret camps in the States. The CIC had been charged by Congress to monitor efforts by former Nazis to enter the United States, and was thorough in its efforts to do so. Thus the CIC reported the dubious background of Stanislaw Stankievich to the US Displaced Persons Commission in the following terms: 'Subject worked first with the Soviets, then with the Nazis, then again for the Soviets. He appears to be an opportunist who will work for anyone who will pay him. Subject is considered a security risk. However, we have additional information in our Secret files still more damning, which can be forwarded.'

But the CIC was often leaned on by higher authority, and its background checks could be circumvented by loopholes in procedure. Thus the State Department was able to smuggle into America the leaders of virtually all the puppet governments set up by the Nazis between the Baltic and the Black Sea, including over 300 Byelorussians and an even larger number of Ukrainians who were smuggled in among the 400,000 DPs from many European nations who finally found a new home in America.

In 1982, after his revelations about these irregularities, John Loftus was asked to comment on the CIC's involvement by members of the Military Intelligence Association of New England, most of whom had served in the CIC during World War Two. Mr Loftus replied:

344 Americas Secret Army

For the record, the American public should know of the superb job done by the Army Counter Intelligence Corps in attempting to prevent Nazi immigration to America. The CIC employed a highly sophisticated central file system to monitor the Nazi underground in the occupied zones of Germany after the war. The CIC brought thousands of war criminals and collaborators to justice in denazification trials conducted by the US military in Germany. In 1948 the CIC was given the responsibility for screening hundreds of thousands of refugees who wished to come to America under the Displaced Persons Act. Of the nearly 8000 CIC employees, I came across only one instance where a CIC agent rewarded the Nazi informant with US visas. The over-whelming evidence is that the CIC did an honest, outstanding, and professional job under the most difficult of circumstances.

In order to circumvent the strict anti-Nazi emigration policy of the CIC, the State Department had to insert its own agents, wearing Army and Air Force uniforms, to sanitize the CIC's files so that their Nazi protégés could slip in to America. To the credit of the CIC, they soon discovered that Nazi war criminals working for the State Department had entered the United States. The local CIC agents in Germany fired off a letter of protest which went up the chain of command all the way to the Pentagon. In 1950, Brigadier General Wecherling personally informed J. Edgar Hoover [the FBI chief] of the CIC's information . . .

From the documents which I have seen [Loftus continued], no one could accuse the CIC of being part of a cover-up. It would be unjust to let a few bad apples, most of whom have recently retired, give all military intelligence officers a bad name. It would be a tragedy to sully the reputation of the intelligence professionals of the CIC, who did their best over thirty years ago to keep the Nazis out of America, and who did their best in recent years to track down the files so that the sad truth could be made public.

The Office of the Army Chief of Staff for Intelligence, the CIC, and the CIA bent over backwards to declassify my account so that I could go public. They, not I, ultimately deserve the credit for exposing the misdeeds of a few reckless individuals some thirty years ago. These men wore the uniforms of military intelligence, and were paid by the CIA, but they were not, in any legitimate sense, ever members of those proud organizations. I hope this helps set the record straight.

The State-assisted immigration of Byelorussian Nazis should, however, be seen in a wider context. Hitherto classified CIC documents, declassified in December 1987, reveal that it was not just the Americans who assisted Nazis in this way. The documents show that immediately after the war the intelligence agencies of France and Britain revived a former Nazi organization called Intermarium, which had originally been founded by a Russian tsarist general after the Bolshevik Revolution in order to fight communism. The intelligence agencies of France, Britain, Australia, Canada, Austria, West Germany and Italy, as well as high Vatican officials, had by then become involved in recruiting former Nazi war criminals for the organization, re-arming and funding them and helping them to emigrate from Europe to safe havens abroad. According to John Loftus, an estimated 10,000 Nazi collaborators were assisted into the USA by this organization, and some 6,500 of these were still living there in 1987. When the CIC found out about the Allied involvement in 1947, the US government decided to get involved and to keep the entire operation secret. Further CIC investigations were stopped and their reports hidden away in order to protect Allied governments and the Vatican, which were unaware of their intelligence agencies' activities, from embarrassing revelations.

This is not the place to develop at length the story of the ill-fated efforts of the Americans (and their allies the British) to foster insurrection and guerrilla war in the Iron Curtain countries of the USSR, Poland and Albania. The point is that at least as far as the Byelorussians were concerned, CIC complicity in the terrible compromises made by the Allied intelligence agencies, especially the OPC, was of a limited, not to say recalcitrant, nature. The CIC did their best to preserve some sense of historical justice; but they could not stop the grand design. Too many other agencies claimed precedence over them.

By 1950 the clandestine army raised by the Americans from the ranks of Russian and East European Waffen-SS veterans numbered some 30,000 fully trained men armed with infantry weapons and chemical warfare equipment. Moreover, the US Joint Chiefs of Staff had given their approval for this underground army to form part of America's nuclear strategy, with the role of conducting an all-out guerrilla war in Russia following any US nuclear strike against that country. Plans for such nuclear strikes had been drawn up as early as a few months after the end of the war in Europe and by 1949 had developed to a point where they entailed the dropping of 70 atomic bombs over a 30-day period with the aim of destroying 40 per cent of the Soviet Union's industrial capacity.

It was, of course, a major problem to conceal such a large underground army and the solution was to hide it within the ranks of the United States' own army in Europe under the guise of Labour Service units (ie non-American service auxiliaries attached to the US Army in Germany). By 1950 these Labour Service units were being used as cover by both the CIC and the CIA for the purpose of training a right-wing German underground organization which called itself a Technical Services unit but whose real name was the BDJ (Bund Deutscher Jungen, or League of Young Germans).

It is at this point that we come to the tricky subject of American-sponsored political assassination programmes, which were under the control of an OPC officer by the name of Colonel Boris Pash, the son of the Metropolitan of the Russian Orthodox Church in America, a veteran of the Russian Civil War, and formerly the chief counter intelligence officer on the Manhattan Project and the leader of the special operation known as the Alsos Mission (the search for the German atomic bomb). After the war Pash was the army's representative on Operation Bloodstone's special operation programme (including assassination) and in March 1949 he was assigned by the army to the OPC division of the CIA. One of the aims of the BDJ was to carry out just such an assassination programme in West Germany in the event of a Soviet attack. BDJ squads would target selected German leaders who were deemed insufficiently anti-Communist and then murder them. The targets not only included German Communists, but members of the Social Democratic Party (the main opposition party during the Adenauer régime), including the party leader, the minister of the interior in Hesse, and the mayors of Hamburg and Bremen. When the plot was uncovered in 1952, CIC officers took custody of arrested BDJ members and hid them away from the German police, and seized all Technical Service records and refused to hand them over to the German authorities.

Pentagon-approved assassination programmes *were* carried out in Germany, however, often in the course of operations in which CIC agents were also involved. Two of these operations, codenamed Hagberry and Lithia, were aimed against foreign agents who had penetrated Anglo-American émigré espionage networks operating under the umbrella codename Rusty. Operation Hagberry was designed to liquidate a Soviet intelligence net in the US Zone known as the Chikalov Ring. Operation Lithia, which began under army auspices in November 1947, authorized 'the liquidation in the United States Zone of the Kindermann Ring, a large-scale Czechoslovakian intelligence net'. Part of the liquidation process apparently involved the murder of all suspected double agents. Army archives no longer have any records of these secret operations; the CIC produced an account of their participation in Lithia, though there is no record of any killings.*

According to the CIC account, CIC agents in Germany eventually had to face the fact that espionage activities in the American Zone were not confined to the Russians. When Czechoslovakia became a Soviet satellite, Czech agents already in place in the American Zone were activated by the Czech Intelligence Chief, a man called Rejoin. To counteract Czech activity, the CIC launched Operation Lithia. By intercepting fresh agents crossing the border into the American Zone with refugee groups, many of whom defected and voluntarily confessed all they knew, the CIC were able to build up a comprehensive, zone-wide picture of Czech espionage in the American Zone, which included the identities of agents in place and agents expected to enter West Germany. The Czech net was under the direction of a Czech controlling officer who operated just across the zonal border in Czechoslovakia and was himself under orders from Czech intelligence in Prague. CIC operatives were able to penetrate the principal courier to this controlling officer and read and photograph the contents of the courier's pouches.

As leads developed and information built up the time approached when the CIC could launch the swoop that would culminate Operation Lithia. The exact time of the swoop was withheld from CIC agents until the very last moment. Finally, at 3 o'clock on a November night in 1948, teletyped Top Secret orders arrived in CIC regional headquarters throughout the American Zone listing the names and addresses of all Czech agents to be rounded up. CIC agents set off in teams to carry out the arrests and by morning the majority of the Czech intelligence nets had been rolled up. All apprehended agents were sent to CIC Region IV in Munich so that they could be interrogated in depth by intelligence officers specially selected for this task. A few months later 11 Czech spies were sentenced by a military tribunal to up to 20 years' imprisonment. By then, as a form of reprisal, the Communist government in Prague had issued a communiqué charging that agents of the United States

---

*In the light of this sort of situation one has to look twice at any document which contains the ambiguous word 'liquidation' – as in the case of a letter sent by a Technical Specialist and CIC Special Agent at Bad Nauheim CIC headquarters on 10 March 1948 on the subject of informant Serge Roukene (alias Karl Orgulski, alias Peter Palcynski, code number P-604-III-BN). This letter reads: 'Subject was sent to this organization *for the purpose of liquidation* [authors' italics]; however, with the verbal approval of 970th CIC Hqs, he was used as a P-type [Penetration] informant whose mission was the penetration of the Soviet Repatriation Mission in Frankfurt and Fulda. His penetration was quite successful and an arrest was planned (i.e. Capt Savaliev); however, higher headquarters procrastinated and the opportunity to make the arrest passed. Subject became extremely fearful of his work and overcautious to the point of being useless to this organization.'

Counter Intelligence Corps were operating inside Czechoslovakia, though no Americans were directly involved. Since the CIC was running informants inside the Soviet Zone of Germany, it is more than possible that they were also running informants inside the frontiers of their new Communist neighbour.

The most notorious assassination programme, of which some accounts do exist, formed part of an operation called Ohio, which employed a squad of ex-Nazi Ukrainians to liquidate double agents and Soviet and Eastern Bloc agents at a DP camp in Mittenwald in the Bavarian Alps. The murders were then blamed on factional violence among rival Ukrainian émigré groups. This is how the story pieces together.

Savage factional rivalries were a characteristic of émigré political groups. Cut off from their homeland, deprived of all sense of reality, trapped in a hothouse atmosphere of intrigue and paranoia in which each faction believed that it alone was the chosen instrument of national liberation, the internecine strife between the rival groups assumed the bitterness of a tribal feud in which treachery was rife and even blood was spilt and the main prize was not so much the fading dream of national freedom and the defeat of Communism as recognition and financial aid from western intelligence agencies. Thus the Byelorussians split into two rival factions – the western Catholic faction and the eastern Orthodox faction – with one group accusing the other of being led by war criminals, and the other of being led by former Gestapo agents.

Even less savoury were the divisions between the Ukrainian émigré groups, who had fled westward with the Nazi retreat. More than half the Ukrainians in the west had settled in the American Zone of Germany, mainly Bavaria. So desperate were competing groups for western money that they cast all other considerations to the wind. One Russian émigré group, known as the Central Association of Post-War Émigrés, actually blew up its own headquarters in Munich and then claimed it was Soviet agents who were responsible, hoping thereby to look more important in the eyes of American intelligence. Another, more significant underground group, called the OUN, or Organization of Ukrainian Nationalists, went even farther, to the point where it deeply compromised the CIC – or so it was supposed to seem.

The OUN was committed to the liberation of the Ukraine from the Soviet Communist yoke and its re-establishment as an independent, non-Communist nation under a right-wing government set up by the leadership of the OUN itself. There were many both inside and outside the Ukrainian independence movement who thought that this was a worthy aim which bestowed honour and legality on the OUN, whatever its background. The OUN stressed the inevitability of war between the Western powers and the USSR and saw this as the perfect opportunity to continue the fight for the liberation of their Ukrainian homeland. As early as the summer of 1946 a CIC intelligence report from Berlin reported that the OUN was using funds allegedly collected from Ukrainian DPs for the purchase of weapons, ammunition and other items necessary to equip and maintain an army.

In fact, there had been an independent Ukrainian government for only three years in the last few centuries, between 1917 and 1920. Moreover, the OUN was actually a thoroughly disreputable organization, and its leader, Stepan Bandera, a notoriously ruthless Fascist. The OUN had a long history of crimes against humanity, starting with the German occupation during World War Two, when the OUN played a significant part in the extermination of the Jews and other 'undesirables', often performing the dirty work of the German Einsatzkommando extermination squads (eg the killing of children), and continuing after the war under American sponsorship.

Though the OUN struck a proudly independent stance, it was totally dependent on outside support, and stooped to many subterfuges to enlist American backing. Its main claim to serious consideration was its alleged contacts with the Ukrainian Insurgent Army, the UPA, an anti-Communist guerrilla force operating in the Soviet Ukraine on the other side of the Iron Curtain. Though the OUN did have some sort of contact with the UPA, it greatly exaggerated both the importance of the UPA and its own role in UPA operations. Photos purporting to show guerrillas in action in the forests of the Ukraine were actually taken in the forests of Bavaria, but the Americans were duly impressed. They were even more impressed when the OUN claimed that the UPA had rigged up a powerful new radio transmitter in the Ukraine and were sending valuable intelligence information which was being picked up by OUN monitors in Munich. When CIC agents were invited to OUN headquarters to hear the broadcasts, they noticed particularly both the clarity of the signal and the value of the information being transmitted. They never guessed that the information was spurious, and that the transmitter, far from broadcasting from the heartland of the Soviet Ukraine, was actually in the apartment next door.

The desperate need to corner the market in dollar backing from American intelligence – the only means by which these expatriate underground groups could survive so far from their natural bases of support at home – was one reason why the OUN resorted to extreme measures. One way of cornering the market was to get rid of rival claimants, and there was no more effective way of getting rid of them than by murdering them. Murder had the extra advantages of eliminating the political opposition, the more moderate anti-Communist groups, and of silencing any rivals who knew the Nazi background of the OUN hierarchy and were thus in a position to denounce them as war criminals liable to automatic arrest, trial and execution, or at the very least as former Soviet citizens subject to forcible repatriation to the Soviet Union. On some occasions, however, the motive for murder sank to the petty level of grudge or the failure to pay protection money to some racketeering camp gang.

At some point after the summer of 1946, therefore, the OUN embarked on a reign of terror amongst their fellow Ukrainians in the American Zone of Germany. The actual killings seem to have been carried out by the secret political police of the OUN, the SB, or Sluzhba Bezpeky, which was modelled on the former Nazi SD. The head of this organization at the time was Mykola Matwiyeko, who disappeared in 1951 while on a secret mission to the Ukraine on behalf of Allied intelligence. Some of Matwiyeko's officers in the SB had themselves worked for the Gestapo in the Ukraine during the war. Today the only man alive who is aware of the full extent of the OUN terror programme is probably Iaroslav Stetsko (or Steczo), who was the Premier of the Ukrainian government formed by the Germans in Lvov in 1941–42, and succeeded Stepan Bandera as head of the OUN when Bandera was killed in Munich in 1959 by a KGB assassin using a cyanide gun. Stetsko now lives in discreet obscurity in Wimbledon, London, not far from the international lawn tennis courts and the local bakery – an ironic location, for it was in a bakery that the worst of the excesses were allegedly carried out by members of the SB in Bavaria during the late 1940s.

According to one report, possibly more than 100 Ukrainians were assassinated in the course of the OUN terror programme, although the exact number has never been made known, and the identities of only a few of the victims were ever revealed. According to an investigation carried out by the left-wing peace magazine *Win* in the mid-1970s, the assassination programme was financed, supervised and condoned by the US Army Counter Intelligence Corps, Naval Intelligence and Air Force Intelligence under the code-name Operation Ohio, and continued into the 1950s with the cognizance of the CIA. Given that the victims were staunch anti-Communists who shared their adversaries' dreams of a free and independent Ukrainian homeland, the killings partake of a more than usually sick and demented quality, especially when the circumstances in which some of them were carried out are taken into account. According to a Russian-born CIA employee who worked at a Displaced Persons camp at Mittenwald in Southern Bavaria – in fact the former training barracks of the German Mountain Infantry – American intelligence at the camp used techniques they had borrowed from the Nazis, and disposed of the corpses of murdered Ukrainian 'undesirables' by burning them in the camp's large bread ovens. After the bodies had been cremated the ovens went back to normal operation and were used to bake the bread for the camp's hungry inmates.

A woman who worked as a secretary for the US authorities at the Mittenwald DP camp also confirmed the killings that took place there. Another informant who witnessed these incidents maintained that the keys to the Mittenwald bread ovens were held by men in US army uniforms, and the OUN murder squads had to apply to the Americans each time they wished to use the ovens. 'Thus the responsibility for the assassinations must rest ultimately with American intelligence,' *Win* concludes, 'first the Army Counter Intelligence Corps, then Naval and Air Force Intelligence and finally, by 1954, the CIA.'

As far as can be ascertained, the OUN's first contact with the CIC took place in 1946 when a member of the SB by the name of Roman Petrenko was directed by the OUN's leadership to establish a liaison with American intelligence. An SB adviser and former Gestapo employee, the Reverend Ivan Grinyokh, who had served as chaplain with the Nazi-OUN Nachtigall battalion in World War Two and been awarded the Iron Cross for his pains, was the instrument of contact with the CIC. However, it was a CIC officer in Rome, Captain Hale, who was responsible for recruiting the Americans' most important agent in the OUN. This was a convicted murderer and graduate of the Gestapo training school in Krakow by the name of Mykola Lebed, who as the Home Secretary and Police Minister in the Nazi puppet administration in Lvov specialized in the mass killing and torturing of Jews, Poles, Communist partisan leaders and rival right-wing Ukrainian nationalists. CIC reports in 1945 and 1946 described Lebed as 'a well known sadist and collaborator of the Germans'. But in 1947 Lebed (who had found refuge in Rome) approached the Rome CIC Detachment offering to trade his intelligence files and personal experience of Soviet matters for American protection. On Captain Hale's recommendation, Lebed was smuggled into Germany, where CIC Region IV in Munich – which was already running Klaus Barbie and Emil Augsburg's network of SS men – took him over.

According to a Munich CIC report, the political standpoint of this Ukrainian terrorist was 'positive ie reliable from the point of view of the Western powers'. In 1949, however, Lebed fell foul of a rival wing of the OUN under Stepan Bandera and with CIA help was smuggled out to the USA, where he continued to work energetically to boost American support for guerrilla warfare in the Ukraine and was even hailed by *Newsweek* magazine as an important underground leader.

CIC official records contain no reference to Operation Ohio or the horrors of Mittenwald – possibly because sensitive records of activities subsequently taken over by the CIA have usually ended up in the closed archives of the CIA itself. Nor have any former CIC agents spoken up about CIC participation in this black episode. The strongest doubt exists as to whether authentic CIC personnel ever took part in the Mittenwald activities. The Ukrainian exiles in general and the OUN in particular were very much the business of Frank Winser's OPC, an organization which was known to use army intelligence cover for its operations, including cover provided by both genuine and dummy CIC units. The fact that Naval and Air Force Intelligence were also involved in the affair at Mittenwald – a small village surrounded by the high peaks of the Bavarian Alps far from a sea or an air base – lends credence to the view that OPC personnel were at work here, as does the statement that the CIA took charge of Operation Ohio in 1954, when OPC had lost its autonomy and was absorbed into the CIA's Directorate of Plans.

Indeed, such documentation as exists indicates that the CIC was as hostile to OPC's Ukrainian Nazis as it was to its Byelorussian ones and kept them both under active surveillance. One CIC agent even managed to photograph eleven volumes of the secret internal files of the OUN, which clearly showed that its members had made a significant contribution to the Nazi war effort by working as policemen, executioners, partisan hunters and officials for the Gestapo and SS and raising several divisions of Ukrainian volunteers for the Waffen-SS. Whatever compromises the CIC may have made in the pursuit of its mission in Germany, it is unlikely that Ohio was one of them.

In any case, it has to be said that there was something decidedly awry as far as the conduct of American intelligence activities in Southern Bavaria were concerned. In many ways this rather remote enclave of the American Zone, bordered to the south by Austria and to the east by Czechoslovakia, seems to have been the very hub of Frank Winser's OPC empire. In Pullach near Munich lay the secret headquarters of the rapidly growing Gehlen Organization, which started up operations against the Russians under the cover of the 7881st CIC Detachment. In Munich itself, where Winser's protégés in the Ukrainian OUN had set up shop, CIC Region IV seemed to all intents and purposes to have taken half the former Munich Gestapo on to their payroll, thereby revealing an apparent fondness for Nazis and Nazism quite at variance with the CIC's normal attitude. In Augsburg, Klaus Barbie's hangout, which one CIC officer described as a CIC 'shambles', the local CIC was administered by a former Gestapo officer in an American uniform, while the 7247th Detachment was probably answerable to the OPC. And then there was Mittenwald.

The OUN had been able to sell itself to the CIC in the early days of the Cold War because it promised that it could eliminate Communist agents in the West. In the hope that the CIC would do the dirty work for them, the OUN then falsely identified their political opponents as Soviet agents. But to their credit the CIC did their own background investigations of the persons named by the OUN. Out of a list supplied by the OUN in July 1946 the CIC found that only 1 per cent of the cases justified further investigation. After that the CIC increasingly distanced itself from the OUN's hustling leadership and eventually pulled out altogether.

Air Force and Naval Intelligence took over and the murder programme continued – until early 1952, when the OUN overdid things by attempting to assassinate the head of the rival Ukrainian Liberation Movement, General Diomid Gulai, who also enjoyed the support of the CIA. The CIA reacted sharply to this indiscreet excess. Assassination was phased out, though American support continued for OUN, in spite of a damning indictment of the organization in an intelligence study, *Soviet Opposition to Stalin*, commissioned by the US Air Force, which condemned the OUN as 'anti-Communist, anti-Russian and, it must be said, anti-democratic'. The study described the OUN's ideology as combining the Nazi colonial *Ostpolitik* of Julius Rosenberg, Hitler's Minister for Eastern Territories, with the fanatical racism of Hitler's and Himmler's *Untermensch* theory.

But so long as the OUN, or any other eastern émigré underground organization, continued to be viewed as a potentially useful tool with which to implement America's major foreign policy objective, that of rolling back Communist gains in Europe, they would continue to enjoy American support, even though they were known to harbour war criminals and mass murderers in their ranks. The covert policy of the Truman administration, according to a top secret National Security Council document (NSC-68, now declassified), was to foment and support unrest and revolt in selected strategic satellite countries by means of covert operations in the fields of economic warfare and political and psychological warfare. The OUN not only claimed it was ready to foment unrest and revolt but boasted that it represented an armed force, the UPA, already at war inside the USSR.

To a limited extent this was possibly true, and some 35,000 persons – Communists, Jews and simple peasants alike – are estimated to have lost their lives as a result of terrorist activities inside the USSR during the late 1940s and early 1950s, most of them in the Ukraine, but some also in Lithuania and Soviet Central Asia. But the dream of rolling back the Iron Curtain proved an illusory one. Though thousands of recruits for the Americans' secret underground army were found among the hordes of homeless, hopeless Byelorussian, Ukrainian, Balt, Russian and Polish refugees in the DP camps, few ever saw any action. But a number of these unfortunate torchbearers of the Western cause, trained by American experts and former Wehrmacht and Waffen-SS instructors in techniques of special operations and espionage work, were indeed parachuted into the Soviet Union from Wisner's planes. Few survived for long. All the émigré groups were riddled by Soviet moles, and the whole American game was in any case reported to the Russians by Kim Philby, a Soviet spy who was the chief of the Soviet section of the British Secret Intelligence Service (MI6) and privy to OPC's operations behind the Iron Curtain. By the early 1950s the plan to overthrow the Communist world from within was exposed as the hollow dream it was. In a sense, the CIC's Nazi hunters had had the last laugh.

Though the impossible dream of destroying the Soviet presence in Europe proved an impractical failure, the mentality that spawned it moved on to greater, and far more extreme and deadly, undercover stratagems elsewhere – most spectacularly in Vietnam (and notoriously in the secret Phoenix assassination programme conducted by US covert operations agents in that country), and later in Central America. Out of the murders of minor double agents and spies at Mittenwald and elsewhere in Germany the CIA developed the concept of assassination, including the assassination of heads of states and other international leaders, as a legitimate political tool, and such techniques of policy implementation as 'scalpel' (the murder of the opposition's infrastructure) and 'bludgeon' (large-scale military operations) – all in the name of the same American security which, back down the line, was the CIC's overriding preoccupation in the early days of the German occupation.

* * *

Though it is to the CIC's credit that they ultimately broke off contact with the murderous OUN, until 1948 they continued to keep a close watch over the Ukrainian leader, Stepan Bandera, in an operation code-named Anyface designed to deny this key figure, the top of the Soviet list of wanted persons, to Soviet agents who might attempt to abduct or assassinate him. The CIC also kept their hand in with a series of anti-Communist operations which arguably crossed the bounds of legality and moved eventually from the sphere of counter intelligence to that of positive intelligence aimed against the Soviets and their allies in Germany and Austria. This anti-Soviet role, which had never been envisaged during the war, began to take shape within a few weeks of VE-Day, when it rapidly became clear that the primary threat against the security of the US Zone of Germany and the rehabilitation of the German nation under American direction came not from dissidents amongst the native populace but from the Soviet Union.

The division of Germany into zones of occupation under the control of the Western Powers and the USSR made it a logical area for intense Soviet subversive activities. The Soviet Zone of East Germany was occupied by the Red Army and soon taken over by the Communist Party, while in the British, French and American Zones of West Germany the KPD (German Communist Party) rapidly established itself as the most active and organized of all the political parties. For the Soviets the KPD was a highly convenient tool for the furtherance of Russian penetration and subversion, since it served as a propaganda machine which could be used for preparing the ground by stirring up dissatisfaction with the existing order of things. To find out more about the ends and means of the KPD, the CIC decided to investigate this organization in a deep-penetration operation code-named Sunrise. During the course of this operation it became clear to the CIC that while the Party was entrusted with the mission of supporting the Soviet objective of destroying the West German government and forcing the withdrawal of Allied forces from Germany, the KPD possessed neither the means nor the potential to accomplish these ends by violence – its most significant potential for violent action was in provoking mass demonstrations and labour unrest.

Early Soviet attempts at actual espionage and subversion in the US Zone were of three kinds. The first involved flooding the area with low-level agents who would each supply a small piece of the overall jig-saw picture of the American Occupation. The second involved the use of legitimate Russian liaison officers (usually working on reparation and repatriation problems in the US Zone) as medium-level intelligence gatherers. The third entailed the infiltration of large numbers of Soviet-indoctrinated agents, mainly DPs and returning POWs, whose aim was to engineer subversion in the US Zone by fomenting unrest and labour troubles and destroying respect for the occupation forces through illegal currency operations, bribery of American personnel, fostering contempt for law and order and the organization of disaffected groups.

The CIC's first major overt operation against Soviet espionage rings was in July 1946. This was Operation Bingo, a swoop operation designed to pick up low-grade agents while leaving the more sensitive Soviet espionage apparatus in place. More than 400 suspect agents were arrested in this Top Secret raid, and though many were released after interrogation without charge, the evidence obtained confirmed the CIC's picture of Soviet espionage techniques, particularly the role of Russian liaison officers in the US Zone, and served notice that the Americans were taking steps to turn back the Soviet flood.

A favourite Soviet technique was the abduction of people wanted for routine questioning from one or other of the Western Zones of Germany and Austria. The practice was particularly prevalent in Berlin, where in the early days of the Occupation armed MVD agents blatantly snatched their victims off the streets in broad daylight. Following a sharp protest from the Americans the MVD modified their procedure and snatched people at night instead. When this also raised an outcry, the Russians sent agents in German police uniform to make the arrests, or tried to lure their targets out of the American sector instead of going in and kidnapping them on the spot.

The Russians were relatively indiscriminate about who they grabbed or their nationality. Allied nationals who happened to stray down the wrong street were just as likely to end up in an MVD cell as anyone else. A German arrested by the Soviets for taking pictures in the Soviet Sector and released after agreeing to work for them as an informant, checked in at the Berlin CIC because he feared abduction and reported that during his incarceration in the MVD cellar at Am Kupfergraben he had seen a small inscription scratched on the cellar wall which bore the poignant message: 'Leslie Golding, 4 Westbury Road, South Church, Southend on Sea, England, Picked up while visiting Marianne Kuenz, Eberswalde [in the Soviet Sector].' Under the inscription were the dates 2.6.47 and 13.10.47. The ultimate fate of this unfortunate Englishman, who seems to have fallen into the Russian security web while surreptitiously visiting a girlfriend in East Berlin, is unknown.

In Austria, where the Russians occupied the eastern part of the country and as one of the four Allied powers enjoyed a strong presence in the capital, Vienna, the situation was particularly troublesome. Agents quickly learnt that the devastation of war and the ensuing occupation did not destroy the espionage nets. New ones sprang up overnight as the occupation forces of four nations and a vast army of displaced persons from many other countries swarmed in. It was an easy matter for a secret agent of a foreign power to slip across the border and lose himself in the throng, and Austria's wild terrain of lakes and mountains offered excellent natural cover if ever the crowds did not. The CIC estimated that two out of every 1000 Austrian civilians were directly or indirectly involved with Soviet-aligned intelligence agencies, and probably much the same was true of Germany. To ferret out Communist suspects the CIC established informant nets within the local community and – perhaps more importantly – throughout the labyrinth of DP camps. By virtue of the Displaced Persons Act the CIC legally controlled these camps and had the power not only to screen the inmates for release and repatriation but to recruit agents and informants from amongst their number for intelligence work on their own side – or interrogate those suspected of working as agents and informants for foreign powers.

For example, a special section of the 430th CIC Detachment in Austria, known as the Displaced Persons Screening Project, utilized a rather oppressive-sounding range of facilities, which included accommodation for the secret solitary confinement of up to 100 detainees at a time, ten cells equipped for the secret monitoring and recording of conversations, and ten private, sound-proof interrogation rooms. This was the background against which incidents such as those at Mittenwald took place, and it is easy to see how operations could get out of hand. As a former Colonel of the 430th CIC confessed: 'In those early days we had some wild ass times in Europe. Now and again a suspected Communist agent would get killed. Things were so tense in those days that it didn't take much, you know.'

The 430th CIC had nothing but trouble from the Russian Repatriation Mission, which had been given permission to operate in the Austrian American Zone, ostensibly to oversee the return of displaced Soviet citizens to the USSR. As in Germany, the Repatriation Mission was a convenient cover for MVD intelligence operations, including kidnapping. One night in January 1946, forewarned of a Russian attempt to kidnap a leading Austrian citizen who was a key counter-espionage agent for the CIC, the 430th laid a trap. When several cars without lights arrived at the CIC employee's home, and a number of men with pistols broke into the house and threatened the

CIC man, American Military Police suddenly switched on a battery of powerful floodlights and moved in to close the trap. Among those arrested were several members of the Soviet Repatriation Mission and Red Army officers, including one wearing the complete uniform of the US Military Police, which had been stolen from the Military Police Battalion in Salzburg. The next day General Mark Clark, the first American High Commissioner for Austria, informed his Soviet counterpart, Marshal Konev, that the Soviet mission was no longer welcome and that Konev's men would be sent back across the line into the Soviet Zone at Linz.

By August 1948 Soviet kidnappings in Austria had reached alarming proportions. In a study analysing the pattern, the CIC concluded:

> Most of the abductions involved persons suspected of espionage or of associations with the United States or other Western intelligence activities. Such kidnappings were the result of Soviet counter intelligence activity, primarily out of considerations of military security. Former German intelligence personnel were added to Western agents on the Soviet wanted lists . . . A special objective of the kidnappings was to destroy networks of Austrian informants employed by CIC. The Russians were relentless in the abduction of their own informants who were believed to have doubled as agents for the West.

Various kidnapping programmes could be identified by the CIC. In May 1947, for example, the Russians began seizing former residents of Soviet satellite countries. In one incident a woman was carried away from her apartment rolled up in a rug. In another a Hungarian repatriation commissioner was hijacked when he was invited to take a lift in a car carrying other Hungarian officials. In a separate programme, the Soviets began abducting Austrian scientists, linguists and other specialists and impressing them into service behind the Iron Curtain. Several students at the University of Vienna were similarly spirited away by Soviet agents. The most spectacular kidnappings involved American personnel. In June 1948 one CIC agent was kidnapped by Soviet counter intelligence, and another was arrested, as was a civilian employee of the Military Intelligence Service. The agent who was kidnapped was guarding an Austrian informant when a Russian snatch team attempted an abduction. This was cut short by the intervention of British Military Police, who arrested one of the Soviet agents along with the CIC agent and took them both off to an Austrian jail. Twenty minutes later a Red Army squad burst into the jail and took the CIC agent and the Soviet agent away by force. But the Soviet agent had left his papers behind and next day these were traded for the CIC agent, who had been so badly beaten up that he had to be hospitalized.

A particular series of kidnappings in the Allied Zones of Austria led to one of the most extensive series of investigations ever carried out by the 430th CIC Detachment. Collectively the operation was known by the code name Snatch Counter-Snatch. The case began in September 1949 when a CIC informant at Linz was reported missing by his wife. Two days later, informants reported that the missing man was being held in the Russian Zone of Vienna. He had been abducted, the informants said, by unidentified persons driving a black 1938 Buick sedan. A little later CIC agents stopped a 1938 Buick in Landstrasse and arrested the three occupants – a man, his mistress and a black marketeer. Under questioning the trio admitted that they had delivered the CIC informant to the Russians in return for the privilege of selling black market cigarettes in the Russian Zone. They went on to explain that they had gone up to the victim in a street in Bad Aussee, hit him on the head with a hammer, thrown him into the back of the Buick, and driven him across the Danube to the village of Uhfar in Russian-controlled territory.

A few weeks later the CIC arrested two men who according to an informant were planning to carry out a similar kidnapping in Salzburg – this time of a Red Army deserter who was then a patient in the Salzburg DP Hospital. The two men told the CIC that they were working for a man in Vienna by the name of Benno Blum, whom they believed to be a Red Army major, though he purported to be a Polish DP and always wore civilian clothes. They alleged that every month Blum employed a network of professional kidnappers to deliver a specified number of people to the Russians in Vienna. In return for this service Blum was given a concession to distribute American cigarettes on the black market. At that time, as in Germany, American (and British) cigarettes were the *de facto* currency of the Austrian economy and Blum was sitting on a fortune. His agents would bulk purchase popular brands of cigarettes in the United States, then send them by air express to Holland or Switzerland. From there the cargo would be despatched by a circuitous route to Hungary, and then taken by Red Army trucks into the Russian Zone of Austria for sale in Austria and Bavaria.

By now well briefed on Blum's plans and methods, the CIC lay in wait for his next kidnap attempt. This time the victim was to be a Rumanian anti-Communist defector, now a CIC informant, who was placed under close surveillance. At the Central Café in Linz, just across the Danube from the Soviet Zone, the Rumanian was approached by a stranger who suggested that they get together, pick up a couple of girls, and do some serious drinking. This proposal so alarmed the poor Rumanian that he leapt up and, startled out of his wits, ran all the way home and bolted the door behind him. With some difficulty his CIC control persuaded him to go ahead with the plan. The next evening the Rumanian's self-appointed companion of the revels returned to the Central Café, but as he was about to depart with the Rumanian in the kidnap car the CIC surveillance team moved in to arrest him. Under interrogation he admitted that he, too, had been hired by Benno Blum.

The net was now closing in on Blum. A little later, acting on a tip-off, CIC and Austrian police arrested two men and a woman at Steyr railway station, near the border of the Russian Zone, just minutes before they were about to abduct another victim designated by Soviet intelligence, a Russian DP by the name of Marjiv. During a search of the two Chevrolets which were to have been the kidnap cars, CIC agents discovered two pistols, a full bottle of cherry brandy heavily laced with chloral hydrate knockout drops, and two sets of Red Army licence plates for getting across the border. Under interrogation at CIC Headquarters the arrested woman – a very good-looking young blond 20-year-old from Berlin by the name of Gisella Sell, who spoke fluent Russian – made a 35-page confession in which she admitted that she had been in the employ of the Russians since the end of the war. She had been the mistress of a Russian Senior Lieutenant, and had continued to work for the Russians even after her lover had returned to Moscow for fear of being exposed to Western intelligence. For kidnapping Marjiv she was to have been rewarded with a fur coat and 5000 Austrian schillings. Her confession implicated a Captain Orlov of the Red Army. It was he who had put the chloral hydrate in the cherry brandy, which was known to be a favourite tipple of the intended target. Needless to say, the whole kidnap plan had been masterminded by Benno Blum, who had accompanied the kidnap team as far as St Valentin and was to have met them there on their return trip.

Because of the co-operation she had given the Americans after her arrest, Gisella Sell's prison sentence was reduced to seven years. Her two companions both got eight. As for Blum, he was arrested by the Russians immediately after the arrest of Fräulein Sell and held for several weeks. On his release he went at once to the apartment of his Austrian girlfriend in the French Zone of Vienna. But his days were now numbered. The Americans wanted Blum and sent two CIC men after him, along with a French agent, since they were in French territory. As they broke through the door of the second-floor apartment, their pistols drawn, Blum scrambled out through a back window. The agents grappled with him and pulled him back inside. Fighting desperately to resist arrest, Blum pulled out a knife and tried to wrest a pistol from one of the agents. He almost succeeded, but the agent managed to place his thumb between the hammer and the firing pin and kept Blum from shooting. As Blum rampaged round the room in a life and death struggle to resist arrest, the other CIC agent and the Frenchman took aim and fired. Blum fell, mortally wounded and bleeding copiously. He died in hospital a short while later. The Russians denied any knowledge of Blum or his activities and his body was unclaimed.

CIC reports from the Snatch Counter-Snatch operation are littered with the personality profiles of the vast flotsam of individuals who were involved with the case or swam into their ken – Russian intelligence officers, Jewish and East European DPs, Austrian and German smugglers and kidnappers, mistresses and molls, gangsters and gunmen, a whole gallery of human types bobbing about in the wake of those two great cataclysms of the twentieth century, the Bolshevik and National Socialist revolutions. For interest's sake, here are a few of the waifs and strays – specifically the MVD men and their aides and victims – who make their brief entrances and alarums in the files of the 430th CIC Detachment:

60-year-old Semyen Chorny, his 55-year-old wife and their daughter Maria, Ukrainian nationals who were sent to Vienna by the Nazis as forced labourers in 1943, arrested by the Russians in 1949, sentenced to 25 years' hard labour for 'treasonable activity' and transferred to an unknown destination on 25 July 1949.

Nikolai Ageev, a Soviet national, mongoloid type, dressed in a grey suit, grey hat, white shirt; sickly, possibly tuberculous, and on the verge of death. Kidnapped by the Blum gang at Linz, confined in Cell 5, the so-called horror cell of the GPU Headquarters confidential prison situated in the basement of the former Spanish Legation in Ploesslgasse, Vienna IV.

Christine Weiss, 24-year-old Hungarian Jewess, apprehended by the Russians as an American espionage agent in March 1949. Subsequent disposition 'unknown'.

Josef Wocilka, 36-year-old Austrian clerk, and a communist involved with Soviet intelligence abduction operations, arrested by the CIC in Vienna in 1949 in possession of two sub-machine guns and six pistols. Fought with the International Brigade in the Spanish Civil War. Imprisoned in Dachau concentration camp during the war, where he was once lashed with 25 double whip lashes and hanged on a tree for two hours as a punishment for escaping. 'His ardent communist nature overshadows all of his statements and remarks. Although he is fully aware that, due to Soviet weapons and uniforms having been found in his apartment, he will probably receive a rather stiff prison sentence, subject laughingly chalks the entire matter up to fate.'

Lieutenant Colonel Karandashov, alias Vasylovsky, alias Shidarov, of Central Soviet Kommandatura in Vienna. Age 38 but looks 50. Frail and thin, with small bones, dark blue civilian suit, wedding ring and gold 'Patek' wrist watch. Speaks educated Russian with Moscow dialect. Has coarse manners, spits a great deal, smokes constantly, speaks very slowly.

Major General at Baden, allegedly Chief of MGB Austria. Aged 55, 5′4″ tall, head shaved completely bald, whitish eyebrows, green uniform with two large stars on shoulder boards, speaks a cultured kind of Russian.

Major Victor, Soviet intelligence officer. A slender, bald, deep-voiced 50-year-old, extremely intelligent and shrewd and a fanatical hard worker, but lacking in physical courage – 'goes for his gun at the slightest provocation; extremely nervous and suspicious.'

Captain Orlov, the Soviet agent of RIS [Russian Intelligence Services] who ran Benno Blum's kidnapping operations. 40-ish, fat, short neck, very bald, heavy jowls, red cheeks, plump hands, egg-shaped bulge on back of head, a brutal, fanatic communist who waddles when he walks. His hobby is hunting and he owns a large German Shepherd dog. He is a very hearty eater and drinker, consuming large quantities of vodka every day. May be contacted at the Soviet Central Kommandatura on extension 153 between 0800 and 1400 hours and again between 2000 and 2400 hours. He resides with his wife Nina in an apartment in Vienna owned by an old woman, phone number U-41506.

Of such stuff are spy romances woven. 'The CIC has more adventure stories buried in its secret files,' wrote a *New York Herald Tribune* reporter in 1947, 'than a month's output of blood and thunder comic books.' But there was rarely anything remotely comic about the CIC's operations during those bleak, dour Cold War days in war-shattered Germany and Austria, where the Russian Intelligence Services occupied the high ground, and just who was doing what was never entirely clear, nor was ever meant to be. Deeply enmeshed with other more clandestine and sinister American agencies, the CIC no doubt did its best in the cause of Western freedom and democracy, as far as it was perceived at that time. If in the process certain principles of honour and justice were compromised, it could be argued that the end probably justified the means. The problem is that in this murky world of mirrors and shadows it was never perfectly plain what that end might be, still less whether it was ever achievable or achieved. As for the means, certain questions may remain for ever obscure. Was the CIC the bed-partner of the CIA, for example, or merely a lady-in-waiting? To what extent was the CIA a kind of succubus, an alien smuggled on board the starship *Enterprise*, so to speak, which suborned the CIC to its cause, or even absorbed it into its ranks? In what degree, if any, was the CIC the CIA?

It is with a slight sense of relief, perhaps, that one turns away from the CIC's mysterious struggle in this grim cockpit of Europe to the faintly fresher air of other arenas in other lands and to the more clear-cut issues and more straightforward roles of a new fighting war in distant Korea.

EPILOGUE

During World War Two the United States had raised a gigantic armed force amounting to some 12 million men and women. After the defeat of Germany in May 1945 and the surrender of Japan three months later, most of this prodigious band of warriors began to return home to civilian life, and by 1947, barely two years after the end of the fighting, only 10 per cent were left under arms, of whom less than 700,000 were serving in the Army.

Many of the soldiers who stayed on in the military did so as occupiers of their country's defeated enemies, taking possession of America's zones of occupation in Germany and Austria, and the whole of Japan and South Korea, a former Japanese dependency. Here, as old enemies were replaced by new ones, intelligence and counter intelligence duties soon proved to be as grave and urgent a matter as they had been during the war. The presence of American troops abroad after VJ-Day had always been expected to be temporary. Most Americans believed that the United Nations Organization founded by the victorious Allies would guarantee a stable and peaceful world. But it rapidly became clear that Russia under Stalin was bent on policies at total variance with the interests of the United States and her Allies. The Soviets suppressed democratic liberties in every country they occupied and through the medium of the Soviet-controlled Communist Parties attempted to subvert the free nations of the West. In the Cold War that now broke out, the CIC were at the sharp end of the intelligence conflict. Though army intelligence was severely hit by the loss of personnel carefully trained in skills that were difficult to replace, the CIC still managed to field a peak strength of over 3000 officers and men in US-occupied Germany, and a 1000-man detachment in Japan.

For a while there was even a CIC presence in China. Communist plans to continue the war until their own objectives were won had long been known to Americans in China. But the flood of Soviet agents intent on learning everything possible about US forces and intentions in that country had scarcely been anticipated. Investigation of pro-Communist employees infiltrating into US installations ranked in importance with the hunt for Japanese war criminals and collaborators. Well before the end of 1945, CIC in China was daily encountering incidents and reliable information to prove that the Soviets were playing for high stakes. In their unremitting efforts to eradicate any traces of American influence in China, the Russians were leaving few stones unturned. The 415th CIC Detachment reported that on 8 July 1946 a group of pro-Russian journalists met at the Soviet Club in Shanghai to discuss means by which political news could be obtained or suppressed. A Soviet expert in press control was charged with the mission of setting up a centralized procedure for the control of all news. News releases under a Soviet-controlled press were to stress the failure of the Americans to support Chinese people and interests in Indo-China and emphasize the toll of Chinese dead and wounded as a consequence of American aid to Chiang Kai-shek's Nationalists.

The CIC presence in China after the end of the Japanese war was clearly finite. In September 1946 the 415th CIC was officially deactivated. In a report to the Director of Intelligence, the head of the remaining CIC personnel explained: 'Due to the requirement of General Marshall that no intelligence work be done within the American Forces in China, the identification of the CIC was changed to Security Control Section and no positive intelligence or counter intelligence work is done where Chinese Forces are concerned.'

From April 1947 the CIC detachment was slowly closed down, while assisting the orderly evacuation of American civilians from trouble spots as the Communists continued their advance. In January 1949, when it became evident that all of the Chinese mainland would soon fall to the Communists, the last few CIC agents departed. Thus ended CIC's sojourn in China.

In spite of the mounting international tension in Asia and Europe, and the overt threat to American interests of increasing Communist power in the post-war world, there seemed little inclination on the part of an economy-minded Secretary of Defense to strengthen America's defences. So when a Soviet proxy embarked on an aggressive adventure, and a real war between the Communist and non-Communist powers broke out in the summer of 1950, the American Army and military intelligence were again caught unprepared, just as they had been in 1941.

The Korean War began in June 1950 when North Korean tanks crossed the 38th parallel that served as a frontier between Communist North and democratic South Korea. It ended in stalemate three years later when an armistice finally stilled the guns. The Communist invasion took the Americans completely by surprise. But the US response when it came was swift and positive. Acting under UN mandate, General MacArthur, the victorious commander of American and Allied forces in the Pacific in World War Two, found himself once again commander of American and Allied troops in yet another major conflict. Initially deploying American occupation troops from Japan to support the hard-pressed South Korean army, MacArthur was soon locked in a highly dynamic but costly campaign against North Korean forces supported in massive strength by Chinese troops, and as the fighting swept up and down the length and breadth of the peninsula there were times when UN forces were within a whisker of both total victory and total defeat.

In a sense the Korean War was a third world war fought in one country: total war fought out on China's frontier. On the Communist side were a North Korean army equipped with Soviet tanks, a Chinese Army of one million men, and a Chinese Air Force of 1500 Soviet MiG jets. On the United Nations side were a South Korean army of half a million men; up to nine American divisions; a British Commonwealth Division of troops from Britain, Australia, Canada and New Zealand; a UN Division of troops from 17 other nations, including France, Belgium, Sweden, Greece, Turkey, Thailand, the Philippines, India and South Africa; more than 2000 warplanes of the US Air Force; and the warships and aircraft carriers of the American and British Navies. To the student of the technique of twentieth-century war, the conflict offered extremes of old and new. On the ground the war was fought at times in the manner of the Western Front in World War One, with trench war along fixed fronts and massed infantry attacks in waves. But in the air the Korean War saw the first jet fighter duels in history; and it was only with difficulty, and at the cost of his own command, that MacArthur was restrained from dropping on China the third atom bomb ever aimed at a human target. By the end, three million lay dead, and another two million wounded; and North and South Korea remained as divided as ever, along the same old 38th parallel.

Swept up in this far-ranging violence was the CIC. The new war posed prodigious problems for US Army intelligence. Peacetime cutbacks and austerity had badly hit military intelligence, as it had the rest of the American Army. The general lack of funding and personnel was as acutely felt by the CIC as any other organization, and when the Korean War began there were no CIC detachments on attachment to the Eighth Army, then on occupation duty in Japan. And though scratch divisional detachments to accompany the Eighth

Army when it embarked for Korea were hastily rustled up from the ranks of a 1000-strong 441st CIC Detachment, the occupation detachment in Japan, they could hardly be described as ready for war. There were by then few veteran agents with combat experience, equipment was sparse, and no one had much idea of how to set about their task in the confusion of a highly fluid war.

One serious handicap was the lack of trained linguists. Few Americans spoke Chinese or Korean, and few of the handful that did could be expected to function efficiently in combat conditions. Trustworthy local civilian interpreters were one solution to the problem. Soon regular divisional detachments were brought into being, 17-man CIC teams which were to perform sterling work in screening the rear areas of their divisions against sabotage, espionage and subversion by an enemy who, operating inside his own country, infiltrated literally everywhere. At the same time, other CIC detachments were assigned in support of Eighth Army and the three Corps operating in Korea. The CIC was thus back in business, and many agents from the last war were rudely recalled from civilian life for another stint of comfortless and dangerous, but vital, duty in the present one.

This is not the place to give a detailed description of CIC's involvement in the Korean War. Nor is it clear that such an account can yet be written, given the paucity of available declassified documentary material. But certain major operations stand out. In the first year of violently fluctuating fortunes, with its routes, retreats and reversals, the war found CIC agents deep in the unexplored, unexploited Korean countryside all the way up to the Yalu River and the Chinese border. It found them screening hundreds of thousands of refugees to weed out Communist infiltrators as they followed the fortunes of war north, south and north again. It found them keeping tabs on 30,000 guerrillas in the Chiri-San hills, where – according to a CIC report – 'penetration of the bands was virtually impossible and amounted to a suicide assignment.' It found them involved in major secret operations, with codenames like Salamander, Big and Little Switch, and Indianhead (the CIC task force for the counter intelligence reduction of the North Korean capital of Pyongyang after its capture by UN forces).

The Korean War was the last foreign conflict in which the CIC took part in any recognizable form under its own name. Successive innovations in the structure of American military intelligence brought about a gradual change in the CIC's individual identity and autonomy throughout the 1950s and 1960s, culminating in its final demise in the early 1970s, at a time when the war in Vietnam and the popular anti-war protests in the United States were reaching their climax. In 1955 the function of positive intelligence gathering was transferred from the CIC, which had been carrying it out on an *ad hoc* basis ever since the OSS was dissolved at the end of World War Two, to the new discipline of field operations intelligence. In 1957 certain counter intelligence personnel were integrated with positive intelligence collectors in new, single, multi-discipline intelligence units to support the tactical commanders. In 1961 the CIC was formally merged with field operations intelligence to form a consolidated organization which was renamed the US Army Intelligence Corps, though it was still the CIC in all but name.

By this time America was beginning to face difficult times at home. The 1960s were a decade of unrest in America, when waves of riots and demonstrations swept the country. When the local authorities could not keep the peace in the inner cities and university campuses, where the disturbances were most acute, the Regular Army was brought in to contain the civil protests – and with the Army came Army Intelligence. Normally the FBI was responsible for counter intelligence investigations of civilians in the United States. However, as the domestic situation progressively deteriorated, national authorities and Army commanders found the domestic intelligence provided by the FBI inadequate, and in 1966, after particularly severe riots in Watts, a suburb of Los Angeles, the Army moved in its own counter intelligence agents to begin the collection of domestic intelligence in likely trouble spots around the USA. These agents, direct linear successors of their predecessors in the CIC, operated under the newly established US Army Intelligence Command, which took over centralized control of the Army counter intelligence groups in the USA, replacing the CIC's successor, the Intelligence Corps. Though the name of the Corps thus passed into history, the mission of military counter intelligence continued much as before.

Controlled from the operations room at Fort Holabird, the former wartime and post-war CIC training headquarters in Maryland, Army counter intelligence agents became deeply involved in the Army's efforts to contain the near chaotic conditions existing in the inner cities and campuses of America as popular feeling against the Vietnam War intensified. In carrying out this difficult mission the Army CI gained unprecedented renown within the national intelligence community, as well as federal and state law enforcement agencies. At the height of the civil disturbances, a CI agent could get a report from the street to Fort Holabird in 20 minutes from practically any city in the United States, and seconds later the report was in the Operations Center in a lower basement of the Pentagon in Washington. But at the same time, this activity was to earn considerable popular opprobrium and inflict serious, virtually fatal injury on Army counter intelligence; for when the extent of military involvement in domestic surveillance in the United States became known, it left the Army open to charges of 'spying on civilians' and led to bitter public outcry and political condemnation.

The death knell for Army CI began to toll in 1970, when a former Army captain, who had served for a time as a law instructor at the Army Intelligence School at Fort Holabird, published an article in which he revealed to the public for the first time the extent of the domestic activities of the Army Intelligence Command. The former captain was a law school graduate and a PhD candidate aspiring to become a professor of American government. He had never spent any time as a CI agent, nor taken part in any investigation or served in any operational position in any intelligence unit. But he expressed his conclusion that 'Army surveillance was not only improper from a constitutional perspective, but was wrong and unnecessary and dangerous for the Army.' Since the article appeared to contain a number of inaccuracies, it was not initially taken very seriously by Army counter intelligence officials or the Pentagon.

But hostility to the military now coloured the mood of the nation. Soon after the article appeared, several Senators spoke out in shocked tones and the influential Senator J. William Fulbright had it read into the *Congressional Record* as if it were a fair reflection of the facts. Some of the news media now joined in the fervour and accepted the original article at its face value, again without checking its veracity. A furore now erupted. Members of the Senate Sub-Committee on Constitutional Rights praised the 'fearless patriotism' of the article's author and referred in insulting terms to the Defense Department representatives. The one lone voice on the Committee who tried to place the case in proper perspective was largely ignored by the news media. Little was said of the Army's constitutional obligation to protect the United States and restore domestic order when so directed by the President. The report of the hearings, published by the *Indiana Law Journal*, spoke of the 'horrors' of having civilians investigated by Army personnel and made no mention of what those civilians were doing that had triggered their investigation in the first place. 'Perhaps no other activity of government poses such a threat to individual liberties as the use of the military for domestic programs. The country can no longer afford to permit any governmental agency to conduct domestic intelligence in a secret and uncontrolled fashion.'

Perhaps a hint of something wrong in the CIC approach and attitude to their business had been foreshadowed a generation previously, when military government critics in American-occupied Korea had complained that CIC enjoyed excessive police power in Korea, employed 'police state methods', exercised 'unlimited powers of arrest, search and seizure', and conducted operations that were 'high, wide and handsome'. Perhaps after all certain checks and balances were necessary in their conduct of civilian surveillances in the democratic USA, since the nation was not, as far as could be perceived, under military occupation. Counter intelligence spokesmen were to complain that the domestic intelligence programme of the late 1960s was not conducted in a 'secret and uncontrolled fashion' but with full constitutional authority and with the knowledge and approval of President Nixon, the Secretaries of Defense, Army, Navy and Air Force, the Joint Chiefs of Staff, the Directors of the FBI and the CIA, and most of the national, state and local law enforcement agencies. The fact remained, however, that in a liberal democracy the intervention of the military in internal political affairs would always be a cause of concern, whatever the justification.

Thus the domestic intelligence programme ended abruptly amid a plethora of lawsuits and press recrimination. Military intelligence suffered a major setback in public esteem and Army counter intelligence and its operational parent, the Army Intelligence Command, were stripped of most of their CI functions. The CIC, or its progeny, had ceased to exist as a unique and separate organization. What President Roosevelt had attempted to do in 1944, when he banished the CIC as a separate entity in the USA, was finally achieved some 30 years later. The Army was thus weaker and less secure than at any time since the beginning of World War Two.

'Even if the decision were carefully made,' wrote CIC historian Ann Bray, who had served 15 years as an agent of the CIC in the USA, Germany and Japan, and as one of her last assignments in the Army had served with the survey team which gathered the data that led to the establishment of the Army Intelligence Command, 'there seems no reasonable logical explanation for the dismantling of an organization that was serving the Army in a proven, highly effective manner, and against which no valid criticism of integrity, efficiency, loyalty and need could be leveled.'

Lieutenant Colonel Arthur S. Hurlburt, whom we have quoted at length in other parts of this book, served in CIC in the South West Pacific Theatre from Australia to Tokyo, was recalled to active duty again in the Korean War, and later taught at the US Army Intelligence School at Fort Holabird. Looking back on those years of CIC's struggle and achievement and final eclipse, he recently wrote in the Anglo-American review, *Intelligence Quarterly*:

> Is abuse inherent in such a free-wheeling group [as CIC]? Does it need the controls and the counter-balance of a constant review and direction from outside its own ranks? In our goal to clean house did we go so far as to throw the baby out with the bath water? Should we now reconstitute what we once had in the military, an organization whose primary tasks were to constantly *think* about what makes the people around them tick, constantly to *explore* the possibilities and recommend to the commander courses of action which would preserve and protect the command and project its combat power? Sitting on the sidelines and observing such incidents as the Marine barracks explosion in Beirut and various acts of terrorism around Europe all lead us to the tragic conclusion that we really did throw the baby out with the bath water.
>
> The honest conclusion is that we must put some of these things back in their former working order. In future we may not have the luxury of time we once enjoyed.

For many years the statue of a sphinx stood in front of the CIC headquarters at Fort Holabird, Maryland. The sphinx, a mythological creature with a lion's body and a woman's head, symbolizing the combination of wisdom and strength, had been the heraldic symbol of American military intelligence since the 1920s. Today this inscrutable creature maintains a constant vigil at the US Army Intelligence Center and School at Fort Huachuca – an informal memorial to the 25,000 men of America's secret army, the almost anonymous protectors of America's military might in three momentous conflicts of arms, the discreet, rarely honoured upholders of those democratic liberties most of us take for granted, of which upholding Arthur Hurlburt was to write in an epistle to his little granddaughter: 'We, you and I, know it or not, and like it or not, were and are the beneficiaries.'

If the CIC exists no more, it lives on enduringly in the memory of that dwindling band of men who were privileged to serve in it. Relatively few of them appear by name in this book. Let two of those who do have the last word. Colonel Earl S. Browning, CIC veteran of Iceland, the campaign in France and the Bulge, and the occupation of defeated Germany, wrote to us: 'After more than 30 years of military service I would say that CIC people in the aggregate were the ablest and most interesting of all the categories I ever encountered.'

And another veteran of World War Two in Europe had this to say, forty-five years on:

'As I look back on the exciting episodes which we experienced, I can truthfully say that having had the opportunity to serve my country in such a unique and interesting way was a privilege and an honour – an adventure I will always cherish.'

APPENDIX

FROM: E. S. Browning   15 June 1988
Virginia

TO: Ian Sayer
Dear Mr Sayer: Here finally is my version of the Barbie affair. I am sorry it
took so long, but I wanted to study the record carefully and be sure that
every statement is documented and every argument supported, by the
documents and other materials in the Ryan report.

I hope that this is helpful, even at this late date.

Best regards,

Earl S. Browning Jr.

MY INVOLVEMENT WITH KLAUS BARBIE

By Earl S. Browning Jr (Col., USA (Ret.))

When the 970th CIC Detachment first became aware of Klaus Barbie,
we knew him only as a former SS captain who had served with the
Gestapo in France and had managed to evade processing as an automatic
arrestee. He had none of the notoriety which has since been attached to
him and the expression 'Butcher of Lyons' had not yet been coined.
Indeed, Allan Ryan [Office of Special Investigation investigator] has
noted that this term never appeared in any of the materials examined by
him in his investigation of the Barbie case for the US Justice Department.

I and most of the headquarters operations staff strongly and steadfastly
opposed the use of Barbie as an informant. This was not necessarily
because we were more virtuous or had better judgment than the agents in
the field who pressed to use him. It was mainly because we had had more
wartime intelligence experience, were more aware of how the Gestapo
had operated and, never having laid eyes on the man or been influenced
by his personality, were more hard-headed in our appraisal of him. We
opposed giving informant status to Gestapo personnel as a matter of
general principle and also it seemed obvious to us that Barbie's wartime
service in France had not given him the background or special knowledge
that would make him a valuable source of information in post-war

374 Americas Secret Army

Germany. Nobody questioned that he was an able and clever individual – this was characteristic of most Gestapo captains – but this seemed to us to be more of a liability than an asset.

To clarify our terminology, we used the title 'Informant' to designate paid, vetted and regularly used sources of information. Other sources of information were simply termed 'Sources'. 'Agent' was used only to identify our own CIC personnel.

Barbie's home was in Trier, in the French zone of occupation, but after the war he had established an identity as Klaus Becker and a residence in Marburg, US zone of occupation. There, at the end of August 1946, he was fingered by a German woman who had worked with him in the SS at the end of the war. He was arrested on the street and was being transported to the Marburg CIC office for interrogation when he leaped from the jeep and managed to escape. The arresting CIC officer was driving the jeep and had no back-up. He fired his pistol at Barbie but only nicked him on a finger. At that time I was the commander of the CIC Region in Bremen. In due course I was notified by CIC headquarters that this automatic arrestee had escaped from the CIC in Marburg and should be arrested if he turned up in our area. He never did, but there were only a few automatic arrestees at large anywhere so my people kept a close watch and Barbie's name was now registered in my mind.

Barbie, who was then helping to organize a clandestine association of former SS officers, reappeared in Hamburg in early November 1946. There, with two associates, he was apprehended by a British intelligence captain who, according to Barbie, said to him: 'Well, my dear friend, we are not Americans. You are not going to run away from *us*.' Nevertheless, though locked in separate cells, Barbie and his two companions managed to escape within three days.

CIC had already become aware of this clandestine association and had penetrated it with one of its German-speaking agents. Since some of the members were in the British zone, British intelligence had been brought into the picture. There was no activity or membership in the Bremen area, however, so I was not then aware of the case although I did know the penetration agent, who had stopped to visit with me on a couple of occasions when his travels took him through Bremen. By January 1947, Klaus Becker and Klaus Barbie had been determined to be the same person. In February it was decided to conduct a swoop operation, in conjunction with the British, to arrest, interrogate and bring to trial all the known members of this illegal association. This swoop operation was given the code name 'Selection Board'. Barbie was still on the run and no new address was known for him. It was decided not to raid his last known address in Marburg in order to protect a source of information who was living at that address, but Barbie himself remained a target as one of the leading members of the association. The arrest order stated that, if found anywhere, his arrest was 'especially desired'.

On 1 February 1947 I was transferred to the headquarters in Frankfurt to replace Lieutenant Colonel Dale M. Garvey as Detachment Operations

Officer. During the month of February I was understudying him while being briefed on current operations, including Selection Board. Being senior to me, Colonel Garvey retained the title of Operations Officer and I did not assume it until he left the headquarters around 1 March to become commander of Region IV (Munich).

When the swoop took effect during the early morning hours of 23 February, Barbie was actually sleeping at the home of another target in Kassel. He would have been arrested then and there had he been discovered and identified, but he realized what was happening, slipped out of a window and managed to make still another escape.

Throughout March, April and May, both Region III (Bad Nauheim) and Region I (Stuttgart) were actively searching for Barbie. Region I even passed leads to Region IV with the reminder that Barbie's arrest was still desired by headquarters. Region III finally decided to raid Barbie's last known address in Marburg and interrogated the other residents as to his whereabouts. Surveillance of the house was maintained after the raid.

In the meantime, Barbie had a chance meeting with a wartime SS friend, Kurt Merk, who was working as an informant for the CIC in Memmingen. Merk recommended Barbie to his handler, Special Agent Robert S. Taylor, who recognized Barbie as an important Selection Board target and therefore obtained Colonel Garvey's personal approval to recruit him. Nothing was said to anyone outside Region IV about Barbie's new whereabouts and status until 3 June when the Selection Board case officer at headquarters raised questions as to the source of information that had been submitted about British recruitment of Selection Board personalities as informants. Taylor then acknowledged Barbie as the source and, because of the outstanding order for Barbie's arrest, requested that Barbie be allowed to remain free as a CIC informant. The Region IV operations officer transmitted this information to headquarters with a concurrence in the request and a further request for confirmation from the British of Barbie's report that they had recruited Selection Board personalities.

Allan Ryan states in his report on Barbie that there is no indication of any action being taken on this correspondence and he concludes that it was simply ignored. My own belief is that the correspondence was inadvertently sent to file during a prolonged absence of the case officer. There is no question that some action should have been taken about Barbie, that the O & G report should have been updated and that the other Regions should have been notified to call off their search.

At this point it is necessary to mention some of the changes that had been made in operational procedures since I had become the detachment operations officer. First of all, I had brought in Captain James Ratliff, the deputy commander of Region III, to be my deputy. Then I had brought in Joseph Vidal, a civilian special agent who had been a CIC officer in the United Kingdom, North Africa, Italy, France and Germany during World War II and who had also been a key member of my staff in Region IX, to head a new 'Technical Specialist' activity that would improve and centralize the control of all CIC informants. Also, while carrying on normal operations, Ratliff, Vidal, Major George Wilson (who had served with CIC in the China-Burma-India theater and was then chief of the case section), and I put our heads together and prepared a detailed SOP (standard operating procedure) that was to be binding on CIC operational personnel at all levels. Simultaneously, the case officers put together a new top secret document, called the Orientation and Guidance Report, that summarized the status of all on-going operations and areas of intelligence interest, listing the Essential Elements of Information (EEIs) needed for each. This was continually updated on a monthly basis.

The Technical Specialist System, the SOP and the O & G Report were all management tools intended to effect greater control, to educate field personnel, to avoid duplication of effort, and to expedite the dissemination of basic information and requirements to all agents in the field. The SOP and O & G report did not go to agents individually but to all offices that were sufficiently secure to protect them, where they were made required reading for the agents. I felt that these new management tools were necessary because the volume and variety of our work were steadily increasing while the quality and experience of our personnel were constantly being eroded by turnover. During the war, CIC had its pick of lawyers, journalists, scholars, investigators and linguists who were mature, well-traveled and skilled in their specialties. At that time, there were only a few of these people left and while CIC still had its pick of the available personnel, the best we could hope for was bright young college graduates and mature Army veterans whose military experience was mostly unrelated to intelligence work. Accordingly, we felt it essential for continued success that we subject our personnel to rigorous standards while pointing their way and providing them with as much guidance and information support as possible.

We were all acutely aware of the need for additional training. All new agents had graduated from the basic course at the CIC school at Fort Holabird, Maryland, and many officers were sent for additional schooling at the European Command Intelligence School at Oberammergau. But this was hardly enough. Major George Sheldon, commander of Region VI (Bamberg), was the first to establish his own regional school and, after I became operations officer, I set up a training section in my office. Headed by Lieutenant Richard B. Snyder, who had been commandant of the Region VI school, its mission was to elevate and systematize training standards throughout the detachment.

The SOP and the O & G report were issued within a week or two. The technical specialist and the training efforts necessarily took longer. First we had to overcome the strong resistance of the regions to the technical specialist concept and the natural reluctance of the agents to allow such extensive control over their informant relationships. Then we had to get each region to divert one its best people to perform the technical specialist function. Then, at each level, began the process of identifying,

vetting and forwarding the names of those informants considered to be
worth keeping. After final approval at the headquarters, informants were
registered with both actual names and coded designations, thenceforth
to be referred to in routine reports only by code number.

Now, to return to Barbie's new status, I personally became aware of it
when my deputy, Jim Ratliff, came to me in a very emotional state and
accused Colonel Garvey of double dealing – of having ordered the
continuing search for Barbie while he was operations officer and then, as
a regional commander, hiding him away as special informant. This is one
of my most vivid memories because Ratliff and I both had then, and still
do to this day, the highest regard for Colonel Garvey and his performance of duty as operations officer. This memory was reinforced by my
own search for Barbie after his escape from the CIC in Marburg and then
subsequently refreshed by news reports that the French were still looking
for him and that he was thought to be in South America.

The documents appended to Ryan's report show only that Colonel
Garvey sent a letter to headquarters on 17 October 1947, referencing
Operation Selection Board, reporting that Barbie had been furnishing
information to a Region IV informant who knew Barbie's location, and
requesting instructions as to the disposition to be made of him. Nothing
was mentioned about Barbie's own status as an informant, which indicates that he had not yet been cleared by Vidal as headquarters technical
specialist. My own recollection is that it was this request for headquarters
technical specialist approval that Ratliff brought to me. In any case there
probably was informal communication between Colonel Garvey's
people and my people that precipitated his letter.

My response, after clearance with my commander (then Colonel
Inskeep), with the EUCOM Intelligence Division and with the European Command Intelligence Center (a separate intelligence entity that
was also under the control of the Intelligence Division), was to order on
29 October that Barbie 'be apprehended and remanded to ECIC for
detailed interrogation.'

This order was strongly resisted by Region IV, both before and after
Colonel Garvey completed his European tour and turned over command
to Lieutenant Colonel Ellington D. Golden. My orders were very rarely
protested by regional commanders, because of their presumed approval
by the detachment commander, but when they *were* protested, over the
signature of the regional commander, protocol required that they be
immediately brought to the detachment commander for decision. In the
only other case that I can recall of a regional commander's protest, that
commander was the next ranking officer and assumed temporary command of the detachment during the emergency absence of the regular
commander. He then had to pass judgment on his own protest. We all
got a chuckle from the fact that he had signed the protest as regional
commander and then over-rode his own protest as detachment commander. In the Barbie case, Colonel Inskeep over-rode the protest signed
by Colonel Golden, though the new order was signed by me. Issued on 1

December, it demanded that Barbie 'be immediately transferred to 7907 ECIC under the provisions' of the previous order.

Barbie was a prisoner at the ECIC from 12 December 1947 until the middle of May 1948. ECIC issued five lengthy interrogation reports detailing his history with Nazi organizations from becoming a Jungvolk-führer in the Hitler Jugend in 1933 until the disintegration of Army Group B on 18 April 1945, and also describing his post-war activities including his work for CIC. On 10 May 1948 ECIC recommended to the Operations Branch of G-2 Division, USFET (new name of Intelligence Division, EUCOM) that Barbie be returned to civilian status because, in their judgment, he was of no further counter intelligence interest. This letter followed a pre-printed format which allowed for alternative dispositions (internment camp, PW camp, or other disposition to be stated). This letter seems especially significant to me because it shows that G-2 Division, USFET, was aware of Barbie's interrogation and had to have approved his return to civilian status.

Region IV naturally wanted Barbie back as an informant. We in the operations office at headquarters opposed it but Colonel David G. Erskine, who had succeeded Colonel Inskeep, decided to allow it under controlled conditions and for specified periods of time, renewable only by explicit approval from headquarters. Colonel Erskine was normally an extremely cautious man whose habitual response to any new proposal was 'Will it hurt us?' In this case, however, he seemed to feel that the ECIC had cleansed Barbie of any former sins and that he should not arbitrarily deprive a subordinate commander of an important resource for carrying out his mission. This is a normal attitude for any US commander on almost any occasion.

So Barbie again became an informant for Region IV. While giving periodic approvals for his continued use, my office was constantly questioning Barbie's value and trying to persuade Region IV to drop him. In fact, some writers have even said I was ambivalent toward Barbie because I only suggested that he be dropped and did not order that it be done. The explanation, of course, is that my hands were tied by Colonel Erskine's decision and that persuasion was the only method open to me.

Finally we were able to get the leverage we needed, in the form of a clipping from the 14 May 1949 issue of a Paris newspaper which said that 'the war veterans and the victims of Nazism have just addressed a letter to the Ambassador of the United States in Paris demanding the immediate arrest of Barbie and trial before the military tribunal of the 8th Region.' Barbie was said to be living as a 'peaceable businessman in Munich' in spite of having used an acetylene torch to make his victims confess and of being 'responsible for the tragic days of Easter 1944, when the region of Saint Claude was literally terrorized.'

I took this immediately to my commander and he was sufficiently shocked to withdraw his approval of Barbie's use as an informant. On 24 May 1949 the order went out, over my name, that Barbie be dropped administratively as an informant but that relations be maintained as in the past until final disposition instructions were issued by the State Department and/or Department of the Army. The regional commander (now a different commander and a different region because of a detachment reorganization to eliminate sub-regions as an echelon of command) confirmed his compliance with this order on 20 July 1949 but defended Barbie as 'the most reliable informant this headquarters has' in spite of having 'frequently been criticized by case officers of Group Headquarters.' (The 970th CIC Detachment had by then been redesignated as the 7970th CIC Group.) He also stated his belief that 'while the charges against SUBJECT may possibly be true they are probably not true.'

Allan Ryan in his report notes that the dropping of Barbie was 'a rather drastic action that could otherwise have been stayed until the truth of the charges had somehow been determined.'

Our general policy toward former Gestapo personnel, while admittedly not carried out in the case of Klaus Barbie, was stated in a directive and covering letter signed by me on 7 June 1949. The letter noted that 'insufficient attention has been paid to the interrogation of former Gestapo specialists on the KPD' and that confusion existed on the part of some CIC personnel as to headquarters policy on the further handling of ex-Gestapo members.

The directive enclosed with the letter contained the following specific guidance:

It is the policy of this Headquarters to discourage the use of Gestapo personnel as further sources of this organization [beyond interview or interrogation] except in unusual circumstances. It may be necessary to use the Gestapo man for the following short term tasks:

1. To introduce the [CIC] agent to other Gestapo personnel
2. To effect a meeting with former sources [of the Gestapo man]
3. To control an ex-source if the relationship is extremely well founded and it is practically impossible for the agent to take over control of the source.

There is no objection to the use of the Gestapo man for purposes of 1 and 2 above provided the amount of time involved is short. A major project involving a long period of time . . . is to be discouraged. All requests for the use of Gestapo personnel to accomplish 3 above will be cleared and approved by this Headquarters. An extremely strong case must be presented and your report must show complete use of your existing facilities and techniques before the request will be approved.

I was reassigned to the US in August 1949 after more than six years with the CIC in Europe – two tours with only a six-month stateside interval between them. I had been integrated into the Regular Army as an Infantry officer, there being then no separate branch for military intelligence, and the Infantry branch sent me to the advanced officer course at the Infantry School in order to requalify me for the Infantry. In one of his last acts as Army Chief of Staff, before becoming Chairman of the Joint Chiefs of Staff, General Omar Bradley had approved a plan for six

Regular Army officers to be permanently assigned to the CIC. I was told that George Sheldon and I were to have been two of those six officers. But General Bradley's successor rescinded the approval to allow further study of the plan. Several years later an intelligence branch was finally established but it was too late for me to benefit and I never returned to intelligence duty.

When I left Germany I thought the Barbie problem had been solved but obviously I was wrong. I have no direct knowledge of what transpired after my departure and only learned the details from Allan Ryan's report. Nevertheless, when speculation about Barbie began to appear in the newspapers during the 1970s, I realized that CIC's connection with him was likely to come to light and I resolved to answer any questions asked of me as fully as possible. I never sought out anyone to hear my story but have responded to every writer and TV reporter who had any questions to ask me.

I believe that Allan Ryan and his staff did an excellent job of investigating Klaus Barbie's relationship with the US government, considering the scope of the investigation and the limited amount of time available for it. I agree generally with most of his conclusions and recommendations, particularly the following:

1. . . . those who made the decision to employ and rely on Klaus Barbie . . . were, on the whole, conscientious and patriotic men faced with a difficult assignment. Under the circumstances, their choice to enlist Barbie's assistance was neither cynical nor corrupt.
2. They were acting within the scope of their official duties. Their actions were taken not for personal gain, or to shield them personally from liability or discipline, but to protect what they believed to be the best interests of the United States Army and the United States government.
3. No other nation in occupied Germany – France, Great Britain or the Soviet Union – is in any position to criticize the decision to use Klaus Barbie now that the United States Government has revealed the facts behind that use. Each of those governments made essentially the same decision at the time: to invoke the available resources of the former German régime to protect and advance what each government perceived to be its national interest.
4. The very nature of intelligence gathering abroad requires the use of informants and it would be grossly unrealistic to require that they be subject to the same standards of character, uprightness and conduct that are required for, say, civil or military service with the United States government.

I disagree with his conclusion that CIC engaged in a continuing obstruction of HICOG's (US High Commissioner for Germany's) efforts to deal with the Barbie case and that CIC and EUCOM representatives made false statements to the HICOG director of intelligence and thereby interfered with the lawful and proper administration of justice.

Various documents make it clear that high-level HICOG officials were quite aware that CIC and the Director of Intelligence at EUCOM did not want to turn Barbie over to the French. If they did not know CIC was in regular touch with Barbie, they knew they could call upon EUCOM to mount a search for him. It seems illogical that one director of intelligence would utter a bald-faced lie to another when they had the same national interest at heart. It is my opinion that the EUCOM and CIC representatives were completely candid, that they asked the HICOG representative to adopt their cover story and that he agreed to do so. In his memorandum about the meeting, the HICOG director of intelligence makes the point rather emphatically that 'the policy question is presented as to whether US–French relations would be more damaged by delivery of Barbie, assuming we could find him, than by non-delivery. We are in a position to make a statement to the French about our termination of his employment and about our loss of contact with him and take a chance that German police will not pick him up even though we make a formal attempt to have that done.' To me that does not indicate any desire on his part or even on HICOG's part, to see Barbie turned over to the French. In another document the deputy political adviser at HICOG states 'I gather we will do nothing here until instructed by the Department to request EUCOM to join in the search . . .' Finally, in a memo dated 20 October 1950, the head of the HICOG Extradition Board reported to the HICOG director of intelligence that he had been advised by telephone that 'it was the policy of the commanding general, EUCOM, that CIC would not attempt to locate any war criminal suspects.' Therefore he suggests that the director of intelligence should make every effort to enlist the efforts of CIC. There is no evidence that anything was ever done about this suggestion.

I further disagree with the recommendation 'that the United States government express to the government of France its regret for its responsibility in delaying the due process of law in the case of Klaus Barbie.' As stated in the documents, on six separate occasions CIC made Barbie available to French intelligence for interrogations: on May 14, May 18 and July 16, 1948, on January 21, 1949, and twice more in early 1949 (specific dates not given). On none of these occasions did the French representatives indicate that Barbie was wanted for any crimes. Furthermore, the extradition efforts later made by the French were perfunctory, sporadic and not presented in the proper form. To me it appears obvious from the record that if the French had made a serious, strong and sustained effort to obtain Barbie that they either would have succeeded or obtained a flat refusal from the US.

Mr Ryan seems confused about the working relationship between CIC and the Intelligence Division of EUCOM. Indeed, there is no evidence that he ever explored the matter. Actually, the relationship was very close. CIC received guidance, missions and specific assignments from the Intelligence Division. Close and constant liaison was maintained. Intelligence Division received written and oral reports from CIC. Intelligence

Division approved Barbie's detention and interrogation at the ECIC, received interrogation reports showing Barbie's status as a CIC informant, and finally approved Barbie's release by the ECIC. Each time that the French interrogated Barbie it was done with the knowledge and implicit approval of the Intelligence Division. When Colonel Erskine made his decision on 4 May 1950 that Barbie would not be placed in the hands of the French, it was done with the expressed concurrence, if not guidance, of Colonel Ligon and Colonel Johnson of EUCOM, presumably representing different branches of the Intelligence Division. To my mind, from that moment on Intelligence Division bore full responsibility for the withholding of Barbie from the French and for his ultimate escape through the rat line.

ADDENDUM

BARBIE: THE TIP OF THE ICEBERG

After the hardback edition of *America's Secret Army* had gone to press, the authors obtained further documentation from the US archives concerning the strange case of Eugene Fischer and Anton Mahler, the two ex-Gestapo officers and war criminals recruited by the CIC in post-war Germany, whose stories are told briefly on pages 331–2 of this book. The new material put this case and the American involvement in it in a completely different light.

The Americans have always claimed that the CIC's employment of Klaus Barbie for intelligence gathering purposes in Germany was a unique case and that the CIC alone were responsible for Barbie's recruitment and continuing employment. The new material makes it clear not only that Barbie was not a unique case but also that the United States Government, and not the CIC alone, bore ultimate responsibility for the employment of Fischer and Mahler, if not of Barbie too.

This is evident from the documentation that was generated when both Fischer and Mahler were put on trial by the Denazification Court in Munich in December 1949 – Fischer on 13 counts of mistreating and torturing prisoners in his custody at the Munich Gestapo headquarters during the war, and Mahler on 14 similar counts. Both were found guilty by the German court and sentenced to five years' and four years' imprisonment with hard labour respectively. Neither was in court to hear the sentence, however. Both had escaped in mysterious circumstances.

In West Germany the escape of two notorious Gestapo convicts was a sensation. 'New Justice Scandal in Munich' ran one newspaper headline at the end of December 1949. The CIC, meanwhile, kept very quiet about the whole affair. Where had the men gone? This was what Mr R. Cunningham, Director of Intelligence at the US High Commission for Germany (or HICOG) – an organ of the US Government in Washington and the ultimate American authority in

Germany – wanted to know. In September 1950 Cunningham wrote to the Director of Intelligence at the US European Command headquarters in Germany to say that the German authorities had requested the High Commission to intercede and help deliver the two fugitives from justice, as both men were known to have had connections with the CIC. 'Since not only a conviction was obtained against the accused,' wrote Cunningham, 'it would appear desirable to deliver the two men to the responsible German authorities UNLESS OTHER OVERRIDING CONDITIONS EXIST.' [Authors' emphasis.]

This unusual comment could be interpreted as a 'red flag'. It implies that the US Government itself, in the shape of its High Commission in Germany, was prepared to pervert the course of justice. That the American High Commission possibly knew what was going on between the lines is indicated by the response of CIC Chief Colonel Erskine to the High Commission's original request. Erskine claimed that he had 'no information concerning the present whereabouts of the two men and no objection to execution of the sentence by German authorities if subjects are apprehended'. He also revealed that it was the High Commission's predecessor, the Office of Director of Intelligence in the US Military Government (OMGUS), that in 1947 had given express authority for Fischer to be sprung from the American internment camp where he was awaiting trial so that he could work as an intelligence informant for the CIC.

In fact, Fischer and Mahler were still under CIC control and hiding out in CIC safe-houses. But by now the careers of the CIC's former Gestapo agents in American intelligence – including Klaus Barbie's – were coming to an end. By the end of 1951, for instance, Mahler was low in funds and in increasing danger. In December of that year he lodged an appeal – from where he was in hiding – against his conviction, which was turned down. 'My extermination is wanted by the KPD [German Communist Party],' he complained, 'in order not to do any more harm to it.' Desperately needing to extricate himself from his predicament, he then threatened to blackmail the CIC by revealing the identity of a secret source – possibly a former Gestapo officer with considerable influence – if the CIC did not contrive to quash the charges against him or help him emigrate to Argentina.

But the CIC was increasingly inclined to dump both Mahler and Fischer. Times were changing; Klaus Barbie had already been shipped off down the 'Rat Line' to a new life in South America in the spring of 1951. Nevertheless, Mahler's CIC file remained active until May 1953, when it appeared that the CIA, the US State department agency that was now taking over the lion's share of secret intelligence work in Germany, requested information about him from CIC HQ. Was Mahler taken over by the CIA? At this point the records peter out and the trail runs cold. But there is every likelihood that the ex-Gestapo officer's special talents were put to good use by the new masters.

Fischer was not so fortunate. When his name appeared on a wanted list put out by the West German police, the CIC appear to have 'shopped' him by notifying the police of his whereabouts. Fischer was arrested during 1953 and incarcerated in Stadelheim prison. All efforts to secure his release failed and by the spring of 1954 he was serving out the sentence passed on him five years before. A little later, his brazen application to the Bavarian Minister of the Interior for a free pardon on the grounds of his former services to the United States was turned down. In March 1956 the former chief of the Munich Gestapo's Communist section was still behind bars. He was still behind bars when his personal file was abruptly terminated a few months later. Fischer's subsequent fate is unknown.

What are we to make of this murky tangle? Recently, one of Klaus Barbie's CIC case officers, Erhard Dabringhaus, admitted that 'Barbie was the tip of the iceberg.' Incredible though it may seem in view of the Barbie scandal, former Gestapo officers Eugene Fischer and Anton Mahler and their colleagues were employed by the CIC in the same network and on the same secret work as Barbie and were run by the same CIC officers from the same CIC office in the same town in Germany – Augsburg. But on the face of it their case is even more alarming than Barbie's, for the sanctioning of Fischer's recruitment by American Military Government and the 'red flag' given by the American High Commission would conclusively establish direct United States Government involvement in the hiring and protection of Nazi war criminals.

If this is true of Fischer, how can it possibly not be true of Barbie also? In his report on the 1983 investigation into the Barbie case for the US Department of Justice – the Ryan Report – US Special Investigator Allan Ryan came to the conclusion that the CIC alone was responsible for the recruitment of Barbie, exonerated the US Government from any knowledge of Barbie's recruitment, and claimed that Barbie's war crimes record was unknown to the CIC for the first two years of his employment. In the light of Ian Sayer's and Douglas Botting's revelations that US Intelligence employed an entire Gestapo network alongside Barbie with the cognizance of the US Government, these conclusions must now be called into question. The light that the Fischer and Mahler files throw on the Barbie case make it clear that there are many more questions to be asked about the Barbie case. The US Government should now answer them.

The authors' examination of the new material relating to Anton Mahler also contained a revelation of a quite different sort – a revelation bearing on a heroic but tragic episode in the history of German resistance to the Hitler tyranny. While Mahler was holed up in a CIC safe-house following his escape from a German court in December 1949, his CIC mentor, Special Agent Herbert Bechtold, spent the lying-low period preparing a lengthy report entitled 'Exploitation of Former Gestapo Personnel'. This included Mahler's original interrogation report on the Scholl case (see page 331). At the time this report was prepared, Mahler was wanted by the West German police for his part in the murder of Hans and Sophie Scholl, the Munich University students whose valiant resistance to Hitler's tyranny was an inspiration to many post-war German democrats, including Nazi-hunter Beate Klarsfeld, the woman who tracked down Klaus Barbie in South America.

Mahler's version – given here for the first time – is completely at variance with the version given in the history books. Mahler was the chief interrogator of Hans Scholl. He claimed he never used torture but was able to extract a confession by other techniques. According to Mahler, Scholl's confession showed that he had been expelled from the Hitler Youth for homosexual activities and had nearly been court-martialled by the German Army for the same reason. For over 40 years it has been assumed that Hans Scholl accepted full responsibility as leader of the White Rose anti-Hitler resistance movement in the Third Reich and never gave his accomplices away. But according to Mahler, who had no obvious reason for lying to his CIC questioners, Hans Scholl betrayed his fellow students Christoph Probst, Alexander Schmorell and Wilhelm Graf as his confederates in the White Rose resistance. It was not until his sister, Sophie Scholl, was shown her brother's full confession that she too broke down and admitted her part in the anti-Hitler conspiracy. The Scholls were then immediately tried, sentenced, and beheaded.

Needless to say, it does not enhance the CIC's or the US Government's image in post-war Germany to know that one of their intelligence informants was the man who interrogated and destroyed one of the few genuine bastions of German resistance to the bloodiest tyranny in human history.

SOURCES

Preliminary quote from 'The Germans Call It a Gestapo' by William
Attwood (*New York Herald Tribune*, 7 March 1947)

INTRODUCTION

Ted Morgan: 'The Barbie File' (*New York Times Magazine*, 10 May 1987)
Tom Bower: *Klaus Barbie – Butcher of Lyons* (London, 1984)
'Fascist Ring Breakup Puts CIC in Spotlight' (*Stars and Stripes*, 23
    December 1943)
Robert H. Hansen: 'CIC in Sicily' (*Look* magazine, 1943)
'G-Men in Khaki' (*The American* magazine, January 1945)
Norbert I. Gagen: 'I Crashed into the Atom Bomb Factory' (*Varsity*, March
    1948, summarized in *CIC Reporter* (Vol No 5, Baltimore, 1948)
Neal M. Sher (and others): *Robert Jan Verbelen and the United States
    Government: A Report to the Assistant Attorney General. Criminal Division.
    US Dept of Justice* (Office of Special Investigations, US Dept of Justice,
    Washington DC, 13 June 1988)
'CIC History on its Way' (*CIC Reporter*, Vol 1 No 12, Baltimore, 1948)

PROLOGUE: AMERICA'S SECRET ARMY

Col. Bruce W. Bidwell: *History of the Military Intelligence Division 1917
    –1919* (Department of the Army, 1954)
History of G-2, SOS, AEF (National Archives, 1919)
Major General R. H. Van Deman: *Memoirs* (CIC Historical File, 1950)
Col. Royden Williamson: *Memoirs* (CIC Historical Project, 1953)
Gilbert Elliot: *History of the CIP in France* (CIP Basic Data File, 1919)
T. M. Johnson: *Our Secret War* (New York, 1929)
Capt. Henry Landau: *The Enemy Within* (New York, 1937)
Dwight D. Eisenhower: *Crusade in Europe* (London, 1948)

WAR GAMES USA

History of the Counter Intelligence Corps 1907–1943 (Central Records Facility)
War Department Technical Manual 30–215, Counter Intelligence Corps
    (22 Sept 1943)

Table of Organization and Equipment 30–500 (CIC) (24 January 1944)

Lt Col. James F. Foothorop: 'History of Office of Chief CIC January 1942 – January 1944' (Historical Section CIC, 1955)

Memoirs of Brig. Gen. W. A. Holbrook (CIC Central Records Facility, no date)

Interview with Col. H. R. Kibler (Fort Holabird, 27 October 1953)

Training History of CIC in World War II (CIC Central Records Facility)

Duval A. Edwards: Correspondence (Seattle, 25 May 1988)

James H. Ratliff: Correspondence (Cincinnati, 19 & 22 February 1988)

Nelson V. N. Dungan: 'Secret Agent X, Counter Intelligence Corps' (unpublished MS, Somerville, NJ, 1988)

Duval A. Edwards: 'Was the Army's "Secret Service" too Secret?' (*CIC Reporter*, Vol 1 No 6, New York, April 1948)

Lt Col. Arthur S. Hurlburt: 'Letter to Julie' (unpublished MS, Medford, Ma, 1987)

Thomas O. Schlesinger: Correspondence (Plymouth, New Hampshire, 26 March 1988)

Ted Morgan: *FDR – A Biography*

Joseph Lash: *Love, Eleanor* (New York, n.d.)

Article on FBI detailing Lash scandal in *US News & World Report*

Lt Col. Anthony W. Lobb: Correspondence (Greenville, NY, 25 March 1987)

THE THIN BLUE LINE

Edward R. Koudelka: *Counter Intelligence: The Conflict and the Conquest* (New York, 1986) [Memoirs of a former CIC agent]

Col Earl S. Browning: Correspondence (Fairfax, Va, 20 April 1987)

'CIC Operations in Iceland' in *A History of G2, ETOUSA* (Historical Section, ETOUSA, April 1945)

Lt Col. D. Hjalmarson: 'CIC Unit History, Iceland Base Command' (Central Records Facility, May 1945)

'History of CIC in Alaska, 467th CIC Detachment' (Kansas City Record Centre, no date)

Special Agents Jack S. Blue and Joseph B. Gilbert: 'Memorandum on Undercover Mission in Newfoundland' (Central Records Facility, 22 August 1943)

Major Elbert D. Turner: 'CIC, Caribbean Defense Command, 1 Jan 42–31 May 45' in 'CIC Operational History of Base and Defense Commands' (June 1945)

Kurt Singer: 'The King of Belize' in *Spies and Traitors of World War Two* (New York, 1945)

'History of the CIC in the Middle East 1942–1945' (400th CIC Detachment, Africa-Middle East Theater, Cairo, May 1945)

Lt Col. John T. McCafferty: 'Historical Report, CIC, Persian Gulf Command, 1942–45' (May 1945)

Earnest R. Oney: 'Drang nach Islam Revisited' (*Intelligence Quarterly*, 1988)
Lt Col. Arthur S. Hurlburt: 'Letter to Julie' op. cit.
Norbert I. Gagen: 'I Crashed into the Atom Bomb Factory' op. cit.
Daniel Lang: 'A Reporter at Large – The Top Top Secret' (*New Yorker*, 27 October 1945), reproduced in *The Infantry Journal* and *Counter Intelligence* (Vol 11, No 1, January 1949)
Henry de Wolf Smyth: *Atomic Energy for Military Purposes: The Official Report on the Development of the Atomic Bomb 1940–1945* (Princeton, 1946)
Lt Col. Arthur S. Hurlburt: 'Whatever Happened to Counter Intelligence?' (*Intelligence Quarterly* Vol 2 No 1, 1987)
Lt Col. Arthur S. Hurlburt: 'Letter to Julie' op. cit.
Samuel A. Goudsmit: *ALSOS – The Search for the German Atom Bomb* (London, 1947)
'CIC with the Manhattan District', Vol 14 'Intelligence and Security', *Manhattan District History* (Atomic Energy Commission, Washington DC)
Lt Col. George R. Eckman: 'Final Report on the ALSOS Mission' (G2 Documents Library, Pentagon, Washington DC)

SAKAKIDA

Interview with Sakakida by Roy Takai, National Japanese American Society, San Francisco, 25 November 1977; and by CIC historians at HQ, Office of Special Investigations (Air Force), Washington DC, 18 March 1955
Document prepared by Arthur Komori, quoted in 'CIC's Lost Detachment' (*CIC in Southwest Pacific Area*, US Army Intelligence Center, Fort Holabird, Baltimore, 1959)
James Rubard: 'The "Lost" Manila Detachment' (unpublished MS, received December 1987)
Duval A. Edwards: Correspondence (San Antonio, Texas, December 1987)
Duval A. Edwards: Anderson's Guerrillas (unpublished MS, 1987)
Joseph D. Harrington: *Yankee Samurai* (Detroit)
Eric Morris: *Corregidor* (London, 1982)
Brig. Gen. Steve Mellnik: *Philippine Diary 1939–1945*
Brig. Gen. Elliot R. Thorpe: *East Wind, Rain* (Boston, 1969)

THE CIC GOES TO WAR

Lt Col. Jack B. Cameron: 'CIC Operations, French Morocco, 8–11 Nov 42' (Letter to Chief CIC, Fort Holabird, 9 February 1954)
2nd Armored Division CIC Detachment War Diary (18 October–23 November 1942)
History of the 202nd CIC Detachment; and summary of interview with Leonard Bessman at NCICA Convention, Chicago, August 1954
History of 305th CIC Detachment

Letter from Lt Col. Horace Miner to CIC Historical Branch, September 1953

John Schwarzwalder: *We Caught Spies* (New York, 1946) [Memoirs of a former CIC agent]

James A. Maxwell: *I Never Saw An Arab Like Him* (Boston, 1948) [Fiction based on North African experiences of a former CIC agent]

Omar N. Bradley: *A Soldier's Story* (London, 1951)

General Mark Clark: *Calculated Risk* (London, 1951)

'CIC's Top Decoration' in *CIC Digest* (Vol 1 No 3, Camp Holabird, Baltimore, August 1948)

Lipps case in Schwarzwalder op. cit. and telephone information from National Archives, Washington DC

THE INVASIONS OF EUROPE

Capt [later Lt Col.] Horace Miner: 'Report of Operations of II Corps CIC Section in the Sicilian Campaign' (CIC Archives)

Lt Dudley M. Matthews: 'Memorandum on Activities of CIC Detachment in Combat' [based on interview with *Look* magazine war reporter Robert H. Hansen in Sicily], 2 October 1943

War Diary of Fifth Army CIC (1 September 43 to 6 January 44)

Interviews with Alfred A. Coppola and Harry Riback by CIC historians at NCICA Convention (Philadelphia, August 1953)

Stephen J. Spingarn (with Milton Lehman): 'How We Caught Spies in World War Two' (*Saturday Evening Post*, 27 November and 4 and 11 December 1948)

Mark Clark: op. cit.

Omar N. Bradley: op. cit.

James H. Ratliff: Correspondence (Cincinnati, 30 May and 2 November 1987)

GUARDIANS OF THE LIBERATION

James H. Ratliff: Correspondence (Cincinnati, 1987)

David Wright: Correspondence (Rockville, Ma, 5 August 1988)

Edward R. Koudelka op. cit.

De Guinzbourg: in Schwarzwalder op. cit. and Dungan op. cit. Also interview with de Guinzbourg by CIC historians at United Nations, New York, August 1955

SHAEF Directive No 7 (Counter Intelligence) (SHAEF, London, 8 February 1944)

Annex to First Army Intelligence Plan NEPTUNE (Operation of the CIC) 'CIC in ETOUSA, 6 June 1944 to 8 May 1945' in 'CIC Operational History of Theaters'

12th Army Group Semi-Monthly Counterintelligence Reports (G2 Twelfth Army Group)

6th Army Group Fortnightly Counterintelligence Reports
7th Army Monthly Counterintelligence Reports

SPY HIGHWAY ITALY

Mark Clark op. cit.
Histories of the 10th, 92nd, 202nd, 305th and 431st CIC Detachments in Italy
Interviews with Sam Freestone and Harry Riback by CIC historians at NCICA Convention (Philadelphia, August 1953)
H. O. Dovey: 'The Unknown War: Security in Italy 1943–45' in *Intelligence and National Security*
Stephen J. Spingarn op. cit.
Michael J. Suszan: 'CIC: The Army's Spy-Hunters' (*Reader's Digest*, January 1952)
'5th Army CIC War Diary' in *CIC Digest* (Vol 1 No 2, July 1948)

THE TROJAN HORSE

12th Army Group op. cit.
6th Army Group op. cit.
'Enemy Agents in the Ardennes' in 'History of Counter Intelligence Activities of the US Army in Europe' (CIC archives)
Glenn B. Infield: *Skorzeny – Hitler's Commando* (New York, 1981)
Charles Foley: *Commando Extraordinary* (London, 1954)
Otto Skorzeny: *Skorzeny's Secret Missions* (New York, 1950)
Rudi Frühbeißer: *Im Rücken der Amerikaner* (Hamburg, 1977)
Dwight D. Eisenhower: *Crusade in Europe* (London, 1948)
William F. Loebl: Correspondence (Chanhassen, Maine, 29 November 1987)
Nelson V. Dungan op. cit.
Col. Earl S. Browning op. cit.
Omar Bradley op. cit.
Harry C. Butcher: *My Three Years with Eisenhower* (New York, 1946)

OVERUNNING THE REICH

Douglas Botting: *From the Ruins of the Reich* (New York, 1985)
Saul K. Padover: *Psychologist in Germany* (London, 1946)
SHAEF Weekly Intelligence Summaries and Counter Intelligence Bulletins
12th Army Group Counter Intelligence Directive for Germany (10 April 1945)
12th Army Group Counter Intelligence Periodic Reports
15th Army Counter Intelligence Bulletins and Monthly Counter Intelligence Reports

9th US Army G2 Periodic Reports

David Kahn: *Hitler's Spies – German Military Intelligence in World War Two* (London, 1978)

Bob Yeargin: 'Bond Tales Dimmed by These Men' (*Sun*, Las Vegas, 5 August 1973)

Kurt Singer: *Spies and Traitors – A Short History of Espionage* (London, 1953)

Thomas Hasler: 'The saga of Greta, the spy' (*Evening Sun*, Baltimore, 17 April 1980)

Martin Hogan: 'Local Lawyer Recalls WWII Encounter With Blond Nazi Spy' (Cincinnati *Enquirer*)

James H. Ratliff: Correspondence op. cit.

'Local Attorney Helped Launch Adenauer Into Postwar Politics' (Cincinnati *Enquirer*, 20 April 1967)

Nelson V. Dungan op. cit.

Ratliff op. cit. 2 March 1988

Vince Cleary: Correspondence (Edgewater, Md, 1988)

Richard W. Beebe: 'Overseas 1944–45' (unpublished MS, Sioux City, Iowa, 5 August 1988)

Koudelka op. cit.

THE MARCH TO JAPAN

Ann Bray and Duval A. Edwards: 'The Counter Intelligence Corps in the War with the Japanese' (unpublished MS, The National Counter Intelligence Corps Association, Dayton, Ohio, 1985)

Major MacKenzie [first name unknown]: 'History of the CIC in the CBI Theater' (CIC Central Records Facility)

Unit History of the Counter Intelligence Corps, China Theater (June 1945)

Brigadier General Elliot R. Thorpe: *History of Counter Intelligence Operations in the Southwest Pacific and United States Armed Forces, Pacific Theater, during World War II* (Office of the Chief Counterintelligence Officer, General Headquarters, Army Forces, Pacific, 1946)

Major General C. A. Willoughby: *Operations of Counter Intelligence Corps in the SWPA* (Vol VIII, Intelligence Series, GHQ, Far East Command, 1948)

Brig. Gen. Elliot R. Thorpe op. cit.

Hurlburt op. cit.

General Walter Krueger: *From Down Under to Nippon* (New York, 1953)

William Owens: *CIC Memoirs of the Pacific War* (Texas, 1988)

IN THE RUINS OF THE REICH

Oliver J. Frederikson: *The American Military Occupation of Germany 1945–53* (Historical Division, US Army, Europe, 1953)

Weekly Intelligence Summaries (Office of Acting Chief of Staff, US Forces, European Theater)

Report on Operation Nursery by 970th CIC Detachment, Frankfurt, 1946

Monthly Information Report from 307th CIC Detachment, 303rd Detachment. Botting op. cit.

Col. Theodor J. Girouard: autobiographical memorandum (Critz, Va, 1987)

Ralph Blumenfeld: 'The Formative Years of Henry Kissinger' (*The Observer* Magazine, London, 29 December 1974)

Arthur D. Kahn: *Betrayal – Our Occupation of Germany* (Warsaw, 1950)

Antony Terry: telephone interview (Nice, France, 1984)

William Larned: telephone interview (Greenwich, Connecticut, 1988)

James H. Ratliff: Correspondence 1987–88; 39-page untitled memorandum on CIC and Cold War intelligence situation in occupied Germany (1949)

James McGovern: *Fräulein* (London, 1957)

Guenther Reinhardt: First Memorandum (48 pp., Frankfurt, November 1947)

Guenther Reinhardt: Second Memorandum (55 pp., Washington DC, Dec 1947)

Guenther Reinhardt: Letter to Tom Agoston (New York, 12 February 1949)

Guenther Reinhardt: *Crime Without Punishment* (New York, 1952) [Memoirs of a former CIC agent]

Orville J. Taylor: Reinhardt Report – Wholesale Irregularities in the Counter Intelligence Corps in the European Theatre (Department of the Army, 29 March 1948)

Mark Seaman: 'The War's Worst Traitor?' (*World War Two Investigator* Vol 1 No 5, August 1988)

Brendan Murphy: *Turncoat* (New York, 1987)

Col. Earl S. Browning op. cit.

Michael J. Suszan: 'The Arrest of Gauleiter Eigruber' (unpublished MS, Birmingham, Michigan, 1958)

CIC Hitler Files (4 volumes, National Archives)

'Adolf Hitler is alive and well and living in . . .' (*World War Two Investigator*, Vol 1 No 2, May 1988)

'Who Identified Hitler's Body?' (*World War Two Investigator* Vol 1 No 6 September 1988)

Hugh Trevor-Roper: *The Last Days of Hitler* (London, 1948)

Arnold Weiss: Correspondence (1987)

THE CIC'S COLD WAR

Christopher Simpson: *Blowback – America's Recruitment of Nazis and Its Effect on the Cold War* (New York, 1988)

John Loftus: *The Belarus Secret* (New York, 1982)

History of the 430th CIC Detachment 1947–48 (Vienna, 1949)

Tom Bower: *Klaus Barbie – Butcher of Lyons* (London, 1984)

Magnus Linklater, Isabel Hilton, Neal Ascherson: *The Fourth Reich – Klaus Barbie and the Neo-Fascist Connection* (London, 1984)

Col. Earl S. Browning Jr: Correspondence 1987–88

Col. Earl S. Browning Jr: 'My Involvement with Klaus Barbie' (unpublished MS, Fairfax, Va, 1988)

Ted Morgan: 'The Barbie File' (*New York Times Magazine*, 10 May 1987)

Allan Ryan: The Ryan Report (Office of Special Investigations, Department of Justice, Washington DC, 1983)

Guenther Reinhardt: *Crime Without Punishment* op. cit.

The Case of Eugene Fischer: CIC Archives

Neal M. Sher (and others): *Robert Jan Verbelen and the United States Government: A Report to the Assistant Attorney General. Criminal Division. US Dept of Justice* (Office of Special Investigations, US Dept of Justice, Washington DC, 13 June 1988)

Heinz Höhne and Hermann Zolling: *The General Was a Spy – The Truth About General Gehlen and His Spy Ring* (London, 1972)

John Loftus: Letter to Isadore Zack, Military Intelligence Association of New England in *Golden Sphinx* (National Counter Intelligence Corps Association, Dayton, Ohio, August 1982)

'Documents link allies to escape of Nazis' (*The Times*, London, 12 May 1988)

Maris Cakars and Barton Osborn: 'Operation Ohio' (*Win*, New York, 18 September 1975)

'Operation Jughead': Appendix to History of 430th CIC Detachment (Vienna, 1949)

CIC Dossier on Operation Snatch Counter-Snatch (US Army Intelligence and Security Command Archives). Also CIC files on Operations Sunrise, Bingo, Rusty and Tobacco.

Operations of the 430th CIC Detachment in Austria (Vienna, 15 May 1947)

US Forces Austria Weekly Intelligence Summaries

Ed Hartrich: 'Czech Spy Ring Smashed' (*New York Herald Tribune*, 22 November 1948)

EPILOGUE

John Patrick Finnegan: *Military Intelligence* (US Army Intelligence and Security Command, Arlington, Va, 1985)

Ann Bray: 'Act Three ... Final Curtain' (unpublished MS, NCICA, Dayton, Ohio, 1986)

Lt Col. Arthur S. Hurlburt: 'Whatever Happened to Counter Intelligence?' (*Intelligence Quarterly* Vol 2 No 1, 1987)

Col Earl S. Browning: Correspondence (Fairfax, Va, 17 March 1988)

Bradley W. Vaughan: 'I Joined Uncle Sam's Counterspies' (unpublished MS, Tempe, Arizona, 1988)

INDEX